T0373291

Bedford/Suzuki
Service and Repair Manual

A K Legg LAE MIMI and S J Drayton

(3015-224-1AG3)

Models covered

Bedford/Vauxhall Rascal and Suzuki (SK410) SuperCarry Van & Pickup models;
970 cc petrol engines

*Does not cover Suzuki ST80 & 90 series Vans, specialist body conversions,
or revised Japanese-built Suzuki SuperCarry range introduced October 1994*

ABCDE
FGHIJ
KLMNO
P
2

© Haynes Group Limited 2003

A book in the **Haynes Service and Repair Manual Series**

ISBN **978 0 85733 993 5**

British Library Cataloguing in Publication Data
A catalogue record for this book is available from the British Library.

Printed in India

Haynes Group Limited
Sparkford, Yeovil, Somerset BA22 7JJ, England

Haynes North America, Inc
2801 Townsgate Road, Suite 340, Thousand Oaks, CA 91361, USA

Disclaimer

There are risks associated with automotive repairs. The ability to make repairs depends on the individual's skill, experience and proper tools. Individuals should act with due care and acknowledge and assume the risk of performing automotive repairs.

The purpose of this manual is to provide comprehensive, useful and accessible automotive repair information, to help you get the best value from your vehicle. However, this manual is not a substitute for a professional certified technician or mechanic.

This repair manual is produced by a third party and is not associated with an individual vehicle manufacturer. If there is any doubt or discrepancy between this manual and the owner's manual or the factory service manual, please refer to the factory service manual or seek assistance from a professional certified technician or mechanic.

Even though we have prepared this manual with extreme care and every attempt is made to ensure that the information in this manual is correct, neither the publisher nor the author can accept responsibility for loss, damage or injury caused by any errors in, or omissions from, the information given.

Contents

LIVING WITH YOUR BEDFORD/SUZUKI

Roadside Repairs

Routine maintenance

Contents

Introduction to the Bedford/Vauxhall Rascal and Suzuki SuperCarry

The Rascal / SuperCarry range was introduced in April 1986, as a joint venture between General Motors and Suzuki. British-built and available in both Van and Pickup derivatives, the vehicle's strengths were its diminutive size and maximum payload weight; 550kg for the Van and 575kg for the Pickup. When the Bedford name ceased to exist in June 1990, General Motors vehicles were rebadged as Vauxhalls. UK production ceased in July 1993 and was resumed in Japan.

All vehicles are fitted with a 970 cc Suzuki engine of four-cylinder overhead camshaft design, mounted longitudinally and inclined to the left, with the transmission mounted at the rear of the engine. All models are rear-wheel-drive, and have either a four or five-speed manual transmission.

Throughout the range, the suspension layout is coil-over-damper struts at the front, and leaf springs with dampers at the rear. In addition, Van derivatives are fitted with a front anti-roll bar. On all models covered by this manual, braking is servo-assisted, utilising discs at the front and drums at the rear.

A range of optional equipment is offered, including tailgate wash/wipe, front foglights, nudge bars and heated rear window.

Provided that regular servicing is carried out in accordance with the manufacturer's recommendations, the vehicle should prove reliable and economical. The engine inspection hatches are well positioned, giving easy access to the majority of components requiring frequent attention.

Acknowledgements

Thanks are due to L.V.S. Commercials, Sparkford for the loan of the Rascal Van used for the majority of this project. Thanks are also due to Draper Tools Limited, who provided some of the workshop tools, and to all those people at Sparkford who helped in the production of this manual.

We take great pride in the accuracy of information given in this manual, but vehicle manufacturers make alterations and design changes during the production run of a particular vehicle of which they do not inform us. No liability can be accepted by the authors or publishers for loss, damage or injury caused by errors in, or omissions from, the information given.

Project vehicles

Various project vehicles were used in the preparation of this manual, and appear in many of the photographic sequences. These include a Bedford Rascal Van and a Vauxhall Rascal Pickup.

Bedford Rascal Van

Vauxhall Rascal Pickup

General dimensions and weights

Note: *All figures are approximate, and may vary according to model. Refer to manufacturer's data for exact figures.*

Dimensions	Van	Pickup
Overall length	3290 mm	3250 mm
Overall width	1660 mm	1660 mm
Overall height (unladen)	1780 mm	1770 mm
Wheelbase	1840 mm	1840 mm
Front track	1210 mm	1210 mm
Rear track	1200 mm	1200 mm

Weights		
Kerb weight (depending on specification)*	820 kg	760 kg
Maximum gross vehicle weight*	1410 kg	1410 kg

*Refer to Bedford/Suzuki dealer for exact recommendations.

Working on your car can be dangerous. This page shows just some of the potential risks and hazards, with the aim of creating a safety-conscious attitude.

General hazards

Scalding

• Don't remove the radiator or expansion tank cap while the engine is hot.
• Engine oil, automatic transmission fluid or power steering fluid may also be dangerously hot if the engine has recently been running.

Burning

• Beware of burns from the exhaust system and from any part of the engine. Brake discs and drums can also be extremely hot immediately after use.

Crushing

• When working under or near a raised vehicle, always supplement the jack with axle stands, or use drive-on ramps. *Never venture under a car which is only supported by a jack.*

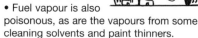

• Take care if loosening or tightening high-torque nuts when the vehicle is on stands. Initial loosening and final tightening should be done with the wheels on the ground.

Fire

• Fuel is highly flammable; fuel vapour is explosive.
• Don't let fuel spill onto a hot engine.
• Do not smoke or allow naked lights (including pilot lights) anywhere near a vehicle being worked on. Also beware of creating sparks (electrically or by use of tools).
• Fuel vapour is heavier than air, so don't work on the fuel system with the vehicle over an inspection pit.
• Another cause of fire is an electrical overload or short-circuit. Take care when repairing or modifying the vehicle wiring.
• Keep a fire extinguisher handy, of a type suitable for use on fuel and electrical fires.

Electric shock

• Ignition HT voltage can be dangerous, especially to people with heart problems or a pacemaker. Don't work on or near the ignition system with the engine running or the ignition switched on.

• Mains voltage is also dangerous. Make sure that any mains-operated equipment is correctly earthed. Mains power points should be protected by a residual current device (RCD) circuit breaker.

Fume or gas intoxication

• Exhaust fumes are poisonous; they often contain carbon monoxide, which is rapidly fatal if inhaled. Never run the engine in a confined space such as a garage with the doors shut.
• Fuel vapour is also poisonous, as are the vapours from some cleaning solvents and paint thinners.

Poisonous or irritant substances

• Avoid skin contact with battery acid and with any fuel, fluid or lubricant, especially antifreeze, brake hydraulic fluid and Diesel fuel. Don't syphon them by mouth. If such a substance is swallowed or gets into the eyes, seek medical advice.
• Prolonged contact with used engine oil can cause skin cancer. Wear gloves or use a barrier cream if necessary. Change out of oil-soaked clothes and do not keep oily rags in your pocket.
• Air conditioning refrigerant forms a poisonous gas if exposed to a naked flame (including a cigarette). It can also cause skin burns on contact.

Asbestos

• Asbestos dust can cause cancer if inhaled or swallowed. Asbestos may be found in gaskets and in brake and clutch linings. When dealing with such components it is safest to assume that they contain asbestos.

Special hazards

Hydrofluoric acid

• This extremely corrosive acid is formed when certain types of synthetic rubber, found in some O-rings, oil seals, fuel hoses etc, are exposed to temperatures above 400°C. The rubber changes into a charred or sticky substance containing the acid. *Once formed, the acid remains dangerous for years. If it gets onto the skin, it may be necessary to amputate the limb concerned.*
• When dealing with a vehicle which has suffered a fire, or with components salvaged from such a vehicle, wear protective gloves and discard them after use.

The battery

• Batteries contain sulphuric acid, which attacks clothing, eyes and skin. Take care when topping-up or carrying the battery.
• The hydrogen gas given off by the battery is highly explosive. Never cause a spark or allow a naked light nearby. Be careful when connecting and disconnecting battery chargers or jump leads.

Air bags

• Air bags can cause injury if they go off accidentally. Take care when removing the steering wheel and/or facia. Special storage instructions may apply.

Diesel injection equipment

• Diesel injection pumps supply fuel at very high pressure. Take care when working on the fuel injectors and fuel pipes.

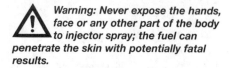

Warning: Never expose the hands, face or any other part of the body to injector spray; the fuel can penetrate the skin with potentially fatal results.

Remember...

DO

• Do use eye protection when using power tools, and when working under the vehicle.

• Do wear gloves or use barrier cream to protect your hands when necessary.

• Do get someone to check periodically that all is well when working alone on the vehicle.

• Do keep loose clothing and long hair well out of the way of moving mechanical parts.

• Do remove rings, wristwatch etc, before working on the vehicle – especially the electrical system.

• Do ensure that any lifting or jacking equipment has a safe working load rating adequate for the job.

DON'T

• Don't attempt to lift a heavy component which may be beyond your capability – get assistance.

• Don't rush to finish a job, or take unverified short cuts.

• Don't use ill-fitting tools which may slip and cause injury.

• Don't leave tools or parts lying around where someone can trip over them. Mop up oil and fuel spills at once.

• Don't allow children or pets to play in or near a vehicle being worked on.

Identifying leaks

Puddles on the garage floor or drive, or obvious wetness under the bonnet or underneath the car, suggest a leak that needs investigating. It can sometimes be difficult to decide where the leak is coming from, especially if the engine bay is very dirty already. Leaking oil or fluid can also be blown rearwards by the passage of air under the car, giving a false impression of where the problem lies.

 Warning: Most automotive oils and fluids are poisonous. Wash them off skin, and change out of contaminated clothing, without delay.

 HAYNES HiNT *The smell of a fluid leaking from the car may provide a clue to what's leaking. Some fluids are distinctively coloured. It may help to clean the car carefully and to park it over some clean paper overnight as an aid to locating the source of the leak.*
Remember that some leaks may only occur while the engine is running.

Sump oil

Engine oil may leak from the drain plug...

Oil from filter

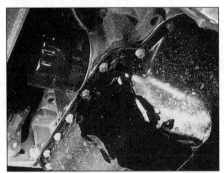

...or from the base of the oil filter.

Gearbox oil

Gearbox oil can leak from the seals at the inboard ends of the driveshafts.

Antifreeze

Leaking antifreeze often leaves a crystalline deposit like this.

Brake fluid

A leak occurring at a wheel is almost certainly brake fluid.

Power steering fluid

Power steering fluid may leak from the pipe connectors on the steering rack.

Jump starting

HAYNES HiNT

Jump starting will get you out of trouble, but you must correct whatever made the battery go flat in the first place. There are three possibilities:

1 *The battery has been drained by repeated attempts to start, or by leaving the lights on.*

2 *The charging system is not working properly (alternator drivebelt slack or broken, alternator wiring fault or alternator itself faulty).*

3 *The battery itself is at fault (electrolyte low, or battery worn out).*

When jump-starting a car using a booster battery, observe the following precautions:

✔ Before connecting the booster battery, make sure that the ignition is switched off.

✔ Ensure that all electrical equipment (lights, heater, wipers, etc) is switched off.

✔ Take note of any special precautions printed on the battery case.

✔ Make sure that the booster battery is the same voltage as the discharged one in the vehicle.

✔ If the battery is being jump-started from the battery in another vehicle, the two vehicles MUST NOT TOUCH each other.

✔ Make sure that the transmission is in neutral (or PARK, in the case of automatic transmission).

1 Connect one end of the red jump lead to the positive (+) terminal of the flat battery

2 Connect the other end of the red lead to the positive (+) terminal of the booster battery.

3 Connect one end of the black jump lead to the negative (-) terminal of the booster battery

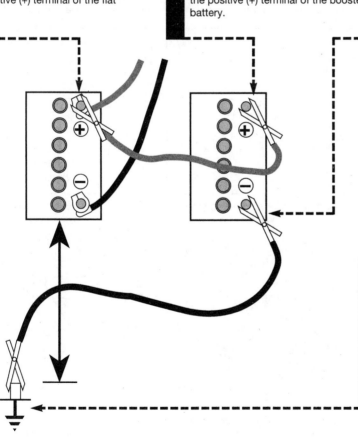

4 Connect the other end of the black jump lead to a bolt or bracket on the engine block, well away from the battery, on the vehicle to be started.

5 Make sure that the jump leads will not come into contact with the fan, drive-belts or other moving parts of the engine.

6 Start the engine using the booster battery and run it at idle speed. Switch on the lights, rear window demister and heater blower motor, then disconnect the jump leads in the reverse order of connection. Turn off the lights etc.

Jacking, towing and wheel changing

Jacking

The jack supplied with the vehicle tool kit should only be used for changing the roadwheels - see *"Wheel changing"* later in this Section. When carrying out any other kind of work, raise the vehicle using a hydraulic jack, and always supplement the jack with axle stands positioned under the vehicle jacking points **(see illustrations)**.

To raise the front of the vehicle using the jack supplied with the vehicle, position the jack underneath the suspension lower arm, as close to the road wheel as possible. **(see illustration)**. **Do not** jack the vehicle under the sump or any of the steering components.

To raise the rear of the vehicle using the jack supplied with the vehicle, position the jack head underneath the rear axle tube **(see illustration)**. **Do not** attempt to raise the vehicle with the jack positioned underneath the spare wheel as the vehicle floor will almost certainly be damaged.

Never *work under, around, or near a raised vehicle, unless it is adequately supported in at least two places.*

Towing

Towing connections must be made either at the towing eye, at the front of the vehicle, or at a main structural member, such as a chassis rail. Body-mounted components such as bumpers should not be used. Always turn the ignition key to the second position when the vehicle is being towed, so that the steering lock is released, and that the direction indicators and brake lights will operate.

Before being towed, release the handbrake and make sure the gear lever is in neutral. Note that greater-than-usual pedal pressure will be required to operate the brakes, since the vacuum servo unit is only operational when the engine is running.

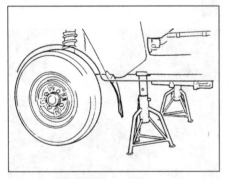
Axle stand position for supporting the front of the vehicle

Axle stand position for supporting the rear of the vehicle

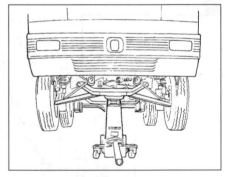
Raising the front of the vehicle with a hydraulic jack

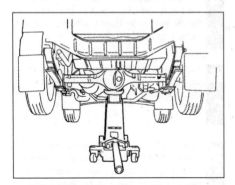
Raising the rear of the vehicle with a hydraulic jack

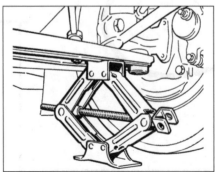
Raising the front of the vehicle with the vehicle jack

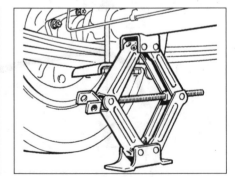
Raising the rear of the vehicle with the vehicle jack

Wheel changing

The jack is located at the front left hand side of the engine bay, adjacent to the radiator. The spare wheel is mounted under the load space, at the rear of the vehicle. For access to the spare wheel, proceed as described under the relevant sub-heading.

Van models

Loosen the cradle securing bolt in the floor of the load area, using the wheel brace **(see illustration)**.

Lift the cradle sufficiently to disengage it from the latch.

Move the latch to one side, then lower the cradle and slide out the spare wheel **(see illustration)**.

Pickup models

Pivot the rear number plate holder upwards.

Slacken and remove the spare wheel retaining bar **(see illustration)**.

Slide out the spare wheel **(see illustration)**.

All models

To change a wheel, remove the spare wheel, jack and wheel brace, as described previously, then proceed as follows.

Make sure that the vehicle is located on firm, level ground. Apply the handbrake, and place chocks at the front and rear of the wheel diagonally opposite the one to be changed. Select first or reverse gear. Prise off, and remove, the wheel trim (if fitted). Slightly loosen the wheel bolts with the wheelbrace provided. Locate the jack head in the jacking point nearest to the wheel to be changed, and raise the jack by turning the handle. When the wheel is clear of the ground, remove the bolts and lift off the wheel. Fit the spare wheel, and

moderately tighten the bolts. Lower the vehicle, and then tighten the bolts fully in a diagonal sequence. Refit the wheel trim, where applicable. Be sure to check the pressure of the spare tyre. Remove chocks, and stow the jack and tools safely.

Temporarily store the punctured wheel in the load area, as a reminder to have it repaired as soon as possible. Hook the cradle back onto the latch, and raise the cradle back into position, or refit the wheel retaining bar, as applicable.

Slacken the cradle securing bolt . . .

. . . and remove the spare wheel (Van)

Pivot the number plate holder upwards, slacken the locknut and remove the retaining bar . . .

. . . then slide out the spare wheel (Pickup)

Buying spare parts

Spare parts are available from many sources; for example, Vauxhall/Suzuki garages, other garages and accessory shops, and motor factors. Our advice regarding spare part sources is as follows.

Officially-appointed Vauxhall/Suzuki garages - This is the best source for parts which are peculiar to your vehicle, and are not generally available (eg complete cylinder heads, internal gearbox components, badges, interior trim etc). It is also the only place at which you should buy parts if the vehicle is still under warranty. To be sure of obtaining the correct parts, it will be necessary to give the storeman the vehicle identification number. If possible, take the old parts along for positive identification. Many parts are available under a factory exchange scheme - any parts returned should always be clean. It obviously makes good sense to go straight to the specialists on your vehicle for this type of part, as they are best equipped to supply you.

Other garages and accessory shops - These are often very good places to buy materials and components needed for the maintenance of your vehicle (eg oil filters, spark plugs, bulbs, drivebelts, oils and greases, touch-up paint, filler paste, etc). They also sell general accessories, usually have convenient opening hours, charge lower prices, and can often be found not far from home.

Motor factors - Good factors will stock all the more important components which wear out comparatively quickly (eg exhaust systems, brake pads, seals and hydraulic parts, clutch components, bearing shells, pistons, valves etc). Motor factors will often provide new or reconditioned components on a part-exchange basis - this can save a considerable amount of money.

Vehicle identification numbers

Modifications are a continuing and unpublicised process in vehicle manufacture, quite apart from major model changes. Spare parts manuals and lists are compiled upon a numerical basis, the individual vehicle identification numbers being essential to correct identification of the component concerned.

When ordering spare parts, always give as much information as possible. Quote the vehicle model, year of manufacture, body and engine numbers as appropriate.

The *Vehicle Identification Number (VIN) and weight specification* plate is situated inside the cabin, riveted to the "B" pillar, adjacent to the seat belt support. The plate carries the VIN and vehicle weight information **(see illustration)**.

The *Service Parts Identification* plate is also riveted to the "B" pillar and indicates model and chassis number, paint code, option codes and the trim code.

The *engine number* is stamped on to the cylinder block, underneath the carburettor and forward of the bellhousing **(see illustration)**. On some models, the engine number is also stamped on the VIN plate.

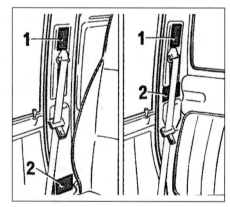

Location of VIN and Service Parts Identification plates; Van (left) and Pickup (right) models

1 Service Parts Identification plate
2 VIN plate

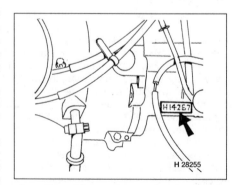

Location of the engine number (arrowed)

Chapter 1
Routine maintenance and servicing

Contents

Degrees of difficulty

| **Easy,** suitable for novice with little experience | **Fairly easy,** suitable for beginner with some experience | **Fairly difficult,** suitable for competent DIY mechanic  | **Difficult,** suitable for experienced DIY mechanic | **Very difficult,** suitable for expert DIY or professional |

Engine

Valve clearances (inlet and exhaust) - engine cold . . . . 0.13 to 0.18 mm (0.005 to 0.007 in)

Cooling system

Antifreeze mixture:
    28% antifreeze . . . . Protection down to -15°C (5°F)
    50% antifreeze . . . . Protection down to -30°C (-22°F)
Note: *Refer to antifreeze manufacturer for latest recommendations..*

Fuel system

Idle speed . . . . 900 rpm
Idle mixture CO content . . . . 1.5 ± 0.5 %

Ignition system

Contact breaker points gap . . . . 0.4 to 0.5 mm (0.016 to 0.019 in)
Dwell angle . . . . 52° ± 3°
Ignition timing . . . . 8° BTDC at 900 rpm
Firing order . . . . 1-3-4-2 (No 1 at front/timing belt end of engine)
Spark plugs . . . . Bosch WR 7 D+
Spark plug electrode gap . . . . 0.8 mm
Ignition HT lead resistance:
    New lead . . . . 16 000 ohms per metre length
    Maximum . . . . 20 000 ohms per lead

Clutch

Pedal free travel . . . . 20 to 30 mm

Brakes

Minimum front brake pad thickness (friction lining plus backing plate) . 6.5 mm
Minimum rear brake shoe lining thickness (lining plus shoe rim) . . . . . . 3.0 mm

Tyres

Tyre size . . . . 155R x 12

	Front	Rear
Pressures (tyres cold) - bars (psi)	1.7 (25)	2.5 (36)

Note: *Pressures given are for a fully-laden vehicle - adjust for a partly-laden vehicle.*
Note: *Pressures apply only to original-equipment tyres, and may vary if any other make or type is fitted; check with the tyre manufacturer or supplier for correct pressures if necessary.*

Torque wrench settings

	Nm	lbf ft
Engine oil drain plug	23	17
Camshaft cover bolts	5	4
Spark plugs	25	18
Transmission filler/level and drain plugs	43	32
Rear axle oil drain plug	6	4
Rear axle oil filler/level plug	4	3
Roadwheel nuts	65	48

Lubricants, fluids and capacities   1•3

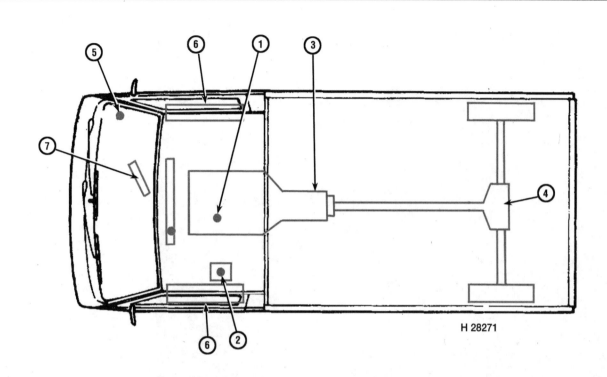

H 28271

Lubricants and fluids

Component or system	Lubricant type/specification
1 Engine	Multigrade engine oil, viscosity 15W/40 or 15W/50, to API-SE, API-SF or GM 6048-M or GM 6136-M or MIL-L-46152
2 Cooling system	Ethylene-glycol based antifreeze to GM 1899-M or GME L 6368
3 Manual transmission	SAE 80W gear oil to API-GL4 or GM 4655-M or MIL-L-2105
4 Rear axle	SAE 80W or 90 gear oil to API-GL5 or GM 4735-M or MIL-L-2105B
5 Braking system	Brake fluid to FMVSS DOT 4
6 Hub/wheel bearings	Multi-purpose lithium based grease
7 Steering rack	Multi-purpose lithium based grease

Capacities

Engine oil
Including filter . . . .   3.5 litres

Cooling system
Including expansion tank . . . .   4.0 litres

Fuel tank
Van . . . .   33 litres
Pickup . . . .   32 litres

Transmission . . . .   1.3 litres

Rear axle . . . .   1.3 litres

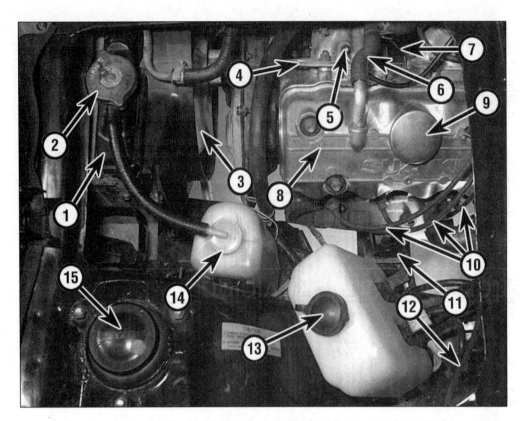

View of the engine beneath the passenger's seat

1 Radiator
2 Radiator filler cap
3 Cooling fan
4 Engine lifting eye
5 Temperature gauge sender unit
6 Crankcase ventilation hose
7 Engine oil level dipstick
8 Cam cover
9 Engine oil filler cap
10 HT leads from spark plugs
11 Left-hand engine mounting
12 HT lead from ignition coil
13 Windscreen washer fluid reservoir
14 Coolant expansion tank filler cap
15 Front suspension strut upper mounting

View of the engine beneath the driver's seat

1 Fuel return hose
2 Carburettor with cable support bracket
3 Crankcase ventilation hose
4 Heater return hose
5 Alternator
6 Auxiliary drivebelt (fanbelt)
7 Radiator top hose
8 Radiator
9 Brake vacuum servo unit vacuum hose
10 Radiator bottom hose
11 Clutch cable
12 Choke cable
13 Air cleaner cover retaining wing nut
14 Air cleaner body

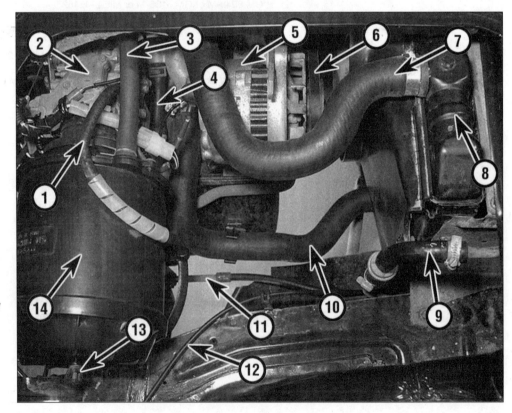

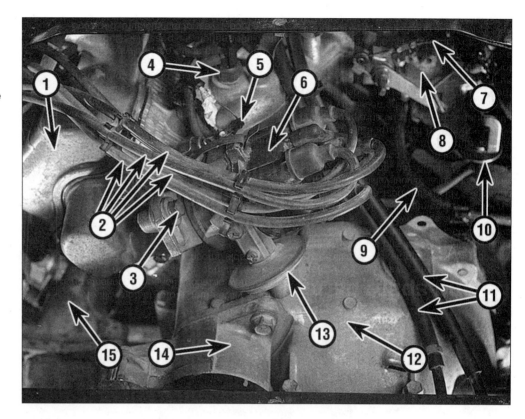

View of the engine beneath the engine rear cover

1 Cam cover
2 HT leads
3 Distributor clamp bolt
4 Choke opener BVSV valve
5 LT wire connector on
   distributor
6 Distributor cap
7 Choke cable
8 Carburettor
9 Fuel feed hose
10 Choke opener
11 Gearchange cables
12 Gearbox
13 Vacuum advance diaphragm
14 Starter motor
15 Exhaust manifold

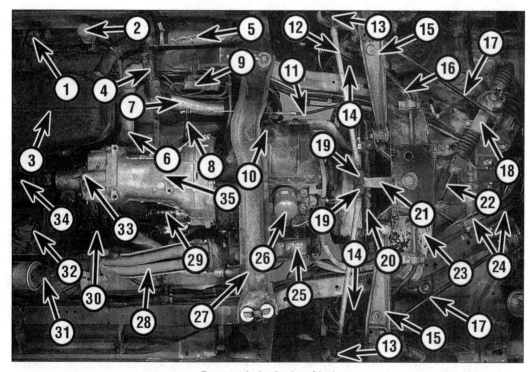

9 Brake pressure-regulating
   valve
10 Engine oil drain plug
11 Clutch cable
12 Steering track rod
13 Outer track rod end
14 Front suspension coil
   spring
15 Front suspension lower
   arm
16 Anti-roll bar
17 Front suspension radius
   arm
18 Steering gear
19 Inner track rod end
20 Radiator
21 Steering linkage centre
   lever
22 Drag link
23 Crossmember
24 Heater hoses
25 Exhaust manifold
26 Oil filter
27 Engine mounting
   crossmember
28 Exhaust front section
29 Starter motor
30 Speedometer cable
31 Exhaust centre section
32 Battery box
33 Gearbox
34 Propeller shaft

Front underbody view (Van)

1 Electric fuel pump
2 Fuel filter
3 Fuel tank

4 Warm-air flap valve
5 Fuel tank filler

6 Warm-air hose from
   exhaust manifold

7 Air inlet hose to air
   cleaner
8 Clutch release arm

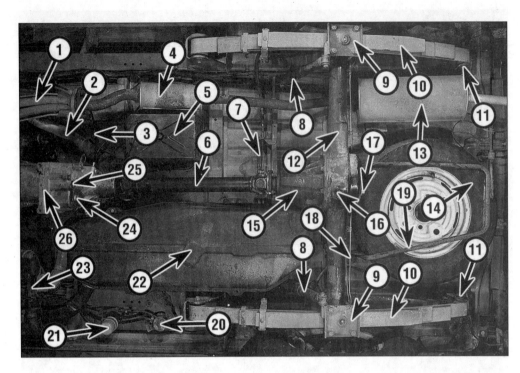

Rear underbody view (Van)

1 Exhaust front section
2 Warm-air hose from exhaust manifold
3 Speedometer cable
4 Exhaust centre section
5 Battery box
6 Propeller shaft
7 Handbrake mechanism
8 Rear shock absorber
9 Rear leaf spring U-bolt plate
10 Rear leaf spring
11 Rear leaf spring shackle
12 Rear axle
13 Exhaust rear section
14 Spare wheel
15 Differential unit
16 Rear axle drain plug
17 Rear axle filler/level plug
18 Brake hydraulic line
19 Spare wheel carrier
20 Electric fuel pump
21 Fuel filter
22 Fuel tank
23 Warm-air flap valve
24 Gearbox filler plug
25 Gearbox drain plug
26 Gearbox

Rear underbody view (Pickup)

1 Exhaust front section
2 Starter motor
3 Speedometer cable
4 Exhaust centre section
5 Handbrake mechanism
6 Rear shock absorber
7 Rear axle
8 Rear leaf spring U-bolt plate
9 Rear leaf spring
10 Exhaust rear section
11 Rear leaf spring shackle
12 Fuel tank
13 Differential unit
14 Rear axle drain plug
15 Rear axle filler/level plug
16 Brake hydraulic line
17 Handbrake cables
18 Propeller shaft
19 Electric fuel pump
20 Fuel filter
21 Warm-air hose from exhaust manifold
22 Gearbox filler plug
23 Gearbox drain plug
24 Gearbox

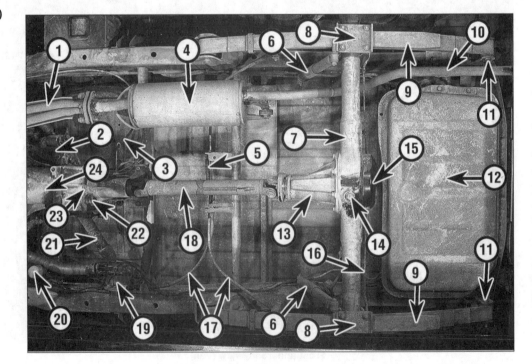

Rascal/SuperCarry maintenance schedule

1 The maintenance intervals in this manual are provided with the assumption that you will be carrying out the work yourself. These are the minimum maintenance intervals recommended by the manufacturer. If you wish to keep your vehicle in peak condition at all times, you may wish to perform some of these procedures more often. We encourage frequent maintenance, because it enhances the efficiency, performance and resale value of your vehicle.
2 If the vehicle is driven in dusty areas, used to tow a trailer, or driven frequently at slow speeds (idling in traffic) or on short journeys, more frequent maintenance intervals are recommended.
3 When the vehicle is new, it should be serviced by a factory-authorised dealer service department, in order to preserve the factory warranty.

Every 250 miles (400 km) or weekly

☐ Check the engine oil level (Section 3)
☐ Check the engine coolant level (Section 3)
☐ Check the brake fluid level (Section 3)
☐ Check the screen washer fluid level (Section 3)
☐ Visually examine the tyres for tread depth, and wear or damage (Section 4)
☐ Check and if necessary adjust the tyre pressures (Section 4)
☐ Check the operation of the horn, all lights, and the wipers and washers (Section 5)
☐ Check the condition of the battery (Section 6)
☐ Check the condition of the wiper blades (Section 7)

Every 6000 miles (10 000 km) or 6 months - whichever comes sooner

In addition to all the items listed above, carry out the following:

☐ Renew the engine oil and filter (Section 8)*
☐ Clean the air cleaner filter element** (Section 9)
☐ Lubricate the accelerator cable and carburettor pivots (Section 10)
☐ Renew the spark plugs (Section 11)
☐ Renew the contact breaker points (Section 12)
☐ Check and adjust the ignition timing (Section 13)
☐ Check and if necessary adjust the clutch cable (Section 14)
☐ Check the condition of the front brake pads, and renew if necessary (Section 15)
☐ Check the condition of the rear brake shoes, and renew if necessary (Section 16)
☐ Check the brake pipes and hoses for condition and correct routing (Section 17)
☐ Check and if necessary adjust the brake pedal height and travel (Section 18)
☐ Check operation of the handbrake lever, and if necessary adjust the cable (Section 19)
☐ Check all hub bearings for correct endfloat (Section 20)
☐ Check the tightness of all roadwheel nuts (Section 20)
☐ Check all shock absorbers for correct operation (Section 20)
☐ Check and if necessary top-up the transmission and rear axle oil levels. Check for leakage (Section 21)
☐ Check the steering and suspension components for condition and security (Section 22)
☐ Lubricate all door hinges (Section 23)
☐ Carry out a road test (Section 24)

Owners of high-mileage vehicles, or those who do a lot of stop-start driving, should renew the engine oil and filter more frequently. Consult a Vauxhall/Suzuki dealer if necessary.
**Owners who use the vehicle in dusty conditions, should clean the air cleaner filter element every 1500 miles (2500 km).*

Every 12 000 miles (20 000 km) or 12 months - whichever comes sooner

In addition to all the items listed above, carry out the following:

☐ Check the condition and adjustment of the auxiliary drivebelt, and renew if necessary (Section 25)
☐ Check and adjust the valve clearances (Section 26)
☐ Check the crankcase ventilation/emission control hoses and throttle positioner system (Section 27)
☐ Check engine compartment for leaks (Section 28)
☐ Check the exhaust system for condition (Section 29)
☐ Check the ignition HT leads for condition (Section 30)
☐ Check the distributor cap and rotor arm for condition (Section 30)
☐ Check the distributor mechanical and vacuum advance (Section 30)
☐ Check the idle speed and mixture adjustment (Section 31)
☐ Check the wiring harness for condition (Section 32)
☐ Check the propeller shaft for condition (Section 33)
☐ Check the headlight beam setting (Section 34)

Every 24 000 miles (40 000 km) or 2 years - whichever comes sooner

In addition to all the items listed above, carry out the following:

☐ Torque-tighten the cylinder head bolts and manifold nuts (Section 35)
☐ Renew the auxiliary drivebelt (Section 36)
☐ Renew the engine coolant/antifreeze mixture (Section 37)
☐ Renew the air cleaner filter element* (Section 38)
☐ Check the fuel tank cap and fuel lines for leaks (Section 39)
☐ Renew the fuel filter (Section 40)
☐ Check the operation of the crankcase ventilation valve, oxygen sensor and fuel cut solenoid (Section 41)
☐ Renew the transmission and rear axle oil. Check for leakage (Section 42)
☐ Renew the brake fluid (Section 43)

Owners of high-mileage vehicles, or those who use the vehicle in dusty conditions, should renew the air cleaner filter element more frequently.

Every 48 000 miles (80 000 km) or 4 years

☐ Renew all brake hoses and rubber components in the master cylinder and wheel cylinders (Section 44)

Every 72 000 miles (120 000 km)

☐ Renew the timing belt (Section 45)*
This is not included in the manufacturer's maintenance schedule, but is strongly recommended as a precaution against the timing belt failing in service. If the timing belt fails while the engine is running, extensive engine damage could be caused.

1 Introduction

1 This Chapter is designed to help the home mechanic maintain his/her vehicle for safety, economy, long life and peak performance.

2 The Chapter contains a master maintenance schedule, followed by Sections dealing specifically with each task in the schedule. Visual checks, adjustments, component renewal and other helpful items are included. Refer to the accompanying illustrations of the engine compartment and the underside of the vehicle for the locations of the various components.

3 Servicing your vehicle in accordance with the mileage/time maintenance schedule and the following Sections will provide a planned maintenance programme, which should result in a long and reliable service life. This is a comprehensive plan, so maintaining some items but not others at the specified service intervals, will not produce the same results.

4 As you service your vehicle, you will discover that many of the procedures can - and should - be grouped together, because of the particular procedure being performed, or because of the close proximity of two otherwise-unrelated components to one another. For example, if the vehicle is raised for any reason, the exhaust can be inspected at the same time as the suspension and steering components.

2 Routine maintenance

1 The first step in this maintenance programme is to prepare yourself before the actual work begins. Read through all the Sections relevant to the work to be carried out, then make a list and gather together all the parts and tools required. If a problem is encountered, seek advice from a parts specialist, or a dealer service department.

2 If, from the time the vehicle is new, the routine maintenance schedule is followed closely, and frequent checks are made of fluid levels and high-wear items, as suggested throughout this manual, the engine will be kept in relatively good running condition, and the need for additional work will be minimised.

3 It is possible that there will be times when the engine is running poorly due to the lack of regular maintenance. This is even more likely if a used vehicle, which has not received regular and frequent maintenance checks, is purchased. In such cases, additional work may need to be carried out, outside of the regular maintenance intervals.

4 If engine wear is suspected, a compression test (refer to Chapter 2A) will provide valuable information regarding the overall performance of the main internal components. Such a test can be used as a basis to decide on the extent of the work to be carried out. If, for example, a compression test indicates serious internal engine wear, conventional maintenance as described in this Chapter will not greatly improve the performance of the engine, and may prove a waste of time and money, unless extensive overhaul work (Chapter 2B) is carried out first.

Weekly checks

3 Fluid level checks

Engine oil

1 The engine oil level is checked with a dipstick that extends through the dipstick tube and into the sump at the bottom of the engine. The dipstick is located above the camshaft cover, and access is gained by lifting or removing (according to model) the left-hand passenger seat and engine inspection cover.

2 The oil level should be checked with the vehicle standing on level ground, before it is driven, or at least 5 minutes after the engine has been switched off.

> **HAYNES HiNT** *If the oil is checked immediately after driving the vehicle, some of the oil will remain in the upper engine components and oil galleries, resulting in an inaccurate reading on the dipstick.*

3 Withdraw the dipstick from the tube, and wipe all the oil from the end with a clean rag or paper towel. Insert the clean dipstick back into the tube as far as it will go, then withdraw it once more. Note the oil level on the end of the dipstick. Add oil as necessary until the level is at the top of the hatched section of the dipstick **(see illustration)**.

4 Always maintain the level within the dipstick hatched section. If the level is allowed to fall below the hatched section, oil starvation may result, which could lead to severe engine damage. If the engine is overfilled by adding too much oil, this may result in oil leaks or oil seal failures.

5 Oil is added to the engine via the filler cap on the camshaft cover. Unscrew the cap and top-up the level **(see illustration)**; an oil can spout or funnel may help to reduce spillage. Always use the correct grade and type of oil as shown in *"Lubricants, fluids and capacities"*.

Coolant

 Warning: DO NOT attempt to remove the radiator pressure cap when the engine is hot, as there is a very great risk of scalding.

6 The vehicles covered by this manual have a pressurised cooling system. An atmospheric pressure expansion tank is incorporated in cooling system, and is located near the left-hand side of the radiator. As engine temperature increases, the coolant expands and is forced past the pressure cap on the top of the radiator into the expansion tank. As the engine cools, the coolant is automatically drawn back into the radiator. The expansion tank always has a reserve amount of coolant in it, which rises or falls according to the temperature of the coolant in the engine. Thus the radiator is always full.

7 The coolant level in the expansion tank should be checked regularly. Access is gained by lifting or removing (according to model) the left-hand passenger seat and engine inspection cover. When the engine is cold, the coolant level should be between the "FULL" and "LOW" marks on the side of the tank. When the engine is hot, the level may rise slightly above the "FULL" mark.

8 If topping-up is necessary and there is still

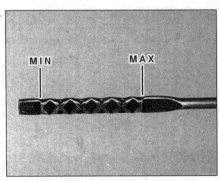
3.3 Engine oil level dipstick markings

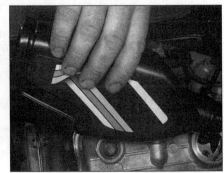
3.5 Topping-up the engine oil

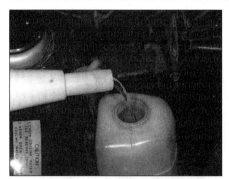

3.8 Topping-up the coolant level in the expansion tank

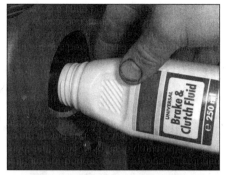

3.13 Topping-up the brake fluid level

3.18 Topping-up the washer fluid level

an amount of coolant in the expansion tank, remove the filler cap and pour in coolant mixture until the level is correct **(see illustration)**. Before refitting the filler cap, check that the inner hose is fitted correctly to the bottom of the cap. Since the expansion tank is not pressurised, there is no need to wait until the engine is cold in this instance.

9 If, through leakage or neglect, there is no coolant in the expansion tank, it will be necessary to remove the filler cap from the top of the radiator (in addition to removing the cap from the expansion tank) and in this instance it is important to wait until the engine is **cold**. Turn the pressure cap on the radiator anti-clockwise until it reaches the first stop. Wait until any pressure remaining in the system is released, then push the cap down, turn it anti-clockwise to the second stop, and lift off.

10 Add a mixture of water and antifreeze (see Section 37) through the expansion tank filler neck until the coolant is approximately halfway between the two level marks, then refit the cap. If the radiator cap has been removed, add the mixture to the radiator until the level reaches the filler neck, then refit the cap, turning it clockwise as far as it will go to secure.

11 The addition of coolant should only be necessary at very infrequent intervals. If frequent topping-up is required, it is likely there is a leak in the system. Check the radiator, and all hoses and joint faces, for any sign of staining or actual wetness, and rectify

as necessary. Coolant leaks will often show up as a white stain in the area of leakage. If no leaks can be found, it is advisable to have the pressure cap and the entire system pressure-tested by a dealer or suitably-equipped garage, as this will often show up a small leak not previously apparent.

Brake fluid

12 The brake fluid reservoir is located through an aperture at the right-hand outer end of the facia, and access is gained by opening the right-hand door. The "MAX" and "MIN" marks are indicated on the side of the reservoir, and the fluid level should be maintained between these marks at all times.

13 If topping-up is necessary, first wipe the area around the filler cap with a clean rag before removing the cap. When adding fluid, pour it carefully into the reservoir, to avoid spilling it (see illustration). Be sure to use only the specified brake hydraulic fluid, since mixing different types of fluid can cause damage to the system. See *"Lubricants, fluids and capacities"* at the beginning of this Chapter.

⚠️ *Warning: Brake hydraulic fluid can harm your eyes and damage painted surfaces, so use extreme caution when handling and pouring it. Do not use fluid that has been standing open for some time, as it absorbs moisture from the air. Excess moisture content can cause a dangerous loss of braking effectiveness.*

14 When adding fluid, it is a good idea to inspect the reservoir for contamination. The system should be drained and refilled if deposits, dirt particles or contamination are seen in the fluid.

15 After filling the reservoir to the correct level, make sure that the cap is refitted securely, to avoid leaks and the entry of foreign matter.

16 The fluid level in the reservoir will drop slightly as the brake pads and shoes wear down during normal operation. If the reservoir requires repeated replenishment to maintain the proper level, this is an indication of a hydraulic leak somewhere in the system, which should be investigated immediately.

Washer fluid

17 The windscreen/tailgate washer fluid reservoir filler is located behind the radiator expansion tank on the left-hand side of the engine compartment. Access is gained by lifting or removing (according to model) the left-hand passenger seat and engine inspection cover.

18 When topping-up the reservoir, a screenwash additive should be added in the quantities recommended on the bottle **(see illustration)**.

4 Tyre checks

1 On later models, the tyres may have tread wear safety bands, which will appear when the tread depth reaches approximately 1.6 mm. Tread wear can be monitored with a simple, inexpensive device known as a tread depth indicator gauge **(see illustration)**.

2 Wheels and tyres should give no real problems in use, provided that a close eye is kept on them with regard to excessive wear or damage. To this end, the following points should be noted.

3 Ensure that the tyre pressures are checked regularly and maintained correctly **(see illustration)**. Checking should be carried out with the tyres cold, **not** immediately after the vehicle has been in use. If the pressures are

4.1 Checking the tyre tread depth with a depth gauge

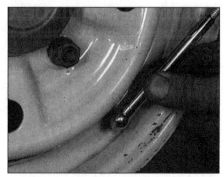

4.3 Checking the tyre pressure with a pressure gauge

Tyre tread wear patterns

Shoulder Wear

Underinflation (wear on both sides)
Under-inflation will cause overheating of the tyre, because the tyre will flex too much, and the tread will not sit correctly on the road surface. This will cause a loss of grip and excessive wear, not to mention the danger of sudden tyre failure due to heat build-up.
Check and adjust pressures
Incorrect wheel camber (wear on one side)
Repair or renew suspension parts
Hard cornering
Reduce speed!

Centre Wear

Overinflation
Over-inflation will cause rapid wear of the centre part of the tyre tread, coupled with reduced grip, harsher ride, and the danger of shock damage occurring in the tyre casing.
Check and adjust pressures

If you sometimes have to inflate your car's tyres to the higher pressures specified for maximum load or sustained high speed, don't forget to reduce the pressures to normal afterwards.

Uneven Wear

Front tyres may wear unevenly as a result of wheel misalignment. Most tyre dealers and garages can check and adjust the wheel alignment (or "tracking") for a modest charge.
Incorrect camber or castor
Repair or renew suspension parts
Malfunctioning suspension
Repair or renew suspension parts
Unbalanced wheel
Balance tyres
Incorrect toe setting
Adjust front wheel alignment
Note: *The feathered edge of the tread which typifies toe wear is best checked by feel.*

checked with the tyres hot, an apparently-high reading will be obtained, owing to heat expansion. **Under no circumstances** should an attempt be made to reduce the pressures to the quoted cold reading in this instance, or effective under-inflation will result.

4 Note any abnormal tread wear **(see illustration)**. Tread pattern irregularities such as feathering, flat spots, and more wear on one side than the other, are indications of front wheel alignment and/or balance problems. If any of these conditions are noted, they should be rectified as soon as possible.

5 Under-inflation will cause overheating of the tyre, owing to excessive flexing of the casing, and the tread will not sit correctly on the road surface. This will cause excessive wear, not to mention the danger of sudden tyre failure due to heat build-up.

6 Over-inflation will cause rapid wear of the centre part of the tyre tread, coupled with reduced adhesion, harsher ride, and the danger of shock damage occurring in the tyre casing.

7 Regularly check the tyres for damage in the form of cuts or bulges, especially in the sidewalls. Remove any nails or stones embedded in the tread, before they penetrate the tyre to cause deflation. If removal of a nail does reveal that the tyre has been punctured, refit the nail so that its point of penetration is marked. Then immediately change the wheel, and have the tyre repaired by a tyre dealer. Do not drive on a tyre in such a condition. If in any doubt as to the possible consequences of any

damage found, consult your local tyre dealer for advice.

8 Periodically remove the wheels, and clean any dirt or mud from the inside and outside surfaces. Examine the wheel rims for signs of rusting, corrosion or other damage. Light alloy wheels are easily damaged by "kerbing" whilst parking, and similarly, steel wheels may become dented or buckled. Renewal of the wheel is very often the only course of remedial action possible.

9 The balance of each wheel and tyre assembly should be maintained to avoid excessive wear, not only to the tyres but also to the steering and suspension components. Wheel imbalance is normally signified by vibration through the vehicle's bodyshell, although in many cases, it is particularly noticeable through the steering wheel. Conversely, it should be noted that wear or damage in suspension or steering components may cause excessive tyre wear. Out-of-round or out-of-true tyres, damaged wheels, and wheel bearing wear also fall into this category. Balancing will not usually cure vibration caused by such wear.

10 Wheel balancing may be carried out with the wheel either on or off the vehicle. If balanced on the vehicle, ensure that the wheel-to-hub relationship is marked in some way prior to subsequent wheel removal, so that it may be refitted in its original position.

11 General tyre wear is influenced to a large degree by driving style - harsh braking and acceleration, or fast cornering, will all produce more rapid tyre wear. Interchanging of tyres

may result in more even wear. However, if this is completely effective, the added expense is incurred of replacing all four tyres at once, which may prove financially-restrictive for many owners.

12 Front tyres may wear unevenly as a result of wheel misalignment. The front wheels should always be correctly aligned according to the settings specified by the vehicle manufacturer (see Chapter 10 Specifications).

13 Legal restrictions apply to many aspects of tyre fitting and usage, and in the UK, this information is contained in the Motor Vehicle Construction and Use Regulations. It is suggested that a copy of these regulations is obtained from your local police if in doubt as to current legal requirements with regard to tyre type and condition, minimum tread depth, etc.

5 Electrical system check

1 Check the operation of all the electrical equipment, ie lights, direction indicators, horn, washers etc. Refer to the appropriate Sections of Chapter 12 for details if any of the circuits are found to be inoperative.

2 Stop-light switch adjustment is described in Chapter 9 if required.

3 Visually check all accessible wiring connectors, harnesses and retaining clips for security, and for signs of chafing or damage. Rectify any faults found.

6.1a On Van models, remove the cover . . .

6.1b . . . for access to the battery

6.1c On Pickup models, remove the metal outer cover for access to the battery

6 Battery check

⚠️ *Caution: Before carrying out any work on the vehicle battery, read through the precautions given in "Safety first!" at the beginning of this manual.*

1 On Van models, the battery is located centrally beneath a cover in the rear load area. On Pickup models, the battery is located in a box beneath the left-hand side of the rear load platform, and access is gained by unbolting a metal outer cover **(see illustrations)**. The exterior of the battery should be inspected periodically for damage such as a cracked case or cover.

2 Check the tightness of the battery cable clamps to ensure good electrical connections, and check the entire length of each cable for cracks and frayed conductors **(see illustration)**.

3 If corrosion (visible as white, fluffy deposits) is evident, remove the cables from the battery terminals, clean away with a small wire brush, then refit the terminals. Corrosion can be kept to a minimum by applying a layer of petroleum jelly to the clamps and terminals after they are reconnected.

4 Make sure that the battery retaining clamp or rod (as applicable) is tight **(see illustrations)**.

5 Corrosion on the retaining clamp/rod and

the battery itself can be removed with a solution of water and baking soda. Thoroughly rinse all cleaned areas with plain water.

6 Any metal parts of the vehicle damaged by corrosion should be covered with a zinc-based primer, then painted.

7 Periodically check the charge condition of the battery as described in Chapter 5A.

8 Further information on the battery, charging and jump starting can be found in Chapter 5A and in the preliminary sections of this manual.

7 Wiper blade check

1 Check the condition of the wiper blades; if they are cracked or show any signs of deterioration, or if the glass swept area is smeared, renew them. For maximum clarity of vision on vehicles used daily, wiper blades should be renewed annually, as a matter of course.

2 To remove a wiper blade, pull the arm fully away from the glass until it locks. For the windscreen wiper blade, swivel the blade so that it is at right-angles to the arm, then press the plastic block from the hooked end of the arm. For the tailgate wiper, depress the small tab in the centre of the blade, and pull the blade off the end of the arm **(see illustrations)**. On refitting, ensure that the blade is fully engaged with the arm.

6.2 Check the tightness of the battery cable clamps

6.4a Battery retaining rod (arrowed) on Van models

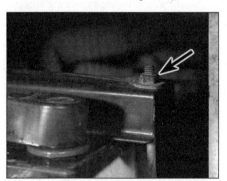

6.4b Battery retaining clamp (arrowed) on Pickup models

7.2a Removing a windscreen wiper blade from the wiper arm

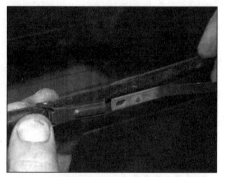

7.2b Removing a tailgate wiper blade from the wiper arm

Every 6000 miles or 6 months - whichever comes sooner

8 Engine oil and filter renewal

1 Frequent oil and filter changes are the most important preventative maintenance procedures which can be undertaken by the DIY owner. As engine oil ages, it becomes diluted and contaminated, which leads to premature engine wear.

2 Before starting this procedure, gather together all the necessary tools and materials. Also make sure that you have plenty of clean rags and newspapers handy, to mop up any spills. Ideally, the engine oil should be warm, as it will drain better, and more built-up sludge will be removed with it. Take care, however, not to touch the exhaust or any other hot parts of the engine when working under the vehicle. To avoid any possibility of scalding, and to protect yourself from possible skin irritants and other harmful contaminants in used engine oils, it is advisable to wear gloves when carrying out this work. Access to the underside of the vehicle will be greatly improved if it can be raised on a lift, driven onto ramps, or jacked up and supported on axle stands (see *"Jacking, towing and wheel changing"*). Whichever method is chosen, make sure that the vehicle remains level, or if it is at an angle, that the drain plug is at the lowest point.

3 Raise or remove (according to model) the front seats and engine covers for access to the engine oil filler cap on top of the engine.

4 Slacken the drain plug about half a turn **(see illustration)**. Position the draining container under the drain plug, then remove the plug completely. If possible, try to keep the plug pressed into the sump while unscrewing it by hand the last couple of turns. As the plug releases from the threads, move it away sharply, so that the stream of oil issuing from the sump runs into the container, not up your sleeve! Recover the sealing ring from the drain plug.

5 Allow some time for the old oil to drain, noting that it may be necessary to reposition the container as the oil flow slows to a trickle.

6 After all the oil has drained, wipe off the drain plug with a clean rag, and fit a new sealing washer. Clean the area around the drain plug opening, and refit the plug. Tighten the plug to the specified torque.

7 Move the container into position under the oil filter, which is located on the left side of the cylinder block, above the front crossmember.

8 Using an oil filter removal tool if necessary, slacken the filter initially, then unscrew it by hand the rest of the way. Empty the oil in the old filter into the container.

9 Use a clean rag to remove all oil, dirt and sludge from the filter sealing area on the engine. Check the old filter to make sure that the rubber sealing ring hasn't stuck to the engine. If it has, carefully remove it.

10 Apply a light coating of clean engine oil to the sealing ring on the new filter, then screw it into position on the engine. Tighten the filter firmly by hand only - **do not** use any tools. The manufacturers recommend that the filter be tightened two-thirds of a turn after the initial contact of the sealing ring with the mounting surface.

11 Remove the old oil and all tools from under the vehicle, then lower the vehicle to the ground (if applicable).

12 Remove the dipstick, then unscrew the oil filler cap from the camshaft cover. Fill the engine, using the correct grade and type of oil (see *"Lubricants, fluids and capacities"*). An oil can spout or funnel may help to reduce spillage. Pour in half the specified quantity of oil first, then wait a few minutes for the oil to fall to the sump. Continue adding oil a small quantity at a time until the level is up to the top of the hatched area on the dipstick. Refit and tighten the filler cap.

13 Start the engine and run it for a few minutes; check for leaks around the oil filter seal and the sump drain plug. Note that there may be a delay of a few seconds before the oil pressure warning light goes out when the engine is first started, as the oil circulates through the engine oil galleries and the new oil filter before the pressure builds up.

14 Switch off the engine, and wait a few minutes for the oil to settle in the sump once more. With the new oil circulated and the filter completely full, recheck the level on the dipstick, and add more oil as necessary.

15 Refit the front seats and engine covers.

Note: It is antisocial and illegal to dump oil down the drain. To find the location of your local oil recycling bank, call this number free.

16 Dispose of the used engine oil safely, with reference to *"General repair procedures"* in the reference Sections of this manual.

9 Air filter element inspection and cleaning

Note: *On vehicles operating in very dusty conditions, the air filter element should be inspected and cleaned more frequently - every 1500 miles/2500 km in extreme conditions.*

1 Raise or remove (according to model) the right-hand seat and engine cover

2 Unscrew the wing nut and remove the washer, then remove the end cap from the air cleaner. Recover the sealing ring.

3 Withdraw the air cleaner element from the housing, and inspect it for excessive clogging and deterioration. If it has completed less than 24 000 miles in service, it is sufficient to clean it. First tap the element lightly on a workbench to dislodge the larger embedded particles of dust and dirt, then blow out the smaller particles, preferably using an air line from the inside surface of the element.

4 Wipe clean the inner surfaces of the air cleaner assembly and end cap.

5 Check the end cap sealing ring condition, and renew if necessary.

6 Insert the element, and refit the end cap together with the sealing ring. Refit the washer and tighten the wing nut.

7 Refit the right-hand seat and engine cover.

10 Accelerator cable and carburettor pivot lubrication

1 Raise or remove (according to model) the right-hand seat and engine cover.

2 Apply a little engine oil to the moving parts (levers, shafts etc) on the carburettor.

3 Pull out the choke control knob, and check that the choke lever on the carburettor operates smoothly. Check that the knob returns to its rest position. If the control is stiff to operate, and lubrication does not improve this, check that the choke cable is correctly routed, and not twisted or bent excessively.

4 Refit the right-hand seat and engine cover.

11 Spark plug renewal

1 The correct functioning of the spark plugs is vital for the correct running and efficiency of the engine. It is essential that the plugs fitted are appropriate for the engine (a suitable type is specified at the beginning of this Chapter). If this type is used and the engine is in good condition, the spark plugs should not need

8.4 Sump drain plug (arrowed)

attention between scheduled replacement intervals. Spark plug cleaning is rarely necessary, and should not be attempted unless specialised equipment is available, as damage can easily be caused to the firing ends.

2 Raise or remove (according to model) the left-hand seat and engine cover. Because the engine is tilted slightly to the left-hand side, access to the spark plugs is restricted, and it may be helpful to remove the windscreen washer reservoir.

3 If there are no marks on the original spark plug (HT) leads, mark the leads "1" to "4", to correspond to the cylinder the lead serves (No 1 cylinder is at the front end of the engine). Pull the leads from the plugs by gripping the end fitting, not the lead, otherwise the lead connection may be fractured.

4 It is advisable to remove the dirt from the spark plug recesses using a clean brush, vacuum cleaner or compressed air before removing the plugs, to prevent dirt dropping into the cylinders.

5 Unscrew the plugs using a spark plug spanner, suitable box spanner or a deep socket and extension bar **(see illustration)**. Keep the socket aligned with the spark plug - if it is forcibly moved to one side, the ceramic insulator may be broken off. As each plug is removed, examine it as follows.

6 Examination of the spark plugs will give a good indication of the condition of the engine. If the insulator nose of the spark plug is clean and white, with no deposits, this is indicative of a weak mixture or too hot a plug (a hot plug transfers heat away from the electrode slowly, a cold plug transfers heat away quickly).

7 If the tip and insulator nose are covered with hard black-looking deposits, then this is indicative that the mixture is too rich. Should the plug be black and oily, then it is likely that the engine is fairly worn, as well as the mixture being too rich.

8 If the insulator nose is covered with light tan to greyish-brown deposits, then the mixture is correct and it is likely that the engine is in good condition.

9 The spark plug electrode gap is of considerable importance as, if it is too large or too small, the size of the spark and its efficiency will be seriously impaired. The gap

should be set to the value given in the Specifications at the beginning of this Chapter.

10 To set the gap, measure it with a feeler blade or wire gauge, and then bend the outer plug electrode until the correct gap is achieved **(see illustrations)**. The centre electrode should never be bent, as this will crack the insulator and cause plug failure, if nothing worse. If using feeler blades, the gap is correct when the appropriate-size blade is a firm sliding fit.

11 Special spark plug electrode gap adjusting tools are available from most motor accessory shops, or from some spark plug manufacturers.

12 Before fitting the spark plugs, check that the threaded connector sleeves are tight, and that the plug exterior surfaces and threads are clean.

13 Refit the spark plugs.

14 Connect the HT leads in their correct order.

HAYNES HINT

It is very often difficult to insert spark plugs into their holes without cross-threading them. To avoid this possibility, fit a short length of 5/16 inch internal diameter rubber hose over the end of the spark plug. The flexible hose acts as a universal joint, to help align the plug with the plug hole. Should the plug begin to cross-thread, the hose will slip on the spark plug, preventing thread damage to the aluminium cylinder head. Remove the rubber hose, and tighten the plug to the specified torque using the spark plug socket and a torque wrench

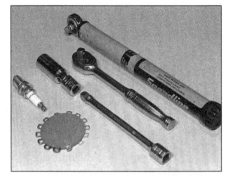

11.5 Tools required for spark plug removal, gap adjustment and refitting

12 Contact breaker points check/renewal

Note: *The manufacturers recommend renewal of the contact breaker points every 6000 miles/10 000 km. However, this Section includes checking and cleaning of the points, which may be necessary in an emergency situation, due to lack of servicing*

1 Remove the engine rear cover - this is located towards the front of the rear load area.

2 Release the two spring clips, and lift off the distributor cap.

3 Carefully pull the rotor arm off the shaft.

4 With the ignition switched off, use a screwdriver to open the contact breaker points, then visually check the points surfaces for pitting, roughness and discoloration. If the points have been arcing, there will be a build-up of metal on the moving contact, and a corresponding hole in the fixed contact; if this is the case, the points should be renewed. In an emergency situation, cleaning the points with a small file or emery tape will enable the engine to be started. However, this is to be regarded as a temporary measure, and they should be renewed at the earliest opportunity.

5 Another method of checking the contact breaker points is by using a points test meter available from most car accessory shops. Turn the engine as necessary (see paragraph 14) until the points are fully shut.

11.10a Measuring the spark plug gap with a wire gauge

11.10b Measuring the spark plug gap with a feeler blade

11.10c Adjusting the gap using a special adjusting tool

12.6 Contact breaker points and mounting screws inside the distributor

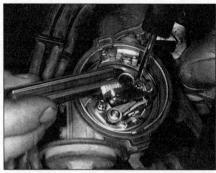

12.15 Adjusting the contact breaker points gap

Connect the meter between the distributor LT wiring terminal and earth, and read off the condition of the points.

6 To remove the points, first loosen the LT terminal nut on the side of the distributor, then use a small pair of pliers to pull the points wiring lead end fitting from the inner end of the terminal. Unscrew the points mounting screws, taking care not to drop them, and noting that the earth lead is attached to one of them. Withdraw the points assembly from the distributor **(see illustration)**.

7 The purpose of the condenser (located externally on the side of the distributor body) is to ensure that when the contact breaker points open, there is no sparking across them, which would cause wear of their faces and prevent the rapid collapse of the magnetic field in the coil. Failure of the condenser would cause a reduction in coil HT voltage, and ultimately lead to engine misfire.

8 If the engine becomes very difficult to start, or begins to miss after several miles of running, and the contact breaker points show signs of excessive burning, the condition of the condenser must be suspect. A further test can be made by carefully separating the points with the ignition switched on, using insulated tools. If this is accompanied by a strong bright flash, it is indicative that the condenser has failed.

9 Without special test equipment, the only sure way to diagnose condenser trouble is to fit a new one, and note if there is any improvement. Refer also to Chapter 5B for more information.

10 To remove the condenser, unscrew the screw securing it to the side of the distributor body, and completely remove the LT nut from the distributor terminal so that the condenser lead may be removed.

11 Refitting of the condenser is a reversal of the removal procedure. Make sure that the mounting point on the distributor body is clean, in order to make good contact.

12 Wipe clean the distributor baseplate, then fit the new set of contact breaker points. Insert the mounting screws together with the earth lead, but do not fully tighten the screws at this stage. They should be just tight enough to hold the points firmly, but enable movement for their adjustment.

13 Fit the points wiring lead end fitting to the inner end of the LT terminal, and tighten the terminal nut.

14 Turn the engine in a clockwise direction, using a socket or spanner on the crankshaft pulley bolt, until the heel of the contact breaker arm is on the peak of one of the four cam lobes. Turning the engine will be much easier if the spark plugs are removed first (see Section 11).

15 With the points fully open, a clean feeler blade equal to the contact breaker points gap as given in the Specifications should now just fit between the contact faces. If the gap is too large or too small, use a screwdriver between the two special pips on the baseplate to move the fixed contact plate until the specified gap is obtained **(see illustration)**.

16 Fully tighten the points mounting screws, and recheck the contact breaker points gap.

17 With the points correctly adjusted, refit the rotor arm and the distributor cap, (and the spark plugs, if removed) then check the ignition timing with reference to Chapter 5B.

18 If a dwell meter is available, a far more accurate method of setting the contact breaker points is by measuring and setting the distributor dwell angle. The dwell angle is the number of degrees of distributor shaft rotation during which the contact breaker points are closed (ie the period from when the points close after being opened by one cam lobe until they are opened again by the next cam lobe). The advantages of setting the points by this method are that any wear of the distributor shaft or cam lobes is taken into account, and also the inaccuracies of using a feeler blade are eliminated.

19 To check and adjust the dwell angle, connect one lead of the meter to the ignition coil "+" terminal, and the other to the coil "-" terminal, or in accordance with the meter maker's instructions.

20 Start the engine, allow it to idle, and observe the reading on the dwell meter scale. If the dwell angle is not as specified, it will be necessary to further adjust the points gap. To increase the dwell angle, decrease the points gap, and to decrease the dwell angle, increase the points gap. **Note:** *Owing to machining tolerances, or wear in the distributor shaft or bushes, it is not*

uncommon for a contact breaker points gap correctly set with feeler blades, to give a dwell angle outside the specified tolerances. If this is the case, the dwell angle should be regarded as the preferred setting.

21 After completing the adjustment, switch off the engine and disconnect the dwell meter. Check the ignition timing as described in Chapter 5B.

22 Refit the engine rear cover.

13 Ignition timing check and adjustment

Refer to Chapter 5B.

14 Clutch cable check and adjustment

1 Check that the clutch pedal moves smoothly and easily through its full travel, and that the clutch itself functions correctly, with no trace of slip or drag.

2 Adjust the clutch cable as described in Chapter 7.

3 If excessive effort is required to operate the clutch, check first that the cable is correctly routed and undamaged, then remove the pedal and check that its pivot is properly greased. Refer to Chapter 7 for further information.

15 Front brake pad check

1 Firmly apply the handbrake, then jack up the front of the car and support it securely on axle stands (see *"Jacking, towing and wheel changing"*). Remove the front roadwheels.

2 For a quick check, the thickness of friction material remaining on each brake pad can be checked through the aperture in the caliper body. Genuine pads will have a wear slot in them **(see illustration)**. If the slot is still visible on both pads, they have not yet reached their

15.2 Brake pad wear can be checked with the pads in place

Arrows indicate pad wear slots

service limit, but if the slots cannot be seen, the pads should be removed with reference to Chapter 9 for further investigation. Where possible, also check the total thickness of each pad with its backing plate, and compare with the minimum thickness given in the Specifications at the beginning of this Chapter. If any pad's friction material is worn to the specified thickness or less, *all four pads must be renewed as a set.*

3 For a comprehensive check, the brake pads should be removed and cleaned. The operation of the caliper can then also be checked, and the condition of the brake disc itself can be fully examined on both sides. Refer to Chapter 9 for further information.

16 Rear brake shoe check

1 Remove the rear brake drums, and check the brake shoes for signs of wear or contamination. At the same time, also inspect the wheel cylinders for signs of leakage, and the brake drum for signs of wear. Refer to the relevant Sections of Chapter 9 for further information. If any brake shoe friction material is worn to the specified thickness or less, *all four shoes must be renewed as a set - NEVER renew the shoes on one wheel only, as uneven braking may result.*

17 Brake pipes and hoses check

1 Apply the handbrake, then raise the front and rear of the vehicle and support on axle stands (see *"Jacking, towing and wheel changing"*).

2 The brake hydraulic system consists of a number of metal hydraulic pipes, which run from the master cylinder around the bulkhead and engine compartment to the front and rear brakes. Flexible hoses are fitted at each front brake and just forward of the rear axle, to cater for steering and suspension movement.

3 When checking the system, first look for signs of leakage at the pipe or hose unions, then examine the flexible hoses for signs of cracking, chafing or deterioration of the rubber. Bend the hoses between your fingers (but do not actually bend them double, or the casing may be damaged) and check that this does not reveal previously-hidden cracks, cuts or splits. Check that all pipes and hoses are securely fastened in their clips.

4 Carefully work along the length of the metal hydraulic pipes, looking for dents, kinks, damage of any sort, or corrosion. Corrosion can be polished off, but if the depth of pitting is significant, the pipe must be renewed (refer to Chapter 9).

5 On completion, lower the vehicle to the ground.

18 Brake pedal height check

Refer to Chapter 9, Section 11.

19 Handbrake check and adjustment

1 Chock the front wheels, then jack up the rear of the vehicle, and support securely on axle stands (see *"Jacking, towing and wheel changing"*).

2 Apply the footbrake firmly several times to establish correct shoe-to-drum clearance, then apply and release the handbrake several times.

3 Fully release the handbrake, and check that the rear wheels rotate freely, without binding. If not, check that all cables are routed correctly, and the cable components and levers move freely.

4 Slowly apply the handbrake to its fully-on position, noting the number of clicks taken by the ratchet. The handbrake is correctly adjusted if the handbrake lever stroke takes between 7 and 9 clicks.

5 To adjust the handbrake cable, first raise the rear of the vehicle and support on axle stands (see *"Jacking, towing and wheel changing"*).

6 Remove the exhaust heat shield (Van models only).

7 Fully release the handbrake, then working under the vehicle, loosen the adjusting nuts on the rear end of the outer cable. Unscrew both nuts to the extremes of the adjuster thread.

8 Apply the footbrake firmly several times to operate the rear brake shoe automatic adjusters.

9 Fully apply the handbrake lever three times, then make sure it is fully released.

10 Working under the rear of the vehicle, pull the left-hand outer cable to the left until the rear brakes are lightly rubbing, then with the cable held in this position, tighten the adjustment nuts on either side of the bracket.

11 Check that the rear wheels are locked when the handbrake lever is applied between 7 and 9 clicks.

12 Fully release the handbrake, and check that both rear wheels turn freely by hand.

13 Check that the handbrake warning light comes on when the handbrake is applied. If necessary, adjust the stop-light switch as described in Chapter 9.

14 On completion, refit the exhaust heat shield on Van models, then apply the handbrake and lower the vehicle to the ground.

20 Hub bearing, wheel nut and shock absorber check

Hub bearings

1 Apply the handbrake, then raise the front of the vehicle, and support securely on axle stands (see *"Jacking, towing and wheel changing"*).

2 Rotate each front wheel in turn (both forwards and backwards) and check that it rotates smoothly, without any noise from the bearings, which would indicate excessive wear of the tracks and ball bearings.

3 Grasp each front wheel in turn at the 12 o'clock and 6 o'clock positions, and attempt to rock the wheel - this will show up wear in the bearings, but do not mistake wear in the suspension with wear in the bearings **(see illustration)**.

4 To confirm wear in the bearings, first remove the wheel centre caps. Attach a dial gauge to an axle stand, with the gauge probe touching the hub. Move the hub in and out, and check that the thrust play does not exceed 0.1 mm.

5 If excessive wear is evident, the bearings should be renewed as described in Chapter 10.

6 Refit the wheel centre caps, and lower the vehicle to the ground.

7 Chock the front wheels, then raise the rear of the vehicle, and support securely on axle stands (see *"Jacking, towing and wheel changing"*).

8 Rotate each rear wheel in turn (both forwards and backwards) and check that it rotates smoothly, without any noise from the bearings, which would indicate excessive wear of the tracks and ball bearings.

9 Grasp each rear wheel in turn at the 3 o'clock and 9 o'clock positions, and attempt to pull the wheel in and out - this will show up wear in the bearings. Make sure the vehicle is adequately supported before carrying out this check.

10 To confirm wear in the bearings, first prise out the wheel centre caps. Attach a dial gauge to an axle stand, with the gauge probe

20.3 Checking for wear in the front wheel bearings

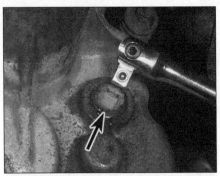

21.2 Using a 3/8 inch drive socket bar to unscrew the transmission filler/level plug (arrowed)

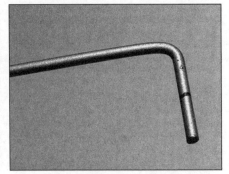

21.3a Bent piece of wire with marking (arrowed) for checking the transmission oil level

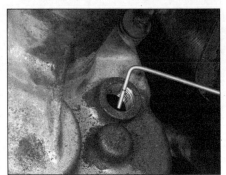

21.3b Checking the transmission oil level

touching the centre of the rear axle flange. Try to move the rear wheel in and out, and check that the thrust play does not exceed 0.8 mm.

11 Renew the bearings as described in Chapter 10 if excessive wear is evident.

12 On completion, lower the vehicle to the ground.

Wheel nuts

13 Using a torque wrench, check that the wheel nuts on each wheel are tightened to the specified torque.

Shock absorbers

14 Depress each corner of the vehicle in turn, and then release it. If the shock absorber is in good condition, the corner of the vehicle will rise and then settle to its normal position; one or two small oscillations are acceptable before the vehicle settles. It is important that the shock absorbers on each side of the vehicle operate in the same way.

15 Inspect the front shock absorbers (from under the front wings) for signs of fluid leakage. If excessive leakage is evident, the strut should be renewed. **Note:** *Both front struts should be renewed at the same time in this case, to maintain equal performance on both sides.* Also check that the front coil spring seats, rebound rubbers and the upper strut mountings are in good condition.

16 Chock the front wheels, then raise the rear of the vehicle and support on axle stands. Inspect the rear shock absorbers for signs of fluid leakage, and renew if necessary. **Note:** *Both rear shock absorbers should be renewed at the same time in this case, to maintain equal performance on both sides.* Also check that the rear shock absorber mounting rubbers are in good condition. On completion, lower the vehicle to the ground.

21 Transmission and rear axle oil level check

Note: *A 3/8 inch square-drive key or socket bar will be required to undo the transmission filler/level and drain plugs. A key can be obtained from most motor factors, or from your Vauxhall/Suzuki dealer; alternatively, a 3/8 inch drive socket bar may be used.*

1 Park the vehicle on level ground, switch off the engine, and apply the handbrake firmly. For improved access, position the vehicle over an inspection pit or on ramps, but note that the vehicle must be level when checking the oil level, to ensure an accurate check.

Transmission

2 Wipe clean the area around the filler/level plug, which is situated on the rear right-hand end of the transmission casing. Unscrew the

filler/level plug from the transmission **(see illustration)**. Note that its threads are tapered, so there is no need for a sealing washer.

3 Check that the oil level is approximately 5.0 mm below the lower edge of the oil filler/level hole on the 5-speed transmission, or approximately 15.0 mm below the lower edge of the oil filler/level hole on the 4-speed transmission. Use a bent piece of wire to make the check **(see illustrations)** - do not use anything which is likely to fall into the plug hole. If necessary, top-up the level with the specified grade of oil.

4 Apply suitable sealant to the threads of the filler/level plug, then insert it and tighten to the specified torque.

Rear axle

5 Wipe clean the area around the filler/level plug, which is situated on the rear of the rear axle casing. Unscrew and remove the plug together with the sealing washer **(see illustration)**.

6 Check that the oil level is up to the bottom of the plug aperture, and if necessary top-up the level with the specified grade of oil **(see illustration)**.

7 Check the condition of the sealing washer and if necessary renew it, then refit the filler/level plug together with the sealing washer, and tighten to the specified torque.

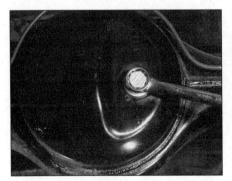

21.5 Removing the rear axle filler/level plug

21.6 Topping-up the rear axle oil level

22.2 Checking the steering rack-and-pinion gaiters for splits

22 Steering and suspension check

Front suspension and steering check

1 Apply the handbrake, then raise the front of the vehicle, and securely support it on axle stands (see *"Jacking, towing and wheel changing"*).

2 Visually inspect the balljoint dust covers and the steering rack-and-pinion gaiters for splits, chafing or deterioration **(see illustration)**. Any wear of these components will cause loss of lubricant, together with dirt and water entry, resulting in rapid deterioration of the balljoints or steering gear.

3 Grasp the roadwheel at the 12 o'clock and 6 o'clock positions, and try to rock it. Very slight free play may be felt, but if the movement is appreciable, further investigation is necessary to determine the source. Continue rocking the wheel while an assistant depresses the footbrake. If the movement is now eliminated or significantly reduced, it is likely that the hub bearings are at fault. If the free play is still evident with the footbrake depressed, then there is wear in the suspension joints or mountings.

4 Now grasp the wheel at the 9 o'clock and 3 o'clock positions, and try to rock it as before. Any movement felt now may again be caused by wear in the hub bearings or the steering track-rod balljoints. If the inner or outer balljoint is worn, the visual movement will be obvious.

5 Using a large screwdriver or flat bar, check for wear in the suspension mounting bushes by levering between the relevant suspension component and its attachment point. Some movement is to be expected as the mountings are made of rubber, but excessive wear should be obvious. Also check the condition of any visible rubber bushes, looking for splits, cracks or contamination of the rubber **(see illustration)**.

6 With the vehicle standing on its wheels and the front wheels in their straight-ahead position, have an assistant turn the steering wheel back and forth about an eighth of a turn each way. There should be very little, if any, lost movement between the steering wheel and roadwheels. If this is not the case, closely observe the joints and mountings previously described, but in addition, check the steering column universal joints for wear, and the rack-and-pinion steering gear itself.

Suspension strut/shock absorber check

7 Check for any signs of fluid leakage around the front suspension strut/rear shock absorber body, or from the piston rod. Should any fluid be noticed, the suspension strut/shock absorber is defective internally, and should be renewed. **Note:** *Suspension struts/shock absorbers should always be renewed in pairs on the same axle.*

8 The efficiency of the suspension strut/shock absorber may be checked by bouncing the vehicle at each corner. Generally speaking, the body will return to its normal position and stop after being depressed. If it rises and returns on a rebound, the suspension strut/shock absorber is probably suspect. Examine also the suspension strut/shock absorber upper and lower mountings for any signs of wear.

Rear suspension check

9 Chock the front wheels, then raise the rear of the vehicle and securely support it on axle stands (see *"Jacking, towing and wheel changing"*).

10 Inspect the rear leaf springs for damage and excessive wear. In particular, check each leaf for cracking and the rubber mountings for deterioration.

11 Check all suspension mountings for tightness.

23 Door hinge lubrication

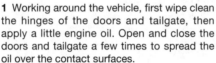

1 Working around the vehicle, first wipe clean the hinges of the doors and tailgate, then apply a little engine oil. Open and close the doors and tailgate a few times to spread the oil over the contact surfaces.

2 Check carefully the security and operation of all hinges, latches and locks, adjusting them where required.

3 Check the condition and operation of the tailgate struts, renewing them if either is leaking or no longer able to support the tailgate securely when raised.

24 Road test

Instruments and electrical equipment

1 Check the operation of all instruments and electrical equipment.

2 Make sure that all instruments read correctly, and switch on all electrical equipment in turn to check that it functions properly.

Steering and suspension

3 Check for any abnormalities in the steering, suspension, handling or road "feel".

4 Drive the vehicle, and check that there are no unusual vibrations or noises.

5 Check that the steering feels positive, with no excessive "sloppiness", or roughness, and check for any suspension noises when cornering, or when driving over bumps.

22.5 This front suspension radius bar mounting rubber is badly perished

Drivetrain

6 Check the performance of the engine, clutch, transmission and rear axle.

7 Listen for any unusual noises from the engine, clutch, transmission and rear axle.

8 Make sure that the engine runs smoothly when idling, and that there is no hesitation when accelerating.

9 Check that the clutch action is smooth and progressive, that the drive is taken up smoothly, and that the pedal travel is correct. Also listen for any noises when the clutch pedal is depressed.

10 Check that all gears can be engaged smoothly, without noise, and that the gear lever action is not abnormally vague or "notchy".

11 Check for any "whining" or "rumbling" noise from the rear axle, which would indicate excessive wear of the differential unit or rear wheel bearings.

Check the operation and performance of the braking system

12 Make sure that the vehicle does not pull to one side when braking, and that the wheels do not lock prematurely when braking hard.

13 Check that there is no vibration through the steering when braking.

14 Check that the handbrake operates correctly, without excessive movement of the lever, and that it holds the vehicle stationary on a slope.

15 Test the operation of the brake servo unit as follows. With the engine off, depress the footbrake four or five times to exhaust the vacuum. Start the engine, holding the brake pedal depressed. As the engine starts, there should be a noticeable "give" in the brake pedal as vacuum builds up. Allow the engine to run for at least two minutes, and then switch it off. If the brake pedal is depressed now, it should be possible to detect a hiss from the servo as the pedal is depressed. After about four or five applications, no further hissing should be heard.

Check seat belt operation

16 Check that the seat belts lock when pulled sharply.

Every 12 000 miles or 12 months - whichever comes sooner

25 Auxiliary drivebelt check

1 The auxiliary drivebelt (fanbelt) drives the water pump and alternator from a pulley on the front of the crankshaft.

2 Disconnect the battery negative lead, then raise or remove (according to model) the front seats for access to the engine.

3 Using a suitable socket and extension bar fitted to the crankshaft sprocket bolt, rotate the crankshaft so that the entire length of the drivebelt can be examined. Examine the drivebelt for cracks, splitting, fraying, or other damage. Check also for signs of glazing (shiny patches), and for separation of the belt plies. Renew the belt if it is worn or damaged. **Note:** *If regular servicing has been carried out in accordance with this Schedule, renewal will only be necessary at the 24 000 mile/ 40 000 km interval.*

4 If the condition of the belt is satisfactory, check the drivebelt tension as follows. Depress the drivebelt with moderate thumb pressure (10 kg/22 lb) midway between the water pump and alternator pulleys **(see illustration)**. The drivebelt is correctly adjusted if it deflects by 6 to 9 mm.

5 If adjustment is necessary, loosen the adjustment and pivot bolts slightly, and use a lever at the pulley end of the alternator housing to reposition it until the drivebelt deflection is correct. Tighten the bolts on completion.

6 Remove the socket and extension bar, and reconnect the battery negative lead. Refit the front seats.

26 Valve clearance check

Note: *The engine must be cold before starting the following procedure.*

1 Raise or remove the front seats and engine covers (according to model). Remove the engine rear cover, located at the front of the rear load area.

2 Disconnect the crankcase ventilation hose from the camshaft cover.

3 To make turning the engine easier, remove the spark plugs with reference to Section 11 of this Chapter.

4 Unscrew the two bolts and remove the camshaft cover from the top of the cylinder head. Recover the gasket.

5 Draw the valve positions on a piece of paper, numbering them 1 to 4, inlet and exhaust, from the front of the engine. As the valve clearances are adjusted, cross them off.

The inlet valves are located on the right-hand side of the engine, and the exhaust valves are on the left-hand side. No 1 cylinder is at the front of the engine.

6 Using a socket or spanner on the crankshaft pulley bolt (on the front of the crankshaft), turn the engine in a clockwise direction until pressure can be felt from the No 1 cylinder (place your finger over the spark plug hole).

7 Remove the rubber plug from the timing hole in the top of the clutch bellhousing, then continue turning the engine until the "T" mark on the flywheel is aligned with the mark on the bellhousing. In this position, No 1 piston is at the top of its stroke on compression. Remove the distributor cap, and check that the rotor arm is pointing in the direction of the No 1 segment position in the cap.

8 Insert a feeler blade of the correct thickness (see Specifications) between the No 1 cylinder inlet valve stem and the end of the rocker arm **(see illustration)**. It should be a firm sliding fit. If adjustment is necessary, loosen the locknut on the rocker arm using a ring spanner, and turn the adjustment screw with a screwdriver until the fit is correct. Tighten the locknut and recheck the adjustment, then repeat the adjustment procedure on No 2 cylinder inlet valve, followed by No 1 cylinder exhaust and No 3 cylinder exhaust. The clearances for the inlet and exhaust valves are the same.

9 Turn the engine exactly one complete turn, making sure that the flywheel "T" mark is correctly aligned with the mark on the bellhousing. Remove the distributor cap, and check that the rotor arm is pointing in the direction of the No 4 segment position in the cap.

10 Using the procedure described in paragraph 8, check and adjust the clearance between the No 3 cylinder inlet valve stem and the end of the rocker arm. Repeat the adjustment procedure on No 4 inlet valve, followed by No 2 exhaust valve and No 4 exhaust valve. The checking procedure is summarised in the following table.

Cylinder at TDC compression	Inlet valves to adjust	Exhaust valves to adjust
1	1(I) and 2(I)	1(E) and 3(E)
4	3(I) and 4(I)	2(E) and 4(E)

11 Remove the socket or spanner from the crankshaft pulley bolt.

12 Refit the distributor cap, and insert the rubber plug in the bellhousing timing hole.

13 Refit the spark plugs with reference to Section 11 of this Chapter.

14 Wipe clean the surfaces of the camshaft cover and cylinder head. Check the condition of the camshaft cover gasket and the cover retaining bolt grommets, and renew if necessary.

15 Refit the camshaft cover together with the gasket, then insert the retaining bolts with grommets and tighten to the specified torque. Reconnect the crankcase ventilation hose.

16 Refit the engine rear cover and front seats.

27 Crankcase ventilation/ emissions control hose and throttle positioner check

1 Details of the emissions control system components are given in Chapter 6.

2 Checking of the crankcase ventilation and emissions control system consists simply of a visual check for obvious signs of damaged or leaking hoses and joints.

3 Checking of the throttle positioner (where fitted) is covered in Chapter 6, Section 2.

28 Coolant and oil leak check

1 Visually inspect the engine joint faces, gaskets and seals for any signs of water or oil leaks. Pay particular attention to the areas around the camshaft cover, cylinder head, oil filter and sump joint faces. Bear in mind that, over a period of time, some very slight

25.4 Checking the auxiliary drivebelt tension

26.8 Adjusting the valve clearances

seepage from these areas is to be expected - what you are really looking for is any indication of a serious leak. Should a leak be found, renew the offending gasket or oil seal by referring to the appropriate Chapters in this manual.

2 Also check the security and condition of all the engine-related pipes and hoses. Ensure that all cable ties or securing clips are in place, and in good condition. Clips which are broken or missing can lead to chafing of the hoses, pipes or wiring, which could cause more serious problems in the future.

3 Carefully check the radiator hoses and heater hoses along their entire length. Renew any hose which is cracked, swollen or deteriorated. Cracks will show up better if the hose is squeezed. Pay close attention to the hose clips that secure the hoses to the cooling system components. Hose clips can pinch and puncture hoses, resulting in cooling system leaks. If crimped-type hose clips are fitted, it may be a good idea to replace them with standard worm-drive clips.

4 Inspect all the cooling system components (hoses, joint faces etc.) for leaks. A leak in the cooling system will usually show up as white- or rust-coloured deposits on the area adjoining the leak. Where any problems of this nature are found on system components, renew the component or gasket with reference to Chapter 3.

29 Exhaust system check

⚠️ **Warning: If the engine has just been running, take care not to touch the exhaust system, especially the front section, as it may still be hot.**

1 Position the vehicle over an inspection pit, or on car ramps. Alternatively, raise the front and rear of the vehicle, and support on axle stands (see *"Jacking, towing and wheel changing"*).

2 Examine the exhaust system over its entire length, checking for any damaged, broken or missing mountings, security of the pipe retaining clamps, and condition of the system with regard to rust and corrosion. If attention is required, refer to Chapter 4 for further information.

3 Lower the vehicle to the ground on completion.

30 Ignition system check

1 The ignition system components should be checked for damage or deterioration as follows. First raise or remove (according to model) the front seats and engine covers, and also remove the engine rear cover located at the front of the rear load area.

2 Ensure that the spark plug (HT) leads are numbered before removing them, to avoid confusion when refitting. The leads are numbered 1 to 4, with No 1 being at the front of the engine. Pull the first lead from the plug by gripping the end fitting, not the lead, otherwise the lead connection may be fractured.

3 Check inside the end fitting for signs of corrosion, which will look like a white crusty powder. Push the end fitting back onto the spark plug, ensuring that it is a tight fit on the plug. If not, remove the lead again, and use pliers to carefully crimp the metal connector inside the end fitting until it fits securely on the end of the spark plug.

4 Using a clean rag, wipe the entire length of the lead to remove any built-up dirt and grease. Once the lead is clean, check for burns, cracks and other damage. Do not bend the lead excessively, nor pull the lead lengthwise - the conductor inside might break.

5 Disconnect the other end of the lead from the distributor cap. Again, pull only on the end fitting. Check for corrosion and a tight fit in the same manner as the spark plug end. If an ohmmeter is available, check the resistance of the lead by connecting the meter between the spark plug end of the lead (disconnected) and the distributor cap end - if the resistance is not similar to that given in the Specifications, the lead should be renewed. Refit the lead securely on completion.

6 Check the remaining leads one at a time, in the same way.

7 If new spark plug (HT) leads are required, purchase a complete set.

8 Release the clips and remove the distributor cap. Wipe it clean, and carefully inspect it inside and out for signs of cracks, black carbon tracks (tracking) and worn, burned or loose contacts; check that the cap's carbon brush is unworn, free to move against spring pressure, and making good contact with the rotor arm. Also inspect the cap seal for signs of wear or damage, and renew if necessary. Remove the rotor arm from the distributor shaft, and inspect the rotor arm. It is common practice to renew the cap and rotor arm whenever new spark plug (HT) leads are fitted. When fitting a new cap, remove the leads from the old cap one at a time, and fit them to the new cap in the exact same location - do not simultaneously remove all the leads from the old cap, or firing-order confusion may occur. Ensure that the rotor arm is located correctly on the shaft cut-out and is fully pressed down, then fit the cap to the distributor, and press the retaining clips firmly into position.

9 Even with the ignition system in first-class condition, some engines may still occasionally experience poor starting attributable to damp ignition components. To disperse moisture, a water-dispersant aerosol can be very effective.

10 The manufacturers recommend checking

the vacuum advance at this service, but not at the 6000 mile/10 000 km service. One way to check the condition of the diaphragm in the vacuum capsule is to disconnect the vacuum hose, then with the distributor cap removed, turn the contact breaker baseplate anti-clockwise, and block the vacuum outlet on the capsule with a finger. If the baseplate is then released, vacuum should be felt at the outlet. For a more accurate check, connect a clean hose to the outlet, and suck - the baseplate should move anti-clockwise, proving that the capsule is working. A further method is to check the difference in ignition timing when the vacuum hose is disconnected and reconnected, with the engine running at a fast idling speed.

31 Idle speed and mixture check and adjustment

1 Before checking the idle speed and mixture setting, check the following:
a) *Check the ignition timing (see Chapter 5B).*
b) *Check that the spark plugs are in good condition and correctly gapped (Section 11).*
c) *Check the valve clearances (Section 26).*
d) *Check that the accelerator cable and choke cable are correctly adjusted (see Chapter 4).*
e) *Check that the crankcase breather hoses are secure, with no leaks or kinks (Section 27).*
f) *Check that the air cleaner filter element is clean (Section 9).*
g) *Check that the exhaust system is in good condition (Section 29).*
h) *If the engine is running very roughly, check the compression pressures and valve clearances (see Chapter 2A and Section 26 of this Chapter).*

2 Take the vehicle on a journey of sufficient length to warm it up to normal operating temperature. **Note:** *The following procedure should be completed within two minutes, without stopping the engine. If this cannot be achieved, clear any excess fuel from the inlet manifold by racing the engine two or three times to between 2000 and 3000 rpm, then allow it to idle again.*

3 Ensure that all electrical loads are switched off, and that the choke knob is pushed fully in. Connect a tachometer to the engine, following the equipment manufacturer's instructions.

4 The idle speed adjusting screw is located on the top of the carburettor, towards the front. The idle mixture adjusting screw is located on the top of the carburettor. Access to both screws is gained by removing the centre console rear mounting screw, moving the rear of the console to the left-hand side, then prising out the rubber grommets located in the panel over the carburettor. Raise or remove (according to model) the right-hand

seat **(see illustrations). Note:** In vehicles produced for some markets, it may be necessary to remove a tamperproof plug in order to gain access to the mixture adjusting screw.

Method using an exhaust gas analyser (CO meter)

5 Connect the exhaust gas analyser to the engine, in accordance with the equipment manufacturer's instructions.
6 Using a screwdriver turn the idle adjusting screw in or out as necessary to obtain the specified idle speed.
7 Using the screwdriver, turn the mixture adjusting screw in or out (in very small increments) until the CO level is as given in the Specifications. Turning the screw in (clockwise) weakens the mixture and reduces the CO level, turning it out will richen the mixture and increase the CO level.
8 If necessary, readjust the idle speed.
9 Temporarily increase the engine speed, then allow it to idle and recheck the settings.
10 When adjustments are complete, stop the engine and disconnect the test equipment. Refit the rubber grommets, centre console and right-hand seat.

Method without using an exhaust gas analyser

Note: *The following procedure cannot be relied upon to obtain an accurate setting.*
11 Using a screwdriver, turn the idle adjusting screw in or out as necessary to obtain an idle speed of 1000 rpm.
12 Using the screwdriver, turn the mixture adjusting screw in or out (in very small increments) to obtain the highest engine speed.
13 Repeat the procedure in paragraphs 11 and 12.
14 Turn the idle adjusting screw as necessary to obtain an idle speed of 1000 rpm.
15 Turn the mixture adjusting screw inwards (clockwise) until the idle speed drops to the specified speed. This will effectively weaken the mixture from the setting obtained in paragraph 12.
16 When adjustments are complete, stop the engine and disconnect the test equipment. Refit the rubber grommets, centre console and right-hand seat.

31.4a Move the rear of the console to the left, and remove the rubber grommets for access to the idle adjustment screws

32 Wiring harness check
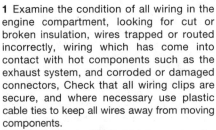

1 Examine the condition of all wiring in the engine compartment, looking for cut or broken insulation, wires trapped or routed incorrectly, wiring which has come into contact with hot components such as the exhaust system, and corroded or damaged connectors, Check that all wiring clips are secure, and where necessary use plastic cable ties to keep all wires away from moving components.
2 Check all earthing points and wire attachment points in the engine compartment for corrosion and tightness.

33 Propeller shaft check

1 Wear in the propeller shaft universal joints is characterised by vibration in the transmission, or a knocking on changing from drive to overrun (applying and releasing the throttle) or vice-versa.
2 To test a universal joint, jack up the vehicle and support on axle stands (see *"Jacking, towing and wheel changing"*). It is only strictly necessary to jack up the rear of the vehicle, but this provides only limited access.
3 Attempt to turn the propeller shaft either side of the joint alternately in opposite directions. Also attempt to lift each side of the joint. Any movement within the universal joint

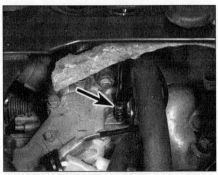

31.4b Adjusting the idle speed (arrow shows screwdriver on adjustment screw)

31.4c Adjusting the idle mixture (arrow shows screwdriver on adjustment screw)

is indicative of considerable wear, and if evident, either the joint or the complete propeller shaft must be renewed.
4 Check for wear of the splines on the front sliding yoke and transmission output shaft by attempting to lift the sliding yoke. If evident, it is possible to obtain the sliding yoke separately, but the splines on the transmission output shaft may also be worn, in which case overhaul of the transmission may be necessary.
5 Check the propeller shaft rear flange bolts for tightness.
6 Lower the vehicle to the ground.

34 Headlight beam adjustment check

Check the headlight beam adjustment with reference to Chapter 12, Section 8.

Every 24 000 miles or 2 years - whichever comes sooner

35 Cylinder head bolt/manifold nut tightness check

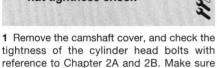

1 Remove the camshaft cover, and check the tightness of the cylinder head bolts with reference to Chapter 2A and 2B. Make sure that the bolts are tightened in the correct sequence.
2 Check the tightness of the inlet and exhaust manifold retaining nuts with reference to Chapter 2B.

36 Auxiliary drivebelt renewal

1 Disconnect the battery negative lead, then raise or remove (according to model) the front seats for access to the engine.
2 Loosen the alternator adjustment and pivot bolts, and swivel the alternator in towards the engine as far as possible.
3 Slip the drivebelt off the crankshaft, water pump and alternator pulleys, and remove it over the fan blades.
4 Locate the new drivebelt on the pulleys, and swivel out the alternator to apply moderate tension. Lightly tighten the adjustment and pivot bolts.
5 Adjust the drivebelt with reference to Section 25, the refit the front seats and reconnect the battery negative lead.

37 Coolant/antifreeze renewal

Cooling system draining

 Warning: Wait until the engine is cold before starting this procedure. Do not allow antifreeze to come in contact with your skin, or with the painted surfaces of the vehicle. Rinse off spills immediately with plenty of water.

1 Raise or remove (according to model) the front seats for access to the engine.
2 With the engine cold, remove the pressure cap from the top of the radiator. Turn the cap anti-clockwise until it reaches the first stop. Wait until any pressure remaining in the system is released, then push the cap down, turn it anti-clockwise to the second stop, and lift it off.
3 Remove the filler cap from the top of the expansion tank.
4 Position a suitable container beneath the lower left-hand side of the radiator.
5 Unscrew the drain plug and allow the coolant to drain into the container **(see illustration)**. Initially it will help if the drain

plug is not completely removed, otherwise the coolant may overshoot the container. Once the initial flow has subsided, fully remove the plug and recover the sealing washer.
6 Remove the expansion tank from its location, and pour its contents into the container. Clean the tank, then refit it.
7 If the coolant has been drained for a reason other than renewal, then provided it is clean and less than two years old, it can be re-used.
8 Refit the radiator drain plug, together with the sealing washer, and tighten it securely.

Cooling system flushing

9 If coolant renewal has been neglected, or if the antifreeze mixture has become diluted, then in time, the cooling system may gradually lose efficiency, as the coolant passages become restricted due to rust, scale deposits, and other sediment. The cooling system efficiency can be restored by flushing the system clean.
10 The radiator should be flushed independently of the engine, to avoid unnecessary contamination.

Radiator flushing

11 To flush the radiator, first loosen the clips and disconnect the top and bottom hoses from the radiator.
12 Insert a garden hose into the radiator top inlet. Direct a flow of clean water through the radiator, and continue flushing until clean water emerges from the radiator bottom outlet.
13 If after a reasonable period, the water still does not run clear, the radiator can be flushed with a good proprietary cleaning agent. It is important that their manufacturer's instructions are followed carefully.
14 If the contamination is particularly bad, remove the radiator (see Chapter 3) then insert the hose in the radiator bottom outlet, and reverse-flush the radiator.

Engine flushing

15 To flush the engine, remove the thermostat as described in Chapter 3, then temporarily refit the thermostat cover leaving the top hose connected to it.

37.5 Drain plug (arrowed) on the radiator bottom tank

16 With the top and bottom hoses disconnected from the radiator, insert a garden hose into the radiator top hose. Direct a clean flow of water through the engine, and continue flushing until clean water emerges from the radiator bottom hose.
17 On completion of flushing, refit the thermostat and reconnect the hoses with reference to Chapter 3.

Cooling system filling

18 Before attempting to fill the cooling system, make sure that all hoses and clips are in good condition, and that the clips are tight. Note that an antifreeze mixture must be used all year round, to prevent corrosion of the engine components (see "Antifreeze mixture" below). Also check that the radiator drain plug is in place and tightened securely.
19 Remove the filler cap, and fill the expansion tank with coolant to the "FULL" level mark.
20 With the pressure cap removed, pour antifreeze mixture into the radiator slowly until it reaches the bottom of the filler neck **(see illustration)**. "Pump" the bottom and top radiator hoses gently by hand, compressing them several times - this will force out any air-pockets from the cooling system.
21 With the radiator cap removed, start the engine and run it at idle until the top hose is hot (indicating that the thermostat has opened and coolant is circulating through the radiator).
22 With the engine still idling, top-up the radiator to the bottom of the filler neck, then refit and tighten the cap.
23 Check that the coolant level in the expansion tank is up to the "FULL" mark, and top-up if necessary.
24 Allow the engine to cool, then check the coolant level with reference to Section 3 of this Chapter. Top-up the level if necessary.

Antifreeze mixture

25 The antifreeze should always be renewed at the specified intervals. This is necessary

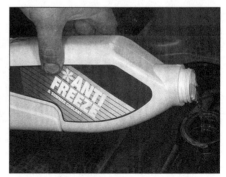
37.20 Topping-up the radiator with coolant

40.5 Fuel filter location (Van models)

42.4a Unscrew the drain plug . . .

42.4b . . . and drain the transmission oil into a suitable container

not only to maintain the antifreeze properties, but also to prevent corrosion which would otherwise occur as the corrosion inhibitors become progressively less effective.

26 Always use an ethylene-glycol based antifreeze which is suitable for use in mixed-metal cooling systems. The quantity of antifreeze and levels of protection are indicated in the Specifications.

27 Before adding antifreeze, the cooling system should be completely drained, preferably flushed, and all hoses checked for condition and security.

28 After filling with antifreeze, a label should be attached to the expansion tank filler neck, stating the type and concentration of antifreeze used, and the date installed. Any subsequent topping-up should be made with the same type and concentration of antifreeze.

29 Do not use engine antifreeze in the windscreen/tailgate washer system, as it will cause damage to the vehicle paintwork. A screenwash additive should be added to the washer system, in the quantities stated on the bottle.

39 Fuel line check

1 With the vehicle raised, inspect the petrol tank, filler neck and hose for punctures, cracks and other damage. The connection between the filler neck and tank is especially critical. Sometimes, a rubber filler neck or connecting hose will leak due to loose retaining clamps or deteriorated rubber.

2 Carefully check all rubber hoses and metal fuel lines leading away from the petrol tank. Check for loose connections, deteriorated hoses, crimped lines, and other damage. Pay particular attention to the vent pipes and hoses, which can become blocked or crimped. Follow the lines to the front of the vehicle, carefully inspecting them all the way. Renew damaged sections as necessary.

3 Inside the engine compartment, check the security of all fuel hose attachments and pipe unions, and inspect the fuel hoses and vacuum hoses for kinks, chafing and deterioration.

4 Open the fuel tank filler flap and remove the filler cap. Check the cap seal for damage, and also check the gasket at the top of the filler neck. Refit the cap on completion.

38 Air filter element renewal

1 Raise or remove (according to model) the right-hand seat and engine cover

2 Unscrew the wing nut and remove the washer, then remove the end cap from the air cleaner. Recover the sealing ring.

3 Withdraw the air cleaner element from the housing.

4 Wipe clean the inner surfaces of the air cleaner assembly and end cap.

5 Check the end cap sealing ring condition, and renew if necessary.

6 Insert the new element, and refit the end cap together with the sealing ring. Refit the washer, and tighten the wing nut.

7 Refit the right-hand seat and engine cover.

40 Fuel filter renewal

⚠️ *Warning: Before carrying out the following operation, refer to the precautions given in "Safety first!" at the beginning of this manual, and follow them implicitly. Petrol is a highly-dangerous and volatile liquid, and the precautions necessary when handling it cannot be overstressed.*

1 On Pickup models, the fuel filter is located on the inside of the right-hand side chassis frame, just forward of the fuel tank. On Van models, the filter is located on the right-hand side of the fuel tank.

2 Disconnect the battery negative lead.

3 Open the fuel filler flap and remove the fuel

tank filler cap, to release any pressure in the fuel tank and feed line. Refit the cap.

4 Apply the handbrake, then raise the front of the vehicle and support on axle stands (see "Jacking, towing and wheel changing").

5 Loosen the clips and disconnect the inlet and outlet hoses from the filter **(see illustration)**. Be prepared for fuel leakage as the hoses are detached, and plug the hose ends to prevent loss of fuel if the new filter is not being fitted immediately.

6 Unscrew the mounting bolt, and remove the filter from its mounting.

7 Fit the new filter using a reversal of the removal procedure, but make sure that the outlet hose is connected to the top stub and the inlet hose to the bottom stub.

8 On completion, restart the engine and check for any signs of leakage from the filter hose connections.

41 Crankcase ventilation valve, oxygen sensor and fuel cut solenoid check

Refer to Chapter 6, Section 2 for details of the procedure for testing the crankcase ventilation (PCV) valve, oxygen sensor and fuel cut solenoid.

42 Transmission and rear axle oil renewal

Note: *A 3/8 inch square-section key is required to undo the transmission drain and filler plugs. These keys can be obtained from most motor factors or your Vauxhall/Suzuki dealer; alternatively, a 3/8 inch drive socket bar may be used.*

1 Park the vehicle on level ground, switch off the engine, and apply the handbrake firmly. For improved access, position the vehicle over an inspection pit or on ramps, but note that the vehicle must be level when checking the oil level, to ensure an accurate check.

2 Examine the transmission and rear axle for signs of oil leakage. In particular, check the transmission rear oil seal and the rear axle differential drive flange oil seal.

Transmission

3 Wipe clean the area around the drain and filler/level plugs, situated respectively on the rear right-hand end and rear bottom of the transmission casing. Unscrew the filler/level plug from the transmission. Note that the threads of both the filler/level and drain plugs are tapered, so there is no need for a sealing washer.

4 Position a suitable container beneath the rear of the transmission, then unscrew the drain plug and allow the oil to drain **(see illustrations)**.

5 Wipe clean the threads of the drain plug, then apply suitable sealant to its threads and insert it in the transmission casing. Tighten the plug to the specified torque.

6 Fill the transmission with the specified quantity and grade of oil, checking the level with reference to Section 21 of this Chapter.

7 Apply suitable sealant to the threads of the filler/level plug, then Insert it and tighten to the specified torque.

Rear axle

8 Wipe clean the area around the drain and filler/level plugs, situated on the rear and bottom of the rear axle casing.

9 Position a suitable container beneath the rear axle, then unscrew the drain plug and allow the oil to drain **(see illustration)**. Also unscrew and remove the filler/level plug, together with the sealing washer.

10 Wipe clean the threads of the drain plug. Check the condition of the sealing washer, and if necessary renew it. Insert the drain plug and washer in the rear axle, and tighten the plug to the specified torque.

11 Fill the rear axle with the specified quantity and grade of oil, checking the level with reference to Section 21.

12 Check the condition of the filler/level plug sealing washer, and if necessary renew it. Refit the filler/level plug together with the sealing washer, and tighten to the specified torque.

43 Brake fluid renewal

 Warning: Brake hydraulic fluid can harm your eyes and damage painted surfaces, so use extreme caution when handling and pouring it. Do not use fluid that has been standing open for some time, as it absorbs moisture from the air. Excess moisture content can cause a dangerous loss of braking effectiveness.

1 The procedure is similar to that for bleeding the hydraulic system as described in Chapter 9, except that allowance should be made for all the old fluid to be expelled when bleeding a section of the circuit.

2 The brake fluid reservoir should first be emptied of old fluid by syphoning, using a clean poultry baster, syringe, or similar, then refilled with fresh fluid. Do not operate the brakes while the reservoir is being emptied, or air will be drawn into the system.

3 Working as described in Chapter 9, open the first bleed screw in the sequence, and pump the brake pedal gently until nearly all the fluid has been emptied from the reservoir.

42.9 Removing the rear axle drain plug

Top-up to the "MAX" level with new fluid, and continue pumping until only new fluid can be seen emerging from the bleed screw. Old hydraulic fluid is invariably much darker in colour than the new, making it easy to distinguish the two. Tighten the screw, and top the reservoir level up to the "MAX" level line.

4 Work through all the remaining bleed screws in the sequence until new fluid can be seen at all of them. Be careful to keep the brake fluid reservoir topped-up to above the "MIN" level at all times, or air may enter the system and greatly increase the length of the task.

5 When the operation is complete, check that all bleed screws are securely tightened, and that their dust caps are refitted. Wash off all traces of spilt fluid, and recheck the fluid level in the master cylinder.

6 Check the operation of the brakes before taking the vehicle on the road.

Every 48 000 miles or 4 years

44 Brake hose and rubber component renewal

Renew all flexible brake hoses and all sealing rubbers of the master cylinder and wheel cylinders with reference to Chapter 9. The brake fluid must be renewed at the same time, so before disconnecting any of the brake lines, all old fluid must be pumped from the hydraulic circuit by opening the bleed screws in turn. Using plastic or rubber tubing connected to the bleed screws, direct the fluid into a suitable container.

Every 72 000 miles

45 Timing belt renewal

Note: *This is not included in the manufacturer's maintenance schedule, but is strongly recommended as a precaution against the timing belt failing in service. If the timing belt fails while the engine is running, extensive engine damage could be caused.*

Refer to Chapter 2A.

Notes

Chapter 2 Part A:
Engine in-vehicle repair procedures

Contents

Degrees of difficulty

Easy, suitable for novice with little experience	Fairly easy, suitable for beginner with some experience	Fairly difficult, suitable for competent DIY mechanic	Difficult, suitable for experienced DIY mechanic	Very difficult, suitable for expert DIY or professional

Specifications

General

Bore . . . . 65.5 mm
Stroke . . . . 72 mm
Displacement . . . . 970 cc
Cylinder compression pressure (at 300 rpm/cranking speed):
  Normal . . . . 13.2 bars (192 psi)
  Limit . . . . 12.0 bars (174 psi)
  Maximum cylinder-to-cylinder difference . . . . 1 bar (14.5 psi)
Fuel octane rating:
  Up to August 1989 (1990 model year) . . . . 92 (RON)
  August 1989 on . . . . 95 (RON)
Compression ratio 8.8:1
Normal operating inlet manifold vacuum (at sea level) . . . . 45 - 50 cm Hg at 900 rpm
Normal operating oil pressure . . . . 3.0 to 4.5 bars (44 to 65 psi) at 3000 rpm
Firing order . . . . 1 - 3 - 4 - 2 (No 1 cylinder at timing belt end)
Idle speed . . . . 900 rpm
Power output . . . . 44 bhp (DIN) at 5300 rpm
Torque . . . . 75 Nm (DIN) at 3200 rpm

Flywheel

Maximum runout . . . . 0.2 mm

Oil pump

Outer gear-to-case radial clearance:
  Standard . . . . 1.12 to 0.20 mm
  Service limit . . . . 0.3 mm
Outer gear-to-crescent clearance . . . . 0.25 to 0.4 mm
Inner gear-to-crescent clearance . . . . 0.6 to 0.8 mm
Gear endfloat:
  Standard . . . . 0.045 to 0.12 mm
  Service limit . . . . 0.17 mm

Torque wrench settings

	Nm	lbf ft
Big-end bearing cap bolts	30	22
Camshaft thrust plate screw	10	7
Camshaft cover bolts	5	4
Camshaft pulley bolt	55	41
Cooling fan bolts	10	7
Crankshaft main bearing cap bolts	45	33
Crankshaft pulley bolt	55	41
Crankshaft rear oil seal housing bolts	10	7
Cylinder head bolts*:		
Revised bolts with 9 mm shank	70	52
Original bolts with 8 mm shank	58	43
Distributor gear case bolts	20	15
Engine mounting block nut	20	15
Engine mounting bracket-to-engine bolt	20	15
Engine mounting crossmember bolt	35	26
Exhaust front pipe bolt and nut	40	30
Exhaust manifold retaining nuts and bolts	20	15
Flywheel retaining bolts*	42	31
Inlet manifold retaining nuts and bolts	20	15
Oil drain plug	22	16
Oil filter assembly	14	10
Oil filter stand	22	16
Oil pressure switch	13	10
Oil pump - case bolt	10	7
Oil pump gear plate screw	10	7
Oil pump pickup bolts	10	7
Rocker shaft retaining screws	10	7
Spark plugs	25	18
Sump retaining bolts	5	4
Timing belt inner cover nuts and bolts	10	7
Timing belt outer cover nuts and bolts	4	3
Timing belt tensioner bolts	20	15
Transmission mounting bracket bolt	20	15
Transmission mounting nut	25	18
Water pump bolts	10	7

*Use new bolts

1 General Information

Using this Chapter

Chapter 2 is divided into parts A and B. Part A describes repair operations that can be carried out with the engine in the vehicle. Part B covers the removal of the engine/transmission and describes the engine dismantling and overhaul procedures.

In this Part, the assumption is made that the engine is installed in the vehicle with all ancillaries connected.

Whilst access to the engine bay can be gained by removing the load area inspection hatch cover and tilting the driver and passenger seats backwards (or forwards, depending on variant), this may be improved by removing the seats from the cab area altogether. This procedure is described in Chapter 11.

Engine description

The engine is a water-cooled, single overhead camshaft, in-line four-cylinder unit, with a cast-iron block and an aluminium-alloy cylinder head. It is mounted longitudinally in

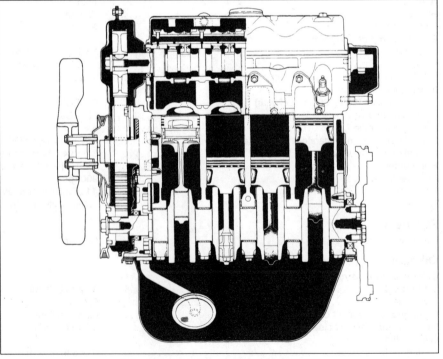

1.4a Cutaway view of engine (side view)

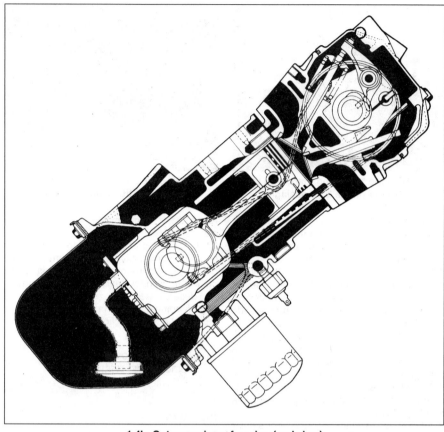

1.4b Cutaway view of engine (end view)

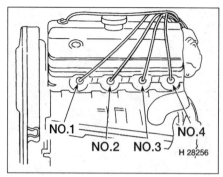

2.1 Cylinder numbering order

the vehicle, slanted towards the left at approximately 45º, with the transmission bolted to the rear of the engine **(see illustrations)**.

The cylinder head carries the camshaft, which is driven by a toothed timing belt. It also houses the inlet and exhaust valves (one each per cylinder) which run in guides pressed into the cylinder head. The camshaft actuates the valves indirectly via rocker arms mounted on rocker shafts. The rocker shafts contain integral oilways which lubricate the rocker arms.

The crankshaft is supported by five main bearings, and endfloat is controlled by a thrust bearing fitted between cylinders No 2 and 3.

Engine coolant is circulated by a pump, driven by the auxiliary drivebelt (which also drives the alternator). For further details on the cooling system, refer to Chapter 3.

A pressurised oil supply is provided by a pump driven directly from the crankshaft. Oil is drawn from the sump through a strainer and then forced through a replaceable screw-on filter. From there, it is distributed to the cylinder head, where it lubricates the camshaft journals, rocker shafts and rocker arms, and also to the crankcase, where it lubricates the main bearings, connecting rod big- and small-ends, gudgeon pins and cylinder bores.

Repairs possible with the engine installed in the vehicle

The following operations can be performed without removing the engine:

a) *Timing belt, sprockets and cover - removal, inspection and refitting.*
b) *Camshaft oil seal - renewal.*
c) *Camshaft sprocket - removal and refitting.*
d) *Cylinder head - removal and refitting.* *
e) *Crankshaft front oil seal - renewal.*
f) *Crankshaft sprocket - removal and refitting.*
g) *Oil pump - removal and refitting.*
h) *Engine mountings - inspection and renewal.*
i) *Sump and oil pickup assembly - removal and refitting.*
j) *Water pump - removal and refitting.*

*The dismantling, overhaul and reassembly of the cylinder head and its components is described in Chapter 2B.

Note: *It is possible to remove the pistons and connecting rods (after removing the cylinder head and sump) without removing the engine from the vehicle. However, this procedure is not recommended. Work of this nature is more easily and thoroughly completed with the engine on the bench, as described in Chapter 2B.*

2 Top Dead Centre (TDC) for No 1 cylinder - locating

Note: *This section assumes that the distributor and HT leads are correctly fitted. If this is not the case, refer to Chapter 5B.*

1 To ensure correct reassembly and synchronisation of the engine components, a method of setting the engine in a "reference" condition during dismantling is required. Setting a particular piston to Top Dead Centre (TDC) achieves this. TDC refers to the highest position a piston reaches within its respective cylinder. In a four-stroke engine, each piston reaches TDC twice per cycle; once on the compression stroke, and once on the exhaust stroke. TDC normally refers to the piston position on the compression stroke. Note that the cylinders are numbered 1 to 4 from the timing belt end **(see illustration)**. The following paragraphs describe the location of TDC on cylinder No 1.

2 Before starting work, disconnect the battery negative cable. Disable the ignition system by removing the distributor centre HT lead and earthing it on the cylinder block using a jumper wire. Prevent any vehicle movement by putting the transmission in neutral, applying the handbrake and chocking the rear wheels.

3 Note the position of the No 1 cylinder HT terminal with respect to the distributor body. If the terminal is not numbered, follow the HT lead from the No 1 cylinder spark plug back to the distributor cap. Using chalk or a pen (**not** a pencil), place a mark on the distributor body directly under the terminal. Unclip and remove the distributor cap.

4 Disconnect the HT leads from the spark plugs, noting their fitted sequence (if the leads are not marked for cylinder number, mark them 1 to 4 from the front of the engine). Remove all four spark plugs (see Chapter 1).

5 To bring any piston up to TDC, it will be necessary to rotate the crankshaft manually. This can be done by using a ratchet wrench and socket on the crankshaft bolt at the front of the engine.

6 Rotate the crankshaft clockwise until the

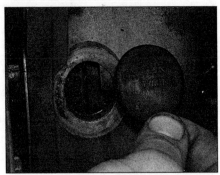

2.7 Remove the bung from the timing inspection hole

2.8 Align the "T" timing mark with the pointer on the bellhousing

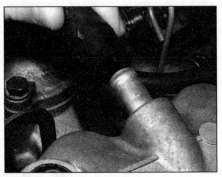

4.3 Disconnect the crankcase breather hose from the camshaft cover

distributor rotor arm electrode approaches the mark that was made on the distributor body.

7 Locate the timing inspection hole on the transmission bellhousing, and remove the rubber bung **(see illustration)**. This exposes the edge of the flywheel, on which there are a number of timing marks.

8 Continue rotating the crankshaft clockwise until the "T" timing mark is aligned exactly with the pointer marked on the bellhousing **(see illustration)**. **Note:** Observe from directly above the inspection hole, to ensure correct alignment.

9 Check that the distributor rotor arm is now aligned with the mark on the distributor body. If it is offset by 180°, then the cylinder is on the exhaust stroke; rotate the crankshaft through one complete revolution, and repeat paragraph 8 above.

10 Cylinder No 1 is now at TDC. This process can also be used to find TDC for cylinder No 4 if required, by repeating the above process but marking the position of the No 4 cylinder HT terminal on the distributor body.

11 Note that the engine can also be set to an a specific angle before top dead centre (BTDC), eg 8° BTDC. This is achieved by aligning the appropriate flywheel timing mark with the pointer on the bellhousing - from the "T" TDC mark, they are graduated in steps of 2°. See Chapter 5B "Ignition timing - static checking and adjustment" for further details.

3 Compression test - description and interpretation

1 When engine performance is down, or if misfiring occurs which cannot be attributed to the ignition or fuel systems, a compression test can provide diagnostic clues as to the engine's condition. If the test is performed regularly, it can give warning of trouble before any other symptoms become apparent.

2 The engine must be fully warmed-up to normal operating temperature, the battery must be fully charged, and all the spark plugs must be removed (refer to Chapter 1). The aid of an assistant will also be required.

3 Disable the ignition system by

disconnecting the ignition HT coil lead from the distributor cap and earthing it on the cylinder block. Use a jumper lead or similar wire to make a good connection.

5 Fit a compression tester to the No 1 cylinder spark plug hole - the type of tester which screws into the plug thread is preferred.

6 Get the assistant to hold the throttle wide open, and crank the engine on the starter motor; after one or two revolutions, the compression pressure should build up to a maximum figure, and then stabilise. Record the highest reading obtained.

7 Repeat the test on the remaining cylinders, recording the pressure in each. Keep the throttle wide open.

8 All cylinders should produce very similar pressures; a difference of more than 2 bars between any two cylinders indicates a fault. Note that the compression should build up quickly in a healthy engine; low compression on the first stroke, followed by gradually-increasing pressure on successive strokes, indicates worn piston rings. A low compression reading on the first stroke, which does not build up during successive strokes, indicates leaking valves or a blown head gasket (a cracked head could also be the cause). Deposits on the undersides of the valve heads can also cause low compression.

9 Refer to the Specifications section in this Chapter, and compare the recorded compression figures with those stated by the manufacturer.

10 If the pressure in any cylinder is low, carry out the following test to isolate the cause. Introduce a teaspoonful of clean oil into that cylinder through its spark plug hole, and repeat the test.

11 If the addition of oil temporarily improves the compression pressure, this indicates that bore or piston wear is responsible for the pressure loss. No improvement suggests that leaking or burnt valves, or a blown head gasket, may be to blame.

12 A low reading from two adjacent cylinders is almost certainly due to the head gasket having blown between them; the presence of coolant in the engine oil will confirm this.

13 If one cylinder is about 20 percent lower than the others and the engine has a slightly

rough idle, a worn camshaft lobe could be the cause.

14 If the compression reading is unusually high, the combustion chambers are probably coated with carbon deposits. If this is the case, the cylinder head should be removed and decarbonised.

15 On completion of the test, refit the spark plugs and refit the ignition coil HT lead.

4 Camshaft cover - removal and refitting

Removal

1 Disconnect the battery negative cable, and position it away from the terminal.

2 Remove the HT leads from the clip on the camshaft cover, and move them to one side.

3 Disconnect the crankcase ventilation hose from the port on the camshaft cover. Retain the hose clip **(see illustration)**.

4 Withdraw the four camshaft cover bolts with their washers, and remove the cover **(see illustrations)**. If it sticks, tap it lightly with a soft-faced mallet. Do not lever it off with an implement that may damage the mating surfaces of the cover or cylinder head.

5 Remove the rubber gasket and examine it carefully. If any damage or deterioration is evident, renew it.

6 Unbolt the breather baffle plate, and remove the paper gasket.

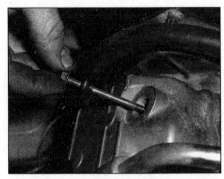

4.4a Withdraw the camshaft cover bolts and washers . . .

4.4b . . . and remove the cover

4.8a Fit a new paper gasket to the cover . . .

4.8b . . . and lay the breather baffle plate in position

7 Clean the cover thoroughly, paying particular attention to the mating surfaces.

⚠ *Caution: Both the camshaft cover and the cylinder head are made of an aluminium alloy, which is softer than steel and easily damaged. Care must be taken when cleaning the mating surfaces to avoid scoring or pitting them, as this may cause leakage.*

Refitting

8 Fit a new paper gasket to the cover, and lay the breather baffle plate in position **(see illustrations)**. Refit and tighten the retaining bolts.

9 Fit the rubber gasket, and place the cover on the cylinder head. Ensure that the gasket is

5.2 Remove the auxiliary drivebelt

evenly seated between the cover and head **(see illustration)**.

10 Refit the four cover retaining bolts with their washers, and tighten them to the specified torque.

11 Reconnect the crankcase breather hose. Push the HT leads into the clip on the camshaft cover, then reconnect the battery negative cable.

5 Timing belt and cover - removal and refitting 🔧

Removal

1 Disconnect the battery negative cable, and position it away from the terminal.

2 Slacken the alternator mounting and adjustment bolts, and pivot the alternator towards the engine. Remove the auxiliary drivebelt **(see illustration)**.

3 Refer to Chapter 3 and remove the cooling fan and spacer. Lift off the auxiliary drivebelt pulley.

4 Referring to Section 2, set the engine to TDC on cylinder No 4 (not No 1 - this is because the timing marks used to align the camshaft sprocket for TDC on No 4 are much easier to see than those for No 1).

5 Remove the crankshaft pulley by extracting the centre bolt **(see illustrations)**. To do this, the crankshaft must be prevented from rotating - this can be achieved by selecting

4.9 Fit the rubber gasket to the cover

fourth gear and firmly applying the handbrake. If this method fails to lock the crankshaft in position, remove the timing mark inspection plug on the bellhousing, and get an assistant to insert a stout, wide-bladed screwdriver between two of the starter ring gear teeth - this should lock the flywheel (and hence, the crankshaft) in position.

6 The timing belt outer cover can now be taken off by removing the bolts securing it to the inner cover **(see illustrations)**. Recover the rubber gasket - if it is serviceable, retain it for refitting later.

7 At this point, identify the timing alignment marks stamped onto both the camshaft and crankshaft sprockets. These should both be lined up with the timing arrows stamped on the inner timing belt cover. Note that there are two

5.5a Remove the crankshaft pulley centre bolt . . .

5.5b . . . and pulley

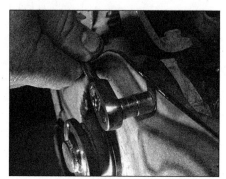

5.6a Remove the timing belt outer cover bolts . . .

5.6b . . . and cover

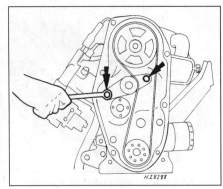

5.8 Tensioner bolts (arrowed)

5.9 Remove the timing belt

arrows provided on the cover for aligning the camshaft sprocket; one at 12 o' clock and one at 6 o' clock. The 12 o' clock arrow is used for setting cylinder No 4 at TDC - the 6 o' clock one is for setting cylinder No 1 at TDC. As the engine has already been set to TDC on No 4, use the 12 o' clock arrow for alignment.

8 Slacken the two bolts securing the timing belt tensioner to the engine block, and prise the tensioner spring off the water pump retaining bolt **(see illustration)**. This will relieve the tension on the belt.

9 Unless they are already printed on, mark the timing belt with arrows indicating its direction of rotation. The belt can now be slid

5.11a Camshaft sprocket correctly aligned with marks on timing belt cover

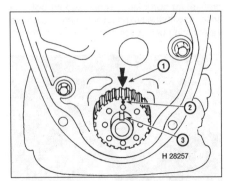

5.11b Crankshaft sprocket correctly aligned with marks on timing belt cover

1 Timing arrow
2 Crankshaft sprocket mark
3 Woodruff key slot

off the timing sprockets **(see illustration)**. Do not allow either the camshaft or crankshaft to rotate until the belt is refitted.

10 Examine the belt carefully for signs of deterioration. If there is evidence of cracking, glazing, chafing, disintegration or oil contamination, renew it. Only refit the existing belt if it is known to have been recently renewed and is still in good condition. The cost of a new belt is minor, compared to the cost of the engine damage which may be caused if it breaks in service.

Refitting

11 Check that both the camshaft and crankshaft are still correctly aligned with the relevant marks on the timing belt inner cover **(see illustrations)**.

12 Fit the timing belt over the camshaft and crankshaft sprockets, ensuring that the arrows on the belt correspond with the rotation of the crankshaft (clockwise) **(see illustration)**. Make

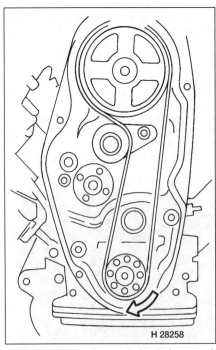

5.12 Correct routing of timing belt around sprockets and tensioner

sure that any slack in the belt is on the tensioner side - the flat side of the belt should pass around the tensioner roller. Ensure that the teeth on the belt engage positively with those on the sprockets.

13 Push the tensioner pulley against the belt to eliminate the slack, and clip the tensioner spring over the water pump retaining bolt..

14 *Temporarily* refit the crankshaft bolt, and put the transmission into neutral. Rotate the crankshaft clockwise through two complete turns, to even out the tension in the belt.

⚠ *Caution: Turn the crankshaft directly - do not apply effort to the camshaft sprocket. Check that the timing marks on both sprockets are again aligned with those on the inner cover. Tighten first the inner, then the outer tensioner bolt to the specified torque.*

15 Rotate the crankshaft through two more clockwise revolutions. The timing belt tension can now be checked using a spring balance and ruler. Hook the spring balance over the timing belt on the side that is not routed around the tensioner roller, at a point mid-way between the two sprockets **(see illustration)**. Pull the balance at right-angles to the belt until 3 kg (6.6 lb) registers on the scale. Use the ruler to measure how much the belt is deflected from its normal position.

16 If the deflection is not between 5.5 and 6.5 mm, the belt tension will have to be adjusted. Loosen the tensioner retaining bolts, slacken or tighten the belt as required, and

5.15 Checking the tension of the timing belt

5.17 Tighten the tensioner retaining bolts to the specified torque

6.2a Unclip the spring from water pump retaining bolt (arrowed) and remove the timing belt tensioner outer . . .

6.2b . . . and inner retaining bolts

repeat the steps in paragraph 15. This process may have to be repeated more than once to achieve the correct belt tension.

17 When the belt deflection is within specification, tighten the tensioner retaining bolts to the correct torque **(see illustration)**. Refit the outer timing belt cover and rubber gasket. If necessary, use a light coating of silicon sealant to hold the gasket in place during refitting.

18 Slide the crankshaft pulley into place, engaging the key and keyway correctly. Refit the bolt and the tighten it to the specified torque, locking the crankshaft using one of the methods described in the removal process.

19 Refit the cooling fan, spacer and water pump drive pulley, and tighten the bolts.

20 Route the auxiliary drivebelt around the crankshaft, water pump and alternator pulleys. Tension the belt using the alternator, as described in Chapter 1.

21 Reconnect the battery negative cable.

6 Timing belt sprockets and tensioner - removal and refitting

Removal

1 Working as described in Section 5, paragraphs 1 to 7 inclusive, remove the auxiliary drivebelt and pulleys, the cooling fan, and the timing belt outer cover.

2 Unclip the belt tensioner spring from water pump retaining bolt, and remove the timing belt tensioner outer and inner retaining bolts **(see illustrations)**. Extract the entire tensioner assembly. Remove the timing belt, and examine it carefully for signs of deterioration. If there is evidence of cracking, glazing, chafing, disintegration or oil contamination, renew it as described in Section 5.

3 Using a suitable implement to hold the sprocket stationary, remove the camshaft sprocket bolt - see illustration 6.6, which shows a forked holding tool. Whatever method is used, hold the sprocket directly - do not be tempted to use the timing belt to hold the sprocket. Slide the sprocket off the camshaft, and recover the Woodruff key **(see illustrations)**.

4 Prise the crankshaft sprocket off the shaft using suitable lever (not a screwdriver). Recover the Woodruff key and the belt guide washer **(see illustrations)**.

6.3a Remove the camshaft sprocket bolt

6.3b Slide the sprocket off the camshaft . . .

6.3c . . . and recover the Woodruff key

6.4a Remove the crankshaft sprocket

6.4b Recover the Woodruff key . . .

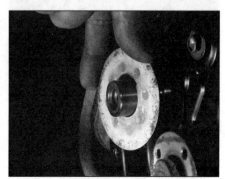

6.4c . . . and the belt guide washer

6.6 Tightening the camshaft sprocket bolt - note the forked holding tool bolted through the sprocket

Refitting

5 Follow the above steps in reverse order. Ensure that the Woodruff keys are inserted correctly when refitting the timing belt sprockets; the curved edge should be inserted into the shaft, with the flat edge facing outwards. Ensure that all fixings are tightened to the correct torque.

6 When tightening the camshaft sprocket bolt, hold it stationary using the same method employed during removal **(see illustration)**.

7 Ensure that the sprockets are correctly aligned as described in Section 5, paragraphs 7 and 11, then refit the timing belt and all other disturbed components.

7 Camshaft oil seal - renewal

1 Remove the auxiliary drivebelt and pulleys, cooling fan, timing belt cover, timing belt, tensioner and sprockets, referring to Sections 5 and 6 of this Chapter.

2 After removing the retaining nuts and bolts, lift the timing belt inner cover away from the engine block **(see illustration)**. (Recover the rubber grommet from the water pump shaft). The oil seal will now be exposed - note how much it protrudes from its housing.

3 Drill two small holes in the existing oil seal, diagonally opposite each other. Thread two

7.2 Lift the timing belt inner cover away from the engine block

self-tapping screws into the holes, and use a pair of pliers to pull on the heads of the screws and extract oil seal. Be careful not to damage the seal housing or camshaft sealing surface during this process.

4 Clean out the seal housing and sealing surface of the camshaft. Remove any swarf or burrs that could cause the seal to leak.

5 Lubricate the lip of the new oil seal with clean engine oil, and push it over the camshaft until it is positioned above its housing.

6 Using a hammer and a long-reach socket of suitable diameter, drift the seal squarely into its housing. Stop when the outer surface of the seal protrudes by the same amount as the original seal. Take care not to damage the seal lip.

7 Refit the timing belt inner cover, timing sprockets, timing belt and outer cover as described in Sections 5 and 6 of this Chapter.

8 Cylinder head, inlet and exhaust manifolds - removal, separation and refitting

Removal

 Caution: The engine must be allowed to cool completely before commencing work.

Note: It is recommended that new cylinder head bolts are used on refitting. Make sure, in any case, that you know which size of bolt you

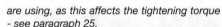are using, as this affects the tightening torque - see paragraph 25.

1 It is possible to remove the inlet and exhaust manifolds with the cylinder head still bolted to the cylinder block. However, access to some of the manifold mounting bolts and studs is very restricted, making their removal difficult. Hence, this section describes the removal of the cylinder head and manifolds as one assembly.

2 Dismantling of the cylinder head and inspection of its components is detailed in Part B of this Chapter. Even if you only intend to fit a new head gasket, removing the cylinder head provides a good opportunity to examine the bearings, camshaft and valve gear for early signs of wear.

3 Disconnect the battery negative cable, and position it away from the terminal.

4 Position the engine at TDC on No 1 cylinder - see Section 2 of this Chapter.

5 Remove the HT leads and distributor - see Chapter 5B.

6 Remove the spark plugs and drain the cooling system - see Chapter 1.

7 After slackening their hose clips, disconnect the breather hose from the PCV valve mounted on the inlet manifold, and remove the brake servo rubber hose completely **(see illustrations)**.

8 Unbolt the gear selector cable retaining bracket from the inlet manifold, and position the cables away from the engine.

9 Disconnect the top hose from the radiator and the thermostat housing, removing it completely. Detach the heater supply hose from the thermostat housing, and position it away from the engine. Pull the coolant bypass hose off the port on the bottom of the thermostat housing **(see illustrations)**.

10 Unplug the coolant temperature sensor cable - pull on the connector housing, not the cable itself. Label it for refitting. Unbolt the engine earth strap from the exhaust manifold heat shield, or if it is too badly corroded, from the bodywork **(see illustrations)**.

11 Remove the carburettor and air cleaner assembly - see Chapter 4.

12 Remove the camshaft cover, cooling fan, auxiliary drivebelt and pulleys, timing belt inner (and outer) covers, timing belt, tensioner

8.7a Disconnect the breather hose from the PCV valve . . .

8.7b . . . then remove the brake servo vacuum supply rubber hose completely

8.9a Disconnect the top hose from the radiator . . .

8.9b . . . and the thermostat housing

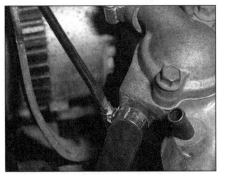

8.9c Detach the heater supply hose from the thermostat housing

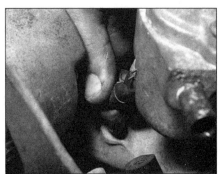

8.9d Pull the coolant bypass hose off the port on the bottom of the thermostat housing

and sprockets - see Sections 4, 5 and 6 of this Chapter.

13 Remove the three bolts securing the exhaust centre pipe to the exhaust manifold flange; refer to Chapter 4 for details. **Note:** *This section of the exhaust pipe is mounted on a ball joint, and hence can be angled away from the manifold flange to give greater clearance.*

14 Pull the warm-air inlet hose off the exhaust manifold heat shield. Take care not to split the aluminium tubing, as it can become very brittle with age.

15 Loosen the cylinder head bolts, one quarter-turn at a time, until they can be removed by hand. Lift the cylinder head and manifolds squarely away from the engine block. If it sticks, carefully lever it up using protrusions on the head and block castings as fulcrums; **do not** lever between the mating surfaces, as this will risk damaging them. Recover the locating dowels. Place the head assembly on a bench, resting it on wooden blocks to protect the mating surfaces and valve heads. Retrieve and discard the head gasket.

Separation

14 Unbolt the heat shield from the exhaust manifold. Take care not shear the studs off when removing the nuts. If they are corroded, use a penetrant oil to release the threads, and carefully work them free by repeatedly slackening and tightening them.

15 Unbolt the exhaust manifold from the

cylinder head and withdraw it, together with its metallic gasket.

16 Unbolt the inlet manifold from the cylinder head, recovering the lifting eyelet and fuel hose clip. Lift the manifold away from the head, tapping it lightly with a mallet if it sticks.

17 Remove all remains of gasket material from the engine block, cylinder head and manifold mating surfaces. With particular regard to the alloy cylinder head and inlet manifold, take care not to score or gouge the surfaces, as this may cause leakage. Do not allow any debris to fall into the cylinder block, as blockages may form at critical points in the lubrication or cooling systems. Use tape to seal up the galleries whilst the cleaning is being carried out. Solvents can be obtained specifically for removing old gasket material from metal surfaces; however as they are corrosive to a wide range of materials, they should be used with extreme caution; delicate items such as valve heads and oil seals may be damaged.

18 Examine all threaded fasteners; if they are damaged or badly corroded, replace them. Pay particular attention to the cylinder head bolts and the condition of their threads. Although the manufacturer does not state that the cylinder head bolts must be renewed when the head is removed, it is strongly recommended that they are, as a complete set.

19 Inspect the surfaces of the manifolds for cracks, especially around the mounting points. A cracked manifold will need to be renewed.

8.10a Unplug the coolant temperature sensor cable

20 The dismantling and overhaul of the cylinder head and its components, including the camshaft, valves and rocker shaft assemblies, is detailed in Part B of this Chapter.

Refitting

21 Fit a new exhaust manifold gasket over the studs on the cylinder head, lining it up such that the preformed indentations allow access to the spark plug holes. Refit the manifold, apply anti-seize grease to the mounting studs, and screw on the retaining nuts, tightening them to the correct torque. Offer up the heat shield to the manifold, and refit the retaining nuts, after smearing anti-seize grease on the stud threads **(see illustrations)**.

8.10b Unbolt the engine earth strap from the exhaust manifold heat shield

8.21a Fit a new exhaust manifold gasket over the studs on the cylinder head . . .

8.21b . . . and refit the manifold

8.21c Offer up the heat shield to the manifold, and refit the retaining nuts

8.22a Fit the two-piece inlet manifold gasket over the studs on the cylinder head . . .

8.22b . . . and refit the inlet manifold

8.23a Push the locating dowels firmly into the cylinder block . . .

8.23b . . . and fit the new cylinder head gasket

22 Fit the two-piece inlet manifold gasket over the studs on the cylinder head, and refit the inlet manifold. Refit the retaining nuts and bolts, including the lifting eyelet and fuel hose clamp **(see illustrations)**.

23 Push the locating dowels firmly into the cylinder block, and fit the new cylinder head gasket - note the orientation marks stamped on the gasket surface **(see illustrations)**.

24 Carefully position the cylinder head assembly on the cylinder block, making sure that it engages with the dowels correctly. Check that the head gasket is seated properly before allowing the full weight of the head to settle on it **(see illustration)**.

25 Apply a smear of high-melting-point grease to the threads and the underside of the heads of the cylinder head bolts. Ensure that the washers are free to move along the shanks of the bolts. **Note:** *that the bolts may have one of two different diameter shanks, and that this affects the final tightening torque. If new bolts are obtained, it is probable that the shanks will be 9 mm in diameter, and the higher specified torque should be used. Seek the advice of your Vauxhall/Suzuki dealer if in doubt.* Fit each bolt in turn, screwing it in until hand-tight. Tighten the bolts to the correct torque, one quarter-turn at a time, following the correct sequence **(see illustrations)**.

26 The remainder of the components can now be refitted by reversing the removal sequence, as follows:

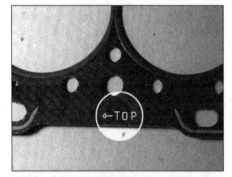

8.23c Orientation marks stamped on the gasket surface

8.24 Position the cylinder head assembly on the cylinder block

8.25a Fit the cylinder head bolts . . .

8.25b Tighten the bolts to the correct torque, one quarter-turn at a time . . .

8.25c . . . following the correct sequence

9.4 Extract the radiator bottom hose from the clip mounted on the sump

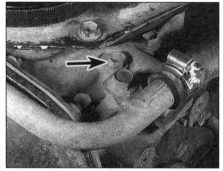

9.5 Underneath the crankshaft pulley, remove the bolt (arrowed) that secures the rigid coolant return hose to the cylinder block

a) *Reconnect exhaust centre pipe, warm-air inlet and earth strap to the exhaust manifold.*
b) *Refit the timing belt inner cover - refer to Section 5 of this Chapter.*
c) *Refit and align camshaft and crankshaft timing sprockets - refer to Section 6 of this Chapter.*
d) *Refit the timing belt and tension it correctly - refer to Section 5 of this Chapter.*
e) *Refit the timing belt outer cover, auxiliary drive pulleys and drivebelt - refer to Section 5 of this Chapter.*
f) *Refit the camshaft cover - refer to Section 4 of this Chapter.*
g) *Refit the carburettor and air cleaner assembly - refer to Chapter 4.*
h) *Refit all disturbed electrical cables, coolant, vacuum and breather hoses.*
i) *Refit the spark plugs, distributor and HT leads, and set the static ignition timing - refer to Chapters 1 and 5B.*

27 With reference to Chapter 1, carry out the following:
a) *Check, and if necessary adjust, the valve clearances.*
b) *Refill the cooling system.*

28 Reconnect the battery negative cable and again referring to Chapter 5B, check the dynamic ignition timing.
29 Run the engine to normal operating temperature, and check for leaks around the newly-gasketed surfaces. As well as looking for coolant or oil leaks, listen for air or exhaust gas leaks.
30 Switch the engine off, and carry out a final coolant and engine oil level check.

9 Sump and oil pickup - removal, inspection and refitting

Removal

1 Disconnect the battery negative cable. Refer to Chapter 1, and drain the coolant and engine oil.
2 From the right-hand engine access hatch, remove the bolt midway between the alternator and right-hand engine mountings that secures the rigid coolant return hose to the engine block.
3 Apply the handbrake, then raise the front of the vehicle and support it securely on axle stands or wheel ramps. Refer to *"Jacking, towing and wheel changing"* at the beginning of this manual for the correct positioning of the axle stands.
4 Slacken the clip securing the bottom coolant hose to the radiator. Pull the hose off the radiator, and extract it from the clip mounted on the sump **(see illustration)**; see Chapter 3 for more details.
5 Remove the bolt located on the engine block, underneath the crankshaft pulley, that secures the rigid coolant return hose from the heater **(see illustration)**. Slacken the two clips at either end of this hose, and detach it from the rubber hose sections.
6 Unbolt the lower baffle plate from the bellhousing **(see illustration)**.
7 Extra working clearance can be gained by removing the clutch cable from its bracket, located on the right-hand engine mounting bracket; refer to Chapter 7.
8 Gradually remove the bolts that secure the sump to the crankcase, together with their washers. Avoid warping the sump by working around the bolts one by one, slackening them a few turns at a time until they are free. Support the sump as the last bolts are withdrawn, tapping it with soft-faced mallet if it sticks to the crankcase. Carefully manoeuvre the sump towards the front of the vehicle and, tilting it to avoid the oil strainer, withdraw it from the engine bay. Recover the rubber gasket.
9 Unbolt the oil pickup assembly from the oil pump flange and the support bracket on the main bearing cap. Withdraw it, recovering the O-ring seal.

Inspection

10 Thoroughly clean the mating surfaces of the sump and the crankcase, removing any traces of old gasket and oil residue. Discard the old gasket, as a new one must be fitted.
11 Examine the gauze filter on the oil strainer/pickup assembly. Remove any residue that may have built up using a suitable solvent or flushing agent. Take care not to push the residue back inside the oil pickup body.

Refitting

12 Seat a new O-ring in the housing on the oil pickup flange, then refit the assembly to the oil pump and main bearing cap, tightening the retaining bolts to the correct torque **(see illustrations)**.
13 Smear the new sump gasket with clean engine oil, and fit it to the sump. Offer up the sump to the crankcase, and refit the retaining bolts; check that the gasket is seated correctly before fully tightening them. As

9.6 Unbolt the lower baffle plate from the bellhousing

9.12a Seat a new O-ring in the housing on the oil pickup flange . . .

9.12b . . . then refit the oil pickup assembly to the oil pump . . .

9.12c . . . and main bearing cap

9.13 Offer up the sump to the crankcase, and refit the retaining bolts

11.4a Remove the alternator . . .

described in the removal process, tighten the bolts to their correct torque progressively, to avoid deforming the sump **(see illustration)**.

14 The remainder of the components can now be refitted by reversing the removal procedure. Upon completion, refill the engine with the correct quantity and grade of oil, and replenish the cooling system, as described in Chapter 1.

15 Run the engine until it reaches its correct operating temperature, and check the newly-gasketed surfaces for leaks.

10 Crankshaft front oil seal - renewal

1 Disconnect the battery negative cable. Remove the auxiliary drivebelt, crankshaft and water pump pulleys, cooling fan, timing belt outer (and inner) cover, timing belt tensioner and sprockets, as described in Sections 5 and 6 of this Chapter.

2 It is advisable to remove the radiator to gain greater clearance around the front of the crankshaft; refer to Chapter 3.

3 Note the fitted depth of the seal, and then prise it out using a narrow-bladed implement, such as screwdriver. Pad the blade to avoid damaging the crankshaft or oil seal housing mating surfaces. If this fails to extract the seal, drill or punch two small-bore holes into it, and

thread two self tapping screws into the holes. Pull on the heads of screws with a pair of grips to draw out the seal.

4 Clean out the seal housing and the crankshaft sealing surface with a clean rag. Examine both surfaces for damage and wear; a new seal fitted to a worn surface will still leak.

5 Lubricate the new oil seal with clean engine oil, and position it over its housing on the crankshaft. Carefully drive it squarely into place using a long-reach socket, until it is inserted to the same depth as the old seal, as noted prior to removal. **Note:** *Select a socket that bears on the rigid outer surface of the seal, not the flexible (and delicate) inner lip.*

6 Remove any remaining oil with a rag. Refit the remaining components, referring to the relevant paragraphs of Sections 5 and 6.

7 Refit the radiator, referring to Chapter 3.

11 Oil pump - removal, inspection and refitting

Removal

1 Disconnect the battery negative cable. With reference to Chapter 1, drain the engine oil.

2 Referring to Sections 5 and 6, remove the cooling fan, auxiliary drivebelt and pulleys, timing belt outer (and inner) cover, timing belt, tensioner and crankshaft sprocket.

3 Refer to Section 9, and remove the sump and oil pickup assembly.

4 Remove the alternator (see Chapter 5A) and unbolt its lower mounting bracket from the cylinder block **(see illustrations)**.

5 Unscrew and withdraw the mounting bolts from the front of the oil pump casing. Grasp the casing and pull it away from the engine, over the crankshaft **(see illustrations)**.

Inspection

6 Carefully scrape any remains of the old gasket from the crankcase and oil pump case mating surfaces, taking care not to score or gouge them.

7 Noting their orientation, extract and clean the gears and the inner body of the pump case. Inspect them for signs of severe scoring or excessive wear, which if evident will necessitate renewal of the complete pump.

8 Using feeler blades, check the clearances between the pump case and the outer gear, and the inner and outer gear-to-crescent clearances. The amount of gear endfloat can be assessed by placing a straight-edge across the pump mounting face, and slipping a feeler blade between the straight-edge and the gear.

9 Check the drivegear for signs of excessive wear or damage.

10 If the clearances measured are outside the specified maximum clearances and/or the drivegear is in poor condition, the complete pump unit must be renewed.

11.4b . . . and unbolt its lower mounting bracket from the cylinder block

11.5a Unscrew and withdraw the mounting bolts from the front of the oil pump casing

11.5b Pull the casing away from the engine

11.12a Fit a new gasket to the front mating surfaces of the oil pump case . . .

11.12b . . . then the underside

11.12c Trim off the excess gasket

11 It is good idea at this point to fit a new crankshaft oil seal to the pump case, while it is out of the engine. Refer to the relevant paragraphs of Section 10 for guidance.

Refitting

12 Fit new gaskets to the front and underside mating surfaces of the oil pump case. Using a sharp blade, trim off the excess gasket. Apply a small quantity of sealant to the trimmed edges of the gasket, to ensure an oil-tight seal **(see illustrations)**.
13 Locate the oil pump over the crankshaft, and slide it into place. Refit the mounting bolts. and progressively tighten them to the correct torque.
14 Refit the remainder of the components by reversing the removal procedure.
15 Refill the engine with the correct grade and quantity of oil. Start the engine, and check the newly-gasketed surfaces for leaks.

12 Engine mountings - inspection and renewal

Inspection

1 Vibration and juddering, particularly when coming off overrun, or during gearchanges, can be attributed to worn engine mountings. Inspect the rubber mounting blocks for signs of major deterioration; surface blemishes that can be scraped away are not a problem. Vulcanisation and deep cracks, however, are signs that the mountings may need to be renewed. Assess their effectiveness by grasping the engine and rocking it around the crankshaft axis. If a significant amount of movement can be induced, then the engine mountings must be renewed.

Renewal

2 Disconnect the battery negative cable.
3 Position a trolley jack directly underneath the engine/bellhousing junction, behind the mounting cross member. Place a block of wood on the head of the jack, to protect the surfaces of the engine and bellhousing. Raise the jack enough to just bear the weight of the

engine, but not enough to strain the engine mountings.
4 After bending back the corners of the lockplates with a pair of pliers, unscrew the four bolts that secure the engine mounting crossmember to the chassis rails, recovering the washers and bushes - note the order of removal **(see illustration)**. Withdraw the crossmember by removing the nuts that secure it to the engine mounting blocks.

 Caution: As the crossmember is removed, check that the engine remains properly balanced on the jack; the angle of inclination can make this difficult to judge until the engine is released from its mountings.

 Warning: Do not position any part of your body underneath the engine whilst it is only supported by a jack.

5 The mounting blocks can be released by removing the nuts that secure them to the engine brackets. **Note:** *The left-hand side mounting block has a steel cover plate mounted over it; be sure to refit this when mounting block is renewed* **(see illustration)**.
6 Fit the new mounting blocks to the engine brackets, and tighten the retaining nuts to the specified figure. Offer the crossmember to the underside of the mounting blocks and refit the retaining nuts, tightening them to the correct torque.
7 With the crossmember located over its mounting holes in the chassis rails, refit the

12.4 Unscrew the four bolts that secure the engine mounting crossmember to the chassis rails

mounting bolts, washers, bushes and lockplate in the correct sequence. Tighten the bolts to the correct torque. Using pliers, bend the corners of the lockplates against the flats of the bolt heads.
8 Carefully lower the jack, and withdraw it from under the vehicle. Grasp the engine and rock it from side to side, to settle it on its mountings. Check that the engine still has a reasonable degree of free movement, and that no part of the engine fouls the engine bay or any other component whilst it is being moved.
9 Reconnect the battery negative cable.

13 Flywheel - removal, inspection and refitting

Removal

1 Disconnect the battery negative cable, and position it away from the terminal. Apply the handbrake, then jack up the front of the vehicle and rest it securely on axle stands, or wheel ramps - refer to *"Jacking, towing and wheel changing"* at the beginning of this manual.
2 Referring to Chapters 7 and 8, remove the propeller shaft, transmission and clutch.
3 Working around the hub of the flywheel,

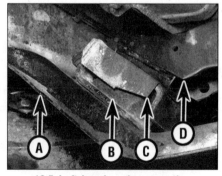

12.5 Left-hand engine mounting arrangement

A *Crossmember*
B *Engine mounting assembly*
C *Cover plate*
D *Engine mounting bracket*

progressively slacken the flywheel retaining bolts. If the flywheel rotates under the applied effort, partially refit two of the clutch pressure plate retaining bolts, and wedge a stout bar between them. Use the bar as a handle to hold the flywheel stationary.

4 As the last bolts are slackened, support the flywheel to prevent it from suddenly dropping and damaging the bolt threads. Note that the flywheel has a holed drilled in it, close to its centre, which is fitted over a locating dowel protruding from the end of the crankshaft. **Note:** *Although the manufacturer does not specify it, renewal of the flywheel retaining bolts is recommended.*

5 Lift the flywheel away from the crankshaft, and lower it onto a work bench. Get an assistant to help, as the flywheel is not only heavy, but also awkward to hold, due to its toothed rim. With the flywheel removed, now is good time to inspect the crankshaft rear oil seal for any evidence of leaking; refer to Section 14 for details.

Inspection

6 Clean the surface of the flywheel with a suitable solvent, paying particular attention to the clutch drive surface. Look for deep scores, cracks, or grooves caused by contact with the rivets on the clutch friction plate. Minor scratches can be eradicated with fine abrasive paper, but deep scoring will mean that the flywheel has to be machined at an engineering workshop, or if the damage is severe, renewed.

7 Examine the ring gear teeth. If any of them are cracked, grooved or even missing, it will be necessary to renew the ring gear. Note that missing teeth not only affect the performance of the cranking system, but may throw the flywheel out of balance, placing increased stress on other components. The job of renewing the ring gear assembly involves heating it to a very specific high temperature; overheating weakens the case-hardening, and will cause accelerated wear. Approach a dealer or an engineering workshop, who will have the equipment necessary to carry out the job correctly.

8 If the flywheel has been removed because of vibration or clutch judder, it is advisable to have the runout checked. This should ideally be carried out by an engineering workshop. Checking the runout with the flywheel mounted on the engine, using a dial gauge, is not possible.

9 Clean the mating surfaces of the end of the crankshaft and the flywheel. Use a tap to clear out any remaining thread-locking compound from the mounting holes in the crankshaft.

10 If they are not already coated, apply thread-locking compound to the new flywheel retaining bolts. Offer up the flywheel to the crankshaft, and engage the locating dowel in the corresponding hole in the flywheel. Loosely insert the bolts, and hand-tighten them. Progressively tighten each bolt with a torque wrench, half a turn at a time, until they are correctly torqued. Prevent the assembly from rotating using the method employed during removal.

11 Refit the clutch, transmission and propeller shaft as described in Chapters 7 and 8. Use a jack to remove the axle stands/wheel ramps, and lower the vehicle to the ground. Reconnect the battery negative cable.

14 Crankshaft rear oil seal - renewal

1 Disconnect the battery negative cable, and position it away from the terminal. Refer to Section 13 and remove the flywheel from the engine.

2 Remove the sump, referring to Section 9 for details.

3 Slacken and withdraw the bolts retaining the oil seal housing. Carefully prise the housing away from the crankcase, and peel off the remaining gasket material. Note the fitted depth of the existing seal in the housing.

4 Rest the housing face down across two

pieces of wood, and using a mallet and punch, drive out the oil seal through the front of the housing **(see illustration)**. Be careful not to score or buckle the housing with the punch, as this will cause leakage when the new seal is fitted.

5 Clean the housing with a suitable solvent, removing any oil deposits and traces of gasket material. Inspect the mating surfaces and the oil seal seat. If they are damaged or worn, a new housing should be fitted. Clean the mating surface of the crankcase in a similar manner.

6 Locate the new oil seal over its seat in the housing. Using a flat block wood, or a section of pipe of suitable diameter, drive the seal squarely into its seat, until it is at the same fitted depth as the old oil seal **(see illustration)**. Be careful not to drive the seal in at an angle as this will cause it to leak.

7 Lubricate the lip of the oil seal and the crankshaft with grease. Position a new gasket on the crankcase. Ease the housing and oil seal onto the crankshaft; it will be quite a tight fit, so use a blunt-ended implement such as a extension bar to push the assembly into place on the crankcase.

8 Refit the housing retaining bolts, and tighten them to the specified torque. Trim off any gasket material that protrudes beyond the housing with a sharp blade, and seal the trimmed edges with a suitable sealant.

9 Refit the sump and flywheel as described in Sections 9 and 13 respectively, and replenish the engine oil and coolant.

10 Reconnect the battery negative cable, and start the engine. Check the area around the bottom of the bellhousing and sump for oil leaks.

14.4 Driving the crankshaft rear oil seal out of its housing (typical example shown)

14.6 Driving the new seal into the housing (typical example shown)

Chapter 2 Part B:
Engine removal and overhaul procedures

Contents

Crankshaft - refitting and main bearing running clearance check .. 10
Crankshaft - removal and inspection 6
Cylinder block/crankcase - cleaning and inspection 7
Cylinder head - dismantling, cleaning, inspection and assembly ... 4
Engine - initial start-up after overhaul and reassembly 13
Engine and transmission - removal, separation and refitting 2
Engine overhaul - preliminary information 3
Engine overhaul - reassembly sequence 9
Flywheel - removal, inspection and refitting .... see Chapter 2A
General Information 1
Main and big-end bearings - inspection and selection 8
Piston and connecting rod assemblies - refitting and big-end
      bearing clearance check 12
Piston rings - refitting 11
Pistons and connecting rods - removal and inspection 5

Degrees of difficulty

Easy, suitable for novice with little experience	Fairly easy, suitable for beginner with some experience	Fairly difficult, suitable for competent DIY mechanic	Difficult, suitable for experienced DIY mechanic	Very difficult, suitable for expert DIY or professional

Specifications

Cylinder head
Maximum distortion:
  Head to block gasket surface .... 0.05 mm
  Manifold gasket surfaces .... 0.10 mm

Rocker shaft assembly
Maximum shaft runout .... 0.06 mm
Shaft diameter .... 14.965 to 14.980 mm
Rocker arm internal diameter .... 14.985 to 15.005 mm
Shaft-to-arm clearance:
  Standard .... 0.005 to 0.040 mm
  Service limit .... 0.07 mm

Camshaft
Maximum shaft runout .... 0.1 mm
Cam height:
  Standard .... 36.152 mm
  Service limit .... 36.100 mm
Endfloat:
  Standard .... 0.050 mm
  Service limit .... 0.150 mm
Camshaft journal external diameters (No 1 at timing sprocket end):
  No 1 .... 43.425 to 43.450 mm
  No 2 .... 43.625 to 43.650 mm
  No 3 .... 43.825 to 43.850 mm
  No 4 .... 44.025 to 44.050 mm
  No 5 .... 44.225 to 44.250 mm
Cylinder head bearing internal diameters (No 1 at timing sprocket end):
  No 1 .... 43.500 to 43.516 mm
  No 2 .... 43.700 to 43.716 mm
  No 3 .... 43.900 to 43.916 mm
  No 4 .... 44.100 to 44.116 mm
  No 5 .... 44.300 to 44.316 mm
Camshaft-to-cylinder head journal clearance:
  Standard .... 0.050 to 0.091 mm
  Service limit .... 0.15 mm

Valve assembly

Valve stem diameter:
Inlet . . . . 6.965 to 6.980 mm
Exhaust . . . . 6.950 to 6.970 mm
Valve guide internal diameter . . . . 7.000 to 7.015 mm
Valve guide protrusion from head (inlet and exhaust) . . . . 14.0 mm
Valve guide oversize . . . . 0.03 mm
Valve guide hole diameter (inlet and exhaust) . . . . 12.030 to 12.048 mm
Stem-to-guide clearance:
Inlet:
Standard . . . . 0.020 to 0.050 mm
Service limit . . . . 0.07 mm
Exhaust:
Standard . . . . 0.030 to 0.065 mm
Service limit . . . . 0.09 mm
Maximum valve stem end deflection:
Inlet . . . . 0.12 mm
Exhaust . . . . 0.16 mm
Valve head thickness:
Inlet:
Standard . . . . 0.80 to 1.20 mm
Service limit . . . . 0.60 mm
Exhaust:
Standard . . . . 0.80 to 1.20 mm
Service limit . . . . 0.70 mm
Maximum valve head radial runout . . . . 0.8 mm
Maximum valve stem end stock allowance . . . . 0.5 mm
Valve seat width . . . . 1.3 to 1.5 mm
Valve spring free length:
Standard . . . . 48.9 mm
Service limit . . . . 47.6 mm
Valve spring preload:
Standard . . . . 23.6 kg/40 mm
Service limit . . . . 22 kg/40 mm
Valve spring squareness limit . . . . 2.0 mm (point of maximum deflection when unloaded)

Pistons and piston rings

Piston diameter:
Standard . . . . 65.450 to 65.475 mm
Oversize 0.25 mm . . . . 65.700 to 65.725 mm
Oversize 0.50 mm . . . . 65.950 to 65.975 mm
Piston-to-cylinder bore clearance . . . . 0.045 to 0.055 mm
Gudgeon pin external diameter . . . . 15.995 to 16.000 mm
Piston ring groove width:
Top compression ring . . . . 1.52 to 1.54 mm
2nd compression ring . . . . 1.51 to 1.53 mm
Oil control ring . . . . 2.81 to 2.83 mm
Piston ring width:
Top compression ring . . . . 1.47 to 1.49 mm
2nd compression ring . . . . 1.47 to 1.49 mm
Oil control ring . . . . 0.45 mm
Piston ring-to-groove wall clearance:
Top compression ring:
Standard . . . . 0.03 to 0.07 mm
Service limit . . . . 0.12 mm
2nd compression ring:
Standard . . . . 0.02 to 0.06 mm
Service limit . . . . 0.10 mm
Piston ring end gap:
Top compression ring:
Standard . . . . 0.15 to 0.30 mm
Service limit . . . . 0.7 mm
2nd compression ring:
Standard . . . . 0.15 to 0.35 mm
Service limit . . . . 0.7 mm
Oil control ring:
Standard . . . . 0.20 to 0.70 mm
Service limit . . . . 1.8 mm

Cylinder block

Maximum distortion of block to head gasket surface	0.05 mm
Bore diameter	65.505 to 65.520 mm
Maximum bore wear	0.05 mm

Connecting rods

Big-end thrust clearance:	
Standard	0.10 to 0.20 mm
Service limit	0.30 mm
Big-end width	21.95 to 22.00 mm
Maximum bow	0.05 mm
Maximum twist	0.10 mm
Small-end internal diameter	16.003 to 16.011 mm
Gudgeon pin-to-small-end clearance:	
Standard	0.003 to 0.016 mm
Service limit	0.05 mm

Crankshaft

Maximum shaft runout	0.06 mm
Endfloat:	
Standard	0.13 to 0.28 mm
Service limit	0.35 mm
Crankpin width	22.10 to 22.15 mm
Crankpin diameter:	
Standard	37.982 to 38.000 mm
Undersize 0.25 mm	37.732 to 37.750 mm
Undersize 0.50 mm	37.482 to 37.500 mm
Big-end bearing-to-crankpin running clearance:	
Standard bearing:	
Standard	0.020 to 0.040 mm
Service limit	0.080 mm
Undersize bearings	0.020 to 0.070 mm
Thrustwasher bearing size:	
Standard	2.500 mm
Oversize 0.125 mm	2.563 mm
Oversize 0.500 mm	2.625 mm
Main bearing journal diameter:	
Standard	49.982 to 50.000 mm
Undersize 0.25 mm	49.732 to 49.750 mm
Undersize 0.50 mm	49.482 to 49.500 mm
Main bearing-to-journal running clearance:	
Standard bearing:	
Standard	0.020 to 0.040 mm
Service limit	0.080 mm
Undersize bearing	0.020 to 0.070 mm

Torque wrench settings

Refer to Part A of this Chapter.

---

1 General Information

Using this Chapter

This part of Chapter 2 deals with the removal, dismantling and overhaul of the engine.

Removal of the engine alone, leaving the transmission in place, is possible, but not recommended. Separation of the two units whilst they are still in the vehicle requires careful manoeuvring, to avoid damaging the surrounding components, and would require the assistance of at least one helper. Hence Part B describes the removal of the engine and transmission as a complete unit. (**Note:** *Removal of the transmission alone is dealt with in Chapter 8.)*

If the engine is to be removed and dismantled for inspection and/or overhaul, some of the operations detailed in Part A will be required. As the operations in Part A describe in-vehicle repairs, any information regarding the disconnection of ancillary components, for example, can be ignored.

Overhauling in general

It is not always easy to determine when, or if, an engine should be completely overhauled - a number of factors need to be taken into consideration.

High mileage is not necessarily an indication that an overhaul is needed, while low mileage does not preclude the need for an overhaul. Frequency of servicing is probably the most important consideration. An engine which has had regular and frequent oil and filter changes, as well as other required maintenance, should give many thousands of miles of reliable service. Conversely, a neglected engine may require an overhaul very early in its life.

Excessive oil consumption is an indication that piston rings, valve seals and/or valve guides are in need of attention. Make sure that oil leaks are not responsible before deciding that the rings and/or guides are worn. Perform a compression test, as described in Part A of this Chapter, to determine the likely cause of the problem.

Check the oil pressure with a gauge fitted in

place of the oil pressure switch, and compare it with that specified. If it is extremely low, the main and big-end bearings, and/or the oil pump, are probably worn out.

Loss of power, rough running, knocking or metallic engine noises, excessive valve gear noise, and high fuel consumption may also point to the need for an overhaul, especially if they are all present at the same time. If a complete service does not remedy the situation, major mechanical work is the only solution.

An engine overhaul involves restoring all internal parts to the specification of a new engine. During an overhaul, the cylinders are rebored, and the pistons and piston rings are renewed. New main and big-end bearings are generally fitted; if necessary, the crankshaft may be reground, to restore the journals. The valves are also serviced as well, since they are usually in less-than-perfect condition at this point. While the engine is being overhauled, other components, such as the distributor, starter and alternator, can be overhauled as well. The end result should be an as-new engine that will give many trouble-free miles.

> **HAYNES HiNT** *Critical cooling system components such as the hoses, thermostat and water pump should be renewed when an engine is overhauled. The radiator should be checked carefully, to ensure that it is not clogged or leaking. Also, it is recommended that the oil pump is renewed as part of the overhaul.*

Before beginning the engine overhaul, read through the entire procedure, to familiarise yourself with the scope and requirements of the job. Overhauling an engine is not difficult if you follow all of the instructions carefully, have the necessary tools and equipment, and pay close attention to all specifications. It can, however, be time-consuming. Plan on the vehicle being off the road for a minimum of two weeks, especially if parts must be taken to an engineering works for repair or reconditioning. Check on the availability of parts, and make sure that any necessary special tools and equipment are obtained in advance. Most work can be done with typical hand tools, although a number of precision measuring tools are required for inspecting parts to determine if they must be renewed. Often, the engineering works will handle the inspection of parts, and offer advice concerning reconditioning and renewal.

Note: *Always wait until the engine has been completely dismantled, and until all components (especially the cylinder block/crankcase and the crankshaft) have been inspected, before deciding what service and repair operations must be completed by an engineering works. The condition of these components will be the major factor to consider when determining whether to overhaul the original engine, or to buy a reconditioned unit. Therefore, do not purchase parts or have overhaul work done on other components until they have been thoroughly inspected.* As a general rule, labour accounts for the largest part of the cost of an overhaul, so it does not pay to fit worn or sub-standard parts.

As a final note, to ensure maximum life and minimum trouble from a reconditioned engine, everything must be assembled with care, in a spotlessly-clean environment.

2 Engine and transmission - removal, separation and refitting

Preparation and precautions

1 If you have decided that the engine must be removed for overhaul or major repair work, several preliminary steps should be taken.

2 Locating a suitable place to work is extremely important. Adequate work space, along with storage space for the vehicle, will be needed. If a workshop or garage is not available, at the very least a solid, level, clean, work surface is required.

3 Clean the engine compartment and engine/transmission before beginning the removal procedure; this will aid access, and help to keep tools clean and organised.

4 A trolley jack rated in excess of the combined weight of the engine and transmission will be required. Safety is of primary importance, considering the potential hazards involved in removing the engine/transmission from the vehicle.

5 If this is the first time you have removed an engine, an assistant should ideally be available. Advice and aid from someone more experienced would also be helpful. There are many instances when one person cannot simultaneously perform all of the operations required when removing the engine from the vehicle.

6 Plan the operation ahead of time. Before starting work, arrange for the hire of (or obtain) all of the tools and equipment you will need. Access to the following equipment will allow the task of removing and refitting the engine/transmission to be completed safely and with relative ease: a heavy-duty trolley jack, complete sets of spanners and sockets as described in the front of this manual, wooden blocks, and plenty of rags and cleaning solvent for mopping up spilled oil, coolant and fuel. A selection of different-sized storage bins will also prove useful for keeping dismantled components grouped together. If any of the equipment must be hired, make sure that you arrange for it in advance, and perform all of the operations possible without it beforehand. This will save you money and time.

7 Plan for the vehicle to be out of use for quite a while. An engineering works will be required to perform some of the work which the do-it-yourself mechanic cannot accomplish without special equipment. These establishments often have a busy schedule, so it would be a good idea to consult them before removing the engine, in order to accurately estimate the amount of time required to rebuild or repair components that may need work.

8 When removing the engine from the vehicle, be methodical about the disconnection of external components. Labelling cables and hoses as they are removed will greatly assist the refitting process.

9 Always be extremely careful when removing and refitting the engine/transmission. Serious injury can result from careless actions. If help is required, it is better to wait until it is available rather than risk personal injury and/or damage to components by continuing alone. By planning ahead and taking your time, a job of this nature, although major, can be accomplished successfully and without incident.

10 The engine and transmission are removed from *under* the vehicle on all models described in this manual.

Removal

11 Select a solid, level surface to park the vehicle on. Give yourself enough space to move around it easily.

12 If the engine is to be dismantled, drain the engine oil, referring to Chapter 1.

13 Drain the cooling system, again referring to Chapter 1. Retain the coolant if it is fit for re-use.

14 Removal of the front seats is recommended, to improve access to the engine bay area. Refer to Chapter 11 for details.

15 Disconnect the battery negative and positive cables. Remove the rear engine cover, referring to Chapter 11 for details.

16 Unscrew the gear lever knob, and lift off the lever gaiter from the centre console.

17 With reference to Chapter 11, remove the five screws securing the console and lift it off, pulling open the plastic flap to allow it to clear the seat belt fasteners. Remove the anchor bolts, and release the seat belt stalks. Referring to Chapter 8, disconnect both the gear shift and selector cables from the transmission, and release them from the bracket on the inlet manifold. This will allow the crossmember to be unbolted and completely removed.

18 Disconnect the earth strap from the exhaust manifold heat shield, and position it clear of the engine.

19 On the distributor body, place a mark under the No 1 cylinder HT terminal, as described in Part A of this Chapter, Section 2, paragraph 3. Unplug the HT leads from the spark plugs and coil. Unclip and remove the distributor cap, with the HT leads still attached.

2.22a Free the fuel feed and return hoses from the clamps mounted on the engine right hand mounting (air cleaner removed for clarity) . . .

20 Disconnect the starter motor cables as described in Chapter 5A.

21 Disconnect the coolant temperature sensor and oil pressure sensor cables as described in Chapter 5B.

22 Release any pressurised vapour contained in the fuel tank by momentarily removing the fuel filler cap. Free the fuel feed and return hoses from the clamps mounted on the right-hand engine mounting bracket and the bellhousing **(see illustrations)**.

⚠️ *Warning: Petrol is extremely flammable - great care must be taken when working on any part of the fuel system. Do not smoke, or allow any naked flames or uncovered light bulbs, near the work area. Note that gas-powered domestic appliances with pilot lights, such as heaters, boilers and tumble-dryers, also present a fire hazard. Bear this in mind if you are working in a garage where such appliances are present. Always keep a suitable fire extinguisher close to the work area; the Aqueous Film-Forming Foam (AFFF) variety is a good choice for dealing with petrol fires. Familiarise yourself with its operation before starting work. Wear eye protection when working on fuel systems, and wash off any fuel spilt on bare skin immediately with soap and water.*

23 Remove the air cleaner assembly and carburettor, with reference to Chapter 4.

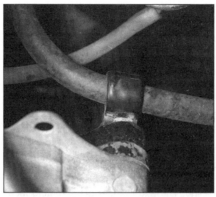

2.22b . . . and on the bellhousing

24 Drain the transmission oil as described in Chapter 1, then refit and tighten the filler and drain plugs.

25 Disconnect the coolant hoses from the heater and radiator. Remove the heater coolant return hose from its mounting bracket on the cylinder block.

26 Disconnect and completely remove the brake servo vacuum hose **(see illustration)**.

27 Unbolt the cooling fan cowling from the radiator, and push it towards the engine, over the cooling fan. Slacken the four bolts securing the cooling fan to the water pump spindle. Remove them and pull the fan off, together with its alloy spacer and the auxiliary drive pulley. If the spacer sticks, tap it lightly with a soft-faced mallet to dislodge it. Unbolt and recover the cooling fan cowling from the engine bay.

28 Apply the handbrake, and chock the rear wheels. Jack up the front of the vehicle and rest it securely on wheel ramps. There must be at least one metre (just over three feet) of clearance between the ground and the bottom of the front number plate to allow the engine and transmission assembly to be removed under the front of the vehicle on a trolley jack. Note that if axle stands are used, they will restrict the removal of the engine assembly from under the front of the vehicle. Alternatively, if this ground clearance cannot be achieved with the equipment available, it is possible to withdraw the engine and

2.26 Disconnect and remove the brake servo vacuum hose

transmission from the side of the vehicle, after the assembly has been lowered to the ground. In this case, the required ground clearance between the same points is 0.8 of a metre (just over two and-a-half feet) and axle stands can be used **(see illustrations)**. See *"Jacking, towing and wheel changing"* at the beginning of this manual for the correct positioning of the axle stands.

29 Disconnect the clutch cable from its mounting bracket and release arm; refer to Chapter 7.

30 Disconnect the transmission earth strap and reversing light switch cable. After slackening the speedometer drive cable pinch-bolt, withdraw the cable, and tie it back to the chassis. Refer to Chapter 8 or 12 for details, as applicable.

31 Remove the three bolts securing the exhaust front pipe to the exhaust manifold flange. This section of the exhaust pipe is mounted on a balljoint, and hence can be angled away from the manifold flange to give greater clearance.

32 Release the warm-air inlet duct from the bracket securing it to the top of the transmission case.

33 Position a trolley jack directly under the engine mounting crossmember, raising it to just take the weight of the engine. Check that nothing remains connected between the engine and vehicle before commencing removal.

34 With reference to Chapter 7, remove the four bolts securing the propeller shaft to the differential input shaft flange. Pull the whole propeller shaft assembly off the transmission output shaft.

35 Remove the two bolts securing the transmission rear mounting. Ensure that the engine and transmission do not tilt away from the horizontal at this point, as the water pump pulley could foul the radiator - get an assistant to provide support whilst the bolts are being withdrawn.

36 Bend back the corners of the lockplates on the engine mounting crossmember to release the four bolts securing it to the chassis. Carefully unscrew and withdraw the

2.28a Removing the engine from under the front of the vehicle

2.28b Removing the engine from under the side of the vehicle

2.36 Bend back the corners of the lockplates on the engine mounting crossmember bolts

bolts, together with their bushes and washers, maintaining firm support of the engine and transmission assembly to prevent it tilting **(see illustration)**.

37 Manoeuvre the assembly towards the rear of the vehicle as it is being withdrawn, to ensure that the water pump pulley clears the radiator. Slowly lower the jack, and pull the assembly clear of the vehicle. Note that if the assembly is to be withdrawn from the side, it must first be lifted from the jack onto a piece of board on the ground - it can then be dragged from under the vehicle. Take great care when doing this, and get an assistant to help.

38 Unbolt the engine mounting brackets from the cylinder block and remove them, together with their support plates. Withdraw the engine support crossmember and unbolt the engine mounting brackets from it, removing the rubber mounting blocks. Inspect the blocks carefully; if any damage or deterioration is evident, renew them. It is good idea at this point to inspect the transmission rubber mounting, and decide whether it also requires renewal. If it does, extract it by removing the two nuts securing it to the upper and lower mounting brackets. When the new rubber mounting is fitted, ensure that the mounting nuts are re-tightened to the correct torque.

Separation

39 Rest the engine and transmission assembly on a firm, flat surface, and use wooden blocks as wedges to keep the unit steady. Unbolt and withdraw the baffle plate from the bottom of the bellhousing.

40 The transmission is secured to the engine block by two nuts screwed onto studs, threaded into the bellhousing, and by two bolts threaded into the cylinder block, which also serve as mountings for the starter motor. Remove these and carefully draw the transmission away from the engine, resting it securely on wooden blocks. Recover the upper baffle plate as the transmission is removed, and collect the locating dowels if they are loose enough to be extracted.

 Caution: Take care to prevent the transmission from tilting, until the input shaft is fully disengaged from the clutch friction plate. Otherwise, potentially-damaging strain will be placed upon the clutch components, the input shaft and its bearings.

Refitting

41 Smear a quantity of high-melting-point grease onto the splines of the transmission input shaft. Do not use an excessive amount, however, as this will risk contaminating the clutch friction plate. Carefully offer up the transmission to the cylinder block, guiding the studs through the mounting holes in cylinder block.

42 Refit the two bolts through the starter motor and bellhousing to the cylinder block, and the two nuts on the bellhousing studs. **Note:** *Do not tighten them to force the engine and transmission together.* Ensure that the bellhousing and cylinder block mating faces are correctly seated before tightening the bolts and nuts securely.

43 Refit the lower baffle plate to the bellhousing. Bolt the left and right-hand engine mounting brackets and rubber blocks to the mounting crossmember, tightening the bolts to the correct torque. Offer up the crossmember to the engine, lining up the engine mounting brackets with the holes on the cylinder block. Refit the bolts and support plates, tightening them to the correct torque.

44 With the help of an assistant, lift the engine assembly onto a trolley jack, resting it on the mounting crossmember. Position the jack under the vehicle, and carefully raise the engine and transmission up into the engine bay, maintaining firm support to prevent tilting and damage to the surrounding components. **Note:** *Raise the assembly to a position slightly to the rear of its final mounting position, pushing it towards the front of the vehicle as it approaches the chassis. This will prevent the water pump pulley from fouling, and possibly damaging, the radiator.*

45 Refit the transmission rear mounting bracket and its two retaining bolts. Do not fully tighten them at this point.

46 Refit the four bolts securing the mounting crossmember to the chassis rails, together with their rubber bushes, washers and lockplates. Do not fully tighten them at this point.

47 Referring to Chapter 7, refit the propeller shaft. Grasp the engine and transmission assembly, and rock it from side to side; this will allow it to settle on its mountings. The engine crossmember and transmission mounting bolts can now be tightened to their correct torque. Fold the corners of the engine crossmember bolt lockplates against the flats of the bolt heads to lock them in position.

48 The remainder of the refitting procedure is the reverse of the removal procedure. In addition, carry out the following:
a) *When refitting the carburettor, adjust the choke and throttle cables with reference to Chapter 4.*
b) *Adjust the clutch cable with reference to Chapter 7.*

c) *Ensure that all hoses are correctly routed, and are secured with the correct hose clips, where applicable. If the hose clips originally fitted are of the crimped variety, they cannot be used again; worm-drive clips must be fitted in their place.*
d) *Connect all cables to their appropriate terminals - if the terminal contacts have become tarnished during the removal process, clean them thoroughly to ensure good electrical continuity.*
e) *Refill the cooling system as described in Chapter 1.*
f) *Refill both the engine and transmission with appropriate grades and quantities of oil, as detailed in Chapter 1.*
g) *Adjust the gear selector cable with reference to Chapter 8.*
h) *Check, and if necessary adjust the ignition timing as described in Chapter 1.*
i) *When the engine is started for the first time, check for air, coolant, lubricant and fuel leaks from manifolds, hoses etc. If the engine has been overhauled, read Section 13 at the end of this Chapter before attempting to start it.*

3 Engine overhaul - preliminary information

1 It is much easier to dismantle and work on the engine if it is mounted on a portable engine stand. These stands can often be hired from a tool hire shop. Before the engine is mounted on a stand, the flywheel should be removed, so that the stand bolts can be tightened into the end of the cylinder block/crankcase.

2 If a stand is not available, it is possible to dismantle the engine with it blocked up on a sturdy workbench, or on the floor. Be extra-careful not to tip or drop the engine when working without a stand.

3 If you are going to obtain a reconditioned engine, all the external components must be removed first, to be transferred to the replacement engine (just as they will if you are doing a complete engine overhaul yourself). These components include the following:
a) *Alternator mounting brackets (Chapter 5A).*
b) *The distributor, HT leads and spark plugs (Chapters 1 and 5B).*
c) *Thermostat housing, and coolant outlet elbow (Chapter 3).*
d) *The dipstick and its tube.*
e) *The carburettor and air cleaner components (Chapter 4).*
f) *All electrical switches and sensors, and the engine wiring harness (Chapters 3 and 5A).*
g) *Inlet and exhaust manifolds (Chapter 2A).*
h) *Oil filter (Chapter 1).*
i) *Engine mountings (Chapter 2A).*
j) *Flywheel (Chapter 2A).*
Note: *When removing the external components from the engine, pay close attention to details*

4.3 Remove the rocker shaft retaining screws from the tops of the camshaft journal bearing posts

4.6 Measure the camshaft endfloat

4.10 Extract the valve stem oil seal

that may be helpful or important during refitting. Note the fitted position of gaskets, seals, spacers, pins, washers, bolts, and other small items.

4 If you are obtaining a "short" engine (which consists of the cylinder block/crankcase, crankshaft, pistons and connecting rods all assembled), then the cylinder head, sump, oil pump, timing belt and water pump will also have to be removed.

5 If you are planning a complete overhaul, the engine can be dismantled in the order given below:
a) *Inlet and exhaust manifolds (Chapter 2A).*
b) *Timing belt, sprockets and tensioner (Chapter 2A).*
c) *Cylinder head (Chapter 2A).*
d) *Flywheel (Chapter 2A).*
e) *Sump (Chapter 2A).*
f) *Oil pump (Chapter 2A).*
g) *Piston/connecting rod assemblies.*
h) *Crankshaft.*

6 Before beginning the dismantling and overhaul procedures, make sure that you have all of the correct tools necessary. Refer to *"Tools and working facilities"* at the end of this manual for further information.

---

4 Cylinder head - dismantling, cleaning, inspection and assembly

1 New and reconditioned cylinder heads will be available from the original manufacturer, and from engine overhaul specialists. It should be noted that some specialist tools are required for the dismantling and inspection procedures, and new components may not be readily available. It may, therefore, be more practical and economical for the home mechanic to purchase a reconditioned head, rather than to dismantle, inspect and recondition the original head.

Dismantling

2 Remove the cylinder head from the engine block, and separate the inlet and exhaust manifolds from it, as described in Part A of this Chapter.

3 Remove the rocker shaft retaining screws from the tops of the camshaft journal bearing posts **(see illustration)**. Use the correct size of Phillips screwdriver bit, to avoid burring the screw heads.

4 It is important that groups of components are kept together when they are removed and, if they are still serviceable, refitted in the same groups. If they are refitted randomly, accelerated wear will occur, leading to early failure. Stowing groups of components in plastic bags or storage bins will help to keep everything in the right order - label them according to their fitted location, eg "No 1 exhaust", "No 1 inlet", etc. Note that No 1 cylinder is nearest the timing belt end of the engine.

5 Push one end of the inlet side rocker shaft into the bearing post, until the other end protrudes enough to grasp. Pull the rocker shaft out gradually, collecting the shaft springs and rocker arms as they are released. Repeat this process on the exhaust side. **Note:** *To help keep the rocker shafts, arms and springs together in the correct sequence, try sliding them as an assembly onto a piece of stout wire or welding rod.*

6 Unbolt the distributor drive gear case from the cylinder head - remove the gasket and discard it. Measure the maximum camshaft endfloat by inserting feeler blades of increasing width between the camshaft and thrust plate, until all endfloat is eliminated **(see illustration)**. Note this measurement for later reference. Take off the camshaft thrust plate by removing its retaining screws.

7 At the timing pulley end of the camshaft, remove the camshaft oil seal - work from the relevant Section of Chapter 2A for guidance.

8 Carefully draw the camshaft out the cylinder head from the distributor drive end. Support the other end of the shaft as it is withdrawn, so that the journals, lobes and bearings are not damaged.

9 Using a valve spring compressor, compress each valve spring in turn, extracting the split collets when the valve spring retainer has been pushed far enough down the valve stem to free them.

 HAYNES HiNT *If the valve spring retainer sticks, lightly tap the upper jaw of the spring compressor with a hammer to loosen it.*

10 Release the valve spring compressor, and remove the retainer, spring and spring seat. Use a pair of pliers to extract the valve stem oil seal **(see illustration)** and withdraw the valve itself through the combustion chamber. If the valve sticks in the guide, deburr the end face with fine abrasive paper. Repeat this process for the remaining valves.

Cleaning

11 Using a suitable degreasing agent, remove all traces of oil deposits from the cylinder head, paying particular attention to the journal bearings, rocker shaft mountings, valve guides and oilways. Scrape any traces of old gasket from the mating surfaces, taking care not to score or gouge them. Turn the head over and using a blunt blade, scrape any carbon deposits from the combustion chambers and ports.

 Caution: Do not erode the sealing surface of the valve seat. Finally, wash the entire head casting with a suitable solvent to remove the remaining debris.

12 Clean the valve heads and stems using a fine wire brush. If the valve is heavily coked, scrape off the majority of the deposits with a blunt blade first, then use the wire brush.

Caution: Do not erode the sealing surface of the valve face.

13 Thoroughly clean the remainder of the components using solvent, and allow them to dry completely. Discard the oil seals, as new items must be fitted when the cylinder head is reassembled.

Inspection

Cylinder head casting

14 Examine the head casting closely, to identify any damage sustained or cracks that may have developed. Pay particular attention to cracking around the areas of the mounting holes, valve seats and spark plug holes. If

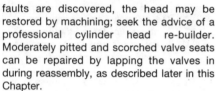

4.15a Measure the distortion of the gasketed surfaces, using a straight-edge and a set of feeler blades

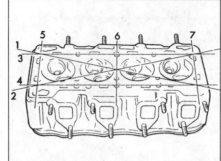

4.15b Take seven measurements on the head gasket surface, to assess the level of distortion in all planes

4.19 Badly-scored or indented rocker arms must be renewed

faults are discovered, the head may be restored by machining; seek the advice of a professional cylinder head re-builder. Moderately pitted and scorched valve seats can be repaired by lapping the valves in during reassembly, as described later in this Chapter.

15 Measure the distortion of the gasketed surfaces, using a straight-edge and a set of feeler blades. Take one measurement longitudinally on both the inlet and exhaust manifold mating surfaces. Take seven measurements on the head gasket surface, to assess the level of distortion in all planes **(see illustrations)**. Compare the measurements with the figures in the Specifications. If the head is distorted out of specification, it may be possible to repair it by grinding down any high-spots on the surface with fine abrasive paper. The manufacturer does not state a minimum cylinder head height, so machining the surface is not recommended.

Rocker shaft assemblies

16 Check that the oil holes are clear of debris. Examine the outer surface of the rocker shafts for wear, in the form of ridges or scoring. A badly-worn rocker shaft must be renewed.

17 Use a micrometer or vernier calipers to measure the outer diameter of the rocker shaft at the points where it passes through the rocker arms. Then, using a bore gauge or internal vernier calipers, measure the internal

diameters of the rocker arm pivots. Use these measurements to establish the clearances. Repeat this process for both shafts, at all the points where the shafts pass through the rocker arms and bearing pillars. Compare the figures obtained with those given in the Specifications. If they are out of tolerance, renew either the rocker shaft or the rocker arm, whichever is outside of its maximum/minimum diameter.

18 Place the rocker shaft between two V-blocks. Using a dial gauge, measure the shaft runout at points midway between the mounting holes. If it is out of tolerance, renew the shaft.

19 Inspect the cam follower face of each rocker arm. If it is badly scored or indented, the arm must be renewed. Check the corresponding lobe on the camshaft, as it will probably be worn as well **(see illustration)**. Examine the ends of the adjusting screws for signs of wear; renew them as required.

20 Although no specifications are given for the rocker arm springs, check them visually for cracking and slackness. Renew them if they appear worn.

Camshaft

21 Visually inspect the camshaft for evidence of wear on the surfaces of the lobes and journals. Normally, their surfaces should be smooth and have a dull shine; look for scoring, erosion or pitting, and for areas that appear highly polished - these are signs that

wear has begun to occur. Accelerated wear will occur once the hardened exterior of the camshaft has been damaged, so always renew worn items. **Note:** *If these symptoms are visible on the tips of the camshaft lobes, check the corresponding rocker arm, as it will probably be worn as well.*

22 Examine the distributor drive gear teeth for signs of wear or damage. Slack in the drive caused by worn gear teeth will affect ignition timing.

23 If the surface of the camshaft appears discoloured or "blued", it is likely that it has been overheated at some point, probably due to inadequate lubrication. This may have distorted the shaft, so check the runout as described later in this Section.

24 Using a micrometer or vernier calipers, measure the camshaft lobe heights and journal diameters **(see illustrations)**. Using internal calipers or a bore gauge, measure the journal bearing internal diameters and use this figure to work out the journal running clearances. Compare these figures with those listed in the Specifications, noting that the journals are numbered 1 to 5 from the timing sprocket end. If they are outside the specified tolerance, renew the camshaft and/or cylinder head.

25 Compare the endfloat measurement recorded earlier with that listed in the Specifications. If it is out of tolerance, renew the thrust plate.

26 Place the camshaft between two V-

4.24a Measure the camshaft lobe heights . . .

4.24b . . . journal diameters . . .

4.24c . . . and journal bearing internal diameters

4.26 Measure the camshaft runout at the centre journal

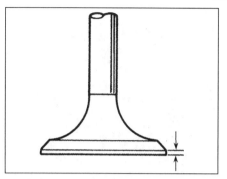

4.27 Measure the valve head thickness; the valve cannot be re-used if this dimension is too small

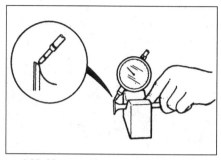

4.28 Measure the runout at the valve head

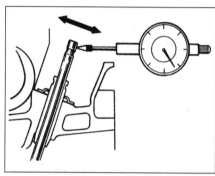

4.29 Measure the maximum side-to-side deflection of the valve in its guide

blocks. Using a dial gauge, measure the runout at the centre journal **(see illustration)**. Compare this figure with that listed in the Specifications. If it is outside the specified tolerance, renew the camshaft.

Valves and associated components

27 Examine each valve closely for signs of wear. Inspect the valve stems for wear ridges, scoring or variations in diameter; measure them at several points along their lengths with a micrometer. The valve heads should not be cracked, badly pitted or charred. Note that light pitting of the valve head can be rectified by grinding the valves in during reassembly, as described later in this Section. Check that the valve stem end face is free from excessive pitting or indentation, caused by incorrect valve clearances. Measure the valve head thickness using a micrometer; the valve cannot be re-used if this dimension is too small **(see illustration)**.

28 Place the valves in a V-block. Using a dial gauge, measure the runout at the valve head **(see illustration)**. Renew the valve if it is out of tolerance.

29 Insert each valve into its respective guide in the cylinder head, and set up a dial gauge against the edge of the valve's end face. With the valve head held a few millimetres away from the seat, measure the maximum side-to-side deflection of the valve in its guide **(see illustration)**. If the measurement is out of tolerance, the valve and valve guide should be

renewed as a pair. **Note:** *Valve guides are an interference fit in the cylinder head, and their removal requires access to professional equipment. For this reason, it would be wise to entrust the job to an engineering workshop or head rebuilding specialist.*

30 Using vernier calipers, measure the free length of each of the valve springs. Stand each spring on its end on a flat surface, against an engineer's square. Check the squareness by measuring the largest gap between the spring and the square. Compare these measurements with the specified figures and if necessary, renew the springs **(see illustrations)**.

31 Measuring valve spring pre-load involves compressing the valve by applying a specified weight, and measuring the reduction in length. This may be a difficult operation to conduct in the home workshop, so it would be wise to approach your local garage or engineering workshop for assistance. Weakened valve springs will at best increase engine running noise, and at worst, cause poor compression, so defective items should be renewed.

Reassembly

⚠️ *Caution: Keep the valve train components in their original groups when refitting - do not mix components between cylinders.*

32 To restore the gas-tight seal between the valves and their seats, it will be necessary to grind, or "lap", the valves in. To complete this

process, you will need a quantity of fine/coarse grinding paste and a grinding tool - this can either be of the dowel and rubber sucker type, or the automatic type, driven by a rotary power tool.

33 Smear a small quantity of fine grinding paste on the sealing face of the valve head. Turn the cylinder head over so that the combustion chambers are facing upwards, and insert the valve into the correct guide. Attach the grinding tool to the valve head, and using a backward/forward rotary action, grind the valve head into its seat. Periodically lift the valve and rotate it, to redistribute the grinding paste. Continue this process until the contact between valve and seat produces an unbroken, matt grey ring of uniform width, between 1.3 and 1.5 mm wide, on both faces **(see illustration)** Repeat the operation for the remaining valves.

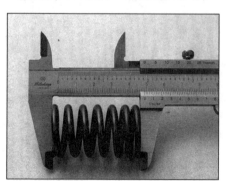

4.30a Using vernier calipers, measure the free length of each valve spring

4.30b Check the squareness of each valve spring

4.33 Grinding-in the valves

4.36a Fit the spring seat into place, with the dimpled side facing upwards

4.36b Use a suitable long-reach socket to press the valve stem seal firmly into position

4.37a Lubricate the valve stem with clean engine oil, and insert it into the guide

34 If the valves and seats are so badly pitted that coarse grinding paste needs to be used, check first that there is enough material left on both components to make this operation worthwhile. If in doubt, consult a professional cylinder head re-builder. Assuming the repair is feasible, work as described in the previous paragraph but use the coarse grinding paste initially, to achieve a dull finish on the valve face and seat. Then wash off coarse paste with solvent, and repeat the process using fine grinding paste to obtain the correct finish.
35 When all the valves have been ground-in, remove all traces of grinding paste from the cylinder head and valves with solvent, and allow them to dry completely.
36 Turn the head over. Working on one valve at a time, fit the spring seat into place, with the dimpled side facing upwards. Dip a new

valve stem seal in clean engine oil, and carefully push it onto the top of the valve guide - use a suitable long-reach socket to press it firmly into position **(see illustrations)**.
37 Lubricate the valve stem with clean engine oil, and insert it into the guide - take care not to damage the stem seal as the valve is being inserted. Locate the valve spring over the seat, and fit the retainer over the top of the spring **(see illustrations)**.
38 Using a valve spring compressor, compress the spring until the retainer is pushed beyond the collet groove in the valve stem. Refit the split collet, using a dab of grease to hold the two halves in the groove **(see illustration)**. Gradually release the spring compressor, checking that the collet remains correctly seated as the spring extends. When correctly seated, the retainer should force the

two halves of the collet together, and hold them securely in the groove.
39 Repeat this process for the remaining sets of valve components. To settle the components after installation, strike the end of each valve stem with a mallet, using a block of wood to protect the stem from damage.
40 Lubricate the camshaft and cylinder head bearing journals with clean engine oil. Working from the distributor drive end of the head, carefully slide the camshaft into position - sprocket mounting end first. Support the ends of the shaft as it is inserted, to avoid damaging the lobes and journals **(see illustrations)**.
41 Refit the camshaft thrust plate, and tighten the retaining screws to the correct torque **(see illustration)**. Rotate the camshaft by hand, to check that it does not bind.

4.37b Locate the valve spring over the seat . . .

4.37c . . . and fit the retainer over the top of the spring

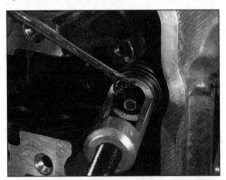

4.38 Using a valve spring compressor, compress the spring and fit the collets

4.40a Lubricate the cylinder head bearings with clean engine oil . . .

4.40b . . . and carefully slide the camshaft into position

4.41 Refit the camshaft thrust plate, and tighten the retaining screws to the correct torque

4.43a Slide the rocker shaft into the bearing pillar (exhaust shaft shown) . . .

4.43b . . . then fit the spring . . .

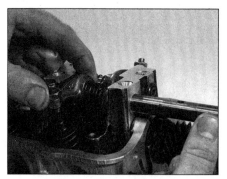

4.43c . . . and rocker arm

42 Examine both rocker shafts, noting that each has flat edges machined into it at one end. It is possible to insert the shafts incorrectly in the cylinder head and as the shafts have integral oil pickup holes, their orientation is critical. Hence, the machined edges are used to identify the ends of the shafts during reassembly.

43 Liberally lubricate the rocker shaft mounting holes in the cylinder head with clean engine oil. Taking the inlet rocker shaft and working from the timing pulley end of the cylinder head, insert the plain end of the shaft (**not** the machined end) into the bearing pillar, until it just protrudes from the other side.

4.43d Orientation of the rocker shafts, viewed from the timing sprocket end

A Inlet rocker shaft - machined end
B Exhaust rocker shaft - plain end

Using the components from the "No 1 inlet" set, fit the rocker arm spring onto the shaft. Lubricate the rocker arm bore, and push it onto the shaft. Slide the shaft into the next bearing pillar, and repeat the process for the remaining inlet rocker arms and springs. When the shaft is fully inserted, rotate it to line up the mounting screw holes with those in the bearing pillars. Refit the mounting screws, and tighten them to the correct torque. Repeat the preceding steps for the exhaust rocker shaft assembly, but this time work from the distributor drive end of the cylinder head, installing the "No 4 exhaust" components first **(see illustrations)**.

44 Slacken all the valve clearance adjusting locknuts and screws to allow the camshaft to rotate without contacting the rocker arms;

4.43e Refit the rocker shaft screws

valve clearance adjustments will be carried out at a later stage.

45 Lubricate the lip of a new camshaft oil seal with clean engine oil, and locate it over its housing **(see illustration)**. Using a mallet and long-reach socket of suitable diameter, drift the seal squarely into place, until the surface of the seal is flush with the outer face of the housing.

46 Place a new gasket over the distributor gear case locating dowels, and refit the case. Insert the retaining bolts and tighten them to the correct torque **(see illustrations)**. Pour a small quantity of clean engine oil into the case, to protect the gear teeth when the engine is started for the first time.

47 Refer to Part A of this Chapter and refit the inlet and exhaust manifolds, complete with new gaskets. Working from the same Chapter, refit the cylinder head to the cylinder block.

---

5 Pistons and connecting rods - removal and inspection

Removal

1 Refer to Part A of this Chapter, and remove the cylinder head, flywheel, sump, oil pickup, oil filter and the alternator (together with its upper and lower mounting brackets).

2 Inspect the tops of the cylinder bores; any wear ridges found at the point where the

4.45 Lubricate the lip of a new camshaft oil seal with clean engine oil, and locate it over its housing

4.46a Place a new gasket over the distributor gear case locating dowels . . .

4.46b . . . refit the case and retaining bolts, and tighten them to the correct torque

5.4 Measure the big-end thrust clearance at each connecting rod

5.5a Mark the bearing caps and connecting rods with their piston numbers, using a centre-punch or a scribe

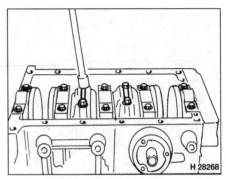

5.5b Unbolt the bearing cap nuts, half a turn at a time, until they can be removed by hand

pistons reach top dead centre must be removed; otherwise the pistons may be damaged when they are pushed out of their bores. This can be accomplished with a scraper or ridge reamer.

3 Scribe the number of each piston on its crown; note that No 1 is at the oil pump end of the engine.

4 Using a set of feeler blades, measure the big-end thrust clearance at each connecting rod **(see illustration)**. Record the measurements for later reference.

5 Rotate the crankshaft until piston Nos 1 and 4 are at bottom dead centre. Unless they are already identified, mark the bearing caps and connecting rods with their piston numbers, using a centre-punch or a scribe. Note the orientation of the bearing caps in relation to the connecting rod; scribe alignment arrows on them both to ensure correct reassembly **(see illustrations)**. Unbolt the bearing cap nuts, half a turn at a time, until they can be removed by hand. Recover the bottom shell bearing, and tape it to the cap for safe-keeping. Note that if the shell bearings are to be re-used, they must be refitted to the same connecting rod.

6 Pad the threads of the big-end bolts with masking tape or pieces of rubber hose; this will prevent them damaging the cylinder bores and bearing journals when the pistons are withdrawn **(see illustration)**. Drive the pistons out of the top of their bores by pushing on the

underside of the piston crown with a piece of dowel or a hammer handle. As the piston and connecting rod emerge, recover the top shell bearing, and tape it to the connecting rod for safe-keeping.

7 Turn the crankshaft through half a turn. Working as described in paragraphs 5 and 6 above, remove Nos 2 and 3 pistons and connecting rods. Remember to maintain the components in their groups while they are dismantled.

8 Using circlip pliers, or a small flat-bladed screwdriver, remove the gudgeon pin circlips from each piston and push out the gudgeon pin, separating the piston and connecting rod **(see illustrations)**. Discard the circlips; new ones must be fitted on reassembly.

Inspection

9 Before an inspection of the pistons can be carried out, the existing piston rings must be removed, using a removal/installation tool. Always remove the upper piston rings first, expanding them to clear the piston crown. The rings are very brittle, and will snap if stretched too much - sharp edges are produced when this happens, so protect your eyes and hands. Discard the rings on removal, as new ones must be fitted when the engine is reassembled.

10 Use a section of old piston ring to scrape the carbon deposits out of the ring grooves, taking care not to score or gouge the edges of the groove.

11 Scrape away all traces of carbon from the top of the piston. A hand-held wire brush (or a piece of fine emery cloth) can be used, once the majority of the deposits have been scraped away. Be careful not to remove any metal from the piston, as it is relatively soft.

12 Once the deposits have been removed, clean the pistons and connecting rods with paraffin or a suitable solvent, and dry thoroughly. Make sure that the oil return holes in the ring grooves are clear.

13 Examine the piston for signs of serious wear or damage. Some normal wear will be apparent, in the form of a vertical "grain" on the piston thrust surfaces, and a slight looseness of the top compression ring in its groove. Abnormal wear should be carefully examined, to assess whether the component is still serviceable, and what the cause of the wear might be.

14 Scuffing or scoring of the piston skirt may indicate that the engine has been overheating, through inadequate cooling, lubrication or abnormal combustion temperatures. Scorch marks on the skirt indicate that blow-by has occurred, perhaps caused by worn bores or piston rings. Burnt areas on the piston crown are usually an indication of pre-ignition, or pinking. In extreme cases, the piston may be holed by operating under these conditions. Corrosion pit marks in the piston crown indicate that coolant has seeped into the combustion chamber and/or the crankcase. The faults causing these symptoms must be

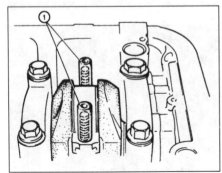

5.6 Pad the threads of the big-end bolts with masking tape or pieces of rubber hose

1 Hose/tape padding

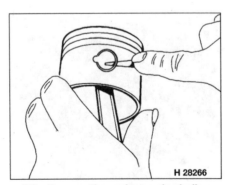

5.8a Remove the gudgeon pin circlips from each piston . . .

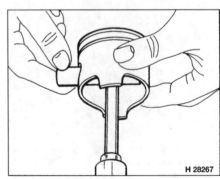

5.8b . . . and push out the gudgeon pin

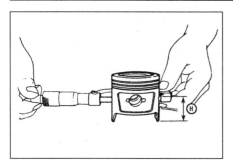

5.16 Measure the diameter of the piston, at right-angles to the gudgeon pin axis

H = 30mm

corrected before the engine is brought back into service, or the same damage will recur.
15 Check the pistons, connecting rods, gudgeon pins and bearing caps for cracks. Lay each connecting rod on a flat surface, and look along its length to see if it appears bent or twisted. If you have doubts about their condition, get them measured at an engineering workshop. Inspect the small-end bush bearing for signs of wear or cracking.
16 Using a micrometer, measure the diameter of all four pistons at a point 30mm from the bottom of the skirt, at right-angles to the gudgeon pin axis **(see illustration)**. Compare the measurements with those listed in the Specifications. If the piston diameter is out of the tolerance band listed for its particular size, then it must be renewed. **Note:** *If the cylinder block was re-bored during a previous overhaul, oversize pistons may have been fitted.* Record the measurements, and use them to check the piston clearances when the cylinder bores are measured, later in this Chapter.
17 Hold a new piston ring in the appropriate groove, and measure the side clearance using a set of feeler blades **(see illustration)**. Note that the rings are of different widths, so use

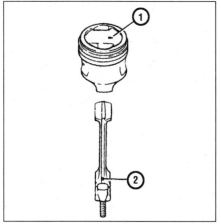

5.19 Orientation of connecting rod and piston

1 Arrow - faces oil pump end of engine
2 Oil hole - faces inlet side of engine

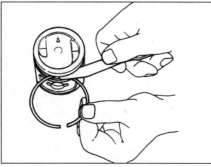

5.17 Measure the piston ring side clearance using feeler blades

the correct ring for the groove. Compare the measurements with those listed; if the clearances are outside of the tolerance band, then the piston must be renewed. Confirm this by checking the width of the piston ring with a micrometer.
18 Using internal/external vernier calipers, measure the connecting rod small-end internal diameter and the gudgeon pin external diameter. Subtract the gudgeon pin diameter from the small-end diameter to obtain the clearance. If this measurement is outside of the stated tolerance band, then the piston and connecting rod bush will have to be resized, and a new gudgeon pin installed. An engineering workshop will have the equipment needed to undertake a job of this nature.
19 The orientation of the piston with respect to the connecting rod must be correct when the two components are reassembled. The piston crown is marked with an arrow; this must point to the oil pump end of the engine when the piston is installed in the bore. The connecting rod has an oil hole drilled into the casting, just above the big-end; this should face the inlet side of the engine when bolted in place **(see illustration)**. Reassemble the two components to satisfy this requirement.
20 Lubricate the gudgeon pin and small-end bush with clean engine oil. Slide the pin into the piston, engaging the connecting rod small-end. Fit two new circlips to the piston at either end of the gudgeon pin, such that their open ends are at 90° to the removal slots **(see illustration)**. Repeat this operation for the remaining pistons.

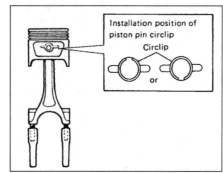

5.20 Orientation of gudgeon pin circlips

6 Crankshaft - removal and inspection

Removal

1 Remove the crankshaft auxiliary drivebelt pulley, timing sprocket, oil pump (including front oil seal), sump, oil pickup, and flywheel, as described in Part A of this Chapter.
2 Remove the pistons and connecting rods, as described in Section 5.

> **HAYNES HINT** *If no work is to be done on the pistons and connecting rods, there is no need to remove the cylinder head, or to push the pistons completely out of the cylinder bores. The pistons should just be pushed far enough up the bores that they are positioned clear of the crankshaft journals.*

3 Remove the crankshaft rear oil seal housing as described in Part A of this Chapter.
4 Check the crankshaft endfloat as follows. **Note:** *This can only be accomplished when the crankshaft is still installed in the cylinder block/crankcase, but is free to move.* Set up a dial gauge so that it is in contact with a fixed point on the crankshaft. Push the crankshaft along its axis to the end of its travel, and then zero the gauge. Push the crankshaft fully the other way, and record the endfloat indicated on the dial **(see illustration)**. The result can be compared with the specified amount, and will give an indication as to whether new thrustwasher bearings are required.
5 If a dial gauge is not available, feeler blades can be used. First push the crankshaft fully towards the flywheel end of the engine, then use a feeler blade to measure the gap between the crankpin web and the main bearing thrustwasher bearing.
6 Observe the identification and orientation marks on the main bearing caps. The number relates to the position in the crankcase, counting from the oil pump end of the engine. The arrow ensures that the caps are installed

6.4 Checking the crankshaft endfloat

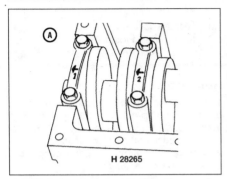

6.6 Main bearing cap identification marks

A Oil pump end of engine

6.12 Use a micrometer to measure the diameter of each main bearing journal

Warning: Wear eye protection when using compressed air!

the correct way around - these should point to the oil pump end of the engine **(see illustration)**.

7 Loosen the main bearing cap bolts one quarter of a turn at a time, until they can be removed by hand. Using a soft-faced mallet, strike the caps lightly to free them from the crankcase. Recover the lower main bearing shells, and tape them to the cap for safe-keeping.

8 Carefully lift the crankshaft out, taking care not to dislodge the upper main bearing shells. It would be wise to get an assistant's help, as the crankshaft is quite heavy. Set it down on a clean, level surface, and chock it with wooden blocks to prevent it from rolling.

9 Extract the upper main bearing shells from the crankcase, and tape them to their respective bearing caps. Remove the two thrustwasher bearings from either side of No 3 crank web.

Inspection

10 Wash the crankshaft in a suitable solvent, and allow it to dry. Flush the oil holes thoroughly, to ensure that are not blocked - use a pipe cleaner or a needle brush if necessary. Remove any sharp edges from the edge of the hole, which may damage the new bearings when they are installed.

11 Inspect the main bearing and crankpin journals for evidence of uneven wear, cracking, scoring or pitting. Rub a penny across each journal several times. If copper tracks are produced on the journal, the surface has suffered too much wear, and must be reground by an engineering workshop; the crankshaft should then be refitted with undersize bearings.

12 Use a micrometer to measure the diameter of each main bearing journal **(see illustration)**. Taking a number of measurements on the surface of each journal will reveal if it is worn unevenly. Differences in diameter measured at 90° intervals indicate that the journal is out-of-round. Differences in diameter measured along the length of the journal, indicate that the journal is tapered. Again, if wear is detected, the crankshaft must be reground by an engineering workshop, and refitted with undersize bearings.

13 Check the oil seal journals at either end of the crankshaft. If they appear worn or damaged, they may cause a new seal to leak when the engine is reassembled. It may be possible to repair the journal; seek the advice of an engineering workshop.

14 Measure the crankshaft runout by setting up a dial gauge on the centre main bearing, and rotating the shaft in V-blocks. The maximum deflection of the gauge will indicate the runout. Take precautions to protect the bearing journals and oil seal mating surfaces from damage during this procedure. Compare the measurement with the figure listed in Specifications.

15 Refer to Section 8 for details of main and big-end bearing inspection.

7 Cylinder block/crankcase - cleaning and inspection

Cleaning

1 Remove all external components and electrical switches/sensors from the block. For complete cleaning, the core plugs should ideally be removed. Drill a small hole in the plugs, then insert a self-tapping screw into the hole. Pull out the plugs by pulling on the screw with a pair of grips, or by using a slide hammer.

2 Scrape all traces of gasket and sealant from the cylinder block/crankcase, taking care not to damage the sealing surfaces.

3 Remove all oil gallery plugs (where fitted). The plugs are usually very tight - they may have to be drilled out, and the holes re-tapped. Use new plugs when the engine is reassembled.

4 If the casting is extremely dirty, it should be steam-cleaned. After this, clean all oil holes and galleries one more time. Flush all internal passages with warm water until the water runs clear. Dry thoroughly, and apply a light film of oil to all mating surfaces and cylinder bores, to prevent rusting. If you have access to compressed air, use it to speed up the drying process, and to blow out all the oil holes and galleries.

5 If the castings are not very dirty, you can do an adequate cleaning job with hot, soapy water and a stiff brush. Take plenty of time, and do a thorough job. Regardless of the cleaning method used, be sure to clean all oil holes and galleries very thoroughly, and to dry all components well. Protect the cylinder bores as described above, to prevent rusting.

6 All threaded holes must be clean, to ensure accurate torque readings during reassembly. To clean the threads, run the correct-size tap into each of the holes to remove rust, corrosion, thread sealant or sludge, and to restore damaged threads. If possible, use compressed air to clear the holes of debris produced by this operation. **Note:** *Take extra care to exclude all cleaning liquid from blind tapped holes, as the casting may be cracked by hydraulic action if a bolt is threaded into a hole containing liquid.*

7 Apply suitable sealant to the new oil gallery plugs, and insert them into the holes in the block. Tighten them securely.

8 If the engine is not going to be reassembled immediately, cover it with a large plastic bag to keep it clean; protect all mating surfaces and the cylinder bores as described above, to prevent rusting.

Inspection

9 Visually check the casting for cracks and corrosion. Look for stripped threads in the threaded holes. If there has been any history of internal water leakage, it may be worthwhile having an engine overhaul specialist check the cylinder block/crankcase with professional equipment. If defects are found, have them repaired if possible, otherwise a new block will be required.

10 Check the cylinder bores for scuffing or scoring. Any evidence of this kind of damage should be cross-checked with an inspection of the pistons - see Section 5 of this Chapter. If the damage is in its early stages, it may be possible to repair the block by reboring it. Seek the advice of an engineering workshop before you progress further.

11 To allow an accurate assessment of the wear in the cylinder bores to be made, their diameter must be measured at a number of points, as follows. Insert a bore gauge into cylinder bore No 1, and take three measurements in line with the crankshaft axis; one at the top of the bore, just below the bottom of the wear ridge, one halfway down the bore, and one at the bottom of the bore, at the lowest point of the piston's travel **(see illustrations)**.

12 Rotate the bore gauge through 90°, so that it is at right-angles to the crankshaft axis, and repeat the measurements detailed in paragraph 11. Record all six measurements, and compare them with the data listed in the Specifications. If the difference in diameter between any two cylinders exceeds the wear

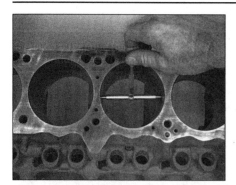

7.11a Measuring cylinder bore diameters with a bore gauge

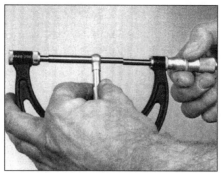

7.11b Measuring the bore gauge with a micrometer

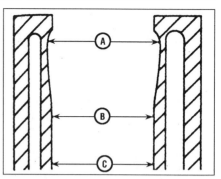

7.11c Take measurements at three depths in the bore, as described in the text

limit, or if any one cylinder exceeds its maximum bore diameter, then *all four* cylinders will have to be rebored, and oversize pistons will have to be fitted. Note that the imbalances produced by not reboring all the cylinders together would render the engine unusable.

13 Use the piston diameter measurements recorded earlier (see Section 5) to calculate the piston-to-cylinder bore clearances. Compare these with the specified maximum, and determine whether reboring and oversize pistons are required.

14 Place the cylinder block on a level work surface, crankcase downwards. Use a straight-edge and a set of feeler blades to measure the distortion of the cylinder head

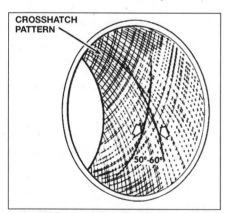

7.17a Ideal cross-hatch pattern produced by honing

7.17b Using a bottle-brush honing tool

mating surface in both planes. Compare the measurement with the limit listed in Specifications. If it is out of tolerance, repair may be possible by machining - consult your dealer for advice.

15 Before the engine can be reassembled, the cylinder bores must be honed. This process involves using an abrasive tool to produce a fine, cross-hatch pattern on the inner surface of the bore. This has the effect of seating the piston rings, resulting in a good seal between the piston and cylinder. There are two types of honing tool available to the home mechanic, both are driven by a power tool, such as a drill. The "bottle brush" hone is a stiff, cylindrical brush with abrasive stones bonded to its bristles. The more conventional surfacing hone has abrasive stones mounted on spring-loaded legs. For the inexperienced home mechanic, satisfactory results will be achieved more easily using the bottle brush hone. **Note:** *If you are unwilling to tackle cylinder bore honing, an engineering workshop will be able to carry out the job for you at a reasonable cost.*

16 Carry out the honing as follows; you will need one of the honing tools described above, a power drill/air wrench, a supply of clean rags, some honing oil, and a pair of safety glasses.

17 Fit the honing tool in the drill chuck. Lubricate the cylinder bores with honing oil, and insert the honing tool into the first bore, compressing the stones to allow it to fit. Turn

on the drill and as the tool rotates, move it up and down in the bore at a rate that produces a fine cross-hatch pattern on the surface. The lines of the pattern should ideally cross at about 50 to 60°, although some piston ring manufacturers may quote a different angle; check the literature supplied with the new rings **(see illustrations)**.

Warning: Wear safety glasses to protect your eyes from debris flying off the honing tool.

18 Use plenty of oil during the honing process. Do not remove any more material than is necessary to produce the required finish. When removing the honing tool from the bore, do not pull it out whilst it is still rotating; maintain the up/down movement until the chuck has stopped, then withdraw the tool whilst rotating the chuck by hand, in the normal direction of rotation.

19 Wipe out the oil and swarf with a rag, and proceed to the next bore. When all four bores have been honed, thoroughly clean the whole cylinder block in hot soapy water to remove all traces of honing oil and debris. The block can be considered clean when a clean rag, moistened with new engine oil, does not pick up any grey residue when wiped along the bore.

20 Apply a light coating of engine oil to the mating surfaces and cylinder bores, to prevent rust forming. Store the block in a plastic bag until reassembly.

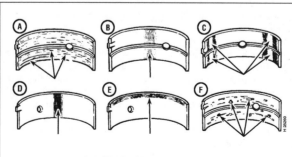

8.1 Typical bearing failures

A *Scratched by dirt; dirt embedded in bearing material*
B *Lack of oil; overlay wiped out*
C *Improper seating; bright (polished) sections*
D *Tapered journal; overlay gone from entire surface*
E *Radius ride*
F *Fatigue failure; craters or pockets*

8 Main and big-end bearings - inspection and selection

Inspection

1 Even though the main and big-end bearings should be renewed during the engine overhaul, the old bearings should be retained for close examination, as they may reveal valuable information about the condition of the engine (see illustration).

2 Bearing failure can occur due to lack of lubrication, the presence of dirt or other foreign particles, overloading the engine, or corrosion. Regardless of the cause of bearing failure, the cause must be corrected before the engine is reassembled, to prevent it from happening again.

3 When examining the bearing shells, remove them from the cylinder block/crankcase, the main bearing caps, the connecting rods and the connecting rod big-end bearing caps. Lay them out on a clean surface, in the same general position as their location in the engine. This will enable you to match any bearing problems with the corresponding crankshaft journal. Do not touch any shell's bearing surface with your fingers while checking it, or the delicate surface may be scratched.

4 Dirt and other foreign matter gets into the engine in a variety of ways. It may be left in the engine during assembly, or it may pass through filters or the crankcase ventilation system. It may get into the oil, and from there into the bearings. Metal chips from machining operations and normal engine wear are often present. Abrasives are sometimes left in engine components after reconditioning, especially when parts are not thoroughly cleaned using the proper cleaning methods. Whatever the source, these foreign objects often end up embedded in the soft bearing material, and are easily recognised. Large particles will not embed in the bearing, but will score or gouge the bearing and journal. The best prevention for this cause of bearing failure is to clean all parts thoroughly, and keep everything spotlessly-clean during engine assembly. Frequent and regular engine oil and filter changes are also recommended.

5 Lack of lubrication (or lubrication breakdown) has a number of interrelated causes. Excessive heat (which thins the oil), overloading (which squeezes the oil from the bearing face) and oil leakage (from excessive bearing clearances, worn oil pump or high engine speeds) all contribute to lubrication breakdown. Blocked oil passages, which usually are the result of misaligned oil holes in a bearing shell, will also oil-starve a bearing, and destroy it. When lack of lubrication is the cause of bearing failure, the bearing material is wiped or extruded from the steel backing of the bearing. Temperatures may increase to the point where the steel backing turns blue from overheating.

6 Driving habits can have a definite effect on bearing life. Full-throttle, low-speed operation (labouring the engine) puts very high loads on bearings, tending to squeeze out the oil film. These loads cause the bearings to flex, which produces fine cracks in the bearing face (fatigue failure). Eventually, the bearing material will loosen in pieces, and tear away from the steel backing.

7 Short-distance driving leads to corrosion of bearings, because insufficient engine heat is produced to drive off the condensed water and corrosive gases. These products collect in the engine oil, forming acid and sludge. As the oil is carried to the engine bearings, the acid attacks and corrodes the bearing material.

8 Incorrect bearing installation during engine assembly will lead to bearing failure as well. Tight-fitting bearings leave insufficient bearing running clearance, and will result in oil starvation. Dirt or foreign particles trapped behind a bearing shell result in high spots on the bearing, which lead to failure.

9 Do not touch any shell's bearing surface with your fingers during reassembly; there is a risk of scratching the delicate surface, or of depositing particles of dirt on it.

10 As mentioned at the beginning of this Section, the bearing shells should be renewed as a matter of course during engine overhaul; to do otherwise is false economy.

Selection - main and big-end bearings

11 Main and big-end bearings for this particular engine are only available in one standard size, and undersizes from 0.25 mm to 1.00 mm, in 0.25 mm increments. There are no intermediate grades of bearing, so the selection criterion is limited to whether or not the crankshaft journals and crankpins have been reground. The engineering workshop will inform you of the undersize diameter that the journals and crankpins were reground to; they may also be able to supply you with the correct undersize bearings.

12 The running clearances will need to be checked when the crankshaft is refitted with its new bearings. This procedure is described in the Section 10.

9 Engine overhaul - reassembly sequence

1 Before reassembly begins, ensure that all new parts have been obtained, and that all necessary tools are available. Read through the entire procedure, to familiarise yourself with the work involved, and to ensure that all items necessary for reassembly of the engine are at hand. In addition to all normal tools and materials, thread-locking compound will be needed. A suitable tube of liquid sealant will also be required for the joint faces that are fitted without gaskets. It is recommended that

the manufacturer's own products are used, which are specially formulated for this purpose; the relevant product names are quoted in the text of each Section where they are required.

2 In order to save time and avoid problems, engine reassembly should ideally be carried out in the following order:
a) Crankshaft.
b) Piston/connecting rod assemblies.
c) Oil pump (see Chapter 2A).
d) Sump (see Chapter 2A).
e) Flywheel (see Chapter 2A).
f) Cylinder head (see Chapter 2A).
g) Timing belt tensioner and sprockets, and timing belt (see Chapter 2A).
h) Engine external components and ancillaries.

3 At this stage, all engine components should be absolutely clean and dry, with all faults repaired. The components should be laid out (or in individual containers) on a completely-clean work surface.

10 Crankshaft - refitting and main bearing running clearance check

1 Crankshaft refitting is the first stage of engine reassembly following overhaul. At this point, it is assumed that the crankshaft, cylinder block/crankcase and bearings have been cleaned, inspected and reconditioned or renewed.

2 Place the cylinder block on a clean, level work surface, with the crankcase facing upwards. Unbolt the bearing caps and carefully release them from the crankcase; lay them out in order to ensure correct reassembly. If they are still in place, remove the bearing shells from the caps and the crankcase, and wipe out the inner surfaces with a clean rag - they must be kept spotlessly-clean.

3 Clean the rear surface of the new bearing shells with a rag, and lay them on the bearing saddles. Ensure that the orientation pegs on the shells engage with the slots in the saddles, and that the oil holes are correctly aligned (see illustration). Do not hammer or

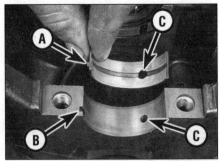

10.3 When fitting the main bearing shells, ensure that the orientation pegs/slots and oil holes (arrowed) are correctly aligned

A Orientation peg   C Oil holes
B Orientation slot

10.7 Lay a piece of Plastigage (arrowed) on each journal, in line with its axis

10.8 Fit the lower main bearing shells to the bearing caps

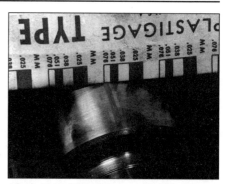

10.11 The width of the crushed Plastigage can now be measured, using the scale provided

otherwise force the bearing shells into place. It is critically important that the surfaces of the bearings are kept free from damage and contamination.

4 Give the newly-fitted bearing shells and the crankshaft journals a final clean with a rag. Check that the oil holes in the crankshaft are free from dirt, as any left here will become embedded in the new bearings when the engine is first started.

5 Carefully lay the crankshaft in the crankcase, taking care not to dislodge the bearing shells.

Running clearance check

6 When the crankshaft and bearings are refitted, a clearance must exist between them, to allow oil to circulate. This clearance is impossible to check using feeler blades, so Plastigage is used. This is a thin strip of soft plastic that is crushed between the bearing shells and journals when the bearing caps are tightened up. The change in its width then indicates the size of the clearance.

7 Cut out five pieces of Plastigage, just shorter than the length of the crankshaft journal. Lay a piece on each journal, in line with its axis **(see illustration)**.

8 Wipe off the rear surfaces of the new lower half main bearing shells, and fit them to the main bearing caps, again ensuring that the locating pegs engage correctly **(see illustration)**.

9 Wipe the front surfaces of the bearing shells, and fit the caps in their correct locations on the bearing saddles. Preserve the order that they were removed in, and ensure that the arrows all face towards the oil pump end of the engine.

10 Working from the centre bearing cap, tighten the bolts one half turn at a time to the specified torque. Do not allow the crankshaft to rotate at all whilst the Plastigage is in place. Progressively unbolt the bearing caps and remove them, taking care not to dislodge the Plastigage.

11 The width of the crushed Plastigage can now be measured, using the scale provided **(see illustration)**. Use the correct scale, as both imperial and metric values are printed on it. This measurement indicates the running

clearance - compare it with that listed in Specifications. If the clearance is outside the tolerance, it may be due to dirt or debris trapped under the bearing surface; try cleaning them again and repeat the clearance check. If the results are still unacceptable, re-check the journal diameters and the bearing sizes. Note that if the Plastigage is thicker at one end, the journals may be tapered, and as such, will require regrinding.

12 When you are satisfied that the clearances are correct, scrape the remains of the Plastigage from the journals and bearing faces. Use a soft plastic or wooden scraper, as anything metallic is likely to damage the surfaces.

Crankshaft - final refitting

13 Lift the crankshaft out of the crankcase. Wipe off the surfaces of the bearings in the crankcase and the bearing caps. Fit the thrustwasher bearings either side of the No 3 bearing saddle, between cylinder Nos 2 and 3. Use a small quantity of grease to hold them in place; ensure that they are seated correctly in the machined recesses, with the oil grooves facing outwards **(see illustration)**.

14 Liberally coat the bearing shells in the crankcase with clean engine oil.

15 Lower the crankshaft into position so that Nos 2 and 3 cylinder crankpins are at TDC; Nos 1 and 4 cylinder crankpins will then be at BDC, ready for fitting No 1 piston.

16 Lubricate the lower bearing shells in the main bearing caps with clean engine oil. Make sure that the locating lugs on the shells are still engaged with the corresponding recesses in the caps.

17 Fit the main bearing caps in the correct order and orientation - the arrows cast into the caps should all point towards the oil pump end of the engine. Insert the bolts and screw them in, *hand-tight* only at this stage.

18 Working from the centre bearing cap outwards, tighten the retaining bolts one half-turn at a time to the specified torque.

19 Refit the crankshaft rear oil seal housing, together with a new oil seal; refer to Part A of this Chapter for details.

20 Check that the crankshaft rotates freely by turning it by manually. If resistance is felt,

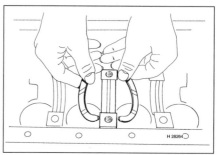

10.13 Fit the thrust bearings either side of the No 3 bearing saddle

1 Thrust bearing   2 Oil grooves

re-check the running clearances, as described above.

21 Carry out a check of the crankshaft endfloat as described at the beginning of Section 6. If the thrust surfaces of the crankshaft have been checked and new thrustwasher bearings have been fitted, then the endfloat should be within specification.

11 Piston rings - refitting

1 At this point it is assumed that the pistons have been correctly assembled to their respective connecting rods, and that the piston ring side clearances have been checked. If not, refer to the end of Section 5.

2 Before the rings can be fitted to the pistons, the end gaps must be checked with the rings fitted into the cylinder bores. Lay out the piston assemblies and the new ring sets on a clean work surface, so that the components are kept together in their groups during and after end gap checking. Place the crankcase on the work surface on its side, allowing access to the top and bottom of the bores.

3 Take the No 1 piston top ring, and insert it into the top of the bore. Using the No 1 piston as a ram, push the ring close to the bottom of the bore, at the lowest point of the piston travel. Ensure that it is perfectly square in the bore by pushing firmly against the piston crown.

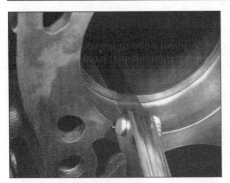

11.4 Use feeler blades to measure the gap between the ends of the piston ring

11.5 Increasing the ring end gap, using a file clamped in a vice

11.6a Fitting the oil ring expander

4 Use a set of feeler blades to measure the gap between the ends of the piston ring; the correct blade will just pass through the gap with a minimal amount of resistance (see illustration). Compare this measurement with that listed in Specifications. Check that you have the correct ring before deciding that a gap is incorrect. Repeat the operation for all twelve rings.

5 If new rings are being fitted, it is unlikely that the end gaps will be too small. If a measurement is found to be undersize, it must be corrected, or there is the risk that the ends of the ring may contact each other during operation, possibly resulting in engine damage. This is achieved by gradually filing

11.6b Fitting the oil ring side rails - do not use a fitting tool at this stage

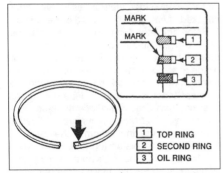

11.6c Correct orientation of the piston rings

Identification markings (arrowed) should face upwards

down the ends of the ring, using a file clamped in a vice (see illustration). Fit the ring over the file, so that both its ends contact opposite faces of the file. Move the ring along the file, removing small amounts of material at a time. Take great care, as the rings are brittle, and form sharp edges if they fracture. Remember to keep the rings and piston assemblies in the correct order.

6 When all the piston ring end gaps have been verified, they can be fitted to the pistons. Work from the lowest ring groove (oil control ring) upwards. Note that the oil control ring comprises two side rails separated by a expander ring. Note also that the two compression rings are different in cross-section, and so must be fitted in the correct groove and the right way up, using a piston ring fitting tool (see illustrations). Both of the compression rings have marks stamped on one side to indicate the top facing surface. Ensure that these marks face upwards when the rings are fitted.

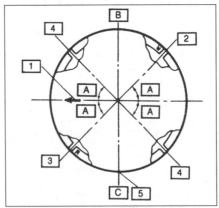

11.7 Distribute the end gaps around the piston, spaced at 45° intervals to the piston centre axis

A 45 degree angle
B Inlet side of engine
C Exhaust side of engine
1 Arrow mark
2 First compression ring end gap
3 Second compression ring end gap
4 Oil ring rail end gaps
5 Oil ring spacer gap

7 Distribute the end gaps around the piston, spaced at 45° intervals to the piston centre axis (see illustration). Position the oil ring expander end gap at 45° to the oil side ring end gap. Note: *If the piston ring manufacturer supplies specific fitting instructions with the rings, follow these exclusively.*

12 Piston and connecting rod assemblies - refitting and big-end bearing clearance check

Big-end bearing running clearance check

Note: *At this point, it is assumed that the crankshaft has been fitted to the engine, as described in Section 10.*

1 As with the main bearings (Section 10), a running clearance must exist between the big-end crankpin and its bearing shells, to allow oil to circulate. There are two methods of checking the size of the running clearance, as described in the following paragraphs.

2 Place the cylinder block on a clean, level work surface, with the crankcase facing upwards. Position the crankshaft such that crankpins No 1 and 4 are at BDC.

3 The first method is the least accurate, and involves bolting the big-end bearing caps to the big-ends, away from the crankshaft, with the bearing shells in place. Note: *Correct orientation of the bearing caps is critical; refer to the notes in Section 5.* The internal diameter formed by the assembled big-end is then measured using internal vernier calipers. The diameter of the respective crankpin is then subtracted from this measurement, and the result is the running clearance.

4 The second method of carrying out this check involves the use of Plastigage, in the same manner as the main bearing running clearance check - this is much more accurate than the previous method. Clean all four crankpins with a clean rag. With crankpins No 1 and 4 at BDC initially, place a strand of Plastigage on each crankpin journal.

5 Fit the upper big-end bearing shells to the connecting rods, ensuring that the locating pegs and slots engage correctly. Temporarily

12.13 Clamp the rings in position using a piston ring compressor

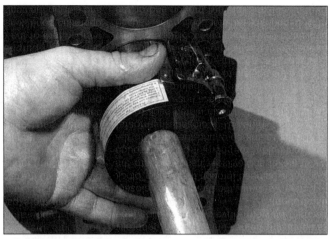

12.14 Insert the piston/connecting rod assembly into the bore - note the use of a hammer handle to tap in the assembly

refit the piston/connecting rod assemblies to the crankshaft; refer to the notes below under *"Final refitting"*. Refit the big-end bearing caps, using the marks made noted on removal to ensure that they are fitted the correct way around.

6 Tighten the bearing cap nuts as described below. Take care not to disturb the Plastigage, nor to rotate the connecting rod during the tightening process.

7 Dismantle the assemblies without rotating the connecting rods. Use the scale printed on the Plastigage envelope to determine the big-end bearing running clearance, and compare it with the figures listed in Specifications.

8 If the clearance is significantly different from that expected, the bearing shells may be the wrong size (or excessively worn, if the original shells are being re-used). Make sure that no dirt or oil was trapped between the bearing shells and the caps or connecting rods when the clearance was measured. Re-check the diameters of the crankpins. Note that if the Plastigage was wider at one end than at the other, the crankpins may be

tapered. When the problem is identified, fit new bearing shells, or have the crankpins reground to a listed undersize, as appropriate.

9 Upon completion, carefully scrape away all traces of the Plastigage material from the crankshaft and bearing shells. Use a soft plastic or wooden scraper, to avoid scoring the bearing surfaces.

Piston and connecting rod assemblies - final refitting

10 Note that the following procedure assumes that the crankshaft main bearing caps are in place (see Section 10).

11 Ensure that the bearing shells are correctly fitted, as described at the beginning of this Section. If new shells are being fitted, ensure that all traces of the protective grease are cleaned off using paraffin. Wipe dry the shells and connecting rods with a lint-free cloth.

12 Lubricate the cylinder bores, the pistons, and piston rings with clean engine oil. Lay out each piston/connecting rod assembly in order on a clean work surface. Fit short sections of

rubber hose or tape over the big-end bolt threads, to protect the cylinder bores during reassembly.

13 Start with piston/connecting rod assembly No 1. Make sure that the piston rings are still spaced as described in Section 11, then clamp them in position with a piston ring compressor **(see illustration)**.

14 Insert the piston/connecting rod assembly into the top of cylinder No 1. Lower the big-end in first, guiding it to protect the big-end bolts and the cylinder bores **(see illustration)**. Ensure that the arrow on the piston crown is pointing towards the oil pump end of the engine. (At this point, check for correct assembly of the connecting rods: the drilled oil hole in the big-end casting should be facing the inlet side of the engine). Using a block of wood or hammer handle against the piston crown, tap the assembly into the cylinder until the piston crown is flush with the top of the cylinder.

15 Ensure that the bearing shell is still correctly installed. Liberally lubricate the crankpin and both bearing shells with clean

12.15 Refit the big-end bearing caps . . .

12.16 . . . and tighten the retaining nuts, half a turn at a time, to the specified torque

engine oil. Taking care not to mark the cylinder bores, tap the piston/connecting rod assembly down the bore and onto the crankpin. Refit the big-end bearing cap, tightening its retaining nuts finger-tight at first **(see illustration)**. Line up the orientation marks made during removal; this also ensures that the locating tabs on the bearing shells engage with each other.

16 Tighten the cap retaining nuts half a turn at a time to the specified torque **(see illustration)**.

17 Refit the remaining three piston/connecting rod assemblies in the same way.

18 Rotate the crankshaft by hand. Check that it turns freely; some stiffness is to be expected if new components have been fitted, but there should be no indication of binding or tight spots.

13 Engine - initial start up after overhaul and reassembly

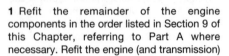

1 Refit the remainder of the engine components in the order listed in Section 9 of this Chapter, referring to Part A where necessary. Refit the engine (and transmission)

to the vehicle as described in Section 2 of this Chapter. Double-check the engine oil and coolant levels, and make a final check that everything has been reconnected. Make sure that there are no tools or rags left in the engine compartment.

2 Remove the spark plugs. Disable the ignition system by disconnecting the ignition coil HT lead from the distributor cap, and earthing it on the cylinder block; refer to Chapter 5B for further information.

3 Turn the engine on the starter until the oil pressure warning light goes out. Refit the spark plugs, and reconnect the spark plug (HT) leads, referring to Chapter 1 for further information. Reconnect the coil HT lead.

4 Start the engine, but be aware that this may take a little longer than usual, due to the fuel system components having been disturbed.

5 While the engine is idling, check for fuel, water and oil leaks. Don't be alarmed if there are some odd smells, and the occasional plume of smoke, as parts heat up and burn off oil deposits.

6 Assuming all is well, keep the engine idling until hot water is felt circulating through the top hose, then switch off the engine.

7 Check the ignition timing and idle speed, as described in Chapter 1, then switch the engine off.

8 After a few minutes, recheck the oil and coolant levels as described in Chapter 1, and top-up as necessary.

9 If the cylinder head bolts were tightened to specification, there is no need to re-tighten them once the engine has been run following reassembly.

10 If new pistons, rings or crankshaft bearings have been fitted, the engine must be treated as new, and run-in for the first 600 miles (1000 km). *Do not* operate the engine at full-throttle, or allow it to labour at low engine speeds in any gear. To keep engine speeds down, it is recommended that whilst running-in, you do not exceed the road speeds listed for the gears shown in the table below. It is also recommended that the oil and filter are changed at the end of this period.

Gear selected	Road speed - mph (km/h)
1st	10 (15)
2nd	16 (25)
3rd	25 (40)
4th	43 (70)
(5th)	50 (80)

Chapter 3
Cooling, heating and ventilation systems

Contents

Degrees of difficulty

Easy, suitable for novice with little experience	Fairly easy, suitable for beginner with some experience	Fairly difficult, suitable for competent DIY mechanic 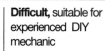	Difficult, suitable for experienced DIY mechanic	Very difficult, suitable for expert DIY or professional

Specifications

General
Radiator cap opening pressure .... 0.9 bars (13 psi)

Thermostat
Type .... Wax pellet. Two types available, with different operating temperatures

	Type "A"	Type "B"
Opening temperature	82°C	88°C
Fully-open temperature	95°C	100°C
Valve lift (fully open)	>8 mm	>8 mm

Coolant temperature sensor
Resistance:
50°C (122°F) .... 134 ohms
80°C (176°F) .... 48 to 57 ohms
100°C (212°F) .... 26 to 29 ohms

Capacities/antifreeze mixture
See Chapter 1.

Torque wrench settings	Nm	lbf ft
Water pump retaining nuts and bolts	10	7
Cooling fan bolts	10	7

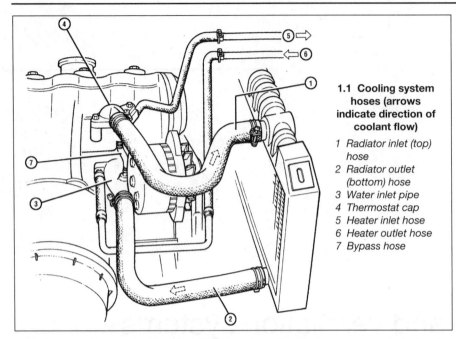

1.1 Cooling system hoses (arrows indicate direction of coolant flow)

1 Radiator inlet (top) hose
2 Radiator outlet (bottom) hose
3 Water inlet pipe
4 Thermostat cap
5 Heater inlet hose
6 Heater outlet hose
7 Bypass hose

1 General information and precautions

The cooling system consists of the water pump, radiator and cap, expansion tank, cooling fan, thermostat, temperature sensor, and associated hoses. The major coolant hoses run to and from the engine block, radiator and heater unit, and are generally secured by worm-drive type hose clips (see illustration).

During warm-up, the thermostat is closed. Coolant is pumped through the cylinder block water jacket and cylinder head, and into the inlet manifold. From here, it passes through the heater matrix core, and then back to the water inlet pipe. The closed thermostat causes coolant to be circulated back to the water pump via the bypass hose. During this period, the radiator is being bypassed, allowing the coolant to heat up rapidly.

When the coolant reaches a specific temperature, the thermostat opens, allowing coolant to flow through the radiator. The flow of air through the radiator cooling fins, caused by the vehicle's forward motion and/or the cooling fan, prevents the coolant temperature from rising any further, and a near-constant temperature is maintained.

The water pump is bolted to the front of the engine, and is driven by the auxiliary drivebelt via pulleys. The unit has sealed bearings, and is not serviceable - a defective unit must therefore be renewed as a complete assembly.

The radiator is constructed from steel, and is composed of a series of core tubes and cooling fins. It relies on a constant flow of air through its cooling fins in order to work.

The radiator cap contains two integral

valves. The first is a pressure-relief valve that vents the cooling system to atmosphere when the pressure exceeds the specified value. The second is a vacuum-relief valve, which allows air into the system when the engine is cooling down. This prevents the radiator core tubes from collapsing due to the vacuum that forms as the coolant contracts.

As the coolant heats up during normal operation, it expands, and the excess coolant flows into the expansion tank. When the coolant temperature falls, it contracts and flows from the expansion tank, back into the radiator. In this manner, the correct level is maintained in the cooling system at all times.

The cooling fan is bolted the water pump drive pulley, and is driven by the auxiliary drivebelt. The fan is positioned between the radiator and the engine, and provides supplementary air flow through the radiator, particularly when the vehicle is stationary in traffic.

The thermostat is a valve, controlled by the expansion and contraction of an integral wax pellet. Its purpose is to control the temperature of the cooling system under all operating conditions. It does this by opening and closing the coolant supply to the radiator, according to coolant temperature.

The coolant temperature sensor contains a thermistor (temperature-dependant resistor). It supplies an electrical signal, which varies with temperature, to the temperature gauge.

The heating system consists of a heater matrix core, blower fan and control levers.

Heated coolant passes through the matrix core, and warms the air flowing through its cooling fins. This warmed air can be directed to the windscreen or different areas of the cabin, either by the ram effect of air entering the vehicle as it moves forward, or by the three-speed blower fan.

Precautions

⚠ **Warning: Do not attempt to remove the radiator filler cap, or to disturb any part of the cooling system, while the engine is hot,** as there is a high risk of scalding. If the radiator filler cap must be removed before the engine and radiator have fully cooled (even though this is not recommended), the pressure in the cooling system must first be relieved. Cover the cap with a thick layer of cloth, to avoid scalding, and slowly unscrew the filler cap until steam is heard to escape. When this has stopped, indicating that the pressure has reduced, slowly unscrew the filler cap until it can be removed; if more steam starts to escape under pressure, wait until it has stopped before unscrewing the cap completely. At all times, keep well away from the filler cap opening, and protect your hands and face.

⚠ **Warning: Do not allow antifreeze to come into contact with your skin, or with the painted surfaces of the vehicle. Rinse off spills** immediately, with plenty of water. Never leave antifreeze lying around in an open container, or in a puddle in the driveway or on the garage floor. Children and pets are attracted by its sweet smell, but antifreeze can be fatal if ingested.

2 Water pump - removal and refitting

1 The water pump is of the centrifugal type, and employs a totally sealed shaft bearing. It cannot be dismantled for overhaul, and must be renewed if it is found to be faulty.

Removal

2 Disconnect the battery negative cable. Refer to Chapter 1 and drain the cooling system, retaining the coolant for re-use if it is in good condition.
3 Set the engine to TDC on cylinder No 4; refer to Chapter 2A. Then remove the cooling fan, auxiliary drivebelt, pulleys, timing belt, timing belt outer (and inner) covers, tensioner

2.4 Unbolting the alternator upper mounting bracket from the engine

2.5a Remove the retaining bolts . . .

2.5b . . . and lift off the water pump

2.7 Fit a new gasket to the cylinder block

and sprockets as described in Section 3 of this Chapter and Chapter 2A.

4 Remove the alternator as described in Chapter 5A. Unbolt the upper mounting bracket from the alternator and cylinder block **(see illustration)**.

5 Remove the water pump retaining bolts and lift off the case, recovering the gasket **(see illustrations)**.

6 Clean the mating surfaces of the pump and the cylinder block, removing any traces of oxide and old gasket. Take care not to score or gouge the surfaces, as this could cause leakage.

Refitting

7 Fit a new gasket to the cylinder block, and locate the water pump in its mounting position **(see illustration)**. Fit the retaining bolts and nuts, and tighten them to the correct torque,

after checking that the gasket is properly seated.

8 Refit all the remaining components by reversing the removal procedure. Reconnect the battery negative cable and refill the cooling system with reference to Chapter 1. Start the engine, and allow it to reach normal operating temperature. Check all newly-gasketed surfaces for leaks.

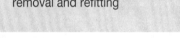

3 Cooling fan - removal and refitting

Removal

1 Disconnect the battery negative cable, and position it away from the terminal.

2 Slacken the alternator mounting and

adjustment bolts, and pivot the alternator towards the engine. Remove the auxiliary drivebelt as described in Chapter 1.

3 Slacken the worm-drive clip, and prise the brake servo vacuum hose off the rigid pipe mounted on the radiator bracket **(see illustration)**.

4 Remove the radiator cowling, to give greater access to the cooling fan bolts, as follows. Remove the bolts securing the cowling, then unclip it from the lower and upper edges of the radiator, and lift it towards the engine. Remove the four retaining bolts and washers, then lift off the cooling fan - recover the alloy spacer if it is loose **(see illustrations)**.

5 Inspect the fan for signs of damage or wear. Any material missing from the fan blades will unbalance it, possibly causing

3.3 Prise the brake servo vacuum hose off the rigid pipe mounted on the radiator bracket

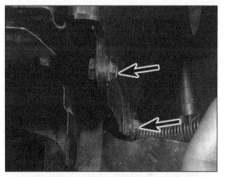

3.4a Remove the bolts securing the cowling (left-hand side bolts arrowed) . . .

3.4b . . . then unclip it from the upper and lower edge of the radiator . . .

3.4c . . . and lift it towards the engine

3.4d Lift off the cooling fan . . .

3.4e . . . recover the alloy spacer if it is loose

vibration and premature bearing failure, so renew it if necessary. If material is missing from the blades, check whether contact with the radiator has occurred and resulted in damage.

Refitting

6 To refit the fan, simply reverse the removal steps, referring to Chapter 1 for details of refitting and tensioning the auxiliary drivebelt.

4 Cooling system hoses - renewal

1 Regular inspection of the cooling system hoses will prevent unexpected and untimely failures. Carry out the check when the engine has cooled - look for chafing, cuts, melting or burns caused by contact with hot components. Hardening and perishing caused by ageing can cause a failure at any time. Also, pay attention to the condition and security of the hose clips; corrosion or deformation caused by over-tightening will cause them to leak.

2 The major coolant hoses run to and from the engine block, radiator and heater unit, and are generally secured by worm-drive type hose clips.

3 If the hoses are to be renewed, have the replacement components to hand before starting work. It is good practice to renew the hose clips at the same time.

4 Ensure that the vehicle has cooled sufficiently, then drain the cooling system as described in Chapter 1. Retain the coolant If it is fit for re-use.

5 Release the clip from the ends of the hose to be renewed. As the clip becomes slack, apply less pressure with the screwdriver, as the clip may rotate around the hose suddenly. Slide the loosened clip back along the hose, away from the joint.

6 Grasp the hose end, and carefully pull it off using a twisting action; position rags underneath the hose, to absorb any coolant that may escape. Some of the hoses are connected to ports that are made of alloy, or are otherwise easily damaged - take care not to damage the port as the hose is pulled off.

7 If a hose has become stuck on its port, it is less damaging to cut it off carefully with a sharp knife, rather than try to lever it off, risking damage to the port beneath.

8 Compare the shape and length of the new hose with the old one, before attempting to fit it. Lubricate each end of the hose with a little washing-up liquid to ease fitting - do not use oil or grease, as this may attack the rubber and contaminate the coolant.

9 Slide the new hose clips over the hose and fit it into place, twisting it carefully onto the port. Make sure that there is adequate overlap between the hose and the port, then slide the hose clip into position and tighten it. Do not be tempted to over-tighten the clip as it may

5.2 Gear cable guide bracket on the inlet manifold

crush the hose, or become deformed itself, and cause leakage.

10 Refill the cooling system as described in Chapter 1. Run the engine up to operating temperature, and examine the new joints for leaks.

11 Check the security of the new joints after a few hundred miles, and top-up the coolant level if necessary.

5 Thermostat - removal, checking and refitting

Removal

1 Disconnect the battery negative cable. Removal of the passenger seat is recommended, to improve access to the engine bay area - refer to Chapter 11 for details.

2 Remove the centre console, seat belt anchor stalks and gear lever crossmember, referring to Chapter 11 where necessary. Release the gear selector and change cables from the guide bracket on the inlet manifold **(see illustration)**. This will allow the seat belt crossmember to be moved to one side, giving access to the thermostat housing on top of the inlet manifold.

3 Ensure that the vehicle has cooled sufficiently, then drain the cooling system as described in Chapter 1. Retain the coolant If it is in good enough condition to be re-used.

4 Loosen the worm-drive clip, and release the radiator top hose from the thermostat housing.

5 Slacken and remove the retaining bolts, then lift off the thermostat housing cap. If it is stuck, tap it lightly with a soft-faced mallet to release it. Lift out the thermostat.

6 Carefully scrape the remains of the original gasket from the mating surfaces of the housing and cap. Avoid scoring or pitting the surfaces, as this will cause leakage.

 HAYNES HINT *Stuff a small (clean) rag into the thermostat housing to keep debris out whilst you carry out this task.*

5.8 The thermostat opening temperature is stamped on its rim

Testing

7 Clean the thermostat in fresh water, using a old paintbrush to loosen any deposits that may have formed on its surface. Clear the air bleed hole of blockages, and examine the valve seat surfaces; deposits on them will prevent the valve from sealing properly, and will allow it to leak.

8 The thermostat opening temperature is stamped on its rim **(see illustration)**. Note that there are two types of thermostat available for the Rascal/SuperCarry, with different operating temperatures - refer to the Specifications. Lower the unit into a saucepan of water, and place it over a source of heat. As the water approaches boiling point, check that the valve plunger has retracted and opened the valve; the spring will compress as this happens. If the action occurs at a much lower temperature - or not at all - renew the thermostat.

9 Check that the valve closes again as the water cools. If it sticks open at any point, renew the thermostat.

10 If a thermometer is available, the exact opening and closing temperatures can be verified, and compared with the values given in the Specifications.

Refitting

11 Lower the thermostat into position, with the spring/wax capsule end facing down. Fit a new gasket to the surface of the thermostat housing **(see illustrations)**.

12 Refit the thermostat housing cap and insert the retaining bolts, tightening them securely **(see illustration)**.

5.11a Lower the thermostat into position, with the spring/wax capsule facing down . . .

5.11b ... and fit a new gasket to the surface of the thermostat housing

 Caution: Over-tightening may crack the cap.

13 Reconnect the radiator top hose to the thermostat housing. Route the gear selector and shift cables back through the guide bracket on the inlet manifold, and tighten the retaining bolts.
14 Refit the seat belt crossmember and passenger seat by reversing the removal steps; refer to Chapter 11 for details.
15 Reconnect the battery negative cable, and refill the cooling system as described in Chapter 1.
16 Start the engine, and allow it to reach its normal operating temperature. Feel the temperature of the hose between the radiator and the thermostat housing. As the coolant

5.12 Refit the thermostat housing cap

temperature rises and the thermostat valve opens, hot coolant will flow through the hose, and the temperature rise can be felt by hand.
17 Finally, check around the newly-gasketed thermostat housing for leaks.

6 Radiator - removal, inspection and refitting

Note: *If the radiator is being removed because it is leaking, note that minor leaks can often be repaired using a proprietary radiator sealant, without removing the radiator.*

Removal

1 Disconnect the battery negative cable, and position it away from the terminal.

2 Drain the cooling system, referring to Chapter 1. Retain the coolant if is fit for re-use.
3 Removal of the front seats, centre console, gear lever crossmember and seat belt stalks will be necessary to gain access to the engine bay area; refer to Chapter 11 for details.
4 Remove the gear change and selector cables from the bracket on the inlet manifold - refer to Section 5, paragraph 2.
5 Slacken the hose clips, and pull the top and bottom hoses off the radiator ports **(see illustrations)**.
6 Remove the coolant expansion tank hose from the radiator filler neck **(see illustration)**.
7 Remove the cooling fan, together with its cowling, as described in Section 3.
8 Unbolt the brake servo rigid pipe from the top of the radiator mounting bracket. Slacken the clips, and prise the rubber vacuum hoses away from either end of the pipe. Lift the pipe clear of the engine bay **(see illustration)**.
9 Remove the four bolts securing the radiator to its mounting bracket **(see illustration)**. Steady the radiator as the last bolt is removed, to prevent it from dropping onto the steering linkage below.
10 Carefully lift the radiator out of the engine bay, taking care not to damage the delicate cooling fins **(see illustration)**.

Inspection

11 If the radiator has been removed to investigate a suspected blockage, reverse-

6.5a Slacken the hose clips and pull the top ...

6.5b ... and bottom hoses off the radiator ports

6.6 Remove the coolant expansion tank hose from the radiator filler neck

6.8 Unbolt the brake servo rigid pipe from the top of the radiator mounting bracket

6.9 Remove the four bolts securing the radiator to its mounting bracket (left-hand bolts arrowed)

6.10 Carefully lift the radiator out of the engine bay

flush it as described in Chapter 1. Use compressed air to clean dirt and debris from the radiator fins. Alternatively, use a soft brush. Be careful, as the radiator fins are not only sharp, but are also easily damaged themselves.

 Warning: Protect your eyes from flying debris by wearing goggles whilst carrying out this task with compressed air.

12 If necessary, a radiator specialist can perform a "flow test" on the radiator, to establish whether an internal blockage exists.
13 A leaking radiator must be referred to a specialist for permanent repair, but refer to the note at the start of this Section if the leak is not too serious. Do not attempt to weld, braze or solder a leaking radiator, as damage to the internal waterways may result.
14 If the radiator is to be renewed or sent for repair, first remove all the attached coolant hoses.
15 Inspect the cooling fins on both sides of the radiator. If they are excessively corroded, or if large areas are bent over and cannot be straightened, air flow will be restricted, and the cooling efficiency of the radiator will be impaired. If this is the case, a new radiator should be fitted.

Refitting

16 Refit the radiator by reversing the removal sequence. Pay particular attention to coolant and vacuum hose refitting; check that all hoses are firmly pushed into place, and that

7.3 Unbolt the sensor from the inlet manifold - use the correct size of spanner (12 mm) as the brass body is easily damaged

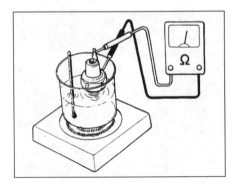

7.6 Testing the resistance of the coolant sensor

the hose clips are securely tightened. Refer to Section 4 for further guidance.
17 Refill the cooling system as detailed in Chapter 1, and reconnect the battery negative cable.
18 Start the engine, and allow it to reach its normal operating temperature. Check all disturbed hose joints for leakage. Road test the vehicle, and check that the coolant temperature is maintained at a satisfactory level.

7 Coolant temperature sensor - removal and refitting

 Warning: Before attempting to remove the coolant sensor, allow the vehicle to cool. Release any pressure in the cooling system by gradually slackening the radiator filler cap, as described in Section 1.

Removal

1 The coolant temperature sensor is located on the inlet manifold, adjacent to the thermostat housing.
2 Pull the cable connector off the spade terminal, on the top of the sensor. Grasp the connector body rather than the cable, to avoid damaging the internal joint.
3 Carefully unbolt the sensor from the manifold - use the correct size of spanner (12 mm) as the brass body is easily damaged **(see illustration)**. Have a rag or small container ready to catch any coolant that may leak out.
4 Clean any traces of thread sealant from the sensor and its mounting hole. Remove any oxide deposits from the sensor probe end, as these may impair its operation.
5 The sensor works by varying its electrical resistance with temperature. Although the exact values are published by the manufacturer, it is possible to check the sensor for obvious faults, without carrying out a time-consuming calibration exercise. Set a multi-meter to its resistance measurement function. Connect one probe to the body of the sensor, and the other to the spade terminal. A short-circuit (zero resistance) or

open-circuit (infinite resistance) means that the sensor is faulty, and must be renewed. Note that when the sensor is very hot, its electrical resistance will be low; do not mistake this for a short-circuit.
6 If a thermometer is available, the calibration curve of the sensor can be checked as follows. Lower the end of the sensor probe into a saucepan of water, and place it over a source of heat. Connect a multi-meter to the sensor as described above, and note the resistance readings obtained at 50, 80 and 100°C **(see illustration)**. Compare these figures with those in the Specifications.

Refitting

7 The sensor can be refitted by simply reversing the removal process. Apply thread sealing tape to the sensor when refitting it. Ensure that the cable connector is pushed firmly onto the sensor's spade terminal. Top-up the coolant level as necessary.

8 Expansion tank - removal and refitting

Removal

1 Drain the cooling system as described in Chapter 1.
2 Pull the coolant hose off the port on the expansion tank filler cap **(see illustration)**.
3 Lift the expansion tank off its bracket and out of the engine bay. Unclip the filler cap, and drain any residual coolant into a suitable container for re-use, if its condition is acceptable.
4 Using fresh water and a stiff brush, clean out the inside of the tank, particularly the bottom, where oxide deposits may have collected.

Refitting

5 Refit the tank by reversing the removal steps. Note that the internal rubber hose should be pushed onto the underside of the filler cap, such that it clears the bottom of the tank by 10 mm. This allows coolant to be siphoned to and from the tank during normal operation.

9 Heating/ventilation components - removal and refitting

Blower fan motor
Removal

1 Disconnect the battery negative cable, and position it away from the terminal.
2 Remove the facia assembly, releasing the heater control levers from their mounting positions as the facia is withdrawn; refer to Chapter 11.
3 Prise the defroster plastic duct out from the bottom right-hand side of the heater unit.

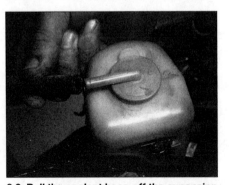

8.2 Pull the coolant hose off the expansion tank filler cap

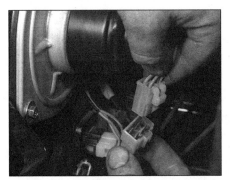

9.4 Disconnect the fan power supply at the connector

9.5a Slacken and withdraw the three bolts that hold the fan assembly in place (arrowed) . . .

9.5b . . . draw the fan assembly out of the heater casing . . .

4 Disconnect the fan power supply at the connector **(see illustration)**.
5 Slacken and withdraw the three bolts that hold the fan assembly in place. Draw the assembly out of the heater casing, and recover the rubber seal **(see illustrations)**.
6 Using a soft brush, clear the fan blades of dust and debris.
7 Separate the fan blade cylinder from the motor by removing the nut from the end of the drive spindle. Grasp the fan motor case, and carefully rock the drive spindle from side to side. Excessive freeplay indicates that the motor bearings are worn; renew the motor if this is the case.

Refitting

8 Reassemble and refit the blower fan by reversing the removal procedure.

Heater core matrix

Removal

9 Drain the cooling system; refer to Chapter 1
10 Remove the facia assembly, releasing the heater control levers from their mounting positions as the facia is withdrawn; refer to Chapter 11 for details. Prise the defroster plastic duct out from the bottom right-hand side of the heater unit. Extract the two facia vent ducts from the top of the heater unit.
11 Apply the handbrake, then raise the front of the vehicle and rest it securely on axle stands; refer to *"Jacking, towing and wheel changing"* at the beginning of this manual for guidance.
12 Working under the front of the vehicle,

slacken the worm-drive clips and prise the heater hoses off the ports protruding from the underside of the floor, just behind the front grille. Remove the nuts and washers from the studs adjacent to the ports **(see illustrations)**.
13 Unclip the three control cables from the heater unit actuator levers. Release the cable outer sheaths from the crimp retaining clips.
14 Extract the retaining screw, and remove the air inlet cowling from the left-hand side of the heater unit **(see illustration)**.
15 Unbolt the top of the heater unit from the bulkhead crossmember **(see illustration)**.
16 Carefully lift the heater unit away from the bulkhead, out of the cabin and onto a work surface **(see illustration)**.

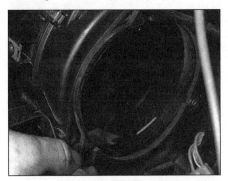

9.5c . . . and recover the rubber seal

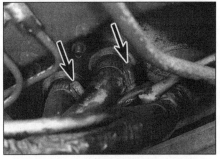

9.12a Slacken the worm-drive clips, and prise the heater hoses off the ports protruding from the underside of the floor, just behind the front grille . . .

9.12b . . . then remove the nuts and washers from the studs adjacent to the ports

9.14 Extract the retaining screw and remove the air inlet cowling from the left-hand side of the heater unit

9.15 Unbolt the top of the heater unit from the bulkhead crossmember

9.16 Carefully lift the heater unit away from the bulkhead

9.17 Remove the heater hose clamp bracket

9.18a Release the clips . . .

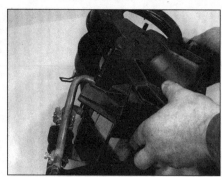

9.18b . . . and separate the two halves of the plastic case

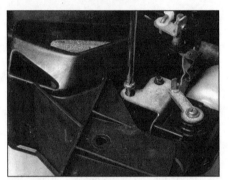

9.19a Remove the retaining screw and lift off the water valve assembly

17 Remove the heater hose clamp bracket **(see illustration)**.
18 Separate the two halves of the plastic case by releasing all the clips **(see illustrations)**.
19 Remove the retaining screw, and lift off the water valve assembly. This will allow the heater core matrix to be withdrawn from the plastic case **(see illustrations)**.
20 The water valve assembly is joined to the heater core matrix by a short section of hose, shielded by a plastic cap. Remove this cap, then slacken the hose clip and pull off the hose **(see illustrations)**.
21 Use proprietary radiator flushing solution to clean out the inside of the matrix core.

Check carefully for leakage, particularly if signs of corrosion are evident. Renew the unit if leaks are found, or if blockages cannot be cleared.

Refitting

22 Reassemble and refit the heater unit by reversing the removal procedure, noting the following:
a) *Ensure that all hoses and clips are correctly refitted and tightened*
b) *Check that the heater control levers/cables operate the actuator levers before re-inserting the facia fixing screws.*
c) *Replenish the engine coolant with reference to Chapter 1*

9.19b Withdrawing the heater matrix core from the plastic case

9.20a Remove the cap . . .

9.20b . . . then slacken the hose clip and pull off the hose

Chapter 4 Fuel and exhaust systems

Contents

Degrees of difficulty

Easy, suitable for novice with little experience	Fairly easy, suitable for beginner with some experience	Fairly difficult, suitable for competent DIY mechanic	Difficult, suitable for experienced DIY mechanic	Very difficult, suitable for expert DIY or professional

Specifications

Fuel pump
Type .... Electric
Fuel delivery rate .... >500 cc/min

Fuel filter
Type .... Replaceable cartridge, non-serviceable

Carburettor
Type .... Mikuni side draught, single venturi
Choke type .... Manual, cable-operated
Idle speed .... 900 ± 50 rev/min
Idle exhaust CO content .... 1.5 ± 0.5%
Float height .... 5.3 to 6.3 mm (see text for details)

Recommended fuel
Octane rating .... 92 to 95 RON (premium unleaded)

Torque wrench settings

	Nm	lbf ft
Front pipe-to-rear section bolts	45	33
Exhaust manifold-to-front pipe nuts	40	30

1 General information and precautions

The fuel system on all models consists of a tank, an electric pump, a cartridge type fuel filter, metal and rubber supply and return hoses, an air cleaner and a carburettor.

On Van models, the fuel tank is mounted on the chassis, underneath the load space floor, with the filler neck positioned behind the front right-hand side wheel arch. On Pickup models, the fuel tank is mounted on the chassis at the rear of the vehicle, with the filler neck behind the rear right-hand side wheel arch.

Fuel is drawn from the tank, through the filter canister, by the fuel pump. It is fed via a supply hose to the carburettor float chamber, where a float and needle valve mechanism regulates the level of fuel held in the chamber. Surplus fuel is directed back to the fuel tank by a fuel return hose.

Cold start mixture enrichment and fast idle is controlled by means of a manually-operated choke. In addition, UK-specification vehicles have a flap valve mounted in the inlet air stream under the vehicle, which can direct hot air from around the exhaust manifold into the air inlet. It can be adjusted, during warmer conditions, to allow ambient air to be drawn in instead.

The air cleaner is mounted directly on the carburettor air inlet, and contains a replaceable paper filter element.

The carburettor is a Mikuni single-venturi, side draught unit, with an integral fuel cut-off solenoid.

Precautions

 Warning: Petrol is extremely flammable - great care must be taken when working on any part of the fuel system:

☐ Do not smoke, or allow any naked flames or uncovered light bulbs, near the work area. Note that gas-powered domestic appliances with pilot lights, such as heaters, boilers and tumble-dryers, also present a fire hazard.

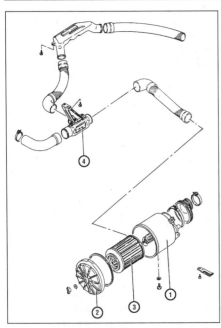

2.1 Air inlet layout (Van model shown)

1 Air cleaner case
2 Air cleaner case cap
3 Air cleaner filter element
4 Warm-air flap valve

Bear this in mind if you are working in an area where such appliances are present.

☐ Always keep a suitable fire extinguisher close to the work area; the Aqueous Film Forming Foam (AFFF) variety is a good choice for dealing with petrol fires. Familiarise yourself with its operation before starting work.

☐ Wear eye protection when working on fuel systems, and wash off any fuel spilt on bare skin immediately with soap and water.

☐ Note that fuel vapour is just as dangerous as liquid fuel; a vessel that has been emptied of liquid fuel and only contains vapour is still potentially explosive.

2 Air cleaner and air inlet assembly - removal, inspection and refitting

Air inlet hoses

1 A section of flexible aluminium hosing routes hot air from the exhaust manifold heat shroud on the left-hand side of the vehicle, over the top of the transmission to the warm-air flap valve, mounted on the right-hand side chassis rail. From here, another section of hosing routes air to the cleaner assembly. Ambient air is drawn through the right-hand chassis rail to the warm-air valve, via a third section of flexible aluminium hosing **(see illustration)**. Note that the layout of the air inlet hoses differs slightly between the Pickup and Van models.

2 Examine closely all sections of hosing, particularly those that follow a tight curve or are subject to a large amount of movement, for example between the engine and body. If necessary, pull the hose off and carefully flex it to expose any cracks. Take care, as the edges of the hoses can be very sharp if they are split. Replace any sections that are found to be damaged.

Warm-air flap valve

3 The valve is located on the right-hand chassis rail, under the load area. On Pickup models, it is mounted adjacent to the gear selector levers. On Van models, it is mounted in front of the fuel tank.

4 Remove the three hoses from the ports on the valve. Slacken and withdraw the screws that hold the valve bracket to the chassis, and remove the valve **(see illustrations)**.

5 Operate the flap lever, and check for resistance or stiffness. Hold it up to a light source, and look for obstructions inside the valve body. Check that the flap can be seen to alternately open and close the inlet ports as the lever is operated.

6 Clear out any debris with a stiff brush, or compressed air if it is available. Apply penetrating oil to the operating lever bush to ease any stiffness.

 Warning: Always protect your eyes from flying debris when using compressed air in this manner.

7 Refit the valve and hoses by reversing the removal steps.

Air cleaner assembly

8 Remove the air filter element, referring to Chapter 1

9 Extract the air inlet hose from the side of the air cleaner barrel. Slacken the worm-drive clip that secures the carburettor air inlet hose to the base of the air cleaner barrel. Prise off the hose using a blunt implement **(see illustrations)**.

10 Release the fuel hose and alternator cables from the clip on the air cleaner barrel. Loosen the clip, and pull off the camshaft cover vent hose.

11 Remove the two bolts that secure the air cleaner barrel to its mounting bracket, and lift the assembly out **(see illustration)**.

12 Clean out any debris that has collected

2.4a Remove the hoses from the ports on the warm-air flap valve . . .

2.4b . . . then slacken and withdraw the valve bracket screws

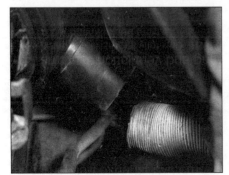

2.9a Extract the air inlet hose from the side of the air cleaner barrel

2.9b Slacken the worm-drive clip (arrowed) that secures the carburettor air inlet hose to the base of the air cleaner barrel

2.11 Remove the two bolts (arrowed) that secure the air cleaner barrel to its mounting bracket

inside the air cleaner, and wipe it clean with soapy water. Inspect the barrel for cracks or splits, and check the condition of the rubber lid seal - renew any items that are found to be faulty.

13 With the air cleaner barrel removed, check the condition of the carburettor air inlet hose. Renew it if it appears perished or split.

14 Refit the components by reversing the removal process - clean or renew the filter element as appropriate.

3 Fuel system - depressurising

1 The fuel delivery and return system is not pumped at high pressure, and hence does not need to be depressurised in the way that a fuel-injected vehicle does before dismantling. However, fuel vapour contained in the fuel tank will, under certain conditions, expand and pressurise the fuel system. If this pressure is not released, it will cause fuel to spurt out when any part of the fuel system is dismantled; the danger in this happening is self-evident.

2 Depressurise the fuel tank by simply removing the fuel filler cap. Replace it after the fuel vapour is heard to escape.

 Warning: Read the precautions in Section 1 before working on the fuel system.

4 Fuel pump - testing, removal and refitting

Testing

 Warning: Read the precautions in Section 1 before working on the fuel system.

1 If you have concerns over the performance of the fuel pump, it is possible to check it on the vehicle. Ensure that the vehicle is allowed to cool before work commences.

2 Relieve any pressure in the fuel system by venting the fuel tank, as described in Section 3.

4.3 Prise the hose off the fuel pump outlet port

3 Prise the hose off the fuel pump outlet port (ie the one that leads to the carburettor, not the one from the fuel filter) **(see illustration)**. Hold a wad of rag under the hose end as you do this, to absorb any spilt fuel.

4 Place a small container under the exposed port, and turn the ignition switch to its second position. Check that regular pulses of fuel emerge from the pump port. At its normal flow rate, the pump should fill a teacup-sized container in about 20 seconds.

5 The fuel pump is a sealed unit, and must be renewed complete if found to be faulty.

6 Push the fuel hose onto the correct pump port, and slide the retaining clip into place. Empty the collected fuel back into the filler neck.

Removal and refitting

 Warning: Read the precautions in Section 1 before working on the fuel system.

7 Disconnect the battery negative cable, and position it away from the terminal.

8 Relieve any pressure that may exist in the fuel system, as described in Section 3.

9 Peel back the protective boot, and disconnect the fuel pump power supply at the two-way connector block.

10 Release the cable from the clamp on the chassis.

11 Squeeze the levers of the quick-release hose clips to slacken them, and pull off the fuel inlet and outlet hoses, labelling them for later reference (the inlet hose is the one connected to the fuel filter). If the hose clips are of the crimp variety, cut them off and discard them; they must be replaced by standard worm-drive clips on reassembly. Hold a wad of dry rag around the ports as you remove the hose, to catch any fuel that may spill out of the hoses and pump. Note the arrows marked on the pump housing indicating the inlet and outlet ports. If these are not visible, make your own using a marker pen - do not scribe or punch the housing.

12 Slacken the bolts that secure the pump mounting bracket to the chassis and withdraw them **(see illustration)**. Recover the anti-vibration rubber bushes, and renew them if they appear worn or perished. Lower the pump away from the chassis, holding it level

4.12 Slacken the bolts that secure the fuel pump mounting bracket to the chassis

to prevent fuel leakage. Rest it on a work surface, and allow the excess fuel to drain out of the pump and soak into a wad of rag.

13 Refitting is the reverse of removal - ensure that the inlet and outlet fuel hoses are connected to the correct ports on the pump. Note that the pump does not need to be primed before it is refitted.

5 Fuel tank - removal and refitting

Removal

 Warning: Read the precautions in Section 1 before working on the fuel system.

1 Relieve any pressure that may exist in the fuel system, as described in Section 3.

2 This operation is more easily completed if the fuel tank is emptied prior to removal.

3 If a drain plug is fitted to the tank, unscrew it and allow the fuel to drain out into an approved storage container. Refit and tighten the plug.

4 If a drain plug is not fitted, carry out the removal of the tank at a time when the level of fuel in it is as low as possible.

5 Disconnect the battery negative cable, and position it away from the terminal.

6 Chock the front wheels, then jack up the rear of the vehicle and rest it securely on axle stands or wheel ramps; refer to *"Jacking, towing and wheel changing"* at the beginning of this manual.

7 Loosen the hose clips, and disconnect the fuel supply and return hoses from the fuel tank. Plug the hoses, to prevent leakage and contamination of the fuel system, and label them to aid the refitting process. If the hose clips are of the crimp type, renew them, using worm-drive clips in their place.

8 Disconnect the tank breather hoses from the connections at the chassis rail and the fuel filler neck (where applicable).

9 Locate the worm-drive clip that secures the fuel filler hose to the tank. Use a screwdriver to slacken the clip, and prise the hose off the tank.

10 Raise a jack under the centre of the tank to support its weight; place a block of wood in the head of the jack to protect the surface of the tank. Slacken and remove the four bolts securing the tank to the chassis mounting pillars - recover the rubber mounting bushes. Carefully lower the tank, until there is enough clearance to gain access to the fuel level sensor. Unplug the sensor cable connector, and lower the fuel tank out of position, disconnecting any additional breather hoses that become visible as the tank clears the vehicle.

11 Place the tank on a work surface. Referring to Section 6, remove the fuel level sensor.

12 Pour about a gallon of hot water into the

tank and agitate it, to dislodge any sediment that may have settled. Continue flushing until the water comes out clean. If particles of rust are visible in the water when it is poured out, the tank is corroded internally. It may be possible to have the tank examined internally using an endoscope; approach an engineering workshop or your local dealer.

 HAYNES HiNT *The sound made by the tank, when struck with a screwdriver or spanner, can give an early warning of failure. If the tank emits a dull tone and buzzes or vibrates when struck, this may mean that welded joints have split or that rust has loosened the inner surface. Renew the tank, or have it repaired, if you have doubts about its condition.*

 Warning: Do not attempt to repair the tank yourself by welding. Even after the tank has been emptied and washed out, fuel vapour - and hence the risk of explosion - will still be present. Take the tank to a welding professional for repair.

Refitting

13 Refit the fuel tank by reversing the removal procedure. Refer to Section 6 for details of refitting the fuel level sensor. Ensure that all fuel and breather hoses are reconnected correctly.

14 Pour any recovered fuel back into the tank, and check all disturbed hoses and repairs for leaks.

15 Reconnect the battery negative cable and start the vehicle, bearing in mind that the cranking period will be longer than usual, due to the fuel system being disturbed.

6 Fuel level sensor -
removal, testing and refitting

Removal

 Warning: Read the precautions in Section 1 before working on the fuel system.

1 Disconnect the battery negative cable, and position it away from the terminal.

2 Remove the fuel tank as described in Section 5.

3 Unplug the level sensor cable at the connector **(see illustration)**.

4 Remove the five retaining screws, and carefully prise the level sensor away from the tank **(see illustration)**.

5 Withdraw the unit slowly, guiding the float arm through the mounting hole. Recover the gasket.

Testing

6 Place the sensor on a clean work surface. Connect a test meter, set to the resistance

6.3 Unplug the level sensor cable at the connector

measurement function, across the sensor's terminals; the positive (+) probe should be connected to the uppermost terminal and the common (-) probe to the metal case of the sensor.

7 Hold the sensor above the work surface, allowing the float arm to dangle at the lowest limit of its travel - this simulates an empty tank. The meter reading should be about 110 ohms.

8 Raise the float arm to its highest limit of travel - this simulates a full tank. The meter reading should be about 3 ohms.

9 Hold the float arm at a point about halfway through its travel - the meter reading should be roughly halfway between the full and empty readings.

10 Move the float up and down through its maximum travel, and watch the meter reading change. Note any abnormally-high or low intermediate readings **(see illustration)**.

11 If the readings obtained are within 10% of the figures quoted, the sensor can be considered healthy. If the readings are out of specification by a large margin, or are intermittent, renew the sensor.

Refitting

12 Fit a new gasket to the fuel tank, and align the screw holes. Guide the level sensor float arm through the mounting hole, and seat the unit securely on the fuel tank, making sure that the gasket is in place.

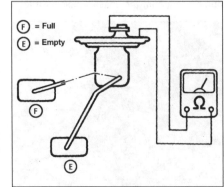

6.10 Checking the resistance of the fuel level sensor

6.4 Remove the five retaining screws, and carefully prise the level sensor away from the tank

13 Refit and tighten the retaining screws. Reconnect the sensor cable.

14 Raise and refit the fuel tank as described in Section 5.

15 Reconnect the battery negative cable.

7 Fuel lines and fittings -
inspection and renewal

 Warning: Read the precautions in Section 1 before working on the fuel system.

1 Whenever the vehicle has to be raised to facilitate repair work, take the opportunity to inspect the fuel lines and fixings for signs of damage or deterioration.

2 Fuel lines are made up of sections of rigid, narrow-bore steel hosing at points where no movement is encountered, and sections of flexible rubber hosing where connections to components, such as pumps and filters, are required.

3 Hose clips are generally used at the joints between hoses and components. These vary from the single-fit, crimp type that are destroyed on removal, to quick-release spring types with finger grips to aid positioning and removal. The most common are the worm-drive type, that are slackened or tightened by turning an integral screw.

4 When inspecting rubber hoses, look for cracks due to perishing or over-stressing, and damage caused by chafing and proximity to sources of heat.

5 When inspecting rigid metal hoses, look for signs of rusting and damage caused by crushing and chafing against bodywork and other components. Rigid hoses are generally secured to the chassis/bodywork by plastic or metal clips. Check that these hold the hoses tightly, and are not cracked (or even missing).

6 Check the security of all hose clips by carefully flexing the joints that they are fastening. If a joint appears loose, tighten the clip to seal it. Avoid the temptation to tighten the clips just out of routine, as this will crush and weaken the joints, if repeated at every inspection.

7 Renew those parts of the fuel lines and fixings which appear worn or damaged. Always use manufacturer's original parts, as incompatible or inferior substitutes could cause leakage, or at worst, a fire.

8 Choke opener system - checking

Description

1 Cold start enrichment and fast idle control is provided by means of a manually-operated choke. This is a butterfly valve that restricts the carburettor air inlet, enriching the fuel/air mixture. The choke actuator lever is mechanically linked to the throttle actuator lever; this allows the engine idle speed to be raised during cold start conditions.

2 When the choke knob is pulled out fully, the choke valve closes and provides maximum enrichment during cranking to assist starting. After the engine has been running for a while, a slightly weaker mixture is required. When the coolant temperature reaches 18°C, a Bi-metal Vacuum Switching Valve (BVSV), mounted in the path of engine coolant, opens and directs manifold vacuum from the running engine to a diaphragm valve. Through a linkage rod, the diaphragm valve then opens the choke valve slightly, weakening the fuel/air mixture as required. Rapid opening of the choke valve would cause erratic idling and possibly stalling, so the opening action is slowed down by the addition of a restrictor in the diaphragm valve vacuum supply.

3 When the engine is fully warmed, enrichment of the fuel/air mixture is not required, so the choke knob should ordinarily be pushed in, fully opening the choke valve. However, certain models, depending on specification, are fitted with an automatic choke knob release system. This consists of a solenoid which holds the choke knob in the open position magnetically, during cold starting and warm-up. When the engine coolant temperature exceeds 63°C, a temperature switch, mounted in the path of the coolant, breaks the power supply to the solenoid and releases the choke knob, allowing it to return to its normal position and hence closing the choke valve.

Automatic choke knob release (where fitted) - operation check

4 Ensure that the engine is allowed to cool (ie coolant temperature below 50°C).

5 With the ignition switch in the OFF position, pull out the choke knob fully. When released, it should recoil back to its normal position. If it does not, check and lubricate the choke actuator lever and cable (see Section 9).

6 Turn the ignition switch to the ON (second) position. Pull the choke knob out fully. When released, it should remain in the extended position, held by the solenoid. If it does not,

check the operation of the temperature-controlled switch as described in paragraph 9. If no fault is found, check the condition of the choke knob solenoid, as described in paragraph 10.

7 Start the engine and allow it to warm up. As the coolant approaches 63°C (indicated by the temperature gauge reading roughly one quarter of its maximum travel), the choke knob should be automatically released and recoil to its normal position. If it does not, check the operation of the temperature-controlled switch as described in paragraph 9.

8 If the system performs as described in the above paragraphs, it is operating properly and requires no corrective action - paragraphs 9 and 10 can therefore be ignored.

Temperature switch (where fitted)

9 Ensure that the engine and ignition are switched off and that the coolant is hot (hotter than 63°C). Locate the temperature switch on the inlet manifold, adjacent to the thermostat housing (do not confuse it with the temperature sensor). Unplug the cable from it, and connect a test meter across its terminals - positive (+) probe on the uppermost terminal, common (-) probe to the metal housing. Set the meter to the lowest scale on the resistance function. With the coolant hot, the switch should be open-circuit, ie a reading of infinity. As the coolant cools and the coolant temperature falls below 53°C, the switch contacts should close, giving a reading close to short-circuit (very low resistance). If the unit does not perform as described, it is faulty and must be renewed.

Choke knob solenoid

10 Remove the dashboard, referring to Chapter 11. Locate the cables leading to the choke knob solenoid, and unplug them at the connector. Using a test meter in the resistance mode, connect one probe to each terminal in the connector, on the choke solenoid side. If it is in good condition, the resistance of the solenoid coil should be between 23 and 43 ohms. If the reading obtained is outside this, renew the choke knob and solenoid assembly.

Choke opener system - operation check

11 Refer to Section 2 and remove the air cleaner assembly. Run the engine until it reaches normal operating temperature.

12 Locate the diaphragm valve, mounted on the side of the carburettor just below the choke cable linkage. Before progressing any further, check the condition of all the vacuum supply hoses in the system. Look for holes and splits that could cause leakage, and renew any items that are found to be defective.

13 The vacuum supply to the diaphragm valve has a restrictor valve mounted in line with it. With the engine still running, pull the vacuum supply hose off the restrictor, and place your finger over the end of the hose to

check that there is vacuum present. If no suction is felt, check the operation of the BVSV, as described in paragraph 17.

14 Connect the vacuum supply hose directly to the diaphragm valve port, taking the restrictor out of line. As you do this, look down the air inlet, and check that the choke valve opens fully when the vacuum hose is connected. If it does not, the diaphragm valve is faulty and must be renewed.

> **Warning: When observing the choke valve, keep your face a safe distance away from the air inlet, in case a backfire occurs.**

15 Reconnect the restrictor and vacuum supply hose as before. As you do this, again look down the air inlet, and check that the choke valve opens, but this time with a slower action. If the opening is just as rapid as without the restrictor, or if the choke valve remains closed, then the restrictor is faulty and must be renewed.

16 If the system performs as described, then it is operating correctly and requires no corrective action - paragraph 17 can therefore be ignored.

Bi-metallic Vacuum Switching Valve (BVSV)

17 Locate the BVSV, mounted on the inlet manifold above cylinder No 4. Pull off the hoses from the upper and lower ports. Blow into the upper port - with the engine coolant at normal operating temperature, air should pass through the valve, and exit from the lower port *only*. With the engine cool, air blown into the upper port should not pass through the valve. In addition, air blown into the lower port should *only* exit through the vent cap on the top of the valve, and *not* through the upper port. If the valve does not perform as described, it is faulty and must be renewed.

18 Refit the hoses, ensuring that the vacuum supply hose leading from the inlet manifold is connected to the upper port.

9 Choke cable - renewal and adjustment

1 Refer to Chapter 11 and remove the dashboard assembly.

2 Remove the air cleaner assembly, referring to Section 2 for details.

3 At the carburettor, release the choke cable inner from the choke opener lever by slackening the pinch-bolt **(see illustration)**. In the cab, pull the choke knob right out of its housing, until the cable inner is visible. Continue pulling and extract the entire cable inner from the outer sheathing.

4 Release the cable outer sheath from the carburettor by slackening the mounting bracket clamp bolt. Unscrew the knurled lock ring from the choke cable housing, to free it from the dashboard. If a choke knob release solenoid is fitted, unplug it from the wiring

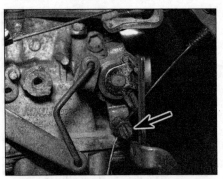

9.3 Release the choke cable inner from the choke opener lever by slackening the pinch-bolt (arrowed)

9.5 Prise the rubber grommet out from the floorpan (arrowed)

harness at the connector. Release the cable outer from any cable ties behind the dashboard area, and allow it to drop to the floor.

5 Working under the front of the vehicle, prise out the rubber grommet that protects the cable as it passes through the floorpan **(see illustration)**.

6 Release the remainder of the cable from any additional clips or ties under the chassis, and withdraw it from the vehicle completely. Note that the cable can be released from the chassis-mounted ties by pressing the release tab. The tie can then be re-used.

7 The new cable can be fitted in the same manner. Draw the inner cable out of its sheath, and put it to one side. Working from the underside of the vehicle, insert the outer sheath into the hole in the floorpan, up to the rubber grommet. Press the grommet into the hole, such that the two lips are positioned on either side of the metal. Securely clip the sheath to the chassis, using the clips provided.

8 In the engine bay, thread the cable sheath up to the carburettor, and loosely fit it to the clamp bracket.

9 In the cab, thread the cable sheath up along the front bulkhead, and insert it through the hole in the dashboard. Fit the knurled lock ring to the other side, and tighten it. Connect the choke knob release solenoid to the wiring harness connector. Strap the sheath securely behind the dash, using the clips provided.

10 Ensure that there are no tight curves in the cable run, as this will impede the process of inserting the new inner cable. If there is more than about 25 mm of sheath protruding past the clamp bracket, trim it off using a pair of cable cutters. Do not use normal pliers, as they will crush the end of the sheath instead of cutting it cleanly.

11 Working from the cab, carefully feed the cable inner into the sheath. Check that the bare end of the cable is not frayed before inserting it, as this may cause it to snag inside the sheath. Continue feeding the inner cable into the sheath until it appears at the other end, in the engine bay. Guide the end of the inner cable through the cable pinch-bolt on the choke opener lever. Pull the remainder of

the cable through, until the choke knob is drawn into its housing.

12 When all the slack in the inner cable has been eliminated, pull the choke knob off its seat by 5 to 10 mm. Ensure that the choke valve is fully open but just starting to close, then tighten the inner cable pinch-bolt. Trim off the excess cable using cable cutters; leave about 25 mm spare at the end.

13 Pull the choke knob out, and check that the choke valve closes fully without the knob pulling out of its housing.

14 Push the knob back onto its seat, and check that the choke valve opens completely. Adjust the choke by slackening the inner pinch-bolt if a fully-open/closed choke valve cannot be obtained.

15 Refit the air cleaner assembly to the carburettor.

16 Refit the dashboard assembly.

10 Accelerator cable - renewal and adjustment

1 Disconnect the battery negative cable, and position it away from the terminal.

2 Remove the pedal assembly cover by extracting the two retaining screws **(see illustration)**.

3 Release the cable outer sheath from its mounting bracket by slackening the locknut. Then release the cable inner by extracting the

10.2 Remove the pedal assembly cover

nipple from the actuator lever **(see illustration)**.

4 The cable runs to the engine bay via a channel in the floorpan. Lift up the floor mat and pull the cable out of the channel, away from the pedal assembly.

5 From the engine bay, carefully pull the cable outer and inner through the grommet in the bulkhead.

6 At the carburettor, release the cable inner from the throttle actuator lever by prising out the cable end nipple; open the throttle by hand slightly to give some slack in the cable. Free the cable outer from its mounting bracket, by slackening the adjustment locknut. Pull the cable away from the carburettor and out of the engine bay.

7 Fit the new accelerator cable in the reverse order to removal. Ensure that the cable passes through the bulkhead grommet, and cannot chafe on the metal bodywork. Clean out of the floorpan channel before laying the cable in it; grit and small stones will quickly wear through the cable outer, as it is in a relatively-exposed position.

8 Once the cable is fitted, check its adjustment as follows (it will be necessary to remove the air cleaner and open the choke to observe the position of the throttle plate):

a) *At the rest position, ie with the accelerator pedal at its highest point of travel, check that the throttle plate is in the idle position, ie almost closed.*

b) *At full throttle, ie with the pedal against the floor-mounted stop, check that the throttle plate is fully open, ie with the throttle lever against its end stop.*

9 If either of these conditions is unobtainable, slacken and reposition the cable adjustment nuts on the carburettor mounting bracket until the correct results are achieved.

11 Carburettor - general information

1 The carburettor is a Mikuni single-venturi, side draught unit, with an integral fuel cut-off solenoid. It has a manually-controlled choke, whose operation is described in Section 8 **(see illustration)**.

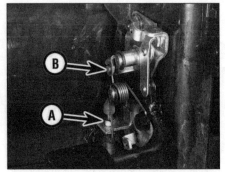

10.3 Accelerator pedal assembly

A Locknut   B Cable nipple

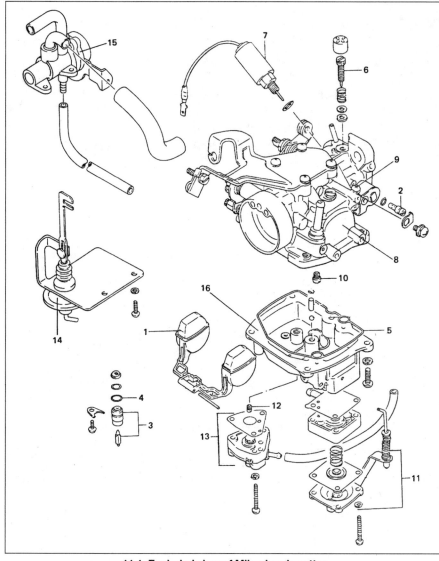

11.1 Exploded view of Mikuni carburettor

1 Float	9 Idle speed adjusting screw
2 Slow jet	10 Main jet
3 Needle valve assembly	11 Accelerator pump
4 O-ring	12 Enrichment jet
5 O-ring	13 Enrichment valve assembly
6 Idle mixture adjusting screw	14 Choke opener assembly
7 Fuel cut-off solenoid valve	15 Bowl vent valve (not fitted to UK vehicles)
8 Carburettor body	16 Float chamber body

2 A reservoir of fuel is accumulated in the float chamber; a float and needle valve mechanism regulates its level. As fuel is drawn from the chamber for mixing, the falling level lowers the float and opens a needle valve, allowing more fuel in. When the chamber fills, the float rises and closes off the valve. This maintains a near-constant fuel level in the float chamber.

3 During steady throttle, low-load conditions at engine speeds above idle, fuel metered through the main jet passes to the emulsion tube, and is drawn into the main bore by the pressure drop at the venturi. Air metered through the main air jet is directed to the emulsion tube, and provides fuel delivery correction as the load on the engine varies.

4 Under steady throttle, high-load conditions, manifold vacuum falls, causing poor carburation and a weak fuel/air mixture. This is compensated for by an enrichment device, which consists of a fuel valve controlled by a vacuum diaphragm valve. As manifold vacuum falls, the diaphragm moves and opens the fuel valve, allowing extra fuel into the emulsion tube. This enriches the fuel/air mixture that is fed into the main bore.

5 Under acceleration and rapid throttle openings, the sudden increase in air flow through the main bore can weaken the fuel/air mixture. To compensate, an accelerator pump is provided. This consists of chamber of fuel controlled by two ball valves, linked indirectly to the throttle shaft through a diaphragm valve. When the throttle is opened sharply, the diaphragm valve forces the fuel in the chamber past the weighted discharge ball valve and through a nozzle into the main bore, enriching the fuel/air mixture.

6 During idling and slow speed conditions, there is not enough air flow in the main venturi to sustain effective carburation, so a slow-running system is provided. Fuel, metered through the main jet, and air, metered through the first of two slow-air jets, is delivered to the slow jet, and mixed. This mixture is then blended with more air, fed from the second slow-air jet and the Air Bleed Control Valve (ABCV). The final mixture is fed through the idle port to the main bore, just downstream of the throttle plate. The mixture then combines with the main air flow in the bore, and is directed to the inlet manifold for combustion. The amount of mixture entering the main bore is regulated by means of the idle mixture screw.

7 A gradual progression from the slow running system to the main running system is essential, to give good throttle response from idle. To achieve this, a bypass port is provided just upstream of the throttle plate. When the throttle is part-opened, air flow over the bypass port causes a pressure drop above it. This allows the slow running fuel/air mixture to enter the main bore through the bypass port, as well as the idle port. This prevents the weakening of the mixture entering the cylinders as the air flow in the main bore rises.

8 A solenoid valve in the slow running system interrupts the fuel/air supply to the idle port when the ignition is switched off.

9 Idle speed is adjusted by a screw mounted on the top of the carburettor body.

12 Carburettor -
check and adjustment

Idle speed adjustment

1 Refer to Chapter 1.

Idle mixture adjustment

2 Refer to Chapter 1.

Throttle travel

3 With the engine and ignition off, press the accelerator to end of its travel, and check on the carburettor that the throttle plate rotates to its end stop. Release the pedal, and check the throttle plate returns to rest on the idle end stop. If necessary, refer to Section 10 and adjust the accelerator cable.

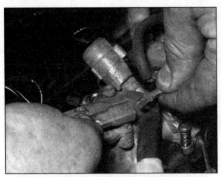

13.5 Disconnect the cable from the fuel cut-off solenoid

13.6 Disconnecting the fuel return hose from the carburettor

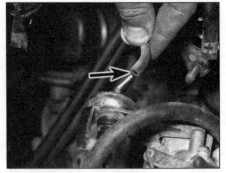

13.9 Pull the vacuum hose (arrowed) off the choke opener diaphragm valve

Accelerator pump

4 Remove the air cleaner assembly from the carburettor - refer to Section 2

5 With engine and ignition off, apply full throttle and look down the air inlet; if the engine is cold, you may have to hold the choke plate open). A steady stream of fuel should eject from the accelerator pump nozzle as the throttle is pressed. If the flow is poor or does not occur at all, the accelerator pump ports may be blocked internally. Refer to Section 14 and carry out an overhaul of the carburettor.

13 Carburettor -
removal and refitting

Removal

⚠ **Warning: Read the precautions in Section 1 before working on the fuel system.**

1 Disconnect the battery negative cable, and position it away form the terminal.
2 When hoses and cables are removed, label them and their points of connection, to aid reassembly.
3 Remove the air cleaner assembly; refer to Section 2.
4 Relieve any pressure that may be built up in the fuel system - refer to Section 3 for details.
5 Disconnect the cable from the fuel cut-off

solenoid, located on the top of the carburettor body **(see illustration)**.
6 Disconnect the fuel supply and return hoses from the carburettor ports **(see illustration)**. Hold a wad of rag underneath the ports as you do this, to absorb any spilt fuel. Note that the fuel supply hose connects to a port on the underside of the carburettor, hidden from view.
7 The throttle and choke cables are secured to their actuator levers by drilled pinch-bolts. Slacken them and pull out the cable cores.
8 Loosen the clamp that retains the choke cable outer, and withdraw the cable assembly. Remove the throttle cable adjuster locknut, then unscrew the adjuster from its support bracket. Withdraw the cable assembly.
9 Locate the choke opener diaphragm valve. Pull off its vacuum supply hose **(see illustration)**.
10 Disconnect the distributor vacuum advance hose from the port on the carburettor body, adjacent to the fuel cut-off solenoid **(see illustration)**.
11 Release the harness cables from the clip on the top of the carburettor body, and disconnect them from the alternator; refer to Chapter 5A for details.
12 Slacken and remove the two nuts securing the carburettor to the inlet manifold. Rock the unit gently from side to side to loosen it, and then draw it off the manifold studs **(see illustration)**.

13 Extract the top paper gasket, insulator gasket and bottom paper gasket.
14 Clean both surfaces of the insulator gasket. Clean the surface of the carburettor, to remove any traces of old gasket. Take care to preserve the surfaces as you do this, particularly on the insulator gasket, as it quite soft and easily damaged.

> **HAYNES HiNT** *If the carburettor is not going to be refitted for some time, seal the inlet manifold orifice with tape or a clean rag, to prevent debris from entering.*

Refitting

15 Fit a new paper gasket over the mounting studs on the inlet manifold. Refit the insulator gasket, and fit the second new paper gasket over the top of it **(see illustration)**.
16 The remainder of the refitting process is the reverse of removal, noting the following:
a) Tighten the carburettor mounting nuts securely.
b) Ensure that all hoses are refitted to their original ports, using the identification labels made during removal.
c) Adjust the choke and accelerator cable; refer to Sections 9 and 10 of this Chapter for details.
17 Start the engine, and check around the area of the carburettor for air and/or fuel leaks. Refer to Chapter 1 for details of checking and adjusting the idle speed and fuel/air mixture.

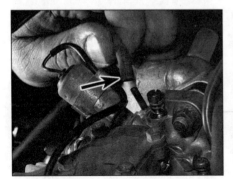

13.10 Disconnect the distributor vacuum advance hose (arrowed)

13.12 Remove the two nuts, and draw the carburettor off the manifold studs

13.15 Fit the second new paper gasket over the inlet manifold studs and insulator gasket

14.9a Remove the circlip (arrowed) from the end of the accelerator pump rod . . .

14.9b . . . and disconnect it from the throttle spindle bracket

14.10 Disconnect the vacuum hose from the enrichment valve

14 Carburettor -
diagnosis and overhaul

1 Carburettor faults generally manifest themselves as engine flooding, difficult starting, stalling, backfiring, poor acceleration, or excessive exhaust emissions. However, before deciding that an internal carburettor fault is responsible for a particular condition, eliminate all other possible causes by checking:

a) *The condition of all LT and HT ignition components, and the ignition timing; refer to Chapter 5B.*
b) *The condition of the air filter element; refer to Chapter 1.*
c) *The valve clearances; refer to Chapter 1.*
d) *The routing and condition of all carburettor vacuum hoses and vacuum-controlled actuators; refer to the relevant Sections of this Chapter.*
e) *The operation of the choke and accelerator pump; refer to the relevant Sections of this Chapter.*
f) *That the carburettor and inlet manifold mounting bolts are correctly torqued; refer to the Specifications Sections of this Chapter and Chapter 2A as required.*
g) *The cylinder compression pressures; refer to Chapter 2A.*
h) *The operation and condition of the fuel pump, filter and hoses; refer to the relevant Sections of this Chapter.*

i) *The positioning of the warm-air flap valve, relative to the ambient conditions.*
j) *Fuel of the correct octane rating is being used; refer to the Specifications Section of this Chapter.*

⚠️ *Warning: It may be necessary during carburettor diagnosis to run the engine with the air cleaner assembly removed. This, together with a potential fault, may cause backfiring through the air inlet. Avoid the risk of being burned by keeping your face and hands away from the air inlet at all times.*

2 If no faults are found with any of the above, it can be assumed that the carburettor is faulty and requires attention. There are two alternative courses of action. The first is to obtain a new or reconditioned carburettor. These are obtainable from dealers or carburettor and fuel system specialists - check the cost and availability of the unit you require.

3 Identify the carburettor by looking for part and serial numbers - these may be stamped on the body of the carburettor, or on a tab, screwed or bolted to the body. Ensure that the new/reconditioned unit is identical to the existing one before attempting to fit it.

4 The second alternative is to overhaul the carburettor yourself. To do this effectively, it is essential that an overhaul kit is obtained. This will contain all the parts that commonly need renewing on a worn carburettor, such as screws, seals and gaskets, as well as details

of how to carry out the overhaul. In addition, a can of carburettor cleaner will be required, to ensure that all internal components are thoroughly cleansed.

5 The design and layout of the fuel system changes frequently over a vehicle's production lifetime, as manufacturers strive to meet increasingly stringent emissions legislation. For this reason, the extent of the carburettor overhaul described in this Section is limited to those components which will be common to all iterations of the carburettor's design.

Dismantling

⚠️ *Warning: Read the precautions in Section 1 before working on the fuel system.*

6 Select a flat, clean, work surface on which to dismantle the carburettor.

7 Remove the carburettor from the inlet manifold, as described in Section 13.

8 Place the carburettor upside-down on the work surface.

9 Locate the accelerator pump throttle linkage rod. Remove the circlip from the end of the rod, and disconnect it from the throttle spindle bracket **(see illustrations)**.

10 Disconnect the vacuum hose from the enrichment valve **(see illustration)**.

11 After removing the retaining screws, gently prise the float chamber housing away from the main carburettor body **(see illustration)**. Release the choke opener linkage from the choke spindle as the two assemblies are separated.

12 Recover the O-ring seal from the main body and discard it, as a new one must be fitted on reassembly. Note the position of the internal components in relation to each other **(see illustrations)**.

13 Using a suitable implement, draw the float hinge pin out from its supports, and lift out the float **(see illustration)**.

14 Examine the float for signs of puncturing or cracking. Renew it if any such damage is evident.

15 Carefully lift the needle valve out of its housing, and inspect it carefully **(see illustration)**. Look for signs of wear around the conical sealing surface; any grooves

14.11 Gently prise the float chamber housing away from the main carburettor body

14.12a Recover the O-ring seal from the main body

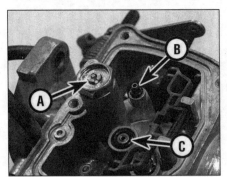

14.12b Location of components

A Main jet and housing
B Enrichment pipe
C Acceleration pump nozzle

14.13a Draw out the float hinge pin (arrowed) . . .

14.13b . . . and lift out the float

14.15 Carefully lift the needle valve out of its housing

caused by contact with the valve seat will allow the valve to leak, possibly flooding the float chamber. Check that the spring-loaded, anti-vibration plunger is free to move, and returns to its rest position if deflected.
16 After removing the retaining screw and plate, lift out the needle valve seat, and prise out the O-ring **(see illustration)**. A shim may have been fitted to correct the float height - lift it out and retain it for refitting. This exposes a mesh filter, which can be withdrawn and cleaned or renewed, depending on its condition.
17 Unscrew the main jet from its housing, then unbolt the housing from the carburettor body. Thoroughly clean both components

with carburettor cleaner, and allow them to dry completely **(see illustrations)**.
18 Squirt carburettor cleaner into the enrichment pipe, emulsion tube (via the main jet housing) and accelerator pump nozzle. Clean out any debris that may have collected in the bottom of the float chamber. Use compressed air, if it is available, to blow out the excess cleaning fluid when you are satisfied that the internal passages are clear.

⚠ **Caution: Wear eye protection when using compressed air for cleaning.**

19 Turn the carburettor body over, so that the float chamber now faces down. Remove the four screws to release the throttle/choke cable mounting bracket from the carburettor body, and prise off the cover plate beneath it.
20 Both the slow and main air jets and the venturi air vent will now be exposed. Use carburettor cleaner to dislodge any foreign material that may have settled in the jets. Ensure that all the cleaning fluid has been expelled before replacing the cover and choke/throttle cable mounting bracket. Refit and tighten the retaining screws.
21 Tighten the idle mixture adjustment screw slowly until it just contacts its seat, counting the exact number of turns required to do this. Then completely slacken the screw and withdraw it. Clean the screw thoroughly, and if it shows signs of wear, renew it. Thread the screw back into its mounting hole until it just contacts its seat. Now unscrew it by the number of turns counted on removal. This will

give a preliminary idle mixture setting to get the engine started and running, whereupon an accurate adjustment can be made.
22 Turn the carburettor back over, and refit the needle valve mesh filter and shim (if fitted). Slide a new O-ring seal into the groove in the needle valve seat, and push the assembly into its recess. Refit the retaining plate and screw to secure the valve seat in position. Carefully drop the needle valve onto its seat, checking that is free to move up and down without resistance.
23 Place the float in the float chamber. Slide the hinge pin through its supports, engaging the float. Check that the float is free to pivot at its hinge, without resistance.

Float height - checking and adjustment

24 To check that the needle valve is opened by the float at the correct point, it is necessary to check the float height, as follows. Rest the carburettor body on a flat surface. Use a finger to hold the float at a height that just allows it to touch the needle valve plunger, without pressing it into the valve. The float height is given by the distance between the mating surface of the carburettor body and the top of the float **(see illustration)**. Compare this measurement with the Specifications.
25 If the float height is too low, it can be increased by fitting a shim underneath the needle valve seat. These are available in thicknesses of 0.2, 0.3, 0.4, and 0.5 mm; a

14.16 Removing the needle valve seat

14.17a Unscrew the main jet from its housing . . .

14.17b . . . then unbolt the housing from the carburettor body

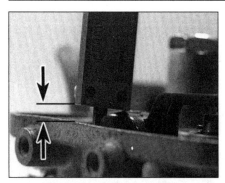

14.24 Measuring the float height (arrowed)

description of the needle valve seat removal is given in paragraph 16. Note that an increase in shim thickness of 0.2 mm results in an increase in float height of 0.8 mm. Select and fit a shim of appropriate thickness, then re-check the float height.

26 Fit a new O-ring seal to the mating surface of the main carburettor body, and refit the float chamber. Insert and tighten the retaining screws.

27 Reconnect the choke opener linkage to the choke spindle, then fit the accelerator pump linkage to the throttle spindle bracket, securing it in place with the circlip. Fit the enrichment valve vacuum hose onto its port.

28 Referring to Section 13, refit the carburettor to the inlet manifold.

15 Exhaust system -
description and component renewal

Description

1 The exhaust system comprises of a 4-into-2 exhaust manifold, a 2-into-1 front pipe, and a rear section that houses two silencers. The system is slung underneath the chassis, suspended by rubber mountings; one just downstream of the front silencer, and two attached to the rear silencer.

Component renewal

2 Raise the vehicle and rest it securely on wheel ramps or axle stands; refer to *"Jacking, towing and wheel changing"* at the beginning of this manual for guidance. Alternatively, position the vehicle over an inspection pit.

Exhaust manifold

3 Separation of the exhaust manifold from the cylinder head is described in Chapter 2A.

Front pipe

4 Slacken the three nuts that secure the front pipe to the exhaust manifold flange. If they are stiff through corrosion, use penetrating oil to loosen them. Periodically rotate the nut back half a turn as it is undone, to clear the threads and prevent the studs from shearing. Recover the metallic gasket and discard it; a new one must be fitted on reassembly.

5 The other end of the front pipe is secured to the rear section by two spring-loaded bolts. Remove these and withdraw the front pipe, recovering the ring seal from the bore as it is freed.

6 Use a wire brush to clean each mating surface, removing all traces of corrosion and carbon. Fit a new gasket over the studs on the exhaust manifold flange, and apply a smear of high melting point grease to the stud threads. Fit a new ring seal to the rear section flange joint and refit the front pipe, tightening all retaining nuts and bolts to the correct torque.

Rear section (including silencers)

7 Unbolt the rear section from the front pipe, at the flange joint. Recover the ring seal, and discard it - a new one should be fitted on reassembly.

8 Unbolt the three rubber mountings from the chassis-mounted hooks, and lower the section to the ground.

9 Inspect the rubber mountings for signs of deterioration, due to damage or ageing. Renew them if they appear cracked, perished or split.

10 Check along the length of the system for evidence of contact.

10 Clean the flange mating face with a wire brush to remove any corrosion and carbon.

11 Offer up the rear section to the vehicle, and bolt the rubber mountings to the fixing points on the chassis.

12 Fit a new ring seal to the flange, then refit the spring-loaded bolts and tighten them.

13 To check that there is adequate clearance between the exhaust system and the underside of the vehicle, grasp the exhaust system at a number of points along its length, and rock it carefully from side to side and up and down. If any contact occurs, check that all components have been refitted correctly, and that none have been omitted.

14 Start the engine and allow it to run. Check that there are no audible exhaust gas leaks where joints have been disturbed. Increase the engine speed through its range, to check that none of the exhaust system components resonate at a particular engine speed.

15 Carry out a road test, and check that no part of the exhaust system fouls the underside of the vehicle, particularly during acceleration/deceleration and gear changes, or when driving over bumps. Note that the exhaust system is subjected to the greatest movement when the engine is started and stopped.

Notes

Chapter 5 Part A:
Starting and charging systems

Contents

Degrees of difficulty

| Easy, suitable for novice with little experience | | Fairly easy, suitable for beginner with some experience | | Fairly difficult, suitable for competent DIY mechanic | | Difficult, suitable for experienced DIY mechanic | | Very difficult, suitable for expert DIY or professional | |

Specifications

Starter motor
Type . . . Nippon Denso
Operating voltage . . . 12V dc
Power . . . 0.6kW or 0.8kW
Direction of rotation . . . Anti-clockwise, viewed from pinion end
Number of pinion teeth . . . 8
No-load characteristic (@ 5000 rpm minimum) . . . 50A maximum @ 11V
Load characteristic (@ 1200 rpm minimum):
  0.6 kW type . . . 230A @ 9.5V
  0.8 kW type . . . 270A @ 9.5V
Locked rotor current:
  0.6 kW type . . . 450A @ 8.5V
  0.8 kW type . . . 600A @ 7.7V
Brush length:
  0.6 kW type . . . 16 mm
  0.8 kW type . . . 18 mm

Starter solenoid
Operating voltage . . . 8V

Alternator
Type . . . Mitsubishi three-phase
Nominal operating voltage . . . 12V
Maximum output current . . . 40A
Direction of rotation . . . Clockwise, viewed from pulley end
Maximum speed . . . 13 500 rpm
No-load speed . . . 1000-1100 rpm @ 14V
Full-load speed . . . 5000 rpm @ 13.5V
Brush length:
  Normal . . . 18.5 mm
  Service limit . . . 8.0 mm

Battery
Voltage . . . 12V
Rating . . . 28Ah or 40Ah
Specific gravity of electrolyte . . . See text

1 General information

This Chapter covers the starting and charging systems as separate, engine-related subjects. The ignition system is covered in Part B of this Chapter. Body electrical systems (such as lighting, instruments) are dealt with in Chapter 12.

This vehicle's electrical system is negative earth.

Precautions

Further details of the various systems are given in the relevant Sections of this Chapter. While some repair procedures are given, the usual course of action is to renew the component concerned. The owner whose interest extends beyond mere component renewal should obtain a copy of the "Automobile Electrical & Electronic Systems Manual", available from the publishers of this manual.

It is necessary to take extra care when working on the electrical system, to avoid damage to semiconductor devices (eg diodes and transistors), and to avoid the risk of personal injury. In addition to the precautions given in "Safety first!" at the beginning of this manual, observe the following when working on the system:

Always remove rings, watches, etc before working on the electrical system. Even with the battery disconnected, capacitive discharge could occur if a component's live terminal is earthed through a metal object. This could cause a shock or nasty burn.

Do not reverse the battery connections. Components such as the alternator, or any others containing semiconductor circuitry, could be irreparably damaged.

If the engine is being started using jump leads and a slave battery, connect the batteries positive-to-positive and negative-to-negative (see "Jump starting" at beginning of this manual). This also applies when connecting a battery charger.

Never disconnect the battery terminals, the alternator, any electrical wiring or any test instruments, when the engine is running.

Do not allow the engine to turn the alternator when the alternator is not connected.

Never test for alternator output by striking the output lead to an earth point.

Never use an ohmmeter of the type incorporating a hand-cranked generator for circuit or continuity testing (unless testing HT leads).

Always ensure that the battery negative lead is disconnected when working on the electrical system.

Before using electric-arc welding equipment on the car, disconnect the battery, alternator and all other electronic components, to protect them from the risk of damage.

Description - starting system

The starting system comprises an ignition switch, battery, a combined starter solenoid and starter motor unit of the pre-engaged type, and associated cabling and fuses **(see illustrations)**.

When the ignition switch is turned to the starting position, current is supplied to the starter solenoid pull-in coil, and the resulting electromagnetic field draws the solenoid armature into the body of the starter solenoid. A plunger, attached to one end of the armature pushes the starter motor pinion, via a pivoted lever, along the main drive shaft, and engages it with the flywheel ring gear.

As this happens, switch contacts at the other end of the armature connect battery current to the starter motor coils - in this manner, the starter motor is energised only after the pinion has engaged with the flywheel. As the starter motor armature moves, it interrupts the current supply to the pull-in coil, and energises the holding coil - this arrangement maintains drive to the flywheel as long as the ignition switch is held in the starting position.

When the engine starts, its speed increases to a normal idle, and the starter motor drive is no longer required. However, if the ignition switch is not released, the engine will now attempt to rotate the starter motor at its own speed, exceeding the motor's maximum rated speed. To prevent damage, an over-running clutch reduces the drive from the flywheel until the ignition switch is released, disengaging the pinion and disconnecting the drive.

Description - charging system

The charging system consists of the alternator, with an integral full-wave diode rectifier and voltage regulator, and its associated cabling **(see illustration)**.

Driven by the crankshaft via the auxiliary drivebelt, the three-phase alternator performs two functions: it charges the battery whilst the engine is running, by supplying it with a charging current, and it provides current to

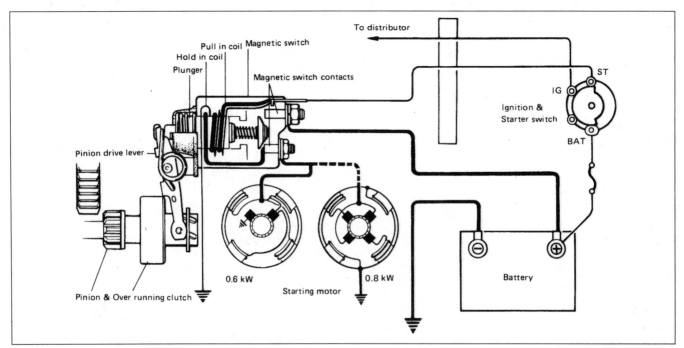

1.14a Starting system schematic, showing solenoid details

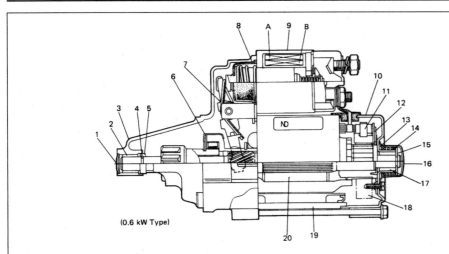

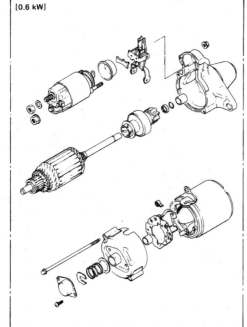

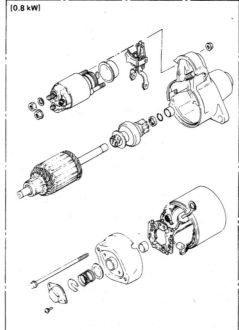

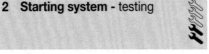

(0.6 kW Type)

[0.6 kW]

[0.8 kW]

1.14b Diagrammatic and exploded views of starter motor

1 Drive housing cover
2 Drive bush
3 Drive housing
4 Armature ring
5 Armature stop ring
6 Over-running clutch
7 Pinion drive lever
8 Solenoid cover
9 Solenoid
10 Commutator end housing
11 Brush spring
12 Brush holder
13 End cap gasket
14 Armature brake spring
15 Armature plate
16 Commutator end cap
17 Commutator end bushing
18 Brush
19 Starting motor yoke
20 Armature
A Hold-in coil
B Pull-in coil

power auxiliary devices and accessories, such as the lights, instruments, fans etc. It should be realised that the battery itself acts only as a reserve of current, used primarily for starting the engine.

The regulator controls the current supplied to the rotor coil windings by monitoring the alternator's output voltage; when the output voltage is low, the regulator increases the current supplied to the rotor coil, raising the output voltage. In this manner, the alternator output voltage and current are kept at a level appropriate to charge the battery and supply any auxiliaries devices currently in use, at any engine speed.

The supply to the rotating rotor coil windings is maintained by a pair of conductive brushes, which rub on a pair of slip ring contacts. The rubbing action erodes the ends of the brushes over time, and because of this,

they need to be inspected and renewed from time to time - an operation which is described later in this Chapter.

2 Starting system - testing

Note: *Refer to the precautions given in "Safety first!" and in Section 1 of this Chapter before starting work.*

1 If the starter motor fails to operate when the ignition key is turned to the appropriate position, the following possible causes may be to blame.
a) *The battery is faulty.*
b) *Poor electrical connections between the ignition switch, starter solenoid, battery and starter motor.*

c) *The starter solenoid is faulty.*
d) *The starter motor is mechanically or electrically faulty.*

2 The importance of good electrical connections cannot be stressed enough. Because of the large currents flowing in the starting system, even a small connection resistance will equate to a substantial volt drop, reducing the effectiveness of the system. Make sure all connections are clean, tight and well-protected from corrosion.

2 To check the battery, switch on the headlights. If they dim after a few seconds, this indicates that the battery is discharged - recharge (see Section 6) or renew the battery. If the headlights glow brightly, turn the ignition switch to the starting position, and observe the lights. If they dim, then this indicates that the starter motor is drawing current, therefore the fault must lie in the starter motor. If the

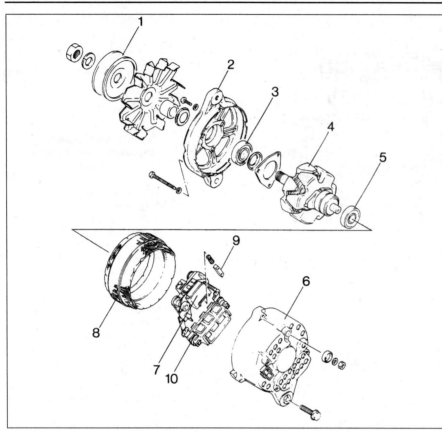

1.18 Exploded view of alternator

1 Drive pulley	5 Rear bearing	8 Stator assembly
2 Drive end frame	6 Rotor housing	9 Brush
3 Front bearing	7 Regulator assembly	10 Rectifier
4 Rotor		

lights continue to glow brightly (and no clicking sound can be heard from the starter motor solenoid), this indicates that there is a fault in the circuit or solenoid - see the following paragraphs. If the starter motor turns slowly when operated, and the battery is in good condition, then this indicates that either the starter motor is faulty, or that there is considerable resistance somewhere in the circuit, possibly in the cables or at a bad connection.

3 If a fault in the circuit is suspected, disconnect the battery leads (including the earth connection to the body), the starter/solenoid wiring and the engine/ transmission earth strap. Thoroughly clean the connections, and reconnect the leads and wiring, then use a voltmeter or test light to check that full battery voltage is available at the battery positive lead connection to the solenoid, and that the earth is sound. Smear petroleum jelly around the battery terminals to prevent corrosion - corroded connections are amongst the most frequent causes of electrical system faults.

4 If the battery and all connections are in good condition, check the circuit by disconnecting the wire from the solenoid blade terminal. Connect a voltmeter or test light between the wire end and a good earth (such as the battery negative terminal), and check that the wire is live when the ignition switch is turned to the "start" position. If it is, then the circuit is sound - if not, then the circuit wiring should be checked for continuity.

5 The solenoid contacts can be checked by connecting a voltmeter or test light between the battery positive feed connection on the starter side of the solenoid, and earth. When

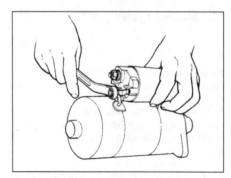

3.3 Unbolt the braided cable between the solenoid and the starter motor body

the ignition switch is turned to the "start" position, there should be a reading or lighted bulb, as applicable. If there is no reading or lighted bulb, the solenoid is faulty and should be renewed.

6 If the circuit and solenoid are proved sound, the fault must lie in the starter motor. Begin checking the starter motor by removing it (see Section 4), and checking the brushes (see Section 5). If the fault does not lie in the brushes, the motor windings are probably faulty. In this event, it may be possible to have the starter motor overhauled by a specialist. Check on the availability and cost of spares before carrying out any overhaul work yourself, as it may prove more economical to obtain a new or exchange motor.

---

3 Starter motor solenoid - removal, inspection and refitting

Removal

1 Disconnect the battery negative cable, and position it away from the terminal.
2 At the rear of the starter solenoid, prise off the rubber boot, and unbolt the main positive supply cable from its terminal.
3 Pull off the two solenoid coil supply cables at the spade connections, labelling them to assist you in refitting them later. **Note:** *Avoid damage by gripping the rubber boot, not the cable itself.* Unbolt the braided cable between the solenoid and the starter motor body **(see illustration)**.
4 Remove the two retaining nuts, and withdraw the starter solenoid assembly. Tilt the back of the assembly up as it is extracted, to release the hooked plunger from the pinion drive lever **(see illustration)**. Prise off the plunger cover cap.

Inspection

5 Press the plunger into its housing, and release it sharply. The plunger should snap

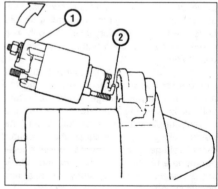

3.4 Tilt the back of the solenoid assembly up as it is extracted, to release the hooked plunger from the pinion drive lever

1 Solenoid assembly terminal end
2 Hooked plunger

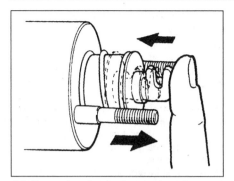

3.5 Press the plunger into its housing, and release it sharply

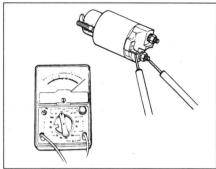

3.6 Testing the continuity of the pull-in coil

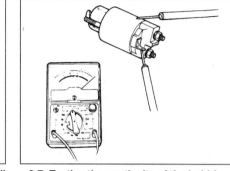

3.7 Testing the continuity of the hold-in coil

back to its original position without resistance **(see illustration)**.

6 To test the continuity of the pull-in coil, connect a multi-meter set to the resistance measurement function, across the "S" and "M" terminals **(see illustration)**. If no continuity exists, the coil is open-circuit and the solenoid assembly must be renewed.

7 To test the continuity of the hold-in coil, connect a multi-meter set to the resistance measurement function, across the "S" terminal and the metal casing **(see illustration)**. If no continuity exists, the coil is open-circuit and the solenoid assembly must be renewed.

8 To test the continuity of the solenoid switch contacts, connect a multi-meter set to the resistance measurement function, across the "M" and "BATTERY" terminals. Press the plunger in by hand, and check that the terminals are short-circuited. Release the plunger, and check that the terminals become open-circuit. If this is not the case, renew the solenoid assembly.

Refitting

9 Apply a small quantity of grease to the plunger hooked end, and refit the solenoid assembly to the starter motor.

10 Refit and tighten the retaining nuts, then reconnect the cables to their respective terminals.

11 Reconnect the battery negative cable.

4.4 Slacken and withdraw the two starter motor retaining bolts

4 Starter motor - removal and refitting

Removal

1 Disconnect the battery negative cable, and position it away from the terminal.

2 At the rear of the starter solenoid, prise off the rubber boot, and unbolt the main positive supply cable from its terminal.

3 Pull off the two solenoid coil supply cables, labelling them to assist you in refitting them later. **Note:** *Avoid damage by gripping the rubber boot, not the cable itself.*

4 Slacken and withdraw the two retaining bolts **(see illustration)**, then lift out the starter motor.

Refitting

5 Refitting is the reverse of removal. Twist the body of the starter motor as it is inserted into the bellhousing, to engage the drive teeth with the ring gear.

5 Starter motor - brush inspection and renewal

1 Disconnect the battery negative cable, and position it away from the terminal.

2 Remove the starter motor from the engine, as described in the Section 4.

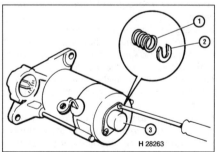

5.4 Remove the two retaining screws, and lift off the commutator end cap

1 *Spring*   3 *Commutator end cap*
2 *Armature plate*

3 Remove the starter solenoid from the motor, as described in Section 3.

4 Remove the two retaining screws, and lift off the commutator end cap. Do this carefully, and be ready to catch the commutator end plate, spring and washer as the cap is removed, as they are installed under tension **(see illustration)**.

5 Slacken and withdraw the two bolts that run the length of the starter motor body, and prise off the commutator end housing **(see illustration)**.

6 Lift out the motor yoke and the brush holder as one unit.

7 Carefully remove the brushes from their guides. Measure the total length of each brush, and compare them with the Specifications. If they excessively worn, the brushes and holder will have to be renewed as a complete assembly.

8 Inspect the coiled brush springs for wear or damage. Press against their ends, to check that they are capable of pressing the brushes against the commutator.

9 The two sides of the brush holder assembly should be electrically isolated. Check that this is the case by holding the probes of a multi-meter, set to the resistance function, against each brush guide **(see illustration)**. If there is electrical continuity, then the insulation has broken down, and the brush holder assembly must be renewed.

10 Reassemble the unit by reversing the dismantling procedure. Apply a smear of

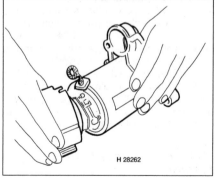

5.5 Prise off the commutator end housing

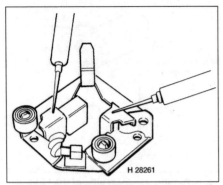

5.9 Checking for electrical isolation between the two sides of the brush holder

grease to the end of the armature shaft as the end cap is refitted.

11 Refit the starter motor and solenoid assembly to the engine, and reconnect the cables.

12 Reconnect the battery negative cable, and test the operation of the starting system.

6 Battery - testing and charging

1 The exact type of battery fitted to this vehicle varies depending on its year of manufacture. In addition, it is possible that, during the vehicle's lifetime, the battery has been renewed. Therefore, the following paragraphs contain a general description of battery testing, intended for use as a guide, rather than a definitive set of instructions.

Standard and low-maintenance battery - testing

2 If the vehicle covers a small annual mileage, it is worthwhile checking the specific gravity of the electrolyte every three months to determine the state of charge of the battery. Use a hydrometer to make the check, and compare the results with the following graph. Note that the ambient temperature affects the readings (see illustration).

3 If the battery condition is suspect, first check the specific gravity of electrolyte in each cell. A variation of 0.040 or more between any cells indicates loss of electrolyte, or deterioration of the internal plates.

4 If the specific gravity variation is 0.040 or more, the battery should be renewed. If the cell variation is satisfactory but the battery is discharged, it should be charged as described later in this Section.

Maintenance-free battery - testing

5 In cases where a "sealed for life" maintenance-free battery is fitted, topping-up

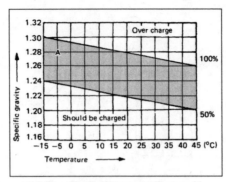

6.2 Graph of battery specific gravity against temperature

Readings obtained should be within the shaded area, as near to the 100% charge line as possible

and testing of the electrolyte in each cell is not possible. The condition of the battery can therefore only be tested using a battery condition indicator or a voltmeter.

6 If the battery is to be tested using a voltmeter, connect the probes across the battery terminals. The test will only be accurate if the battery has not been subjected to any kind of charge for the previous six hours. If this is not the case, switch on the headlights for 30 seconds, then wait four to five minutes before testing the battery after switching off the headlights. All other electrical circuits must be switched off, so check that the doors and tailgate (as applicable) are fully shut when conducting the test.

7 If the voltage reading is less than 12.2 volts, then the battery is discharged, whilst a reading of 12.2 to 12.4 volts indicates a partially discharged condition.

8 If the battery is to be charged, remove it from the vehicle (Section 7) and charge it as described later in this Section.

Standard and low-maintenance battery - charging

Note: *The following is intended as a guide only. Always refer to the manufacturer's recommendations (often printed on a label attached to the battery) before charging a battery.*

9 Charge the battery at a rate of 3.5 to 4 amps, and continue to charge the battery at this rate until no further rise in specific gravity is noted over a four-hour period.

10 Alternatively, a trickle charger charging at the rate of 1.5 amps can safely be used overnight.

11 Specially rapid "boost" charges which are claimed to restore the power of the battery in 1 to 2 hours are not recommended, as they can cause serious damage to the battery plates through overheating.

12 While charging the battery, note that the temperature of the electrolyte should never exceed 37.8°C (100°F).

Maintenance-free battery - charging

Note: *The following is intended as a guide only. Always refer to the manufacturer's recommendations (often printed on a label attached to the battery) before charging a battery.*

13 This battery type takes considerably longer to fully recharge than the standard type, the time taken being dependent on the extent of discharge, but it can take anything up to three days.

14 A constant-voltage type charger is required, to be set to 13.9 to 14.9 volts, with a charger current below 25 amps. Using this method, the battery should be usable within three hours, giving a voltage reading of 12.5 volts, but this is for a partially-discharged battery and, as mentioned, full charging can take considerably longer.

15 If the battery is to be charged from a fully-discharged state (condition reading less than 12.2 volts), have it recharged by your dealer or local automotive electrician, as the charge rate is higher, and constant supervision during charging is necessary.

7 Battery - removal and refitting

Removal

1 On Van models, remove the battery carrier cover located on the floor of the load area, and unbolt the battery retaining bar, removing it completely.

2 On Pickup models, unscrew the front cover, and slacken the retaining bar nuts. Pivot the left-hand threaded rod away from the battery box, and rotate the retaining bar clear of the battery.

3 After slackening the terminal pinch-bolts, disconnect first the negative, then positive battery cables, and position them clear of the terminal posts.

4 Lift out the battery, and place it upright on a suitable work surface. Do not tilt the battery at all.

Refitting

5 Refitting is the reverse of removal, noting the following:

a) *On Van models, be sure to refit the dust seals correctly. It is recommended that, to prevent water ingress via the battery carrier, a bead of silicone rubber sealant is applied to the joint between the carrier and its cover.*

b) *Apply a small quantity of petroleum jelly to the battery and cable terminals after they have been reconnected, to protect them from corrosion.*

c) *Always reconnect the negative battery cable last.*

8 Alternator/charging system - testing in vehicle

⚠️ **Warning: A number of the following procedures involve working around the engine whilst it is running. Under these circumstances, take great care to keep clear of any rotating or high-temperature components. Tie back long hair and loose clothing.**

⚠️ **Caution: Only disconnect alternator cables when the engine is not running and the ignition switch is turned to the "off" position. In addition, if alternator battery connections are to be removed, disconnect the battery negative cable first, to avoid the possibility of causing a short-circuit.**

1 If the dashboard-mounted charge warning light fails to come on when the ignition switch is turned to the second position, or if it fails to go out when the engine is running, this is an indication that the charging system is not functioning correctly. However if, in the absence of any such warning indications, the charging system's operation is still suspected, carry out the checks described in the following paragraphs.

Charging system check

2 Check that the battery is in good condition and sufficiently charged before commencing this test. To assess whether the alternator is capable of charging the battery, first discharge it partially by switching on a number of major electrical loads, such as the blower fan, headlights, heated rear windscreen for 4 or 5 minutes.

3 Start the engine, and run it at 3000 rpm for a few minutes. This will cause the alternator to supply a charging current to the battery.

4 Switch off the loads and the engine. The battery voltage should now have reached around 13.5V. If it does not, the charging system is faulty; use the following paragraphs to help identify the area of failure.

Auxiliary drivebelt check

5 Refer to Chapter 1.

Cable continuity check

6 Switch the ignition to the "off" position. Disconnect first the battery negative cable, then all three alternator cables.

7 Reconnect the battery negative cable, and turn the ignition switch to the second position.

8 Using a multi-meter, check that battery voltage is present at all three alternator cable connectors (harness side). If this is not the case, investigate where the bad connection is and rectify it. **Note:** *If the "L" terminal is at anything less than battery voltage, the charge warning light bulb may have blown.*

9 Switch off the ignition, and reconnect all cables.

Circuit volt drops

10 Because of the large currents flowing in the charging system, a small resistance caused by a dirty or corroded contact can translate to a substantial volt drop. This will reduce the efficiency of the charging system.

11 Connect one probe of a multi-meter to the battery positive terminal, and the other to the "B" terminal on the alternator. Set the meter to the voltage measurement function, and start the engine.

12 Run the engine at about 3000 rpm, and switch on a number of electrical loads. The meter should indicate a volt drop of no more than about 0.5V.

13 Now connect the probes between the battery negative terminal and the point where the engine earth strap bolts to the vehicle body. With the engine still running and the loads still turned on, the volt drop should not exceed 0.5V.

14 If the readings are higher, check the security and condition of the battery terminal connections and engine earth strap connections.

Regulator operation

15 With the engine running at about 3000 rpm, use a multi-meter to measure the battery voltage; it should rise to between 14.2 and 15.0V (measured at 25ºC) and remain at this level without fluctuation outside of these limits. If it does not, then the regulator is not operating correctly and requires renewal.

16 The only economically-serviceable component in the alternator is the regulator/brush holder module. The renewal of this item is described in Section 10.

17 If the fault appears to be more complex, the alternator should be taken to an automotive electrical specialist for testing and repair or renewal. He may also be able to supply you with a rebuilt alternator, as a cost-effective alternative to a brand new unit.

9 Alternator - removal and refitting

Removal

1 Disconnect the battery negative cable, and position it away from the terminal.

2 Pull back the rubber boot, and unbolt the main battery cable from the alternator "B" terminal. Pull off the connector from the "L" and "IG" terminals **(see illustrations)**.

3 Slacken the upper and lower mounting bolts, and pivot the alternator towards the engine, allowing the auxiliary drivebelt to slacken.

4 Pull off the auxiliary drivebelt, and put it to one side. Remove the upper and lower mounting bolts, then lift the alternator away from the engine **(see illustrations)**.

5 Refer to Section 10 for details of the regulator/brush holder module inspection and renewal.

Refitting

6 Refit the alternator by reversing the removal procedure; refer to Chapter 1 for details of refitting and tensioning the auxiliary drivebelt.

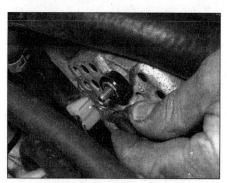
9.2a Unbolt the main battery cable from the alternator "B" terminal . . .

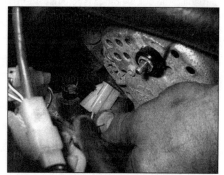
9.2b . . . and pull off the connector from the "L" and "IG" terminals

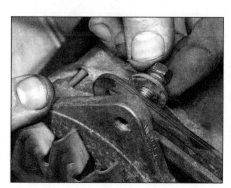
9.4a Removing the upper mounting bolt

9.4b Lifting out the alternator

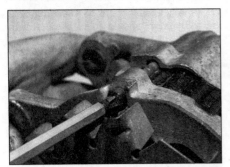

10.2 Slacken and withdraw the three bolts holding the two halves of the alternator housing together

10.4a Removing the rectifier and brush holder/regulator module mounting screws

10.4b Remove the "B" terminal nut, washer and insulating bush from the outside of the housing

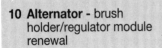
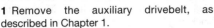

10 Alternator - brush holder/regulator module renewal

1 Remove the auxiliary drivebelt, as described in Chapter 1.

2 Remove the alternator as described in Section 9, and place it on a clean work surface. Slacken and withdraw the three bolts that hold the two halves of the alternator housing together **(see illustration)**. Scribe an alignment mark on the surface of the alternator, across both halves of the housing - this will aid correct reassembly later.

3 Use a soft-faced mallet to tap the rotor housing and stator coil away from the end frame and rotor. Do not use a screwdriver as a lever against the stator core, as this will risk damaging the coil windings **(see illustration)**.

4 Release the rectifier and brush holder/regulator modules from the rotor housing, by removing the two mounting screws. One of the screws also serves as the "B" terminal post, and can be withdrawn after removing the nut, washer and insulating bush from the outside of the housing **(see illustrations)**. Note that the two modules and the stator assembly are connected, and so must be removed together.

5 Place the stator face down on the work surface, with the brush holder/regulator uppermost. Slide the plastic blade terminal housing out of its seat, and put it to one side. Recover the insulating bushes from the

module mounting holes, and if they are in good condition, retain them for refitting later.

6 Lift out the brush holder/regulator module. Examine the brush springs - if they corroded or damaged to the extent that they are not capable of pressing the brushes against the slip rings, renew the module. Examine the brushes themselves; they have the manufacturer's emblem stamped into the conductive material, to act as a depth gauge. When the brushes are worn down to the bottom of this emblem, they are exhausted and must be renewed **(see illustrations)**.

7 Inspect the surfaces of the slip rings, on the end of the rotor. If they appear worn or burnt, it may be possible to restore them with fine abrasive paper.

8 Renew the module if the regulator is suspected of being faulty. See Section 8 for details of fault diagnosis.

9 Reassemble the components by reversing the removal sequence. Take care not to overtighten fasteners with insulating bushes, as they are brittle, and break easily. Lubricate the rotor rear bearing with a smear of grease before reassembly.

10 To allow the rotor to be refitted into its bearing in the rotor housing, the brushes must be temporarily compressed inside their holder. This can be achieved by holding up the brushes with one finger, and then inserting a stout length of wire through the hole provided in the rotor casing to keep them in position **(see illustrations)**. When the rotor is refitted to its bearing, the wire can then be

removed, and the brushes will seat correctly on the slip rings.

11 Refit the alternator to the engine, and connect the cables to their respective terminals.

12 Refer to Chapter 1 for details of fitting and tensioning the auxiliary drivebelt.

11 Oil pressure switch - removal and refitting

Removal

1 The operation of the oil pressure switch can be verified by removing it as described below, and screwing in a proprietary oil pressure gauge in its place. These can be obtained from an auto-accessories retailer, or your local dealer will be able to carry out the task for a nominal fee.

2 The oil pressure switch is located on the cylinder block, just above the oil filter. Unplug the harness cable from the oil switch spade terminal.

3 Unscrew the oil switch from the engine block - hold a rag underneath the switch as it is withdrawn, to catch any oil that drains out.

4 Wipe the switch clean, and inspect it for signs of corrosion or fouling.

Refitting

5 Refit the switch by reversing the removal steps. Smear the threads with anti-seize grease before screwing it into place, then tighten it securely.

10.6a Lift out the brush holder/regulator module

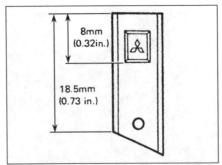

10.6b Examine the brushes; use the manufacturer's emblem as a depth gauge

8mm (0.32in.)

18.5mm (0.73 in.)

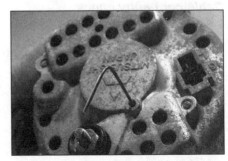

10.10 Hold up the brushes with one finger then insert a stout length of wire into the brush setting hole

Chapter 5 Part B: Ignition system

Contents

Degrees of difficulty

Easy, suitable for novice with little experience	Fairly easy, suitable for beginner with some experience	Fairly difficult, suitable for competent DIY mechanic 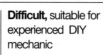	Difficult, suitable for experienced DIY mechanic 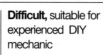	Very difficult, suitable for expert DIY or professional

Specifications

General

Type	Contact breaker
Static ignition timing	8° BTDC @ 900 rpm (vacuum advance disconnected)

Ignition coil

Type	Bosch
Primary winding resistance	1.3 ohms
Secondary resistance	6.2 kilohms
Ballast resistor	In line with harness, 1.5 ohms

Distributor

Type	Nippon Denso
Dwell angle	53 ± 3°
Contact breaker points gap	0.40 to 0.50 mm
Condenser capacitance	0.25 microfarads
Direction of rotation	Clockwise

Spark plugs and HT leads

See Chapter 1 Specifications

---

1 General information

The ignition system major components include four spark plugs, HT leads, distributor, contact breaker points, ignition coil, ignition switch, ballast resistor and battery **(see illustration)**.

The basic system operation is as follows: battery voltage is supplied to the primary side of the coil (referred to as the LT voltage), and this supply is periodically interrupted by the contact breaker points opening. The collapsing primary magnetic field induces a much larger voltage in the secondary coil, called the HT voltage. This voltage is directed, by the distributor via the HT leads, to the spark plug in the cylinder currently on its ignition stroke. The spark plug electrodes form a gap small enough for the HT voltage to arc across, and the resulting spark ignites the

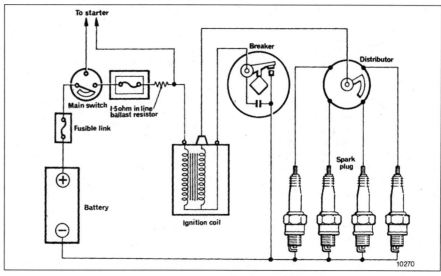

1.1 Ignition system schematic diagram

fuel/air mixture in the cylinder. The timing of this sequence of events is critical, and is regulated by the mechanical synchronisation between the camshaft and the distributor drive. Details of setting the ignition timing are given later in this Chapter.

The distributor is driven by a gear on the end of the camshaft. The common shaft drives both the rotor arm, which distributes the HT voltage, and the cam which opens and closes the contact breaker points. It contains integral mechanisms for introducing engine speed and load-related mechanical and vacuum ignition timing advance.

When the engine is running normally, the ignition switch is in the second position, and battery current is supplied to the primary side of the ignition coil via a ballast resistor, built into the wiring harness. Note that the normal operating voltage of the coil is considerably less than normal battery voltage - the ballast resistor introduces the necessary volt drop. During cranking, however, the ignition switch is turned to the "Start" position, and battery current is supplied to the coil via the starter solenoid contacts, bypassing the ballast resistor. This arrangement has three advantages: during cold start cranking, the starter motor draws a large current, and this can reduce the battery voltage to a level where the coil cannot produce sufficient HT voltage to start the engine. By bypassing the ballast resistor, a higher proportion of the available battery voltage is supplied to the coil, maintaining an adequate HT output, and improving the chances of starting the engine. The second advantage is that during normal running, the ballast resistor alters the impedance of the primary coil circuit, which reduces the voltage oscillations caused by the contact breaker points opening. This gives a stabilised HT voltage output, and allows a much more consistent spark to be produced at the spark plug. In addition, the resistor acts as a current control device, allowing more current to flow to the coil primary windings at high engine speeds, to maintain an adequate spark.

2 Ignition system - fault-finding

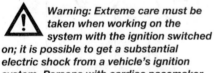

⚠️ **Warning: Extreme care must be taken when working on the system with the ignition switched on; it is possible to get a substantial electric shock from a vehicle's ignition system. Persons with cardiac pacemaker devices should keep well clear of the ignition circuits, components and test equipment.**

Note: *Refer to the warning given in Section 1 of Part A of this Chapter before starting work. Always switch off the ignition before disconnecting or connecting any component, and when using a multi-meter to check resistances.*

General

1 Most ignition system faults are likely to be due to loose or dirty connections or to "tracking" (unintentional earthing) of HT voltage due to dirt, dampness or damaged insulation, rather than by the failure of any of the system's components. **Always** check all wiring thoroughly before condemning an electrical component, and work methodically to eliminate all other possibilities before deciding that a particular component is faulty.

2 The old practice of checking for a spark by holding the live end of an HT lead a short distance away from the engine is **not** recommended; not only is there a high risk of an electric shock, but the HT coil could be damaged. Similarly, **never** try to "diagnose" misfires by pulling off one HT lead at a time.

Engine will not start

3 If the engine either will not turn over at all, or only turns very slowly, check the battery and starter motor. Connect a voltmeter across the battery terminals (meter positive probe to battery positive terminal), disconnect the ignition coil HT lead from the distributor cap and earth it, then note the voltage reading obtained while turning over the engine on the starter for (no more than) ten seconds. If the reading obtained is less than approximately 9.5V, first check the battery, starter motor and charging systems (see Chapter 5A).

4 If the engine turns over at normal speed but will not start, check the HT circuit by connecting a timing light (following its manufacturer's instructions) and turning the engine over on the starter motor; if the light flashes, voltage is reaching the spark plugs, so these should be checked first. If the light does not flash, check the HT leads themselves, followed by the distributor cap, carbon brush and rotor arm, using the information given in Chapter 1.

5 If there is a spark, check the fuel system for faults, referring to Chapter 4 for further information.

6 If there is still no spark, check the voltage at the ignition HT coil positive terminal, with the ignition switch at the second position; it should be approximately 7.0V. If the voltage at the coil is less than this, check the supply through the fusebox, starter solenoid contacts and ignition switch to the battery and its earth, until the fault is found.

7 If the feed to the HT coil is sound, check the condition of the contact breaker points; see Chapter 1.

8 Assuming that the contact breaker points are in good condition, check the coil's primary and secondary winding resistance as described later in this Chapter; renew the coil if faulty, but check carefully the condition of the LT connections themselves before doing so, to ensure that the fault is not due to dirty or poorly-fastened connectors.

Engine misfires

9 An irregular misfire suggests either a loose connection or intermittent fault on the primary circuit, or an HT fault on the coil side of the rotor arm.

10 With the ignition switched off, check carefully through the system, ensuring that all connections are clean and securely fastened. If the equipment is available, check the LT circuit as described above.

11 Check that the HT coil, the distributor cap and the HT leads are clean and dry. Check the leads themselves and the spark plugs (by substitution, if necessary), then check the distributor cap, carbon brush and rotor arm as described in Chapter 1.

12 Regular misfiring is almost certainly due to a fault in the distributor cap, HT leads or spark plugs. Use a timing light (paragraph 4 above) to check whether HT voltage is present at all leads.

13 If HT voltage is not present on one particular lead, the fault will be in that lead, or in the distributor cap. If HT is present on all leads, the fault will be in the spark plugs; check and renew them if there is any doubt about their condition.

14 If no HT voltage is present, check the HT coil; its secondary windings may be breaking down under load.

3 Ignition timing - dynamic checking and setting

1 To accurately set the dynamic ignition timing, a stroboscopic timing light will be required. The type that uses a clip-on inductive pick-up is preferable to the type that plugs in between the HT lead and the spark plug.

2 Check the contact breaker points gap, and adjust the idle speed to its correct setting; refer to Chapter 1 for details.

3 Run the engine until it reaches normal operating temperature, then switch it off. Connect the timing light to No 1 spark plug HT lead; note that No 1 cylinder is at the timing pulley end. Connect the light's power supply according to its manufacturer's instructions. Pull the vacuum advance hose off the port on the distributor body, and plug or clamp the end of it (see Section 7 for details).

4 Locate the timing inspection hole on the transmission bellhousing, and prise out the rubber bung. This will expose the edge of the flywheel. Using a wrench and socket, manually turn the engine over using the crankshaft pulley bolt, until the timing marks stamped onto the edge of the flywheel are visible. Find the mark which represents 8° BTDC (Before Top Dead Centre) and carefully highlight it, and the mark on the edge of the

3.4 Find the mark (arrowed) which represents 8° BTDC (Before Top Dead Centre) and carefully highlight it with typists' correction fluid

bellhousing, with typists' correction fluid **(see illustration)**.

HAYNES HINT *Turning the engine will be much easier if the spark plugs are removed first (see Chapter 1).*

5 Start the engine again, and allow it to idle. Aim the (now flashing) timing light at the inspection hole in the bellhousing. The stroboscopic effect will "freeze" the movement of the flywheel, and allow you to read the timing setting. The edge of the inspection hole has a pointer marked on it - if the ignition timing is set correctly, the 8° BTDC mark highlighted earlier should line up with the mark on the edge of the bellhousing. View from directly above the inspection hole to make an accurate reading.

6 If the timing is incorrect to the extent that none of the timing marks coincide with the bellhousing mark, the distributor may have been incorrectly fitted. Refer to Section 4.

7 The ignition timing may be adjusted by slackening the distributor clamp bolt (see Section 7 for details) and slowly rotating the distributor body until the timing marks coincide; anti-clockwise to advance the timing, and clockwise to retard it. When you are satisfied that the ignition timing is correct, tighten the distributor clamp bolt and check the setting once more, as tightening the bolt may disturb the setting.

8 Raise the engine speed, and check that as it rises, the ignition timing advances until it is no longer readable on the marked scale. This proves that the mechanical advance mechanism is at least operating - a calibration check would have to be performed by a dealer with appropriate equipment, and should only be contemplated if persistent engine speed-related timing problems are encountered.

9 If the timing does not change with engine speed, then remove the distributor and check the mechanical advance mechanism, as described in Section 7.

10 Reconnect the vacuum advance hose to the distributor, and check that a further increase in ignition advance can be seen as the engine speed is raised just above idle to about 2000 rpm.

11 If this does not occur, or the ignition timing appears erratic or unstable, remove and inspect the distributor, as described in Section 7.

4 Ignition timing - static checking and adjustment

1 This Section describes the method of achieving a safe, approximate ignition timing setting to enable the engine to be started if the distributor reassembly alignment marks have been lost. Following this, the dynamic ignition timing setting must be checked, using the method described in Section 3.

2 The first thing to do is set the engine to TDC on cylinder No 1 - refer to the description of this operation given in Chapter 2A. To be sure that No 1 cylinder is on the compression stroke (and not No 4), remove the No 1 spark plug, and hold your finger over the hole; pressure will be felt when the cylinder is on its compression stroke. Use the flywheel/bellhousing timing marks for final alignment, as described in Chapter 2A.

3 On the distributor cap, identify No 1 cylinder terminal. If necessary, trace the HT lead back from No 1 spark plug (nearest the front of the engine) to the distributor cap. Temporarily fit the cap, and scribe a mark on the distributor body, directly underneath the No 1 terminal. Remove the cap again, and put it to one side.

4 Refit the distributor to the drive case (if applicable), referring to Section 7 for guidance.

5 Using a wrench and socket, rotate the crankshaft slightly until the 8° BTDC mark on the flywheel is now lined up with the pointer

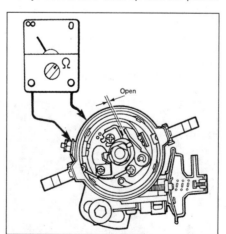

4.7 Using a multi-meter to determine when the contact breaker points are open

Meter shown is set to resistance function - points are open when meter reads infinity (open-circuit)

on the bellhousing - refer to Section 3 for details.

6 Connect a multi-meter, set to measure continuity, to the distributor body and the LT cable connection. The meter will be used to determine whether the contact breaker points are open or closed.

7 Turn the distributor body anti-clockwise, to allow the points to close, then slowly rotate it clockwise and watch the meter - the timing is set correctly when the meter reading indicates that the contact breaker points have *just* opened **(see illustration)**. At this point, tighten the distributor clamp bolt. Then, referring to Chapter 1, set the contact breaker points to the correct gap.

8 To test this setting, turn the engine through two complete crankshaft revolutions, and check that the contact breaker points open as the 8° BTDC mark passes the pointer on the bellhousing.

9 Fit the distributor cap, and press the retaining clips firmly into place. Working from No 1 terminal, connect the HT leads between the spark plugs and the distributor cap. Note that the firing order is 1-3-4-2, and that the rotor arm rotates clockwise inside the distributor. Finally, fit the HT "king" lead between the coil and the centre terminal on the distributor cap, and reconnect the wiring harness LT cable.

10 The engine now has an ignition timing setting that will allow it to be started. However, before it is brought back in to normal service, fine-tune the timing by carrying out a dynamic check; see Section 3.

5 Ignition coil - testing, removal and refitting

Testing

1 To test the coil under the correct conditions, the vehicle should be run until it reaches its normal operating temperature. Stop the engine, and switch off the ignition. Disconnect the battery negative cable, positioning it away from the terminal.

2 To measure the resistance of the coil primary

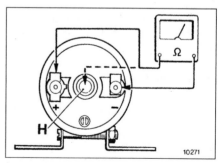

10271

5.2 Using a multi-meter to measure the resistance of the coil primary and (dotted line) secondary windings

H King lead HT terminal

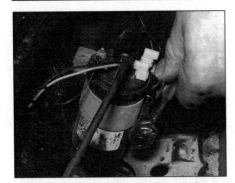

5.6 Removing the two coil mounting bracket screws (windscreen washer reservoir bottle removed for clarity)

windings, pull off the positive and negative LT connectors, and apply the probes of a multimeter, set to the resistance measurement function, across the terminals on the coil. Compare the measurement with that listed in the Specifications. Measure the coil secondary windings in the same manner, this time applying the meter probes to the HT king lead (centre) terminal and the negative LT terminal **(see illustration)**. Compare the measurement with that listed in the Specifications.

3 If either of the readings are out of tolerance, the coil should be renewed. **Note:** *If the readings are only just outside the acceptable limits, it may be due to the coil not being at the correct temperature; seek the advice of your dealer before condemning the coil.*

Removal

4 Disconnect the battery negative cable.

5 Unplug all HT and LT cables from the coil - label them if necessary, to assist refitting.

6 Remove the two screws that secure the coil mounting bracket to the bodywork, and lift out the coil **(see illustration)**.

Refitting

7 Ensure that the mounting bracket is securely fastened around the coil body by tightening the clamp bolt.

8 The coil makes an electrical earth through its bracket and the vehicle bodywork, so make sure that all traces of corrosion and dirt are removed from the mounting holes and screws.

9 Refit and tighten the mounting screws, then reconnect the LT and HT cables to the coil terminals.

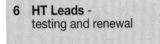

6 HT Leads -
testing and renewal

1 The HT leads are highly insulated, to enable them to carry HT voltages of tens of thousands of volts. This insulation can break down if the leads are damaged, or are allowed to get dirty and trap moisture. Tracking (unintentional earthing) can then occur - the HT voltage conducts through the water in the

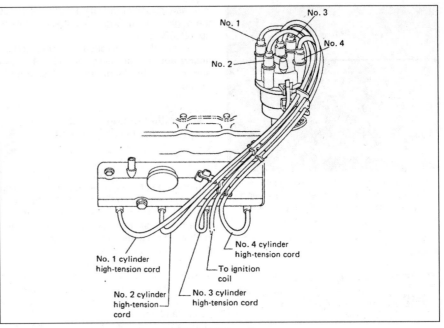

6.4 HT lead fitting diagram

dirt on the outside of the cable, and earths through the engine or bodywork, instead of reaching the spark plugs. The result is at best, a misfire, and at worst, an engine that will not start.

2 Inspect the cables for signs of damage or wear, in the form of splits, cracks, abrasion or melting from contact with hot components. Wipe the leads clean with a non-conductive cleaning solution, and allow them to dry thoroughly. Examine the connector contacts at either end, and remove any traces of corrosion - this will appear as white, powdery deposits on the surface of the metal. Be careful not to pit or score the contacts, as this will encourage new corrosion to form more readily.

3 The leads can be tested electrically, if access to a generative-type resistance meter is available - a normal multi-meter will not be adequate. Measure the resistance of each lead by connecting a probe to each end, and divide this figure by the length of the lead -

this will give the resistance per unit length. Compare the figure with the Chapter 1 Specifications, and renew the leads if they are out of tolerance.

4 If the leads are to be renewed, remove them one at a time, fitting the new lead as the old one is removed. This will preserve the correct firing order **(see illustration)**.

7 Distributor -
removal, inspection and refitting

Removal

1 Disconnect the battery negative cable, and position it away from the terminal.

2 Set the engine to 8° BTDC on cylinder No 1, referring to Section 3 and/or Chapter 2A for guidance.

3 Disconnect the LT cable from the distributor. Pull off the vacuum advance hose, and plug or clamp the end of it **(see illustrations)**.

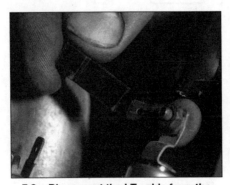

7.3a Disconnect the LT cable from the distributor

7.3b Pull the vacuum advance hose off the port on the distributor body, and plug or clamp the end of it

7.4 Recover the distributor cap rubber seal

7.5a Slacken and remove the clamp bolt (arrowed) . . .

7.5b . . . and withdraw the distributor body

4 Unclip the distributor cap retaining clips, lift off the cap and put it to one side, with the HT cables still attached. Recover the rubber seal **(see illustration)**.

5 Mark the relationship between the distributor and the drive gear case flange by scribing arrows on each. Then slacken and remove the clamp bolt, and withdraw the distributor body **(see illustrations)**.

Inspection

6 Recover the O-ring seal from the bottom of the distributor, and discard it; a new one must be fitted on reassembly.

7 Inspect the distributor cap rubber seal for signs of deterioration - renew it if necessary.

8 Refer to Section 8 for details of condenser inspection and renewal. Refer to Chapter 1 for details of contact breaker points inspection, renewal and adjustment.

Centrifugal (mechanical) advance mechanism

9 Grasp the drive gear at the bottom of the distributor with one hand. With the other, turn the rotor arm clockwise as far as it will travel; check that the movement is smooth, and free from binding. Release the rotor arm, and check that it springs back anti-clockwise to its rest position, without sticking **(see illustration)**.

Vacuum advance mechanism

10 Connect a hand vacuum pump to the vacuum advance diaphragm port, and apply a vacuum of about 400 mmHg whilst watching the baseplate **(see illustration)**. As the vacuum is applied, the baseplate should rotate with respect to the distributor body, freely and without resistance.

11 Release the applied vacuum, and check that the plate returns to its rest position without sticking.

Drive gear mechanism

12 Inspect the teeth of the distributor drive gear for signs of wear or damage. Any slack in the distributor drive train will affect ignition timing and engine efficiency. Renew the distributor if the teeth of the drive gear appear worn or chipped.

Refitting

13 Fit a new O-ring seal to the bottom of the distributor.

14 Pour about 60 cc of clean engine oil into the drive gear case, then install the distributor and loosely fit the clamp bolt; it may be necessary to rotate the shaft slightly, to allow it to engage with the camshaft drive gear. Rotate the distributor body such that the alignment marks made during removal line up.

If the alignment marks have been lost, line up the pointer cast into the distributor mounting flange **(see illustration)** with the centre of the clamp bolt shaft - this will give an approximate setting. The shaft is engaged at the correct angle if the rotor arm is pointing directly at the No 1 HT terminal mark, scribed on the distributor body earlier. It may take a few attempts to get this right, as the helical drive gears make the alignment difficult to judge. Do not tighten the distributor clamp bolt fully at this point.

15 Refer to Section 4 for details of setting the static timing.

16 Refit the distributor cap, and press the retaining clips firmly into place. Working from the No 1 terminal, connect the HT leads between the spark plugs and the distributor cap. Note that the firing order is 1-3-4-2, and that the rotor arm rotates clockwise inside the distributor. Finally, fit the HT king lead between the coil and the centre terminal on the distributor cap, and reconnect the wiring harness LT cable. Push the vacuum advance hose firmly onto the diaphragm assembly port.

16 Using the information given in Section 3, check and if necessary adjust the dynamic timing with a strobe light.

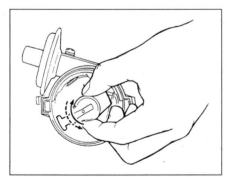

7.9 Turn the rotor arm clockwise, and check that it springs back anti-clockwise to its rest position, without resistance

7.10 Using a vacuum hand pump to check the operation of the vacuum advance mechanism

7.14 Line up the pointer (arrowed), cast into the distributor mounting flange, with the centre of the distributor clamp bolt, if no other marks are available

8 Condenser - testing and renewal

1 Disconnect the battery negative cable, and position it away from the terminal.

2 Unscrew the condenser from the distributor body and LT terminal. Momentarily touch the end of the fly lead onto the metal case of the condenser - this will cancel any residual capacitance.

3 Connect a multi-meter, set to the resistance measurement function, to the condenser, with one probe on the metal case and one on the end terminal.

4 As the probes are connected, the meter should briefly rise to a low resistance reading, then fall back to an open-circuit reading. If the meter has a capacitance measurement facility, the condenser should read 0.25 microfarads **(see illustration)**.

5 If the readings differ from those expected, renew the condenser.

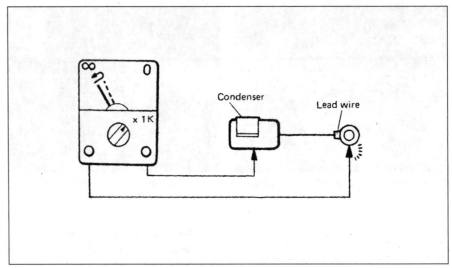

8.4 As the probes are connected, the meter should briefly rise to a low resistance reading, then fall back to an open-circuit reading

Chapter 6 Emissions control systems

Contents

Degrees of difficulty

Easy, suitable for novice with little experience	Fairly easy, suitable for beginner with some experience	Fairly difficult, suitable for competent DIY mechanic	Difficult, suitable for experienced DIY mechanic	Very difficult, suitable for expert DIY or professional

1 General information

All models have the ability to use unleaded petrol, and have various features built into the fuel system to help minimise harmful emissions. All models have a crankcase emissions control system and a fuel cut system.

Certain non-UK models from late 1992 are equipped with a throttle positioner system, deceleration mixture control system, evaporative emissions control system, and computer-controlled emissions control system, together with a 3-way catalytic converter **(see illustration)**. On these models, an oxygen sensor in the exhaust system provides the system engine control module (ECM) with constant feedback on the oxygen content of the exhaust gases. This enables

the ECM to adjust the mixture, to provide the best possible conditions for the converter to operate. The sensor has a special element which sends a varying voltage to the ECM depending on the amount of oxygen in the exhaust gases; if the air/fuel mixture is too rich, the exhaust gases are low in oxygen, and the sensor sends a high-voltage signal. The voltage decreases as the mixture weakens and the amount of oxygen in the exhaust gases rises. Peak conversion efficiency of all

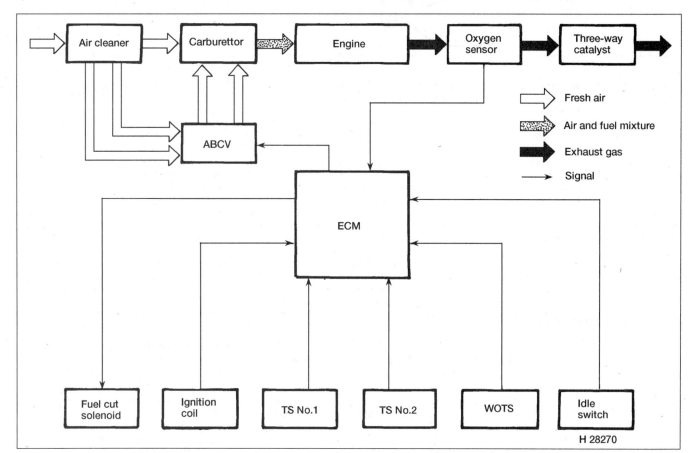

1.2 Computer-controlled emissions control system fitted to certain non-UK models

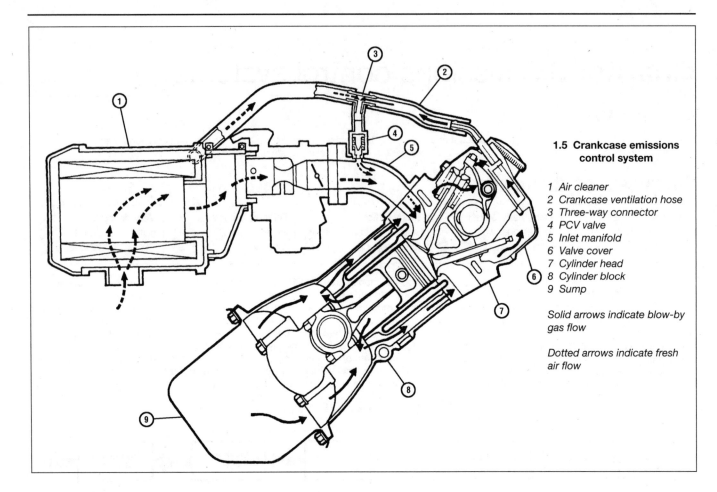

1.5 Crankcase emissions control system

1 Air cleaner
2 Crankcase ventilation hose
3 Three-way connector
4 PCV valve
5 Inlet manifold
6 Valve cover
7 Cylinder head
8 Cylinder block
9 Sump

Solid arrows indicate blow-by gas flow

Dotted arrows indicate fresh air flow

major pollutants occurs if the intake air/fuel mixture is maintained at the chemically-correct ratio for the complete combustion of petrol - 14.7 parts (by weight) of air to 1 part of fuel (the "stoichiometric" ratio). The sensor output voltage alters in a large step at this point, the ECM using the signal change as a reference point, and correcting the intake air/fuel mixture accordingly.

At the time of writing, it is thought that catalytic converters are to be introduced on Suzuki UK models in late 1994 or early 1995, however there is no confirmation that these models will have the same emissions control components described above and later in this Section.

The emissions control systems function as follows.

Crankcase emissions control

To reduce the emissions of unburned hydrocarbons from the crankcase into the atmosphere, the engine is sealed, and the blow-by gases and oil vapour are drawn from inside the crankcase to the top of the engine. From here, they are drawn through an oil separator in the valve cover, and through a hose to the PCV (Positive Crankcase Ventilation) valve located on the inlet manifold. Air from the air cleaner is mixed with the gases before they are drawn through the PCV valve into the inlet manifold

and burned by the engine during normal combustion **(see illustration)**.

The PCV valve incorporates a valve and spring. When inlet manifold vacuum is low (ie the throttle valve is open) the PCV valve is wide open, and maximum scavenging of blow-by gases occurs. When the vacuum is high (ie the throttle valve is closed) the PCV valve closes, and scavenging of the gases ceases. The operation of the PCV valve is varied between the wide open and closed positions of the throttle valve in order to correspond to the amount of blow-by gases passing the pistons into the crankcase.

With a worn engine, the amount of blow-by gases may be excessive, and the PCV valve may not pass all of them to the inlet manifold. In this case, the excess gases will be passed to the air cleaner. Ultimately, this will affect the fuel mixture and cause the engine to misfire or run unevenly.

Throttle positioner system

The throttle positioner system incorporates a diaphragm actuator and spring, which controls the return of the throttle valve to the idle position. Without the positioner, an excessively rich mixture occurs when the throttle pedal is released quickly during deceleration (overrun), due to high vacuum in the inlet manifold. The positioner slows down

the return of the throttle valve, and thus reduces the amount of unburnt hydrocarbon produced during the deceleration phase.

The system incorporates a vacuum delay valve. Before starting the engine, a spring in the actuator keeps the throttle valve slightly open, to provide an increased initial engine speed. The spring does not act directly on the throttle valve, but moves the throttle positioner lever, which in turn moves the throttle valve. When the engine runs, vacuum is gradually applied through the delay valve, and the throttle valve is returned to its normal idle position. When the throttle valve is opened, vacuum to the delay valve decreases and the actuator spring moves the throttle positioner lever to its pre-start position. If the throttle valve is closed quickly at this time, it will be returned to the idle position slowly as described in the previous paragraph.

Deceleration mixture control system

The deceleration mixture control system introduces fresh air into the inlet manifold, in order to counteract the temporary rich mixture which occurs during rapid deceleration, and during periods when the throttle valve is closed. The system is operated by a mixture control valve (MCV).

During rapid deceleration when the throttle

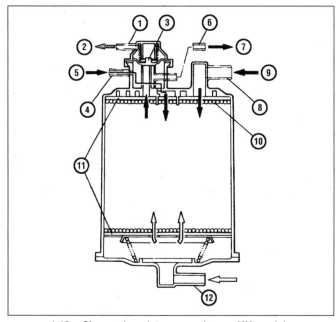

1.13a Charcoal canister on early non-UK models

1 Purge control nozzle	7 To inlet manifold
2 To carburettor	8 Float chamber nozzle
3 Purge control valve	9 From float chamber
4 Tank nozzle	10 Carbon charcoal
5 Front fuel tank	11 Filter
6 Purge nozzle	12 Air inlet nozzle

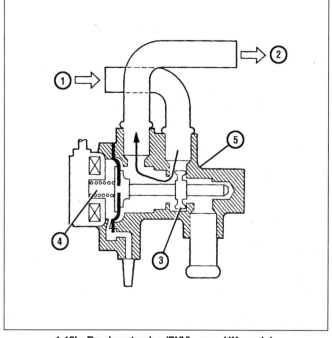

1.13b Bowl vent valve (BVV) - non-UK models

1 Fuel vapour from float chamber	4 Spring
2 Fuel vapour to canister	5 Valve casing
3 Valve	

valve is closed, there is a noticeable difference in vacuum between the inlet manifold area near the carburettor throttle valve and the inlet manifold area near the cylinder head. The MCV valve senses the two vacuum levels, and introduces fresh air through its internal air filter. When deceleration ceases, the vacuum levels equalise, and the MCV valve closes.

Evaporative emissions control system

The evaporative emissions control system minimises the escape into the atmosphere of unburned hydrocarbons from the fuel tank. The fuel tank filler cap is sealed, and a charcoal canister collects the petrol vapours generated in the tank when the vehicle is parked. It stores them until the engine is started, and they are cleared from the canister and burned by the engine during normal combustion.

On certain early models, petrol vapours from the carburettor float chamber are also channelled to the charcoal canister when the engine is stopped, using a bowl vent valve (BVV) **(see illustrations)**. With the engine stopped, an internal spring moves the valve to open the channel from the carburettor float chamber to the charcoal canister, but when the engine is started, initially inlet manifold vacuum is used to move the valve, so that the float chamber is vented to the air cleaner.

After the initial movement, the valve is held in this position by a solenoid as long as the engine is running (as long as the ignition is switched on).

On later models, the system is controlled by a bi-metal vacuum switching valve (BVSV). When the engine reaches the predetermined temperature, the BVSV opens the purge control valve on the canister, and the fuel vapour is discharged into the inlet manifold, together with fresh air.

Computer-controlled emissions control system

The computer-controlled emissions control system consists of an engine control module (ECM), oxygen sensor, idle switch, air bleed control valve (ABCV), wide open throttle switch (WOTS), and two thermal switches. The ECM varies the air/fuel mixture ratio by way of the ABCV valve at all times, except when the engine is cold, the throttle valve is fully open, or during deceleration. Under each of the three latter conditions, the ECM applies a pre-programmed air/fuel ratio.

The ECM receives input signals from the oxygen sensor, the wide open throttle switch, the idle switch, the ignition coil (engine speed), and the thermal switches (engine temperature). After processing the signals, the ECM controls the ABCV valve, to vary the amount of air in the main and slow circuits of the carburettor. The air-fuel mixture is therefore controlled within the most efficient

parameters, and the three-way catalytic converter is able to function correctly.

The computer-controlled emissions control system also incorporates a fuel cut system, which is activated with the ignition switched on if the engine stops, or during deceleration if the idle switch, neutral switch, clutch switch and engine speed sensor are in "off" mode at the same time. If the system is activated while the engine is running, this helps to improve fuel economy, and to prevent misfiring which would damage the catalytic converter. The system is also activated when the ignition is switched off. "Off" modes occur at the idle switch when the throttle valve is open by more than 5°, at the neutral switch when the transmission is not in neutral, at the clutch switch when the clutch is engaged and the pedal released, and at the engine speed sensor when the engine speed is between 2700 rpm and 2900 rpm.

The catalytic converter is fitted in a central position in the exhaust system, at the front of the tailpipe and silencer section, behind the front section of the exhaust system which goes from twin-bore to single-bore.

General information

Although some of the systems described in this Chapter are not fitted to UK models, some of the individual components (such as the BVSV valve for the choke opener) *are* fitted, and the information and tests for these items may be used.

2 Emissions control systems - testing and component renewal

Crankcase emissions control

Testing

1 Should the engine not idle correctly, the crankcase emissions control hoses and PCV valve may be blocked with sludge, or the hoses may be perished. Disconnect the hoses and clean them out thoroughly.

2 Check the PCV valve for blockage by disconnecting the three-way connector, then starting the engine. With the engine idling, place a finger over the end of the hose leading to the PCV valve - it should be possible to feel vacuum, however if this is not the case, the PCV valve should be removed and cleaned or renewed.

3 The PCV valve can be checked while removed by attempting to blow through it from the inlet manifold side. If this is possible, the valve is not seating correctly, and should be renewed. Conversely, it *should* be possible to blow through the valve from the outside, although resistance will be felt, from the internal spring holding the valve shut.

Renewal

4 Disconnect the hoses from the three-way connector, and from the PCV valve.

5 Unscrew the PCV valve from the inlet manifold.

6 Apply suitable sealant or sealing tape to the threads of the new valve, then screw it into the inlet manifold and tighten securely.

Throttle positioner

Testing

Note: *The ignition timing must be correctly set before carrying out the following test (see Chapter 5B).*

7 Run the engine until the temperature gauge needle registers between a quarter and half on the scale.

8 With the engine stopped, disconnect the wiring for the wide open throttle switch (WOTS).

9 Disconnect the hose between the throttle positioner diaphragm unit and the delay valve, then plug the vacant apertures with suitable caps.

10 Connect a tachometer to the engine, then start the engine without depressing the accelerator pedal, and check that the engine speed is between 1800 and 3000 rpm. If not, check the hose between the delay valve and the carburettor for cracks and deterioration.

11 A vacuum pump is required for further checks. Connect the pump to the throttle positioner actuator, and apply a vacuum of 400 mmHg. The diaphragm rod should move smoothly, and be held without any loss of vacuum - if not, the positioner actuator should be renewed.

12 Disconnect and remove the delay valve. Close the dark blue side of the valve with a finger, then apply 500 mmHg to the white side with the vacuum pump. When the finger is removed, the vacuum should die away gradually - if not, renew the delay valve.

Renewal

13 Disconnect the hose from the throttle positioner actuator, then unscrew the mounting screws and remove the unit from the carburettor.

14 Fit the new unit using a reversal of the removal procedure.

Mixture control valve

Testing

15 Check that the hoses from the mixture control valve to the inlet manifold are in good condition, clean and secure. Renew the hoses as necessary.

16 Start the engine and run to normal operating temperature, then allow to idle.

17 Have a piece of paper ready to cover the bottom air inlet of the MCV valve.

18 Disconnect the small vacuum hose from the MCV valve, then with the engine still idling, bring the piece of paper close to the air inlet on the bottom of the valve. The paper should not be drawn against the valve, since the valve should be shut. Note that the engine will not idle evenly while the vacuum hose is disconnected.

19 Reconnect the hose to the valve, and check that the paper is now drawn against the air inlet, proving that the valve is now open.

20 If the valve does not function as described, it should be renewed.

Renewal

21 Disconnect the two hoses from the MCV, then detach it from its mounting.

22 Fit the new unit using a reversal of the removal procedure.

Evaporative emissions control

Testing

23 Check that all hoses connected to the charcoal canister, bowl vent valve (BVV) or bi-metal vacuum switching valve (BVSV) and inlet manifold are in good condition and secure. Also check that the hoses between the two-way check valve, liquid vapour separator and fuel tank are in good condition and secure.

24 Identify the hoses connected to the charcoal canister, then disconnect them and remove the canister from the mounting bracket. Blow into the nozzle on the bottom of the unit, and check that air comes out of the tank nozzle (or float chamber vent nozzle on early models) on the top. Now blow into the purge nozzle (ie the nozzle connected directly to the inlet manifold) and check that no air comes out of any of the remaining nozzles. If available, use a vacuum pump to apply a vacuum of 80 mmHg to the purge control nozzle, then blow again into the purge nozzle

and check that air comes out of the tank nozzle and the nozzle on the bottom of the unit. If the charcoal canister does not function as described it should be renewed.

25 To check the bi-metal vacuum switching valve (BVSV), ideally it should be removed and checked for operation in a container of water. Check that it is not possible to blow through the valve with it at a temperature lower than 40° C, but check that **it is** possible to blow through it at a temperature higher than 50° C.

26 To test the two-way check valve, remove it and check that it is possible to blow hard through it from the black side (ie tank side). From the orange side, it should only be possible to blow through the valve softly.

27 To check the bowl vent valve (BVV), disconnect the hoses, and blow through the float chamber nozzle - air should only come out of the canister nozzle. Now apply vacuum to the control nozzle and blow through the float chamber nozzle again - check that air only comes out of the air cleaner nozzle.

Charcoal canister - renewal

28 Identify the hoses connected to the charcoal canister, then disconnect them and remove the canister from the mounting bracket.

29 Fit the new canister using a reversal of the removal procedure.

Bi-metal vacuum switching valve - renewal

30 Drain the cooling system with reference to Chapter 1.

31 Disconnect the hoses, then unscrew the valve from the inlet manifold.

32 Apply suitable sealant to the threads of the new valve, then screw it into the inlet manifold and tighten securely.

33 Reconnect the hoses, and refill the cooling system with reference to Chapter 1.

Two-way check valve - renewal

34 Disconnect the hoses from the check valve, and remove it from the tank-to-charcoal canister line.

35 When refitting the valve, make sure that the orange side is facing towards the charcoal canister.

Computer-controlled emissions control system

Testing

Note: *Only use a low-resistance analogue voltmeter for the following tests.*

36 Before making an in-depth test, check all hoses for cracking and deterioration, and renew as necessary.

37 Check that battery voltage is available at terminal 6 on the ECM.

38 Check that the wire to terminal 9 is earthed correctly. If not, check the earthing cable on the cylinder head, and remake the earth if necessary.

39 The engine control module (ECM) has a self-diagnosis function, which can be accessed by using a low-resistance analogue voltmeter. The diagnosis connector is located under the facia, and the voltmeter is connected as follows. Connect the positive probe of the voltmeter to the pink wire terminal on the connector, and the negative probe of the voltmeter to the black wire terminal on the connector.

40 The engine should be at normal operating temperature, and the battery must be in good condition. Run the engine at 2000 rpm for approximately 30 seconds, then allow the engine to idle, and note the coded pulses on the voltmeter needle. The module will output the two-digit code every 3 seconds, and there will be a 1 second gap between the digits. There are four possible codes, as shown in the following table. Note that code "44" may occur before the accelerator pedal is depressed, but this is normal.

Code	Fault area	Action
12	Normal	None required
13	Oxygen sensor and circuit	Check oxygen sensor
44	Idle switch and circuit	Check idle switch
54	ABCV and circuit	Check ABCV

Oxygen sensor

Testing

41 Check that the wiring between the oxygen sensor and ECM is intact and connected correctly. If checking the wiring for continuity, the wire must be disconnected from the ECM and oxygen sensor. **Note:** *Do not connect on ohmmeter to the oxygen sensor, as it will be damaged.* Renew the sensor if the wiring is proved good but the code 13 still occurs.

Renewal

42 Wait until the engine is cold, then apply the handbrake, jack up the front of the vehicle and support on axle stands (see *"Jacking, towing and wheel changing"*).

43 Disconnect the wiring, then unscrew the oxygen sensor from the exhaust manifold.

44 Apply a little anti-seize compound to the threads of the new sensor, then screw it into the exhaust manifold and tighten securely.

Idle switch

Testing

45 Check that the wiring between the idle switch and ECM is intact and connected correctly. If checking the wiring for continuity, the wire must be disconnected from the ECM and idle switch.

46 Check the operation of the switch by disconnecting the wiring at the connector (front right side panel) then connecting an ohmmeter to the switch wire and the earthing point on the carburettor. With the accelerator pedal released, the switch contacts should be closed, and the resistance reading should be less than 50 ohms. With the pedal depressed

about halfway, the switch contacts should be open, and the resistance reading should be infinity.

47 If an infinity reading is obtained with the accelerator pedal released, the switch is either faulty or in need of adjustment. To adjust the switch, first remove the carburettor (Chapter 4), then with the ohmmeter connected as for the previous test, open the throttle plate until a 0.3 mm feeler blade can be inserted between the throttle plate and the wall of the carburettor. Turn the switch adjusting screw until the switch contacts just open and the resistance value moves to infinity.

48 On completion, refit the carburettor with reference to Chapter 4.

Renewal

49 Remove the carburettor as described in Chapter 4, then unscrew the switch mounting screws and remove the switch from the carburettor.

50 Fit the new switch using a reversal of the removal procedure, and tighten the mounting screws securely. On completion, adjust the switch as described in paragraph 47.

Air bleed control valve (ABCV)

Testing

51 Check that the wiring between the valve and the ECM is intact and connected correctly. If checking the wiring for continuity, the wire must be disconnected from the ECM and ABCV. Also check the hoses for cracking and deterioration.

52 To check the valve internal circuits, disconnect the wiring at the connector, and connect an ohmmeter between the red wire terminal and each of the other terminals (blue, white, green and yellow wire terminals). The resistance should be 95 ohms in each case. If this is not the case, the valve should be renewed.

Renewal

53 Identify each hose position on the valve, then disconnect the hoses.

54 Disconnect the wiring at the connector, then detach the valve unit and remove.

55 Fit the new valve using a reversal of the removal procedure.

Wide open throttle switch (WOTS)

Testing

56 Check that the wiring between the wide open throttle switch and ECM is intact and connected correctly. If checking the wiring for continuity, the wire must be disconnected from the ECM and wide open throttle switch.

57 Check the operation of the switch by disconnecting the wiring at the connector (front right side panel) then connecting an ohmmeter to the switch wire and the earthing point on the carburettor. With the accelerator pedal released, the switch contacts should be closed, and the resistance reading should be

less than 50 ohms. With the pedal fully depressed, the switch contacts should be open, and the resistance reading should be infinity.

58 If a reading of less than 50 ohms is obtained with the accelerator pedal fully depressed, the switch is either faulty or in need of adjustment. To adjust the switch, first remove the carburettor (Chapter 4), then with the ohmmeter connected as in paragraph 57, open the throttle plate until the distance between the throttle plate and the wall of the carburettor is approximately 9.0 mm. Turn the switch adjusting screw until the switch contacts just open and the resistance value moves to infinity.

59 On completion, refit the carburettor with reference to Chapter 4.

Renewal

60 Remove the carburettor as described in Chapter 4, then unscrew the switch mounting screws and remove the switch from the carburettor.

61 Fit the new switch using a reversal of the removal procedure. On completion, adjust the switch as described in paragraph 58.

Thermal switches

Testing

62 For an accurate test, the thermal switch must be removed and suspended in heated water. However, if the approximate temperature of the coolant in the engine is known, the following test can be carried out.

63 There are two thermal switches located on the inlet manifold next to the BVSV valve. The one furthest from the BVSV valve is No 1 switch (coloured yellow and green), and the one nearest the BVSV valve is No 2 switch (coloured red).

64 To test thermal switch No 1, disconnect the wiring, and connect an ohmmeter between the terminal and the switch body. If the coolant is below 13° C, the internal contacts should be closed and there should be continuity, but if the coolant is above 23° C, the internal contacts should be open and the reading should be infinity.

65 Connect the ohmmeter to thermal switch No 2 as in paragraph 64. If the coolant is below 53° C, the internal contacts should be closed and there should be continuity, but if the coolant is above 63° C, the internal contacts should be open and the reading should be infinity.

66 Renew the thermal switches if they do not function correctly.

Renewal

67 Drain the cooling system as described in Chapter 1.

68 Disconnect the wiring, then unscrew the thermal switch from the inlet manifold.

69 Apply a little sealant to the threads of the new switch, then fit it to the inlet manifold and tighten securely.

70 Reconnect the wiring, and refill the cooling system with reference to Chapter 1.

Fuel cut solenoid

Testing

71 Have an assistant switch the ignition on and off without starting the engine. The solenoid should make a clicking sound, proving its correct operation.

72 Disconnect the neutral and clutch switch wiring at the connectors, then run the engine to normal operating temperature.

73 Connect a tachometer to the engine, and run the engine at 3500 rpm. While holding the engine at this speed, use a screwdriver to move the idle switch rod into the switch housing - the solenoid is functioning correctly if the engine speed reduces while the rod is held into the switch.

74 On completion of the test, reconnect the neutral and clutch switch wiring.

75 Renew the solenoid if it does not function correctly.

Renewal

76 Disconnect the wiring, and unscrew the solenoid from the carburettor. Recover the sealing washer.

77 Insert the new solenoid together with a new sealing washer, and tighten securely. Reconnect the wiring.

Catalytic converter

Testing

78 The performance of the catalytic converter can be checked only by measuring the exhaust gases using a good-quality, carefully-calibrated exhaust gas analyser. An accurate result obtained with this method will depend on the condition and adjustment of the carburettor and the general condition of the engine.

Renewal

79 The catalytic converter is part of the exhaust system. Refer to Chapter 4 for guidance, as the same general principles will apply as for the rest of the exhaust system.

---

3 Catalytic converter - general information and precautions

1 The catalytic converter is a reliable and simple device which needs no maintenance in itself, but there are some facts of which an owner should be aware if the converter is to function properly for its full service life.

a) DO NOT use leaded petrol in a vehicle equipped with a catalytic converter - the lead will coat the precious metals, reducing their converting efficiency, and will eventually destroy the converter.

b) Always keep the ignition and fuel system well-maintained in accordance with the manufacturer's schedule (see Chapter 1).

c) If the engine develops a misfire, do not drive the vehicle at all (or at least as little as possible) until the fault is cured.

d) DO NOT push- or tow-start the vehicle - this will soak the catalytic converter in unburned fuel, causing it to overheat when the engine does start.

e) DO NOT switch off the ignition at high engine speeds - ie do not "blip" the throttle immediately before switching off.

f) DO NOT use fuel or engine oil additives - these may contain substances harmful to the catalytic converter.

g) DO NOT continue to use the vehicle if the engine burns oil to the extent of leaving a visible trail of blue smoke.

h) Remember that the catalytic converter operates at very high temperatures. DO NOT, therefore, park the vehicle in dry undergrowth, over long grass or piles of dead leaves after a long run.

i) Remember that the catalytic converter is FRAGILE - do not strike it with tools during servicing work.

j) In some cases a sulphurous smell (like that of rotten eggs) may be noticed from the exhaust. This is common to many catalytic converter-equipped vehicles. Once the vehicle has covered a few thousand miles, the problem should disappear. In the meantime, try changing the brand of petrol used.

k) The catalytic converter, used on a well-maintained and well-driven vehicle, should last for between 50 000 and 100 000 miles - if the converter is no longer effective, it must be renewed.

Chapter 7
Clutch, propeller shaft and rear axle

Contents

Degrees of difficulty

Easy, suitable for novice with little experience		Fairly easy, suitable for beginner with some experience		Fairly difficult, suitable for competent DIY mechanic		Difficult, suitable for experienced DIY mechanic		Very difficult, suitable for expert DIY or professional	

Specifications

Clutch

Type	Single dry plate with diaphragm spring. Cable-operated release mechanism
Pedal free travel	20 to 30 mm
Friction plate:	
Diameter	180 mm
Minimum depth of rivets below friction material	0.5 mm

Propeller shaft

Type	Single-piece tubular steel, with Hardy-Spicer universal joints front and rear

Rear axle

Type	Rigid, with hypoid bevel gear differential unit
Lubrication	See "Lubricants, fluids and capacities"

Torque wrench settings

	Nm	lbf ft
Clutch cover bolts	23	17
Clutch release arm bolt and nut	13	10
Clutch cable locknut	20	15
Brake/clutch pedal pivot bolt	23	17
Propeller shaft rear flange bolt	38	28
Differential unit-to-rear axle casing	23	17
Rear axle oil drain plug	6	4
Rear axle oil filler/level plug	4	3
Rear leaf spring U-bolt nuts	38	28

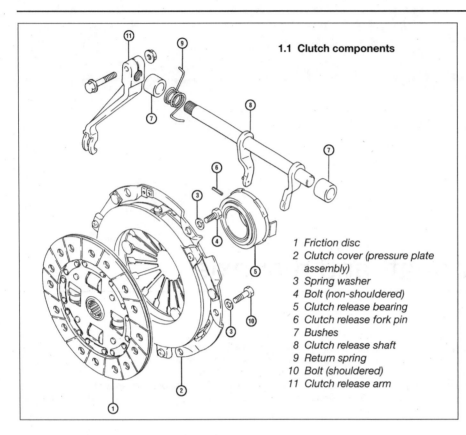

1.1 Clutch components

1 Friction disc
2 Clutch cover (pressure plate assembly)
3 Spring washer
4 Bolt (non-shouldered)
5 Clutch release bearing
6 Clutch release fork pin
7 Bushes
8 Clutch release shaft
9 Return spring
10 Bolt (shouldered)
11 Clutch release arm

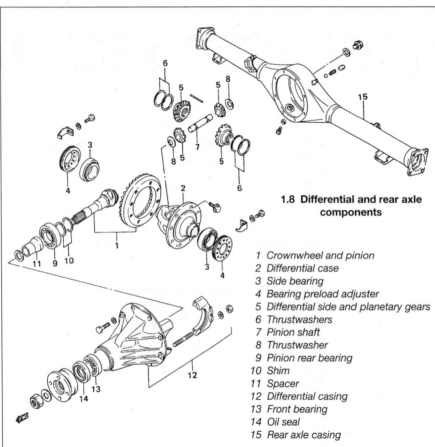

1.8 Differential and rear axle components

1 Crownwheel and pinion
2 Differential case
3 Side bearing
4 Bearing preload adjuster
5 Differential side and planetary gears
6 Thrustwashers
7 Pinion shaft
8 Thrustwasher
9 Pinion rear bearing
10 Shim
11 Spacer
12 Differential casing
13 Front bearing
14 Oil seal
15 Rear axle casing

1 General information

The clutch consists of a friction plate, a pressure plate (cover) assembly, a release bearing, and the release mechanism; all of these components are contained inside the transmission bellhousing, sandwiched between the engine and the transmission. The release mechanism is mechanical, being operated by a cable **(see illustration)**.

The friction plate is fitted between the engine flywheel and the clutch pressure plate, and is allowed to slide on the transmission input shaft splines. It consists of two circular facings of friction material riveted in position to provide the clutch bearing surface, and a spring-cushioned hub to damp out transmission shocks.

The pressure plate (cover) assembly is bolted to the engine flywheel, and is located by shouldered bolts. When the engine is running, drive is transmitted from the crankshaft via the flywheel to the friction plate (these components being clamped securely together by the pressure plate assembly) and from the friction plate to the transmission input shaft.

The clutch is disengaged by a sealed release bearing fitted concentrically around the transmission input shaft; when the driver depresses the clutch pedal, the release bearing is pressed against the fingers at the centre of the diaphragm spring. Since the spring is held by rivets between two annular fulcrum rings, the pressure at its centre causes it to deform, so that it releases the clamping force from the pressure plate.

Depressing the clutch pedal pulls the control cable, and this in turn pulls the release lever and fork. The release fork forces the release bearing against the fingers on the diaphragm spring.

As the friction plate facings wear, the pressure plate moves towards the flywheel; this causes the diaphragm spring fingers to push against the release bearing, thus changing the position of the clutch pedal. To ensure correct operation, the clutch cable must be regularly adjusted.

Drive is taken from the rear of the transmission to the rear axle by a single-piece propeller shaft having a Hardy-Spicer universal joint at its front and rear ends. The propeller shaft is of tubular form, and is balanced.

The differential unit is of hypoid bevel gear type. Drive from the differential pinion is transmitted to the crownwheel, and then through side gears to the axle shafts and rear wheels **(see illustration)**. The purpose of the differential unit is to allow the rear wheels to rotate at different speeds while the vehicle is cornering, and at the same time be driven from the propeller shaft.

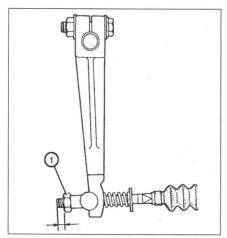

2.5 After adjustment, the length of the visible thread on the end of the clutch cable must be between 1.0 mm and 5.0 mm

1 Adjustment nut

2 Clutch - adjustment

1 The clutch adjustment is made by measuring the clutch pedal free travel, and adjusting it as required.

2 Using a ruler for this check might prove awkward - as an alternative, mark the positions of the clutch pedal on a strip of wood, then measure the distance between them. First make a mark on the wood corresponding to the rest position of the pedal. Now depress the pedal until resistance is just felt, and make another mark on the wood. The distance between the two marks represents the clutch pedal free travel. If this is not as given in the Specifications at the start of this Chapter, adjust the clutch as follows.

3 Locate the adjustment nut on the release lever, on the right-hand side of the transmission. For improved access, first apply the handbrake, then jack up the front of the vehicle and support on axle stands (see *"Jacking, towing and wheel changing"*).

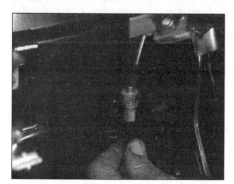

3.4 Removing the outer cable from the pedal bracket

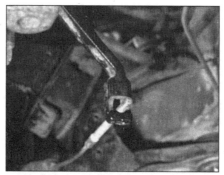

3.2 Clutch cable attachment to release arm

4 Turn the adjustment nut as necessary until the clutch pedal free travel is correct. There is no locknut provided, as the adjustment nut is held in position by the tension spring and the curved section of the nut on the pivot pin.

5 After making the adjustment, check that the length of the visible thread on the end of the cable (ie between the end of the cable and the adjustment nut) is between 1.0 mm and 5.0 mm **(see illustration)**.

3 Clutch cable - removal and refitting

Removal

1 Apply the handbrake, then jack up the front of the vehicle and support on axle stands (see *"Jacking, towing and wheel changing"*).

2 Working under the vehicle, note the position of the clutch cable adjustment nut in relation to the end of the cable, then unscrew the nut and remove the pivot pin. Remove the washer, spring and final washer from the end of the cable, and disconnect the cable from the release arm **(see illustration)**.

3 Inside the vehicle, reach up behind the clutch pedal, and disconnect the inner cable from the top hooked end of the pedal **(see illustration)**.

4 Unscrew the nut securing the outer cable to the clutch pedal bracket, and move the cable sideways from the slot in the bracket **(see**

3.5 Clutch cable attachment to right-hand engine mounting bracket

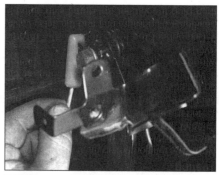

3.3 Disconnecting the inner cable from the clutch pedal

illustration). Release the cable from the support clip.

5 Loosen the locknuts and disconnect the clutch outer cable from the right-hand engine mounting bracket **(see illustration)**, then withdraw the cable down through the floor, at the same time prising out the rubber grommet. Release the cable from the support clips, noting its routing, and withdraw it from under the vehicle.

6 Examine the cable, looking for worn end fittings or a damaged outer casing, and for signs of fraying of the inner wire. Check the cable's operation - the inner wire should move smoothly and easily through the outer casing. Remember, however, that a cable that appears serviceable when tested off the vehicle may well be much heavier in operation, when compressed into its working position. Renew the cable if it shows any signs of excessive wear or damage.

Refitting

7 Apply a thin smear of multi-purpose grease to the cable end fittings and exposed inner cable, then pass the cable through the floor, and refit the rubber grommet. Clip the cable into position, making sure that it is routed as noted during removal.

8 Locate the cable in the bracket, and tighten the nut.

9 Locate the inner cable end fitting on the hooked end of the clutch pedal.

10 Fit the washer and tension spring on the end of the inner cable, then locate the cable on the release arm, and refit the pivot pin and adjustment nut.

11 Adjust the clutch pedal free travel as described in Section 2.

12 Lower the vehicle to the ground.

4 Clutch pedal - removal and refitting

Removal

1 Remove the facia panel as described in Chapter 11.

2 Loosen the clip, and disconnect the vacuum servo hose from the servo unit.

4.10 Pedal pivot shaft and return spring locations

5.4a Removing the clutch cover . . .

5.4b . . . and friction plate

3 Disconnect the clutch cable from the clutch pedal and bracket with reference to Section 3.
4 Disconnect the wiring from the stop-light switch on the pedal bracket.
5 Remove the fusebox cover, then unbolt the fusebox from the pedal bracket.
6 Unscrew the mounting nuts securing the master cylinder to the rear of the vacuum servo unit. Also unscrew the master cylinder upper mounting bolt at the small bracket on the servo unit.
7 Withdraw the master cylinder away from the servo unit, bending the brake lines only a minimum amount.
8 Unscrew the lower mounting bolt, and withdraw the pedal bracket together with the vacuum servo unit, leaving the master cylinder suspended by the brake lines.
9 Unscrew the nut from the right-hand end of the pedal pivot bolt.
10 Note the location of the pedal return springs (see illustration), then withdraw the pivot bolt to the left-hand side of the bracket until the brake pedal can be removed. If necessary, remove the pedal return spring.
11 Withdraw the pivot bolt further, and remove the spacer, return spring, clutch pedal and final spacer. Note the positions of the spacers, as they are of different lengths.
12 Withdraw the pivot bolt completely from the bracket, and recover the washer.
13 Carefully clean all components, renewing any that are worn or damaged; check the bearing surfaces of the pivot bushes and bolt with particular care. It is not possible to renew the bushes, and if they are excessively worn, the pedals must be renewed.

Refitting

14 Lubricate the clutch and brake pedal bores with a little grease, then refit the components using a reversal of the removal procedure. Make sure that the pedal return springs are correctly located.
15 Refit and tighten the pivot bolt nut to the specified torque.
16 Check that the wiring harness near the pedal bracket position is located correctly, so that it will not obstruct the refitting procedure. Locate the pedal bracket on the bulkhead.

Check again that the wiring is not trapped beneath the bracket. Refit and tighten the lower mounting bolt.
17 Locate the master cylinder on the rear of the vacuum servo unit, and tighten the mounting nuts and bolt to the specified torque.
18 Refit the fusebox, and tighten the mounting bolt.
19 Reconnect the wiring to the stop-light switch on the pedal bracket.
20 Reconnect the clutch cable to the clutch pedal, and adjust the clutch cable with reference to Section 2.
21 Reconnect the vacuum servo hose to the servo unit, and tighten the clip.
22 Refit the facia panel with reference to Chapter 11.

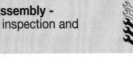

5 Clutch assembly - removal, inspection and refitting

⚠️ **Warning: Dust created by clutch wear and deposited on the clutch components may contain asbestos, which is a health hazard. DO NOT blow it out with compressed air, or inhale any of it. DO NOT use petrol or petroleum-based solvents to clean off the dust. Brake system cleaner or methylated spirit should be used to flush the dust into a suitable receptacle. After the clutch components are wiped clean with rags, dispose of the contaminated rags and cleaner in a sealed, marked container. Although some friction materials may no longer contain asbestos, it is safest to assume that they DO, and to take precautions accordingly.**

Removal

1 Unless the engine/transmission is to be removed from the vehicle and separated for major overhaul (Chapter 2B), the clutch can be reached by removing the transmission alone, as described in Chapter 8.
2 Before disturbing the clutch, use chalk or a marker pen to mark the relationship of the

pressure plate/cover assembly to the flywheel.
3 Working in a diagonal sequence, slacken the cover bolts by half a turn at a time, until the spring pressure is released and the bolts can be unscrewed by hand. Leave two opposite bolts loosely in position, to hold the cover on the flywheel. Note that two of the bolts are shouldered, in order to positively locate the cover.
4 Remove the final two bolts, and collect the cover and friction plate, noting which way round the friction plate is fitted (see illustrations).

Inspection

Note: *Due to the amount of work necessary to gain access to the clutch components, it is usually considered good practice to renew the clutch friction plate, pressure plate assembly and release bearing as a matched set, even if only one of these is actually worn enough to require renewal. The input shaft spigot bearing in the flywheel should also be examined and renewed if necessary.*

5 When cleaning clutch components, read first the warning at the beginning of this Section; remove any dust using a clean, dry cloth, and working in a well-ventilated atmosphere.
6 Check the friction plate facings for signs of wear, damage or oil contamination. If the friction material is cracked, burnt, scored or damaged, or if it is contaminated with oil or grease (shown by shiny black patches), the friction plate must be renewed.
7 If the friction material is still serviceable, check that the centre boss splines are unworn, that the torsion springs are in good condition and securely fastened, and that all the rivets are tightly fastened. Using vernier calipers if possible (a tyre tread depth gauge may suffice), check the depth of the rivets below the surface of the friction material. If this is less than the minimum amount given in the Specifications, or if excessive wear or damage is found, the friction plate must be renewed.
8 If the friction material is fouled with oil, this must be due to an oil leak from the crankshaft

5.10 Flywheel with the clutch removed, showing the friction disc contact surface (arrowed)

5.18 Tightening the clutch cover mounting bolts with a torque wrench

6.2 Removing the clutch release bearing

rear oil seal, from the sump-to-cylinder block joint, rear oil seal housing joint, or from the transmission input shaft oil seal. If a leak is evident, renew the seal or fit a new joint (as appropriate) as described in Chapter 2 or 8, before installing the new friction plate, or the new plate will go the same way.

9 Check the pressure plate/cover assembly for obvious signs of wear or damage. Shake it to check for loose rivets or damaged fulcrum rings; check that the drive straps securing the pressure plate to the cover do not show signs of overheating (such as a deep yellow or blue discoloration). If the diaphragm spring is worn or damaged, or if its pressure is in any way suspect, the pressure plate/cover assembly should be renewed.

10 Examine the surfaces of the pressure plate and of the flywheel; they should be clean, completely flat, and free from scratches or scoring (minor damage of this nature can sometimes be polished away using emery paper). If either is discoloured from excessive heat, or shows signs of cracking, it should be renewed **(see illustration)**.

11 Check that the release bearing inner rotates smoothly and easily, with no sign of noise or roughness, and that the surface itself is smooth and unworn, with no signs of cracks, pitting or scoring. If there is any doubt about its condition, the bearing must be renewed.

12 Check the spigot bearing in the centre of the flywheel for smooth action. If it is worn or dry, it should be renewed. To remove it, use a suitable puller engaged with the inner race. An alternative method which sometimes works is to fill the cavity in the rear of the crankshaft with heavy grease, then insert a close fitting metal rod through the bearing. Using a hammer, drive the rod through the bearing - the force applied to the heavy grease will be applied to the rear of the bearing, which will be forced from the crankshaft. If this method is used, take adequate precautions to prevent personal injury and damage to the rear of the crankshaft. Clean the cavity, then drive the new bearing into the rear of the crankshaft, making sure that it is the correct way round, and using a metal tube on the outer race only.

Refitting

13 On reassembly, ensure that the bearing surfaces of the flywheel and pressure plate are completely clean, smooth, and free from oil or grease. Use solvent to remove any protective grease from new components.

14 Fit the friction plate so that its spring hub assembly faces away from the flywheel; there may also be a marking showing which way round the plate is to be refitted.

15 Refit the cover assembly, aligning the marks made on dismantling if the original assembly is re-used. Fit the pressure plate bolts, but tighten them only finger-tight, so that the friction plate can still be moved. The two shouldered bolts should be fitted diagonally opposite each other.

16 The friction plate must now be centralised, so that when the transmission is refitted, its input shaft will pass through the splines at the centre of the friction plate.

17 Centralisation can be achieved by passing a loose-fitting long bar through the centre hub of the friction plate and into the centre of the spigot bearing in the crankshaft; the friction plate can then be moved around until it is centred on the bearing hole and with the diaphragm spring fingers. Alternatively, a clutch-aligning tool can be used to eliminate the guesswork; these can be obtained from most accessory shops, or can be made up from a length of metal rod or wooden dowel which fits closely inside the spigot bearing, and has insulating tape wound around it to match the diameter of the friction plate splined hole.

18 When the friction plate is centralised, tighten the cover bolts evenly and in a diagonal sequence to the specified torque setting **(see illustration)**.

19 Apply a thin smear of high-melting point grease to the splines of the friction plate and the transmission input shaft, also to the release bearing guide tube and release fork shaft. Do not apply too much, otherwise there is a danger of it finding its way onto the clutch friction surfaces.

20 Refit the transmission as described in Chapter 8.

6 Clutch release mechanism - removal, inspection and refitting

Note: *Refer to the warning concerning the dangers of asbestos dust at the beginning of Section 5.*

Removal

1 Unless the engine/transmission is to be removed from the vehicle and separated for major overhaul (Chapter 2B), the clutch release mechanism can be reached by removing the transmission alone, as described in Chapter 8.

2 Unhook the release bearing from the fork, and slide it from the guide tube and over the end of the input shaft **(see illustration)**.

3 Using a screwdriver, unhook the return spring from the fork arm on the release arm shaft.

4 Mark the release arm in relation to the shaft to ensure correct refitting, then unscrew and remove the clamp bolt, and remove the arm from the splines on the shaft.

5 Using a thin punch from inside, drive out the bush from the release arm end of the transmission bellhousing. If the bush is particularly tight, it may be possible to use grips on its outer end to pull it out.

6 Move the shaft firstly to the right-hand side of the transmission, so that its inner end can be removed from the left-hand bush, then withdraw the arm from inside the bellhousing. Recover the return spring from the right-hand end of the shaft, noting which way round it is fitted.

7 Extract the left-hand bush from the bellhousing.

Inspection

8 Check the release arm and shaft for wear and damage. In particular, check the ends of the fork which contact the release bearing. Renew the components as necessary.

9 Check the release bearing itself, noting that it is often considered worthwhile to renew it as a matter of course. Check that the bearing inner rotates smoothly and easily, with no sign

7.2 Propeller shaft rear universal joint and differential flanges

7.3 Removing the four bolts securing the propeller shaft to the differential unit flange

of noise or roughness, and that the surface itself is smooth and unworn, with no signs of cracks, pitting or scoring. If there is any doubt about its condition, the bearing must be renewed. While access is easily obtained to the other clutch components, it would be worth removing and inspecting them also (see Section 5).

Refitting

10 Clean the bush bores in the transmission bellhousing, and the inside surface of the bellhousing itself. Apply high-melting point grease to the inner bores of the bushes.

11 Drive the left-hand bush into its bore until level with the inside surface of the bellhousing. Using a centre-punch, lightly stake the bellhousing at two diagonally-opposite points to lock the bush in position.

12 Locate the return spring on the right-hand end of the release shaft, ensuring that it is the correct way round.

13 From inside the bellhousing, insert the right-hand end of the shaft through the bush aperture, then locate its left-hand end in the bush already fitted.

14 Locate the right-hand bush over the end of the release arm shaft, and drive it in until level with the inside surface of the bellhousing. Lock the bush using the same method used for the left-hand bush.

15 Locate the release arm on the right-hand end of the shaft, making sure that the previously-made marks are aligned. Insert the clamp bolt, and tighten to the specified torque.

16 Using a screwdriver, hook the return spring onto the fork arm on the release arm shaft.

17 Apply a little high-melting point grease to the guide tube, then slide on the release bearing, at the same time engaging it with the release arm fork.

18 Refit the transmission as described in Chapter 8.

7 Propeller shaft - removal and refitting

Note: *New rear flange bolts are required when refitting.*

Removal

1 Chock the front roadwheels, then jack up the rear of the vehicle and support on axle stands (see *"Jacking, towing and wheel changing"*). Note that if the rear of the vehicle is raised, or even if the vehicle is level over an inspection pit, it will not be necessary to drain the oil from the transmission. If the front of the vehicle is raised for any reason, however, it will be necessary to drain the transmission oil before removing the propeller shaft.

2 Mark the rear universal joint flange and differential unit flange in relation to each other, if the original propeller shaft is to be refitted **(see illustration)**. This is not necessary if a new propeller shaft is to be fitted.

3 Unscrew and remove the four bolts securing the propeller shaft to the differential

unit flange, noting which way round they are fitted **(see illustration)**. In order to hold the shaft stationary as the bolts are unscrewed, apply the handbrake, or alternatively, insert a suitable bar or screwdriver through the universal joint yoke.

4 Detach the propeller shaft flange from the differential unit flange, then pull the shaft rearwards from the transmission output shaft splines **(see illustration)**. A small amount of oil may drip from the rear of the transmission, so be prepared for this - place a cloth rag around the extension housing.

5 Withdraw the propeller shaft from under the vehicle.

Refitting

6 Wipe clean the front sliding yoke of the propeller shaft, and smear it with a little transmission oil.

7 Carefully slide the sliding yoke on the front end of the propeller shaft onto the transmission output shaft splines, taking care not to damage the transmission rear oil seal.

8 Locate the propeller shaft rear flange on the differential unit flange, aligning the previously-made marks (where applicable).

9 Insert the four *new* bolts from the front (ie through the propeller shaft rear flange first), then fit the nuts and tighten to the specified torque. Hold the shaft stationary as during the removal procedure.

10 If necessary, check and top-up the transmission oil level as described in Chapter 8, but note that the vehicle must be level for this.

11 Lower the vehicle to the ground.

8 Propeller shaft universal joints - renewal

1 Remove the propeller shaft as described in Section 7.

2 Remove the circlips from the bearing cups. Use a punch to free them if they are stuck.

3 Place the propeller shaft onto a vice, so that the yokes of the propeller shaft (not the flange) are resting on the open vice jaws. Remember that the propeller shaft is hollow, and would easily be damaged by too much vice pressure.

7.4 Propeller shaft connection at rear of transmission housing

8.4a Tap the flange yoke downwards and remove the bearing cup

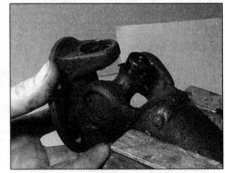

8.6 Removing the flange

8.8 Spider, bearings and circlips

8.9a Placing the spider in the yoke . . .

8.9b . . . and fitting a bearing cup

4 Using a socket which will just fit over the bearing cups, and a hammer, gently tap the flange yoke (rear universal joint) or sliding yoke (front universal joint) downwards so that the uppermost bearing cup protrudes about 3.0 to 4.0 mm. Remove the cup **(see illustration)**.
5 Turn the propeller shaft through 180°, and repeat the operation on the opposite bearing.
6 The flange or sliding yoke (as applicable) can now be removed from the propeller shaft, and the same procedure used to remove the spider from the shaft **(see illustration)**.
7 Clean the bearing seats in the flange and propeller shaft yokes.
8 Remove the bearings from the new spider, and ensure that the needle bearings are well-greased **(see illustration)**. This will ensure that the needle bearings stay in place during the following fitting procedure.
9 Place the spider in the flange/sliding yoke, and install one bearing cup onto the yoke **(see illustrations)**.
10 Using the vice and a socket of suitable diameter, press the bearing cup into the yoke by about 3.0 to 4.0 mm. Fit the circlip **(see illustrations)**.
11 Repeat on the opposite side, then fit the flange/sliding yoke and spider to the propeller shaft yoke, and fit the remaining bearing cups **(see illustrations)**.
12 Fit the remaining bearing retaining circlips.
13 Check the joint for full and free movement. If it feels excessively tight, rest it on the vice and just gently tap it with a plastic mallet, which will centralise the bearings and free the joint.

14 Refit the propeller shaft as described in Section 7.

9 Differential unit - removal and refitting

Note: *New propeller shaft rear flange bolts are required when refitting.*

Removal

1 Chock the front roadwheels, then jack up the rear of the vehicle and support on axle stands (see *"Jacking, towing and wheel changing"*).
2 Position a suitable clean container beneath the rear axle, then unscrew the oil drain plug and drain the oil. To aid draining, also remove the filler plug. On completion, check the condition of the sealing washer, renew if necessary, then refit and tighten the drain plug.
3 Remove both rear axle shafts with reference to Chapter 10.
4 Mark the propeller shaft rear universal joint flange and differential unit flange in relation to each other, then unscrew and remove the four bolts and spring washers securing the propeller shaft to the differential unit, noting which way round they are fitted. In order to hold the shaft stationary as the bolts are unscrewed, insert a suitable bar or screwdriver through the universal joint yoke.
5 Detach the propeller shaft from the differential unit, and support it on an axle stand.

6 Unscrew and remove the bolts securing the differential unit to the rear axle casing. Leave one of the upper two bolts loosely in position until you are ready to remove the differential unit.
7 The unit is quite heavy, and the help of an assistant will make its removal easier. Unscrew the final bolt, and remove the differential unit from the rear axle casing. Lower it to the floor, and remove it from under the vehicle.

Refitting

8 Thoroughly clean the mating surfaces of the differential unit and rear axle casing, then apply an even coating of suitable sealant to them.
9 Lift the differential unit into position in the rear axle casing, and insert the mounting bolts. Progressively tighten the bolts to the specified torque.

8.10a Pressing the bearing cup into the yoke

8.10b Fitting the circlip

8.11a Tap the first cup into the shaft yoke . . .

8.11b . . . fit the other cup and press it home in the vice

10 Locate the propeller shaft rear flange on the differential unit flange, aligning the previously-made marks.

11 Insert the four *new* flange bolts from the front (ie through the propeller shaft rear flange first), then fit the spring washers and nuts, and tighten to the specified torque. Hold the shaft stationary as during the removal procedure.

12 Refit the rear axle shafts with reference to Chapter 10.

13 Fill the rear axle with the correct quantity and grade of oil, with reference to Chapter 1. Note that the vehicle must be level in order to obtain an accurate oil level. Tighten the filler/level plug.

14 Lower the vehicle to the ground.

10 Differential unit pinion oil seal - renewal

Note: *The pinion bearing preload is determined on original assembly by the deformation of a collapsible spacer and a shim. The preload, together with the correct torque of the pinion nut, must be maintained after fitting the new pinion oil seal. It is most important not to alter the length of the collapsible spacer, otherwise the complete differential unit will have to be dismantled, and a new collapsible spacer fitted. The latter work cannot be undertaken by the home mechanic, due to the need for special tooling. If you have not renewed a pinion oil seal before, you may decide to have the work carried out by a Vauxhall or Suzuki dealer.*

Note: *New propeller shaft rear flange bolts are required when refitting.*

1 The pinion oil seal can be renewed without removing the differential unit from the rear axle. First chock the front roadwheels, then jack up the rear of the vehicle and support on axle stands (see "Jacking, towing and wheel changing").

2 Mark the propeller shaft rear universal joint flange and differential unit flange in relation to each other, then unscrew and remove the four bolts and spring washers securing the propeller shaft to the differential unit, noting which way round they are fitted. In order to hold the shaft stationary as the bolts are unscrewed, insert a suitable bar or screwdriver through the universal joint yoke.

3 Detach the propeller shaft from the differential unit, and support it on an axle stand.

4 Using a marker pen or centre-punch, mark the differential drive flange, pinion and nut in relation to each other, to ensure correct refitting.

5 Hold the differential flange stationary by applying the handbrake. Alternatively, bolt a long bar to the flange, or screw two bolts into adjacent holes, and insert a long bar between them.

6 Unscrew the drive flange self-locking nut, and recover the washer. Note the exact number of turns necessary to remove the nut, as a further precaution to refit it in its original position.

7 Place a suitable container beneath the differential unit, to catch any oil which may be lost as the drive flange is removed.

8 Pull the drive flange from the splined pinion. If it is tight, use a suitable puller to remove it.

9 Note the fitted depth of the oil seal in the differential casing, then use a screwdriver to prise it out.

10 Clean the area of the differential casing where the oil seal locates, and clean the drive flange and the end of the pinion.

11 Locate the new oil seal on the differential casing. Drive it in squarely to its previously-noted depth, using a suitable tube drift or socket. Smear a little oil on the sealing lip of the oil seal.

12 Slide the drive flange on the splined pinion, taking care not to damage the oil seal - make sure the previously-made marks are correctly aligned.

13 Locate the washer on the pinion, and screw on the self-locking nut. Hold the drive flange stationary using one of the methods already described, and tighten the nut to its previously-noted position.

14 Locate the propeller shaft rear flange on the differential unit flange, aligning the previously-made marks.

15 Insert the four new flange bolts from the front (ie through the propeller shaft rear flange first), then fit the spring washers and nuts, and tighten to the specified torque. Hold the shaft stationary as during the removal procedure.

16 Check and if necessary top-up the rear axle oil level with reference to Chapter 1. Note that the vehicle must be level in order to obtain an accurate oil level.

17 Lower the vehicle to the ground.

11 Rear axle - removal and refitting

Note: *New propeller shaft rear flange bolts are required when refitting.*

Removal

1 Chock the front wheels, release the handbrake, then jack up the rear of the vehicle and support on axle stands (see *"Jacking, towing and wheel changing"*). Remove the relevant rear roadwheel.

2 Position a suitable clean container beneath the rear axle, then unscrew the oil drain plug and drain the oil. To aid draining, also remove the filler plug. Refit and tighten the drain plug to the specified torque.

3 Remove the brake drums and rear brake shoes, with reference to Chapter 9.

4 Extract the spring clips securing the handbrake cables to the rear brake backplates, then pull out the cables from the backplates.

5 Fit a brake hose clamp to the rear brake hose in front of the rear axle. Alternatively, syphon out the brake fluid from the master cylinder reservoir (refer to Chapter 9 if necessary).

6 Disconnect the rear brake hose from the rigid brake pipe on the rear axle, with reference to Chapter 9. Tie a small polythene bag to the pipe end, to prevent entry of dust and dirt.

7 Mark the propeller shaft rear universal joint flange and differential unit flange in relation to each other, then unscrew and remove the four bolts and spring washers securing the propeller shaft to the differential unit, noting which way round they are fitted. In order to hold the shaft stationary as the bolts are unscrewed, insert a suitable bar or screwdriver through the universal joint yoke.

8 Detach the propeller shaft from the differential unit, and support it on an axle stand.

9 Working on the rear leaf springs, unscrew and remove the nuts from the bottom of the U-bolts, and remove the U-bolts from the top of the rear axle. Recover the upper saddle/bump stops.

10 With the help of an assistant, lift the rear axle from the top of the rear leaf springs, and withdraw it from under the vehicle.

11 If necessary, the rear axle shafts and differential unit may be removed with reference to Section 9.

Refitting

12 Where removed, refit the differential unit and rear axle shafts with reference to Section 9.

13 Lift the rear axle into position on top of the rear leaf springs, making sure that it is correctly located.

14 Locate the upper saddle/bump stops on the top of the rear axle, and refit the U-bolts through the lower plate. Fit the nuts to the U-bolts, and progressively tighten them to the specified torque. With all the nuts tightened, check that the number of threads visible on the bottom of the U-bolts is the same on all of them.

15 Locate the propeller shaft rear flange on the differential unit flange, aligning the previously-made marks.

16 Insert the four *new* bolts from the front (ie through the propeller shaft rear flange first), then fit the spring washers and nuts, and tighten to the specified torque. Hold the shaft stationary as during the removal procedure.

17 Reconnect the rear brake hose to the rigid brake pipe on the rear axle, with reference to Chapter 9.

18 Fill the rear axle with the correct quantity and grade of oil with reference to Chapter 1. Note that the vehicle must be level in order to obtain an accurate oil level. Tighten the filler/level plug to the specified torque.

19 Lower the vehicle to the ground.

Chapter 8 Manual transmission

Contents

Degrees of difficulty

Easy, suitable for novice with little experience	Fairly easy, suitable for beginner with some experience	Fairly difficult, suitable for competent DIY mechanic	Difficult, suitable for experienced DIY mechanic	Very difficult, suitable for expert DIY or professional

Specifications

General

Type . . . . Manual, four or five forward speeds and reverse. Synchromesh on all forward speeds

Gear ratios

1st	3.652 : 1
2nd	1.947 : 1
3rd	1.423 : 1
4th	1.000 : 1
5th (where applicable)	0.795 : 1
Reverse	3.466 : 1

Lubrication

Refer to "Lubricants, fluids and capacities"

Torque wrench settings	Nm	lbf ft
Oil filler/level plug (with sealant on threads)	43	32
Oil drain plug	43	32
Gear selector shaft lever nut	23	17
Gear selector housing mounting bolt	13	10
Gear shift control lever nut	23	17
Speedometer drive gear	6	4
Clutch release arm nut	13	10
Reverse detent bolt	29	21
Guide tube housing bolt	23	17
Transmission mounting bracket bolt	20	15
Transmission mounting nut	25	18

1 General information

The 4- or 5-speed manual transmission is bolted to the rear of the engine, being located approximately midway between the front and rear wheels.

Drive is transmitted from the crankshaft via the flywheel and clutch to the input shaft, which rotates in sealed ball-bearings, and has a splined extension to accept the clutch friction plate. From the input shaft, drive is transmitted to the countershaft, which also rotates in roller bearings at each end. When a gear other than 4th is selected, drive is transmitted from the countershaft to the mainshaft (output shaft). With 4th gear selected, drive is direct through the transmission, as the input shaft is locked to the mainshaft.

All of the gears on the countershaft are fixed (reverse and 5th gears are splined to the shaft). However, the gears on the mainshaft are free to rotate independently, and are in constant mesh with the countershaft gears. Gear selection is by means of synchromesh units splined to the mainshaft - the units incorporate outer rings which are moved into engagement with the gears on the mainshaft (or input shaft in the case of 4th gear), and thus lock the free rotating gears to the output shaft (or input shaft, in the case of 4th gear). The speeds of the synchro outer ring and the gear being engaged are "synchronised" by a tapered baulk ring before the gears are locked together, as the splines on the outer ring engage the dog teeth on the gear. Reverse gear is obtained by an idler gear in constant mesh with the countershaft and the reverse gear on the mainshaft; unlike the normal method of moving the idler gear into engagement with the other gears, the synchro outer ring is moved onto dog teeth on the

3.4 Gearchange cable adjustment at the front of the inner cable

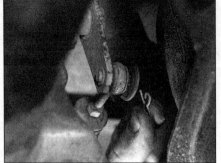

4.6a Extract the spring clip . . .

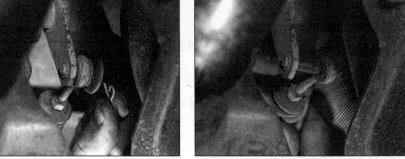

4.6b . . . and disconnect the cables from the levers on the transmission

driven gear, and thus locks the driven gear to the mainshaft.

From the transmission, drive is transmitted via the propeller shaft and rear axle to the rear wheels.

Gear selection is via a lever mounted on the engine cover crossmember; two cables are utilised to move the gear selection mechanism in the transmission.

All forward gears incorporate synchromesh on both 4 and 5-speed transmissions. Reverse gear is not synchronised.

2 Manual transmission oil - draining and refilling

Note: *A 3/8 inch square-drive key or socket bar will be required to undo the transmission filler/level and drain plugs. A key can be obtained from most motor factors, or from your Vauxhall/Suzuki dealer.*

1 This operation is much quicker and more effective if the vehicle is first taken on a journey of sufficient length to warm the engine and transmission up to normal operating temperature.

2 Park the vehicle on level ground, switch off the engine, and apply the handbrake firmly. For improved access, position the vehicle over an inspection pit or on ramps, but note that the vehicle must be level when checking the oil level, to ensure that the correct amount of oil is contained in the transmission.

3 Wipe clean the area around the filler/level plug, which is situated on the rear right-hand end of the casing. Unscrew the filler/level plug from the transmission. Note that its threads are tapered, so that there is no need for a sealing washer.

4 Position a suitable container under the drain plug (situated centrally on the lower rear of the transmission) and unscrew the plug from the transmission.

5 Allow the oil to drain completely into the container. If the oil is hot, take precautions against scalding. Clean both the filler/level and the drain plugs, being especially careful to wipe any metallic particles off them.

6 When the oil has finished draining, clean the drain plug threads in the transmission casing, then insert the plug and tighten to the specified torque.

7 Make sure that the vehicle is parked on flat level ground, then refill the transmission with the specified amount and grade of oil.

8 Check that the oil level is approximately 5.0 mm below the lower edge of the oil filler/level hole on the 5-speed transmission, or approximately 15.0 mm below the lower edge of the oil filler/level hole on the 4-speed transmission. Use a bent piece of wire to make the check (see Chapter 1 for more details).

9 Clean the threads of the filler/level plug, then insert it and tighten to the specified torque.

3 Gearchange lever and cables - general information and adjustment

General information

1 If a stiff, sloppy or imprecise gearchange leads you to suspect that a fault exists within the lever assembly or cables, first dismantle the assembly completely, and check for wear or damage as described in Section 4. Reassemble, applying a smear of multi-purpose grease to all bearing surfaces.

2 The test for correctly-adjusted cables and linkage is to attempt to engage 3rd and 4th from the neutral position. If this is smooth, then the cables are adjusted correctly; if not, carry out the following adjustment.

3 If the fault is not cured by adjustment of the cables, the vehicle should be examined by an expert, as the fault must lie within the transmission itself. There is no adjustment as such within the transmission.

Adjustment

4 Move the gear lever slightly to the left (ie towards the 1st/2nd side of neutral), then from here attempt to engage the 3rd and 4th positions. If it is now possible to engage the 3rd and 4th gears smoothly, then loosen the left-hand cable rear locknut, and tighten the front nut until it is possible to engage the gears smoothly from the normal rest position

in neutral. Depending on the year of manufacture, the cable adjustment nuts are located on the outer cable at the gear lever bracket, or on the front of the inner cable at the bottom of the gear lever **(see illustration)**.

5 If the procedure described in the previous paragraph did not apply to the fault, move the gear lever slightly to the right (ie towards the reverse side of neutral), and attempt to engage the 3rd and 4th positions. If it is now possible to engage the 3rd and 4th gears smoothly, then loosen the left-hand cable front locknut, and tighten the rear nut until it is possible to engage the gears smoothly from the normal rest position in neutral.

6 Once the adjustment has been made, check that all gears can be selected, and that the gearchange lever returns properly to its correct at-rest neutral position.

4 Gearchange lever and cables - removal, inspection and refitting

Removal

1 Firmly apply the handbrake, then jack up the front of the vehicle and support it on axle stands.

2 Ensure that the gear lever is in neutral.

3 Remove both front seats and the centre console, as described in Chapter 11.

4 Extract the spring clip and remove the washer, then disconnect the shift control cable from the bottom of the gear lever.

5 If necessary, unscrew the nut and remove the gear lever from the pivot on the lever assembly.

6 Working under the vehicle, extract the spring clips, remove the washers, and disconnect the shift and selector cables from the levers on the transmission. Also loosen the nuts and disconnect the cables from the transmission bracket **(see illustrations)**. To avoid confusing them during refitting, identify each cable with masking tape.

7 Unscrew the nut(s) from the end of the selector control cable, and disconnect the cable from the pivot on the bellcrank arm **(see illustration)**.

4.6c Gearchange cable mounting on the transmission bracket

4.7 Selector control cable connection to the bellcrank arm

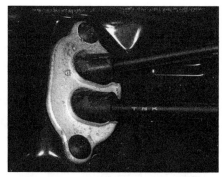

4.8a Gearchange cable guide bracket

8 Unscrew the screws, and detach the front cable guide bracket from the body. Also pull out the spring clips, and disconnect the outer cables from the gearchange lever bracket **(see illustrations)**. Note that on some early models, one of the cables is attached with locknuts instead of a spring clip - on these models, the locknuts are used for adjustment.

9 Loosen the nuts, and release the rear ends of the cables from the support bracket **(see illustration)**. Remove the cables from under the vehicle.

10 Unbolt the gear lever bracket from the body **(see illustration)**.

11 If required, the selector housing may be unbolted from the top of the transmission. Make sure that the transmission is in neutral before doing this.

12 To dismantle the selector housing, prise off the rubber boot, then unscrew the nut and remove the selector shaft lever and selector shaft. Note the position of all components for correct reassembly, and recover the oil seal O-ring.

13 Unscrew the bolt, and remove the reverse detent spring and detent ball.

14 Extract the pin, then pull out the gear shift shaft, spring, lever, washer and spring. On 5-speed models, unscrew the pivot bolt and remove the reverse shift limit dog, after noting which way round it is fitted.

Inspection

15 Thoroughly clean all components, and

examine them for signs of wear or damage **(see illustration)** - renew as necessary. In particular, check the ends of the selector lever fingers for excessive wear - if excessive wear is evident on the transmission selector shafts, it may be necessary to overhaul the transmission itself; however, this work is considered outside the scope of the home mechanic (see Section 9). Also check the springs for signs of wear or weakness. Obtain new seals, and fit them to the shafts.

Refitting

16 Before reassembling the selector housing, apply transmission oil to all moving parts.

17 On 5-speed models, refit the reverse shift limit dog, making sure it is the same way round as noted during removal. Tighten the pivot bolt.

18 Refit the gear shift shaft, spring, lever, washer and spring, then align the pin holes and insert the pin to secure. The lever on the outside of the housing must be at the same angle as the inner levers. On 4-speed models, make sure that the spacer is fitted between the No 2 spring and the gear shift lever.

19 Refit the selector shaft lever and selector shaft, using a reversal of the removal procedure. Tighten the selector shaft nut to the specified torque. Fit the new rubber boot.

20 Refit the reverse detent spring and ball, and tighten the bolt to the specified torque.

21 Clean the selector housing and transmission joint faces, and apply suitable sealant. Locate the housing in position, insert the mounting bolts, and tighten to the specified torque.

22 Refit the gear lever bracket to the body, and tighten the mounting bolts.

23 Refit the selector cables to the support bracket and front bracket, and tighten the screws. To prevent entry of water inside the vehicle, apply sealant to the front bracket before refitting it. Refit the cable guide bracket.

24 During the remaining procedure, apply a little grease to the bearing surfaces of all components.

25 Reconnect the selector control cable to the bellcrank arm, and tighten the nut(s).

26 Reconnect the shift and selector cables to the levers on the transmission, and refit the washers and spring clips. Make sure the cables are refitted in the positions noted during removal.

27 Refit the gear lever to the pivot on the lever assembly, and tighten the nut.

28 Reconnect the shift control cable to the bottom of the gear lever, then refit the washer and spring clip.

29 Adjust the cables as described in Section 3, and check that all gears can be selected easily.

30 Refit the centre console and the front seats with reference to Chapter 11.

31 Lower the vehicle to the ground.

4.8b Disconnecting the outer cables from the gearchange lever bracket

4.9 Loosen the nuts, and release the rear ends of the cables from the support bracket

4.10 Gear lever bracket mounting bolts (arrowed)

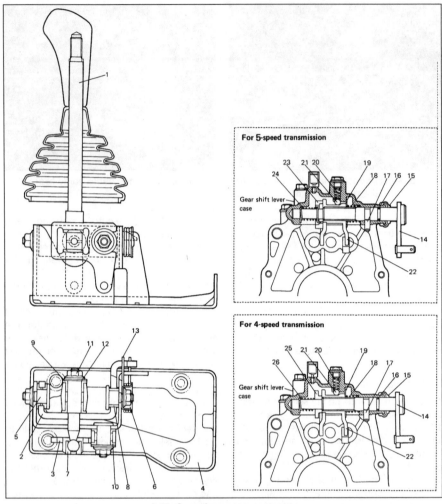

4.15 Gearchange components

1 Gear lever	11 Lever pin nut	20 Reverse check spring
2 Gear shift control yoke	12 Washer	21 Reverse detent ball
3 Gear selector arm	13 Selector arm return spring	22 Reverse shift lever
4 Control guide	14 Gear shift shaft lever	23 Reverse shift limit dog
5 Lever pin	15 Rubber boot	24 Shift lever hold No 2
6 Select return spring spacer	16 O-ring	spring
7 Guide bush	17 Lever case pin	25 Reverse gear shift spacer
8 Lever yoke bush	18 Shift lever hold No 1	26 Shift lever hold No 2
9 Control lever bush	spring	spring
10 Lever yoke bush	19 Lever hold washer	

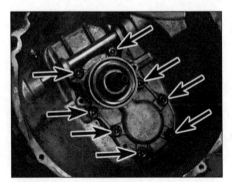

5.3 Bolts (arrowed) retaining the guide tube housing to the transmission casing

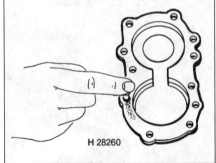

5.7 Apply sealant to the mating surface of the guide tube housing

5 Oil seals - renewal

Input shaft oil seal

1 Remove the transmission as described in Section 8.

2 Remove the clutch release bearing from the release arm fork, as described in Chapter 7. Turn the release arm so that the fork is pointing away from the guide tube housing.

3 Unscrew the bolts retaining the guide tube housing to the transmission casing **(see illustration)**. Use three 6 mm bolts in the threaded holes provided, to force the housing off the input and countershaft bearings. Withdraw the housing over the input shaft.

4 Prise the oil seal from inside the guide tube housing, using a screwdriver.

5 Clean the guide tube housing, then apply a little transmission oil to the lips of the new oil seal.

6 Drive in the new oil seal squarely, using a suitable metal tube or socket, and making sure that the seal lips are facing into the transmission.

7 Apply sealant to the mating surface of the guide tube housing **(see illustration)**.

8 Locate the guide tube housing over the input shaft onto the transmission casing, and insert the retaining bolts. Tighten the bolts to the specified torque.

9 Refit the clutch release bearing with reference to Chapter 7.

10 Refit the transmission with reference to Section 8.

Output shaft oil seal

11 Remove the propeller shaft as described in Chapter 7.

12 Using a screwdriver, prise the old oil seal from the transmission extension casing. If the oil seal is tight, a small puller may be required to remove it. Due to the curved end of the oil seal, it will not be possible to use self-tapping screws and grips as a means of removing the oil seal.

13 Clean the oil seal seating in the extension casing.

14 Smear a little transmission oil on the lip of the new oil seal, then press it into the extension casing with the lip facing inwards - use a suitable metal tube or socket on the outer part of the oil seal only.

15 Refit the propeller shaft with reference to Chapter 7.

Speedometer drive oil seal

16 Refer to Section 7.

6 Reversing light switch - testing, removal and refitting

Testing

1 The reversing light circuit is controlled by a plunger-type switch, screwed into the top of the transmission casing. If a fault develops in the circuit, first ensure that the circuit fuse has not blown, and that the reversing light bulbs are intact.

2 To test the switch, disconnect the wiring connector, and use a multi-meter (set to the resistance function) or a battery-and-bulb test circuit, to check that there is continuity between the switch terminals only when reverse gear is selected. If this is not the case, the switch is faulty, and must be renewed. A further test may be made by connecting a link wire between the two terminals on the disconnected wiring connector - with the ignition switched on, the reversing lights should be on, proving that the wiring is in good condition.

3 If the switch functions correctly, check the associated wiring for possible open- or short-circuits.

Removal

4 Access to the reversing light switch is gained by removing the left-hand seat (refer to Chapter 11). The switch is located on the top of the transmission. On models with a catalytic converter, do not confuse it with the neutral switch located a little lower down on the transmission casing.

5 Disconnect the wiring at the connector, then unscrew the switch from the transmission casing. Remove the switch, together with the sealing O-ring.

Refitting

6 Fit a new sealing O-ring to the switch, then screw it back into position in the top of the transmission housing and tighten securely. Reconnect the wiring, then refit the left-hand seat.

7.2 Removing the end of the speedometer cable from the transmission extension casing (shown with propeller shaft removed)

7 Speedometer drive - removal and refitting

Removal

1 Access to the speedometer drive is best gained from below the front of the vehicle. Apply the handbrake, then raise the front of the vehicle and support on axle stands (see *"Jacking, towing and wheel changing"*).

2 Unscrew and remove the speedometer drive retaining bolt located on the transmission extension casing, and pull out the speedometer cable end fitting **(see illustration)**.

3 Using a pair of grips, ease the driven gear bush out of the casing **(see illustration)**. On older vehicles, the bush may be quite tight, in which case it will be necessary to turn it back and forth several times before removing it.

4 The pinion will normally come out with the bush, and the two components may then be separated. If it remains in the transmission, use pliers to lift it out **(see illustration)**.

5 Examine the pinion and bush for signs of damage, and renew if necessary. Renew the O-rings as a matter of course.

Refitting

6 Wipe clean the aperture in the transmission extension casing.

7.3 Removing the speedometer drive driven gear bush out of the transmission casing

7 Apply transmission oil to the pinion, and locate it in the bush. Insert the assembly into the extension casing, making sure that the bolt holes are correctly aligned with each other.

8 Apply a smear of oil to the O-rings, then insert the speedometer cable end fitting in the bush. Insert and tighten the retaining bolt.

9 Lower the vehicle to the ground.

8 Manual transmission - removal and refitting

Note: *The transmission can be removed on its own, or as a unit with the engine. If the latter method is to be employed, refer to Chapter 2B for details of the removal and separation procedure. This Section describes the removal of the transmission on its own, leaving the engine in situ.*

Removal

1 Position the vehicle over an inspection pit, or raise it and support on axle stands (see *"Jacking, towing and wheel changing"*). Alternatively, raise just the front of the vehicle and support on axle stands. Make sure that the clearance between the transmission and the ground is sufficient to allow easy removal of the transmission.

2 Disconnect the battery negative lead.

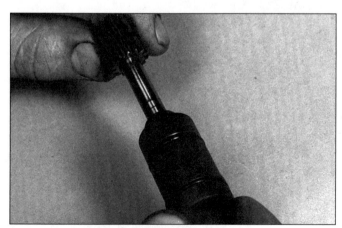

7.4 Separating the pinion from the bush

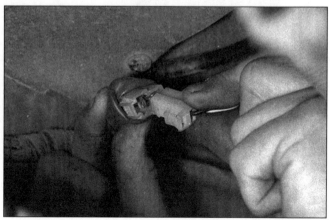

8.4 Disconnecting the reversing light wiring at the connector

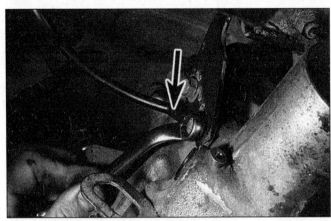

8.10 Unbolting the earth cable (arrowed) from the transmission casing

8.14 Removing the lower bellhousing cover from the lower front of the transmission

3 Remove both front seats as described in Chapter 11. Also remove the rear engine compartment cover.

4 Disconnect the reversing light wiring at the connector, and release the wiring from the clamps **(see illustration)**.

5 Disconnect the wiring from the starter motor (refer to Chapter 5A if necessary).

6 Unscrew the starter mounting bolts, so that it is detached from the transmission. There is no need to remove it from the engine.

7 Remove the propeller shaft as described in Chapter 7.

8 Loosen the bolt on the extension casing, and disconnect the speedometer cable. Refit the bolt after removing the cable, and screw it in loosely.

9 Drain the transmission oil as described in Section 2, then refit the drain and filler/level plugs and tighten them to their specified torque settings.

10 Unbolt the earth cable from the transmission casing **(see illustration)**.

11 Disconnect the clutch cable from the release lever, with reference to Chapter 7.

12 Disconnect the gear shift and selector cables from the transmission, with reference to Section 4.

13 Release the warm-air hose clamp from the bracket on the transmission casing.

14 Unbolt the lower bellhousing cover from the lower front of the transmission **(see illustration)**.

15 Support the weight of the transmission on a trolley jack, then unbolt the rear mounting bracket from the underbody **(see illustrations)**.

16 The help of an assistant will be helpful at this stage.

17 Unscrew the lower nuts and upper bolts securing the transmission to the rear of the engine, while the assistant holds the transmission against the rear of the engine.

18 Take the weight of the transmission, and withdraw it directly from the rear of the engine. Do not allow the weight of the transmission to hang on the clutch. There may be some initial resistance to movement if the transmission casing binds on the locating dowels. There is no need to support the engine, since its mountings are positioned so that it will remain balanced horizontally.

19 Remove the transmission from under the vehicle. If they are loose, remove the locating dowels from the transmission or engine, and keep them in a safe place.

Refitting

20 The transmission is refitted using a reversal of the removal procedure, bearing in mind the following points:

a) *Apply a little high-melting-point grease to the splines of the transmission input shaft. Do not apply too much, otherwise there is a possibility of the grease contaminating the clutch friction plate.*

b) *Ensure that the locating dowels are correctly positioned prior to installation.*

c) *Tighten all nuts and bolts to the specified torque (where given).*

d) *On completion, refill the transmission with the specified type and quantity of oil, as described in Section 2.*

e) *Check and if necessary adjust the clutch cable, with reference to Chapter 7.*

9 Manual transmission overhaul - general information

1 Overhauling a manual transmission is a difficult and involved job for the DIY home mechanic. In addition to dismantling and reassembling many small parts, clearances

8.15a Transmission rear mounting bracket bolts (arrowed) on Van models

8.15b Transmission rear mounting on Pick-up models

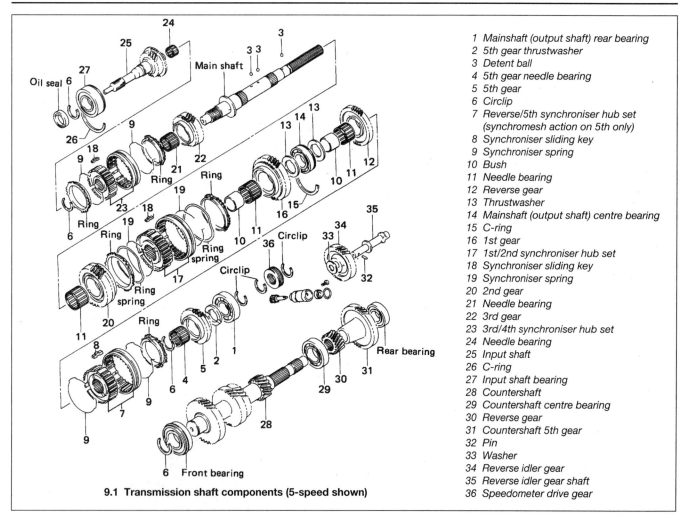

1 Mainshaft (output shaft) rear bearing
2 5th gear thrustwasher
3 Detent ball
4 5th gear needle bearing
5 5th gear
6 Circlip
7 Reverse/5th synchroniser hub set
  (synchromesh action on 5th only)
8 Synchroniser sliding key
9 Synchroniser spring
10 Bush
11 Needle bearing
12 Reverse gear
13 Thrustwasher
14 Mainshaft (output shaft) centre bearing
15 C-ring
16 1st gear
17 1st/2nd synchroniser hub set
18 Synchroniser sliding key
19 Synchroniser spring
20 2nd gear
21 Needle bearing
22 3rd gear
23 3rd/4th synchroniser hub set
24 Needle bearing
25 Input shaft
26 C-ring
27 Input shaft bearing
28 Countershaft
29 Countershaft centre bearing
30 Reverse gear
31 Countershaft 5th gear
32 Pin
33 Washer
34 Reverse idler gear
35 Reverse idler gear shaft
36 Speedometer drive gear

9.1 Transmission shaft components (5-speed shown)

must be precisely measured and, if necessary, changed by selecting shims and spacers. Internal transmission components are also often difficult to obtain and, in many instances, extremely expensive. Because of this, if the transmission develops a fault or becomes noisy, the best course of action is to have the unit overhauled by a specialist repairer, or to obtain an exchange reconditioned unit.

2 Nevertheless, it is not impossible for the more experienced mechanic to overhaul the transmission, provided the special tools are available, and the job is done in a deliberate step-by-step manner so that nothing is overlooked.

3 The tools necessary for an overhaul include internal and external circlip pliers, bearing pullers, a slide hammer, a set of pin punches, a dial test indicator, and (possibly) a hydraulic press. In addition, a large, sturdy workbench and a vice will be required.

4 During dismantling of the transmission, make careful notes of how each component is fitted, to make reassembly easier and more accurate **(see illustration)**.

5 Before dismantling the transmission, it will help if you have some idea of which area is malfunctioning. Certain problems can be closely related to specific areas in the transmission, which can reduce the amount of dismantling and component examination required. Refer to the *"Fault finding"* Section at the end of this manual for more information.

Notes

Chapter 9 Braking system

Contents

Degrees of difficulty

Easy, suitable for novice with little experience	Fairly easy, suitable for beginner with some experience	Fairly difficult, suitable for competent DIY mechanic	Difficult, suitable for experienced DIY mechanic	Very difficult, suitable for expert DIY or professional

Specifications

General

System type . . . .   Dual hydraulic circuit, split front/rear. Front disc brakes and rear drum brakes fitted on all models. Vacuum servo-assistance on all models. Cable-operated handbrake acting on rear wheels.

Front brakes

Type	Disc, with single-piston sliding caliper
Disc diameter	215 mm
Disc thickness:	
New	10.0 mm
Minimum thickness (1.0 mm maximum variation between sides) . . .	8.5 mm
Maximum disc run-out (disc mounted on hub)	0.15 mm
Minimum pad thickness (friction lining plus backing plate)	6.5 mm

Rear brakes

Type	Drum with leading and trailing shoes
Drum diameter:	
New	220 mm
Maximum diameter after machining	222 mm
Minimum shoe lining thickness (lining plus shoe rim)	3.0 mm

Torque wrench settings	Nm	lbf ft
Brake disc to hub	50	37
Front brake caliper	85	63
Front brake caliper guide bolt	27	20
Master cylinder to vacuum servo	13	10
Vacuum servo mounting nuts	13	10
Brake pressure proportioning valve	10	7
Rear wheel cylinder:		
6 mm bolt	10	7
8 mm bolt	19	14
Brake pipe union nut	16	12
Brake/clutch pedal pivot bolt	23	17
Flexible brake hose to caliper	23	17
Bleed screw	9	7
Stop-light switch locknut	13	10
Roadwheel nuts	65	48

1 General information

The braking system is of dual-circuit hydraulic type, split front (primary circuit) and rear (secondary circuit) and all models are fitted with a vacuum servo. The arrangement of the hydraulic system is such that the front and rear brakes are operated independently from a tandem master cylinder. Under normal circumstances, both circuits operate in unison. However, in the event of hydraulic failure in one circuit, full braking force will still be available at the remaining circuit.

All models are fitted with front disc brakes and rear drum brakes.

The front disc brakes are actuated by single-piston sliding type calipers, which ensure that equal pressure is applied to each disc pad.

The rear drum brakes incorporate leading and trailing shoes, which are actuated by twin-piston wheel cylinders. A self-adjusting mechanism is incorporated, to automatically compensate for rear brake shoe wear. As the brake shoe linings wear, operating the footbrake automatically operates the adjuster mechanism, which effectively lengthens the shoe strut and repositions the brake shoes, to adjust the lining-to-drum clearance.

On all models, the handbrake provides an independent mechanical means of rear brake application. The handbrake cable arrangement is unusual, in that the front primary inner cable pulls the rear secondary **outer** cable.

Various types of brake proportioning valves are fitted (according to model year), to ensure that the braking effort applied to each wheel is most efficient for the load being carried and the road conditions encountered. This helps to counteract wheel lock-up, especially during emergency braking.

Note: *When servicing any part of the system, work carefully and methodically, and observe scrupulous cleanliness when overhauling any part of the hydraulic system. Always renew components in axle sets (where applicable) if in doubt about their condition, and use only genuine replacement parts, or at least those of known good quality. Note the warnings given in "Safety first!", and at relevant points in this Chapter, concerning the dangers of asbestos dust and hydraulic fluid.*

2 Hydraulic system - bleeding

⚠ *Warning: Hydraulic fluid is poisonous; wash off immediately and thoroughly in the case of skin contact, and seek immediate medical advice if any fluid is swallowed or gets into the eyes. Certain types of*

hydraulic fluid are inflammable, and may ignite when allowed into contact with hot components; when servicing the hydraulic system, it is safest to assume that the fluid IS inflammable, and to take precautions against the risk of fire as though it is petrol that is being handled. Finally, it is hygroscopic (it absorbs moisture from the air) - old fluid may be contaminated and unfit for further use. When topping-up or renewing the fluid, always use the recommended type, and ensure that it comes from a freshly-opened sealed container.

> **HAYNES HiNT** *Hydraulic fluid is an effective paint stripper, and will attack plastics; if any is spilt, it should be washed off immediately, using copious quantities of fresh water*

General

1 The correct operation of the brake hydraulic system is only possible after removing all air from the components and circuit; and this is achieved by bleeding the system.

2 During the bleeding procedure, add only clean, unused brake hydraulic fluid of the recommended type; never re-use fluid that has already been bled from the system. Ensure that sufficient fluid is available before starting work.

3 If there is any possibility of incorrect fluid being already in the system, the brake components and circuit must be flushed completely with uncontaminated, correct fluid, and new seals should be fitted throughout the system.

4 If hydraulic fluid has been lost from the system, or air has entered because of a leak, ensure that the fault is cured before proceeding further.

5 Park the vehicle on level ground, and apply the handbrake. Switch off the engine, then depress the brake pedal several times to dissipate the vacuum from the servo unit.

6 Check that all pipes and hoses are secure, unions tight and bleed screws closed. Remove the dust caps (where applicable), and clean any dirt from around the bleed screws.

7 The brake fluid reservoir is located through an aperture on the right-hand end of the facia, accessible after opening the door. Unscrew the cap, and top-up the reservoir to the "MAX" level line; refit the cap loosely, and remember to maintain the fluid level at least above the "MIN" level line throughout the procedure, otherwise there is a risk of further air entering the system.

8 There are a number of one-man, do-it-yourself brake bleeding kits currently available from motor accessory shops. It is recommended that one of these kits is used whenever possible, as they greatly simplify the bleeding operation, and also reduce the risk of expelled air and fluid being drawn back

into the system. If such a kit is not available, the basic (two-man) method must be used, which is described in detail below.

9 If a kit is to be used, prepare the vehicle as described previously, and follow the kit manufacturer's instructions, as the procedure may vary slightly according to the type being used; generally, they are as outlined below in the relevant sub-section.

10 Whichever method is used, the same sequence must be followed (paragraphs 11 and 12) to ensure that the removal of all air from the system.

Bleeding sequence

11 If the system has been only partially disconnected, and suitable precautions were taken to minimise fluid loss, it should be necessary to bleed only that part of the system (ie the primary or secondary circuit). Note that the rear brake circuit has only one bleed screw located on the left-hand rear wheel cylinder - hydraulic fluid is supplied to the right-hand rear wheel cylinder, and a brake pipe located on the rear axle connects the two rear wheel cylinders together.

12 If the complete system is to be bled, then it should be done working in the following sequence.
a) Right-hand front wheel.
b) Left-hand front wheel.
c) Rear brake deceleration-sensing proportioning (DSP) valve (where fitted)
d) Left-hand rear wheel.

Bleeding - basic (two-man) method

13 Collect a clean glass jar, a suitable length of plastic or rubber tubing which is a tight fit over the bleed screw, and a ring spanner to fit the screw. The help of an assistant will also be required.

14 Remove the dust cap **(see illustration)** from the first screw in the sequence (if not already done). Fit a suitable spanner and tube to the screw, place the other end of the tube in the jar, and pour in sufficient fluid to cover the end of the tube.

15 Ensure that the brake fluid reservoir fluid level is maintained at least above the "MIN" level line throughout the procedure.

16 Have the assistant fully depress the brake

2.14 Dust cap (arrowed) on the front brake caliper bleed screw

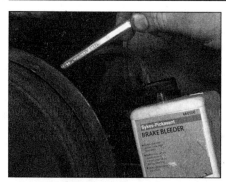

2.22 Bleeding the rear brake hydraulic system (left-hand rear brake)

pedal several times to build up pressure, then maintain it down on the final downstroke.

17 While pedal pressure is maintained, unscrew the bleed screw (approximately one turn) and allow the compressed fluid and air to flow into the jar. The assistant should maintain pedal pressure, following the pedal down to the floor, and should not release the pedal until instructed to do so. When the flow stops, tighten the bleed screw again, have the assistant release the pedal slowly, and recheck the reservoir fluid level.

18 Repeat the steps given in paragraphs 16 and 17 until the fluid emerging from the bleed screw is free from air bubbles. If the master cylinder has been drained and refilled, and air is being bled from the first screw in the sequence, allow at least five seconds between cycles for the master cylinder passages to refill.

19 When no more air bubbles appear, tighten the bleed screw securely, remove the tube and spanner, and refit the dust cap (where applicable). Do not overtighten the bleed screw.

20 Repeat the procedure on the remaining screws in the sequence, until all air is removed from the system and the brake pedal feels firm again.

Bleeding - using a one-way valve kit

21 As their name implies, these kits consist of a length of tubing with a one-way valve fitted, to prevent expelled air and fluid being

drawn back into the system; some kits include a translucent container, which can be positioned so that the air bubbles can be more easily seen flowing from the end of the tube.

22 The kit is connected to the bleed screw, which is then opened **(see illustration)**. The user returns to the driver's seat, depresses the brake pedal with a smooth, steady stroke, and slowly releases it; this is repeated until the expelled fluid is clear of air bubbles.

23 Note that these kits simplify work so much that it is easy to forget the brake fluid reservoir fluid level; ensure that this is maintained at least above the "MIN" level line at all times.

Bleeding - using a pressure-bleeding kit

24 These kits are usually operated by the reservoir of pressurised air contained in the spare tyre. However, note that it will probably be necessary to reduce the pressure to a lower level than normal; refer to the instructions supplied with the kit.

25 By connecting a pressurised, fluid-filled container to the brake fluid reservoir, bleeding can be carried out simply by opening each screw in turn (in the specified sequence), and allowing the fluid to flow out until no more air bubbles can be seen in the expelled fluid.

26 This method has the advantage that the large reservoir of fluid provides an additional safeguard against air being drawn into the system during bleeding.

27 Pressure-bleeding is particularly effective when bleeding "difficult" systems, or when bleeding the complete system at the time of routine fluid renewal.

All methods

28 When bleeding is complete, and firm pedal feel is restored, wash off any spilt fluid, tighten the bleed screws securely, and refit their dust caps.

29 Check the hydraulic fluid level in the brake fluid reservoir, and top-up if necessary (Chapter 1).

30 Discard any hydraulic fluid that has been bled from the system; it will not be fit for re-use.

31 Check the feel of the brake pedal. If it feels at all spongy, air must still be present in the system, and further bleeding is required. Failure to bleed satisfactorily after a reasonable repetition of the bleeding procedure may be due to worn master cylinder seals.

3 Hydraulic pipes and hoses - renewal

Note: *Before starting work, refer to the note at the beginning of Section 2 concerning the dangers of hydraulic fluid.*

1 If any pipe or hose is to be renewed, minimise fluid loss by first removing the brake fluid reservoir cap; tighten it down onto a piece of polythene to obtain an airtight seal. Alternatively, flexible hoses can be sealed, if required, using a proprietary brake hose clamp; metal brake pipe unions can be plugged (if care is taken not to allow dirt into the system) or capped immediately they are disconnected. Place a wad of rag under any union that is to be disconnected, to catch any spilt fluid.

2 If a flexible hose is to be disconnected, unscrew the brake pipe union nut before removing the spring clip which secures the hose to its mounting bracket **(see illustrations)**.

3 To unscrew the union nuts, it is preferable to obtain a brake pipe spanner of the correct size; these are available from most large motor accessory shops. Failing this, a close-fitting open-ended spanner will be required, though if the nuts are tight or corroded, their flats may be rounded-off if the spanner slips. In such a case, a self-locking wrench is often the only way to unscrew a stubborn union, but it follows that the pipe and the damaged nuts must be renewed on reassembly. Always clean a union and surrounding area before disconnecting it. If disconnecting a component with more than one union, make a careful note of the connections before disturbing any of them.

4 If a brake pipe is to be renewed, it can be obtained, cut to length and with the union

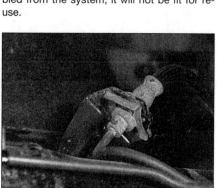

3.2b Flexible brake hose connection to brake line on rear axle casing

3.6 Brake pipe mounting clip on the rear axle

3.2a Flexible brake hose connection to brake line on mounting bracket beneath front wheel arch

nuts and end flares in place, from a Vauxhall or Suzuki dealer. All that is then necessary is to bend it to shape, following the line of the original, before fitting it to the vehicle. Alternatively, most motor accessory shops can make up brake pipes, but this requires very careful measurement of the original, to ensure that the replacement is of the correct length. The safest answer is usually to take the original to the shop as a pattern.

5 On refitting, do not overtighten the union nuts. It is not necessary to exercise brute force to obtain a sound joint.

6 Ensure that the pipes and hoses are correctly routed, with no kinks, and that they are secured in the clips or brackets provided **(see illustration)**. After fitting, remove the polythene from the reservoir, and bleed the hydraulic system as described in Section 2. Wash off any spilt fluid, and check carefully for fluid leaks.

4 Front brake pads - renewal

⚠️ **Warning: Renew BOTH sets of front brake pads at the same time - NEVER renew the pads on only one wheel, as uneven braking may result. Note that the dust created by wear of the pads may contain asbestos, which is a health hazard. Never blow it out with compressed air, and don't inhale any of it. An approved filtering mask should be worn when working on the brakes. DO NOT use petrol or petroleum-based solvents to clean brake parts; use brake cleaner or methylated spirit only.**

1 Apply the handbrake, then jack up the front of the vehicle and support it on axle stands (see *"Jacking, towing and wheel changing"*). Remove the front roadwheels.

2 Push the piston into its bore by pulling the caliper outwards.

3 Unscrew and remove the caliper upper and lower guide pin bolts **(see illustration)**.

4 With the guide pins removed, lift the caliper away from the brake pads and mounting bracket **(see illustration)**, and tie it to the

4.3 Unscrewing a caliper guide pin bolt (arrowed)

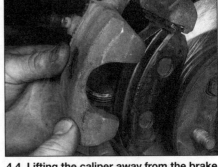

4.4 Lifting the caliper away from the brake pads and mounting bracket

suspension strut using a suitable piece of wire. Do not allow the caliper to hang unsupported on the flexible hose. Also **do not** depress the brake pedal with the caliper removed from the mounting bracket.

5 Withdraw the two brake pads from the caliper mounting bracket **(see illustration)**, and examine them as follows. First measure the thickness of each brake pad (friction material and backing plate). If any pad is worn at any point to the specified minimum thickness or less, **all four** pads must be renewed. Note that the wear grooves in the friction linings are machined so that they disappear when the minimum thickness has been reached. Also, the pads should be renewed if any are fouled with oil or grease; there is no satisfactory way of degreasing friction material, once contaminated. If any of the brake pads are worn unevenly or fouled with oil or grease, trace and rectify the cause before reassembly. New brake pads and spring kits are available from Vauxhall/Suzuki dealers, motor factors or car accessory shops.

6 If the brake pads are still serviceable, carefully clean them using a clean, fine wire brush or similar, paying particular attention to the sides and back of the metal backing. Clean out the grooves in the friction material, and pick out any large embedded particles of dirt or debris. Carefully clean the pad locations in the caliper body/mounting bracket.

7 Prior to fitting the pads, check that the guide sleeves are free to slide easily in the caliper body, and check that the rubber guide sleeve gaiters are undamaged. Brush the dust and dirt from the caliper and piston, but do not inhale it, as it is a health hazard. Inspect the dust seal around the piston for damage, and the piston for evidence of fluid leaks, corrosion or damage. If attention to any of these components is necessary, refer to Section 8. Also inspect the brake disc as described in Section 6.

8 If new brake pads are to be fitted, the caliper piston must be pushed back into the cylinder to make room for them. Either use a G-clamp or similar tool, or use suitable pieces of wood as levers. Provided that the brake fluid reservoir has not been overfilled with hydraulic fluid, there should be no spillage, but keep a careful watch on the fluid level while retracting the piston. If the fluid level rises above the "MAX" level line at any time, the surplus should be siphoned off (not by mouth - use an old syringe or a poultry baster) or ejected via a plastic tube connected to an opened bleed screw.

9 Apply a smear of copper grease to the backing plates of the pads, then install them in the caliper bracket, ensuring that the friction material of each pad is against the brake disc **(see illustrations)**.

10 Position the caliper over the pads. Coat the threads of the new lower guide pin bolt with locking fluid, and fit the bolt. Apply

4.5 Removing the brake pads from the caliper mounting bracket

4.9a Apply a smear of copper grease to the backing plates of the pads . . .

4.9b . . . then install them in the caliper bracket

4.10a Position the caliper over the brake pads . . .

4.10b . . . and refit the bolts

5.2 Rear brake shoes ready for dismantling

locking fluid to the new upper guide pin bolt, press the caliper into position, and fit the bolt **(see illustrations)**. Check that the anti-rattle springs are correctly located.

11 Tighten the guide pin bolts to the specified torque, starting with the lower bolt.

12 Depress the brake pedal several times, to bring the pads into firm contact with the brake disc.

13 Repeat the above procedure on the other front brake caliper.

14 Refit the roadwheels, then lower the vehicle to the ground, and tighten the roadwheel nuts to the specified torque.

15 Check the hydraulic fluid level as described in Chapter 1.

16 If new pads have been fitted, full braking efficiency will not be obtained until the linings have bedded-in. Be prepared for longer stopping distances, and avoid harsh braking as far as possible for the first hundred miles or so after fitting new pads.

5 Rear brake shoes - renewal

⚠ **Warning:** Renew BOTH sets of rear brake shoes at the same time - NEVER renew the shoes on only one wheel, as uneven braking may result. Note that the dust created by wear of the shoes may contain

asbestos, which is a health hazard. Never blow it out with compressed air, and don't inhale any of it. An approved filtering mask should be worn when working on the brakes. DO NOT use petrol or petroleum-based solvents to clean brake parts; use brake cleaner or methylated spirit only.

1 Remove the rear brake drums, as described in Section 7.

2 Working on one side of the vehicle, brush the dirt and dust from the brake shoes, backplate and drum **(see illustration)**. Do not inhale the dust, as it may be a health hazard.

3 Note the position of each shoe, and the location of the return and steady springs.

4 Remove the trailing shoe hold-down spring. Use a pair of pliers to depress the spring and

turn it through 90°, then release the spring from the pin and remove it **(see illustration)**.

5 Recover the special spring retainer pin from the backplate **(see illustration)**.

6 Release the bottom of the trailing brake shoe from the backplate bottom anchor, then unhook and remove the lower return spring **(see illustrations)**.

7 Using a pair of pliers, unhook the end of the handbrake cable from the lever on the trailing shoe **(see illustration)**.

8 Unhook the small spring securing the trailing shoe to the automatic adjustment link, and remove the shoe from the link **(see illustration)**.

9 Remove the leading shoe hold-down spring. Use a pair of pliers to depress the

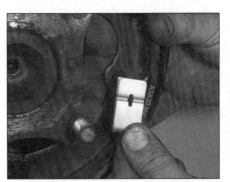

5.4 Removing the trailing shoe hold-down spring

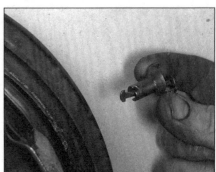

5.5 Removing the special spring retainer spring from the backplate

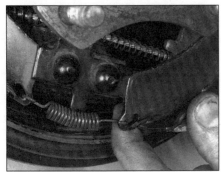

5.6a Release the bottom of the trailing brake shoe from the backplate bottom anchor . . .

5.6b . . . then unhook and remove the lower return spring

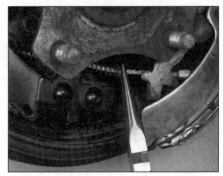

5.7 Unhook the end of the handbrake cable from the lever on the trailing shoe

5.8 Unhook the small spring securing the trailing shoe to the link, and remove the shoe

5.9a Use a pair of pliers to depress the spring and turn it through 90° . . .

5.9b . . . then remove the spring

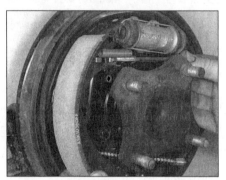

5.10 Removing the leading shoe and adjustment link

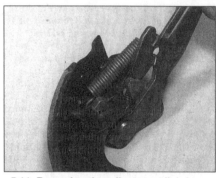

5.11 Removing the adjustment link from the leading shoe

spring and turn it through 90°, then release the spring from the pin and remove it (see illustrations).

10 Withdraw the leading shoe together with the adjustment link from the backplate (see illustration).

11 Remove the adjustment link from the leading shoe, and unhook the spring (see illustration).

12 Position a rubber band or a cable-tie over the wheel cylinder, to prevent the pistons from being ejected (see illustration). If there is any evidence of fluid leakage from the wheel cylinder, renew it or overhaul it as described in Section 9.

13 Transfer the handbrake and automatic adjuster levers to the new shoes, as required (prise off the spring clips to remove the levers) (see illustrations). Note that the levers and strut on each rear wheel are different.

14 Apply brake grease sparingly to the shoe contact areas of the brake backplate (see illustration), and where applicable, remove the rubber band or cable-tie from the wheel cylinder.

15 Fit the adjustment link to the leading shoe, making sure that the spring is correctly located.

16 Remove the rubber band or cable-tie from the wheel cylinder, then locate the leading shoe and link on the backplate.

17 Refit the leading shoe hold-down spring.

18 Locate the trailing shoe onto the

5.12 An elastic band positioned on the wheel cylinder, to prevent the pistons from being ejected

5.13a Prise off the spring clip with a screwdriver . . .

5.13b . . . and remove the pin

5.13c Use a pair of pliers to press the new clip in position

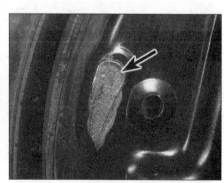

5.14 Apply brake grease sparingly to the shoe contact areas of the brake backplate

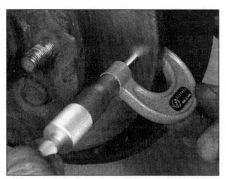

6.3 Using a micrometer to measure disc thickness

adjustment link, and refit the small spring while twisting the shoe outwards.

19 Engage the end of the handbrake cable with the lever on the trailing shoe.

20 Attach the lower return spring, then locate the bottom of the trailing brake shoe in the backplate bottom anchor.

21 Insert the special spring retainer pin in the backplate and through the trailing shoe, then refit the hold-down spring.

22 Set the automatic adjuster link to its minimum length by prising the serrated quadrant out from the leading shoe end.

23 Repeat the procedure on the remaining side of the vehicle, then refit the brake drums as described in Section 7.

24 On completion, check the handbrake adjustment as described in Chapter 1.

6 Front brake disc -
inspection, removal and refitting

Note: Before starting work, refer to the warning at the beginning of Section 4 concerning the dangers of asbestos dust. If either disc requires renewal, BOTH should be renewed at the same time, to ensure even and consistent braking. New brake pads should also be fitted.

Inspection

1 Apply the handbrake, then jack up the front of the vehicle and support it on axle stands (see *"Jacking, towing and wheel changing"*). Remove the appropriate front roadwheel.

2 Slowly rotate the brake disc so that the full area of both sides can be checked; remove the brake pads (see Section 4) if better access is required to the inboard surface. Light scoring is normal in the area swept by the brake pads, but if heavy scoring or cracks are found, the disc must be renewed.

3 It is normal to find some rust around the disc's perimeter; this can be scraped off if required. If, however, a lip has formed due to excessive wear of the brake pad swept area, then the disc's thickness must be measured using a micrometer **(see illustration)**. Take measurements at several places around the disc, at the inside and outside of the pad

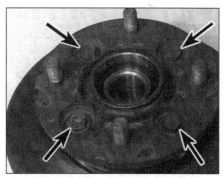

6.7 Bolts (arrowed) securing the brake disc to the hub

swept area; if the disc has worn at any point to the specified minimum thickness or less, the disc must be renewed.

4 If the disc is thought to be warped, it can be checked for run-out. Either use a dial gauge mounted on any convenient fixed point, while the disc is slowly rotated, or use feeler blades to measure (at several points all around the disc) the clearance between the disc and a fixed point, such as the caliper mounting bracket. If the measurements obtained are at the specified maximum or beyond, the disc is excessively warped, and must be renewed; however, it is worth checking first that the hub bearing is in good condition (Chapters 1 and/or 10). Also, try the effect of removing the disc and turning it through 180°, to reposition it on the hub; if the run-out is still excessive, the disc must be renewed.

5 Check the disc for cracks and any other wear or damage, and renew if necessary.

Removal

6 Remove the front hub with reference to Chapter 10, Section 2.

7 Unscrew the bolts, and separate the brake disc from the hub **(see illustration)**. If the disc is rusted onto the hub, tap it free with a hide or rubber mallet.

Refitting

8 Ensure that the contact faces of the disc and hub are clean. If a new disc is being fitted, use a suitable solvent to wipe any preservative coating from the disc.

9 Locate the disc on the inner face of the hub,

7.2 The trailing brake shoe hold-down spring pin stopper (arrowed)

and insert the retaining bolts from the outside, loosely at this stage.

10 Refit the front hub with reference to Chapter 10, Section 2.

11 Have an assistant depress the brake pedal, then tighten the bolts securing the brake disc to the hub to the specified torque.

12 Refit the front roadwheel, lower the vehicle to the ground, and tighten the roadwheel nuts to the specified torque.

7 Rear brake drum -
removal, inspection and refitting

Note: Before starting work, refer to the warning at the beginning of Section 5 concerning the dangers of asbestos dust. If either drum requires renewal, BOTH should be renewed at the same time, to ensure even and consistent braking. New brake shoes should also be fitted.

Removal

1 Chock the front wheels, then release the handbrake, jack up the rear of the vehicle, and support it on axle stands (see *"Jacking, towing and wheel changing"*). Remove the appropriate rear wheel.

2 Before attempting to remove the brake drum, the rear brake shoes must be positioned so that the maximum clearance exists between the shoes and the drum inner surface. **Note:** *It is best not to attempt to remove the drum without doing this, as it may not be possible to determine whether the drum is tight on the rear axle shaft flange, or tight on the rear brake shoes.* On the inner-facing side of the backplate, and towards the rear of the vehicle, is located the trailing shoe hold-down spring pin stopper **(see illustration)**. Using a pair of pliers or grips, pull out this stopper approximately 5 mm - this will allow the handbrake lever on the trailing shoe to move rearwards, increasing the clearance between the shoes and the drum.

3 The brake drum incorporates two 8 mm threaded holes for the purpose of forcing the drum off the rear axle - insert two 8 mm bolts in the holes, and tighten them evenly until the

7.3a Using 8 mm bolts to pull the rear brake drum off the axle shaft flange

7.3b Removing a rear brake drum - note the accumulated dust on the shoes and wheel cylinder

7.10 Locating the brake drum over the wheel studs

drum is forced off the flange. Withdraw the drum over the wheel studs **(see illustrations)**.

Inspection

4 Working carefully, remove all traces of brake dust from the drum, but *avoid inhaling the dust, as it is a health hazard.*
5 Clean the outside of the drum, and check it for obvious signs of wear or damage, such as cracks around the roadwheel stud holes; renew the drum if necessary.
6 Carefully examine the inside of the drum. Light scoring of the friction surface is normal, but if heavy scoring is found, the drum must be renewed. It is usual to find a lip on the outer edge of the drum, which consists of rust; this should be scraped away to leave a smooth surface. If, however, the lip is due to the friction surface being recessed by excessive wear, then the drum must be renewed.
7 If the drum is thought to be excessively worn, or oval, its internal diameter must be measured at several points using an internal micrometer. Take measurements in pairs, the second at right-angles to the first, and compare the two, to check for signs of ovality. Provided that it does not enlarge the drum to beyond the specified maximum diameter, it may be possible to have the drum refinished by skimming or grinding; if this is not possible, the drums on both sides must be renewed. Note that if the drum is to be skimmed, BOTH drums must be refinished, to maintain a consistent internal diameter on both sides.

Refitting

8 Before refitting the drum, have an assistant apply the handbrake lever, then refit the trailing shoe hold-down spring pin stopper. Release the handbrake, then make sure that the rear brake shoes are located on the wheel cylinder and bottom anchor correctly. Move the serrated automatic adjuster lever quadrant against the spring tension, to set the shoes at their minimum diameter, by inserting a screwdriver to prise out the quadrant.
9 If a new brake drum is to be fitted, use a suitable solvent to remove any preservative coating that may have been applied to its internal friction surfaces.

10 Locate the drum over the wheel studs, and tap it fully onto the rear axle flange using a hammer **(see illustration)**.
11 Depress the footbrake several times to operate the self-adjusting mechanism.
12 Repeat the above procedure on the remaining rear brake assembly (where necessary), then check and, if necessary, adjust the handbrake cable as described in Chapter 1.
13 On completion, refit the roadwheel(s), then lower the vehicle to the ground and tighten the wheel nuts to the specified torque.

8 Front brake caliper - removal, overhaul and refitting

Note: *Before starting work, refer to the note at the beginning of Section 2 concerning the dangers of hydraulic fluid, and to the warning at the beginning of Section 4 concerning the dangers of asbestos dust.*

Removal

1 Apply the handbrake, then jack up the front of the vehicle and support it on axle stands (see *"Jacking, towing and wheel changing"*). Remove the appropriate roadwheel.
2 Before disconnecting the hydraulic circuit, push the caliper piston into its bore by pulling the caliper outwards.
3 To minimise fluid loss, first remove the brake fluid reservoir cap, then tighten it down onto a piece of polythene, to obtain an airtight seal. Alternatively, and preferably, use a brake hose clamp to clamp the flexible hose running to the caliper.
4 Clean the area around the flexible hose union bolt on the caliper. Unscrew and remove the bolt, and recover the two washers either side of the union. Tie a small plastic bag over the union, to prevent dust and dirt entering the hydraulic system.
5 Slacken and remove the caliper upper and lower guide pin bolts, using a slim open-ended spanner to prevent the guide pin itself from rotating.
6 With the guide pins removed, lift the caliper away from the brake pads and mounting

bracket. **Do not** depress the brake pedal with the caliper removed. Note that the brake pads need not be disturbed, and can be left in position in the caliper mounting bracket.

Overhaul

7 With the caliper on the bench, wipe away all traces of dust and dirt, but *avoid inhaling the dust, as it is a health hazard.*
8 Use a small screwdriver to carefully prise the dust seal retaining clip out of the caliper bore.
9 Withdraw the piston from the caliper body, and remove the dust seal. The piston can be withdrawn by hand, or if necessary pushed out by applying compressed air to the brake hose union hole. Only low pressure should be required, such as is generated by a foot pump.

⚠️ *Caution: The piston may be ejected with some force.*

10 Using a small screwdriver, extract the piston hydraulic seal, taking great care not to damage the caliper bore.
11 Where applicable, prise off the retaining clips, then withdraw the guide sleeve pins from the caliper mounting bracket, and remove the rubber gaiters.
12 Thoroughly clean all components, using only methylated spirit or clean hydraulic fluid as a cleaning agent. Never use mineral-based solvents such as petrol or paraffin, as they will attack the hydraulic system's rubber components. Dry the components immediately, using compressed air or a clean, lint-free cloth. Use compressed air to blow clear the fluid passages.
13 Check all components, and renew any that are worn or damaged. Check particularly the cylinder bore and piston; these should be renewed if they are scratched, worn or corroded in any way. Similarly check the condition of the guide sleeve pins and their bores in the caliper mounting bracket; both pins should be undamaged and a reasonably tight sliding fit in the mounting bracket bores. If there is any doubt about the condition of any component, renew it.
14 If the assembly is fit for further use, obtain the appropriate repair kit.
15 Renew all rubber seals, dust covers and caps disturbed on dismantling as a matter of course.
16 On reassembly, ensure that all components are absolutely clean and dry.
17 Dip the piston and the new piston (fluid) seal in clean hydraulic fluid. Smear clean fluid on the cylinder bore surface.
18 Fit the new piston (fluid) seal, using only your fingers to manipulate it into the cylinder bore groove. Fit the new dust seal to the piston, and refit the piston to the cylinder bore using a twisting motion; ensure that the piston enters squarely into the bore. Press the piston fully into the bore, then press the dust seal into the caliper body.
19 Where fitted, install the dust seal retaining

clip, ensuring that it is correctly seated in the caliper groove.

20 Apply the grease supplied in the repair kit, or a good quality high-temperature brake grease or anti-seize compound (eg Duckhams Copper 10), to the guide sleeve pins. Fit the guide sleeve pins to the caliper body mounting bracket, and fit the new rubber gaiters, ensuring that they are correctly located in the grooves on both the pin and body mounting bracket.

Refitting

21 Check that the brake pads are still correctly fitted in the caliper mounting bracket.

22 Position the caliper over the brake pads, and align the mounting bolt holes with the guide pins.

23 If the threads of the caliper guide pin bolts are not already pre-coated with locking compound (new ones usually are), apply a suitable locking compound to them. Refit the bolts, and tighten them to the specified torque while holding the flats on the pins with a spanner.

24 Refit the flexible hose union to the caliper, together with two new washers, and tighten the bolt to the specified torque. The hose should be positioned so that it curves upwards from the caliper.

25 Remove the brake hose clamp, or remove the polythene from the fluid reservoir, as applicable, and bleed the hydraulic system as described in Section 2. Note that, providing the precautions described were taken to minimise brake fluid loss, it should only be necessary to bleed the relevant front brake circuit.

26 Refit the roadwheel, then lower the vehicle to the ground, and tighten the roadwheel nuts to the specified torque.

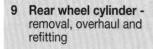

9 Rear wheel cylinder -
removal, overhaul and
refitting

Note: *Before starting work, refer to the warning at the beginning of Section 2 concerning the dangers of hydraulic fluid.*

Removal

1 Remove the brake drum as described in Section 7, and the rear brake shoes as described in Section 5.

2 To minimise fluid loss, first remove the brake fluid reservoir cap, then tighten it down onto a piece of polythene, to obtain an airtight seal. Alternatively, use a brake hose clamp to clamp the rear brake flexible hose in front of the rear axle on the right-hand side **(see illustration)**.

3 Wipe away all traces of dirt around the brake pipe union(s) at the rear of the wheel cylinder. The right-hand rear wheel cylinder has two brake pipes connected to it, and is not fitted with a bleed screw; the left-hand

9.2 To minimise fluid loss, fit a brake hose clamp (arrowed) to the flexible hose in front of the rear axle on the right-hand side

rear wheel cylinder has only one brake pipe fitted to it, but has a bleed screw for bleeding the rear brake circuit **(see illustration)**.

4 Unscrew the brake pipe union(s) from the rear of the wheel cylinder. Ideally, a proper brake pipe spanner should be used to do this, but a close-fitting open-ended spanner may be used (refer to Section 3 if necessary). To prevent the entry of dust and dirt in the hydraulic system, tie a plastic bag over the end of the pipe(s), or fit rubber caps to the pipe(s). Wipe any spilt fluid from the brake backplate.

5 Unscrew the two retaining bolts from the rear of the backplate, and remove the wheel cylinder **(see illustration)**. Wipe any spilt fluid from the brake backplate.

Overhaul

6 Clean the exterior of the cylinder, removing all traces of dirt and brake dust.

7 Pull the dust seals from the grooves in the ends of the cylinder **(see illustration)**.

8 Extract the pistons and seals, and return spring, noting the locations of all components to ensure correct refitting.

9 Examine the surfaces of the cylinder bore and pistons for signs of scoring and corrosion, and if evident, renew the complete wheel cylinder. If the components are in good condition, discard the seals and obtain a

9.5 Removing the wheel cylinder from the backplate

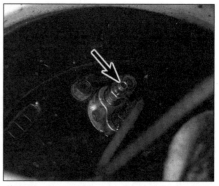

9.3 The left-hand rear wheel cylinder has only one brake pipe fitted to it, but also has the rear brake bleed screw (arrowed)

repair kit, which will contain all the necessary renewable components.

10 Clean the pistons, the cylinder and return spring with methylated spirit or clean brake fluid, and reassemble in reverse order, making sure that the components are fitted in the correct sequence and orientated correctly, as noted before removal. Dip the pistons in clean brake fluid before inserting them into the cylinder. Ensure that the lips of the seals face into the cylinder.

11 On completion, wipe away any excess brake fluid.

Refitting

12 Clean the backplate, then place the wheel cylinder in position, and tighten the retaining bolts.

13 Reconnect and tighten the brake pipe union(s) to the rear of the wheel cylinder, taking care not to allow dirt into the system.

14 Refit the rear brake shoes and drum with reference to Sections 5 and 7.

15 On completion, remove the brake hose clamp, or remove the polythene from the fluid reservoir, as applicable, and bleed the hydraulic system as described in Section 2. Note that, providing the precautions described were taken to minimise brake fluid loss, it should only be necessary to bleed the rear brake circuit.

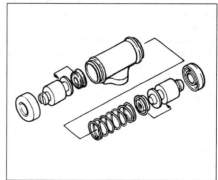

9.7 Exploded view of the rear wheel cylinder

10.1 Brake fluid reservoir mounted on the A-pillar - seen with facia panel removed, for clarity

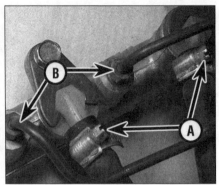

10.4 Brake master cylinder, showing supply hose (A) and brake line (B) connections - unit removed for clarity

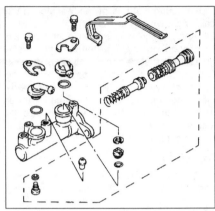

10.6 Exploded view of the master cylinder

10 Master cylinder -
removal, overhaul and refitting

Note: *Before starting work, refer to the warning at the beginning of Section 2 concerning the dangers of hydraulic fluid.*

Removal

1 Remove the facia panel as described in Chapter 11. Although it is *just* possible to remove the master cylinder without removing the facia, its removal will provide much more working room, and make the task that much easier **(see illustration)**.
2 Unscrew the brake fluid reservoir cap, and use a syringe or poultry baster to draw out the hydraulic fluid. Alternatively, brake hose clamps may be fitted to both of the hoses leading from the master cylinder to the fluid reservoir.
3 Loosen the worm-drive clips, and disconnect the two reservoir rubber hoses from the master cylinder. Wipe away any excess hydraulic fluid.
4 Wipe clean the area around the master cylinder, and place absorbent rags beneath the pipe unions to catch any surplus fluid. Unscrew the two unions and disconnect the brake pipes from the master cylinder. Note their fitted positions for correct refitting. If necessary, release the pipes from the support bracket, and plug or tape over their ends **(see illustration)**.
5 Unscrew the main mounting nuts and the upper mounting bracket bolt, and withdraw the master cylinder from the rear face of the vacuum servo unit.

Overhaul

Note: *Note the order of removal of each item as it is removed from the master cylinder, to ensure correct refitting.*

6 Note the orientation of the hydraulic fluid inlet stubs on the top of the master cylinder to ensure correct refitting, then unscrew the clamp bolts and remove the clamps **(see illustration)**.

7 Carefully prise out the fluid inlet stubs from the top of the master cylinder. Check the sealing rings, and if necessary extract them from the grooves.
8 Extract the circlips from the inlet apertures, then remove the check valves and sealing rings.
9 Position a piece of clean rag over the open end of the master cylinder, then apply air pressure (such as from a foot pump) to the primary circuit fluid aperture to force out the primary piston. **Note:** *Take extreme care if using an air line, as the piston will be ejected with considerable force.*
10 Depress the secondary piston using a screwdriver, then unscrew the stopper screw from the side of the master cylinder.
11 Using the same method used to remove the primary piston, remove the secondary piston by applying air pressure in the stopper screw hole.
12 Thoroughly clean all components, using only methylated spirit or clean hydraulic fluid as a cleaning agent. Never use mineral-based solvents such as petrol or paraffin, as they will attack the hydraulic system rubber components. Dry the components immediately, using compressed air or a clean, lint-free cloth.
13 Check all components, and renew any that are worn or damaged. Check particularly the cylinder bores and pistons; the complete assembly should be renewed if these are scratched, worn or corroded. If there is any doubt about the condition of the assembly or any of its components, renew it. Check that the cylinder body fluid passages are clear.

 Warning: where a cast-aluminium master cylinder is fitted, do not under any circumstances polish the piston bore.

14 If the assembly is fit for further use, obtain a repair kit of all seals and washers.
15 Before reassembly, dip the pistons and the new seals in clean hydraulic fluid. Smear clean fluid onto the cylinder bore.
16 Insert the secondary piston assembly into the cylinder bore, using a twisting motion to avoid trapping the seal lips. Using a

screwdriver, depress the secondary piston, then refit and tighten the stopper screw.
17 Using the same method as for the secondary piston, insert the primary piston assembly into the cylinder bore.
18 Insert the sealing rings and check valves into the inlet apertures, and secure with the circlips.
19 Check that the sealing rings are in place in the fluid inlet stubs, then press the stubs into the master cylinder apertures.
20 Turn the stubs to their previously-noted positions, and refit the clamps. Tighten the clamp bolts.

Refitting

21 Clean the contact surfaces of the master cylinder and vacuum servo unit, then locate the master cylinder on the mounting studs, and tighten the nuts to the specified torque. Also tighten the upper mounting bolt.
22 Locate the two brake pipes in the support bracket, then insert the unions in the master cylinder and tighten to the specified torque.
23 Reconnect the fluid reservoir hoses to the master cylinder, and tighten the clips.
24 Remove the brake hose clamps (where used).
25 Check and if necessary adjust the brake pedal height, with reference to Section 11.
26 Fill the brake fluid reservoir with new fluid, and bleed the complete hydraulic system as described in Section 2.

11 Brake pedal -
removal and refitting

Removal

1 Remove the facia panel as described in Chapter 11.
2 Loosen the clip and disconnect the vacuum servo hose from the servo unit.
3 Disconnect the clutch cable from the clutch pedal and bracket, with reference to Chapter 7.
4 Disconnect the wiring from the stop-light switch on the pedal bracket.

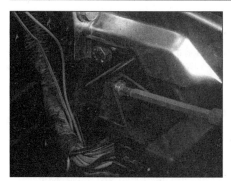

11.5a Unscrew the screws . . .

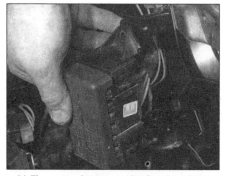

11.5b . . . and remove the fusebox from the pedal bracket

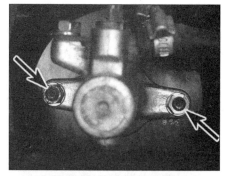

11.6 Master cylinder mounting nuts (arrowed) on the rear face of the servo

5 Unscrew the screws and remove the fusebox from the pedal bracket **(see illustrations)**.

6 Unscrew the mounting nuts securing the master cylinder to the rear face of the vacuum servo unit **(see illustrations)**. Also, where necessary, unscrew the master cylinder upper mounting bolt at the small bracket on the servo unit.

7 Withdraw the master cylinder away from the servo unit, bending the brake lines only a minimum amount **(see illustration)**.

8 Unscrew the mounting bolts and withdraw the pedal bracket together with the vacuum servo unit, leaving the master cylinder suspended by the brake lines **(see illustrations)**.

9 Unscrew the nut from the right-hand end of the pedal pivot bolt **(see illustration)**.

10 Note the location of the pedal return springs, then withdraw the pivot bolt to the left-hand side of the bracket until the brake pedal can be removed. If necessary, remove the pedal return spring.

11 Carefully clean all components, renewing any that are worn or damaged; check the bearing surfaces of the pivot bush and bolt with particular care. It is not possible to renew the bush, and if it is excessively worn, the pedal must be renewed.

Refitting

12 Lubricate the brake pedal bore with a little grease, then locate the pedal in the bracket,

and fully push in the pivot bolt from the left-hand side. Make sure the pedal return spring is correctly located.

13 Refit and tighten the pedal pivot bolt nut to the specified torque.

14 The brake pedal should be set at the same height as the clutch pedal (assuming that the clutch cable adjustment is also correct). If necessary, check that the measurement between the brake vacuum servo mounting surface and the centre of the pushrod clevis pin hole is between 106.5 mm and 107.5 mm. Adjust if required.

15 Check that the wiring harness near the pedal bracket position is located correctly, so that it will not obstruct the refitting procedure. Locate the pedal bracket on the bulkhead.

11.7 Withdrawing the master cylinder from the servo unit, leaving the brake lines still attached

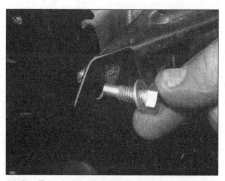

11.8a Removing the side mounting bolt . . .

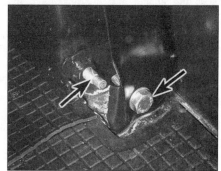

11.8b . . . lower mounting bolts (arrowed) . . .

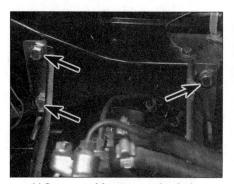

11.8c . . . and front mounting bolts (arrowed)

11.8d Removing the pedal bracket, leaving the master cylinder in position

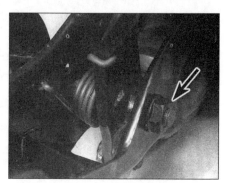

11.9 Brake pedal and pivot shaft nut (arrowed) located at the right-hand end

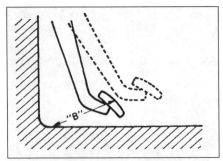

11.22 Brake pedal travel dimension (B) with specified force applied

B = 95 mm

Check again that the wiring is not trapped beneath the bracket. Refit and tighten the lower mounting bolt.

16 Locate the master cylinder on the rear of the vacuum servo unit, and tighten the mounting nuts and bolt to the specified torque.

17 Refit the fusebox and tighten the mounting bolt.

18 Reconnect the wiring to the stop-light switch on the pedal bracket.

19 Reconnect the clutch cable to the clutch pedal. If necessary, adjust the clutch cable with reference to Chapter 7.

20 Reconnect the vacuum servo hose to the servo unit, and tighten the clip.

21 Refit the facia panel with reference to Chapter 11.

22 Check the brake pedal travel as follows. Start the engine and depress the pedal several times, then apply a force of approximately 66 lbs (30 kg) to the pedal, and measure the distance from the top of the pedal footpad to the bulkhead **(see illustration)**. This distance must not be less than 95 mm. If it is, the probable cause is that the rear brakes are worn excessively, or that there is air in the hydraulic circuit.

23 Adjust the brake stop-light switch as described in Section 16.

---

12 Brake pressure proportioning valves - description, testing, removal and refitting

Description

1 The deceleration-sensing proportioning (DSP) valve reduces the pressure to the rear brakes at or above a predetermined rate of deceleration. The valve incorporates an inertia ball which controls the brake pressure, and is fitted to models manufactured before September 1990. The valve is located on the right-hand chassis member, midway along on Van models, or towards the front of the vehicle on Pickup models **(see illustration)**.

2 A gravity proportioning (GP) valve is fitted to some models. On early models, the valve was located at the front of the vehicle, and

12.1 Deceleration-sensing proportioning (DSP) valve (Van model)

controlled the pressure to both the front and rear braking circuits. As from September 1990, the GP valve is only fitted in the rear brake circuit, and incorporates a bypass for the rear circuit, which applies full line pressure to the rear brakes in the event of a front circuit failure.

3 A proportioning and bypass (P&B) valve is fitted to some models, and is located in the master cylinder outlet hydraulic pipes.

4 The valves are fitted in various positions and in various combinations, according to model.

Testing

5 The purpose of the proportioning valve(s) is to maintain equal braking effect on the front and rear wheels, regardless of the load being carried, and (specifically) to prevent the rear brakes from locking up.

6 If you find that, on applying the brakes, the effect is mainly on the front wheels, or alternatively, that the rear brakes invariably lock under heavy braking, it is likely that the valve is defective.

7 A Vauxhall or Suzuki dealer will have to test the component if its performance is in doubt, as pressure-testing equipment is necessary. No attempt must be made to dismantle the unit.

Removal

8 To remove the valve, first chock the front or rear wheels (as appropriate), then jack up the front or rear of the vehicle, and support on axle stands.

13.5a Extract the split pin (arrowed) . . .

9 To minimise fluid loss, remove the brake fluid reservoir cap, then tighten it down onto a piece of polythene, to obtain an airtight seal.

10 Identify the location of the brake pipes on the valve, then unscrew the union nuts and carefully pull out the pipes so that they are clear of the unit.

11 Unbolt and remove the unit.

Refitting

12 Refitting is a reversal of removal, but tighten the union nuts to the specified torque, and tighten the mounting bolt(s) securely. Bleed the complete hydraulic circuit as described in Section 2.

---

13 Vacuum servo unit - testing, removal and refitting

Testing

1 To test the operation of the servo unit, with the engine off, depress the footbrake several times to exhaust the vacuum. Keep the pedal firmly depressed, and start the engine. As the engine starts, there should be a noticeable "give" in the brake pedal as the vacuum builds up. Allow the engine to run for about one minute, then switch it off. If the brake pedal is now depressed it should feel normal, but further applications should result in the pedal feeling firmer, with the pedal stroke decreasing with each application.

2 If the servo does not operate as described, the fault lies within the unit itself.

3 The servo is very much a sealed unit, with little in the way of repairs being possible. It may be possible to obtain a reconditioned unit from a Vauxhall or Suzuki dealer, or from a motor factor.

Removal

4 Follow the procedure described for the master cylinder removal in Section 10, paragraphs 1 to 5.

5 Extract the split pin, and remove the clevis pin securing the top of the brake pedal to the vacuum servo pushrod clevis **(see illustrations)**.

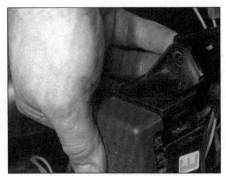

13.5b . . . and remove the clevis pin

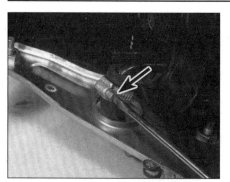
13.6a Loosen the clip (arrowed) . . .

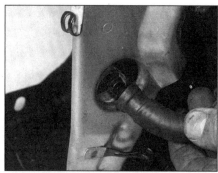
13.6b . . . and disconnect the vacuum hose from the servo unit

13.7 Unbolting the side bracket

6 Loosen the clip, and disconnect the vacuum hose from the servo unit **(see illustrations)**. Note that the arrows on the hose point towards the direction of the inlet manifold.
7 For improved access, unbolt the side bracket **(see illustration)**.
8 Unscrew the mounting nuts, and remove the vacuum servo unit from the pedal bracket **(see illustrations)**.

Refitting

9 Before refitting the servo unit, check the length of the pushrod between the mounting face and the centre of the clevis pin hole **(see**

illustration). If this is not between 106.5 mm and 107.5 mm, loosen the locknut and reposition the clevis as required. Tighten the locknut on completion.
10 Locate the vacuum servo unit on the pedal bracket, and tighten the nuts to the specified torque.
11 Reconnect the top of the brake pedal to the vacuum servo pushrod clevis, by inserting the clevis pin and fitting a new split pin **(see illustrations)**.
12 Reconnect the vacuum hose to the servo unit, and tighten the clip. Note that the arrows on the hose point towards the inlet manifold.

13 The remaining procedure is a reversal of the master cylinder refitting procedure described in Section 10, paragraphs 21 to 26.

14 Handbrake lever - removal and refitting

Removal

1 Working inside the vehicle, remove the centre console as described in Chapter 11.
2 Remove the retaining screw located on the

13.8a Servo unit mounting nuts (arrowed)

13.8b Removing the servo unit from the pedal bracket

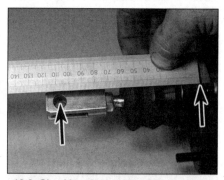
13.9 Checking the length of the pushrod between the mounting face and the centre of the clevis pin hole (arrowed)

13.11a Insert the clevis pin . . .

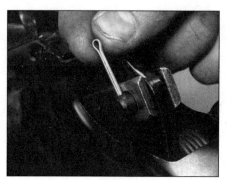
13.11b . . . and fit a new split pin

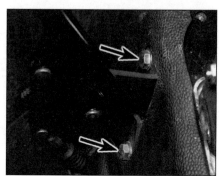
14.5 Handbrake lever mounting bolts (arrowed)

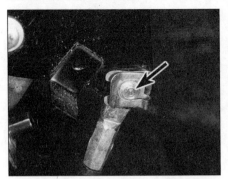

15.4 Clevis pin (arrowed) securing the front of the primary handbrake cable to the bottom of the handbrake lever

15.5a Remove the splash guard on Van models . . .

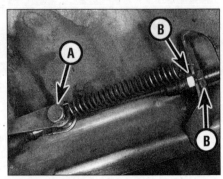

15.5b . . . then unhook return spring from pin (A) and remove pin. Note mounting and adjustment nuts (B)

right-hand side of the seat base panel, then pull back the rubber floor mat for access to the handbrake lever mounting bolts.

3 Release the handbrake. Extract the split pin, or remove the special spring clip, and remove the clevis pin securing the front of the primary handbrake cable to the bottom of the handbrake lever (see illustration 15.4).

4 Remove the handbrake warning light switch as described in Section 17.

5 Unscrew the mounting bolts, and remove the handbrake lever from the body crossmember (see illustration).

Refitting

6 Refitting is a reversal of removal, but adjust the handbrake as described in Chapter 1, and check for correct operation.

15.6 Clip (arrowed) securing the front of the outer cable to the body

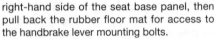

15 Handbrake cables - removal and refitting

Primary cable
Removal

1 Apply the handbrake, then jack up the front of the vehicle and support on axle stands (see *"Jacking, towing and wheel changing"*). Chock the rear wheels, then fully release the handbrake lever.

2 Working inside the vehicle, remove the centre console as described in Chapter 11.

3 Remove the retaining screw located on the right-hand side of the seat base panel, then pull back the rubber floor mat for access to the handbrake lever mounting bolts.

4 Release the handbrake. Extract the split pin, or remove the special spring clip, and remove the clevis pin securing the front of the primary handbrake inner cable to the bottom of the handbrake lever (see illustration).

5 Working beneath the vehicle, remove the splash guard (Van models only), then unhook the return spring from the pin on the secondary cable. Remove the pin, and disconnect the rear end of the primary cable (see illustrations).

6 Extract the clip from the front of the primary outer cable, then release the cable from the body clips and withdraw it from under the vehicle (see illustration).

Refitting

7 Refitting is a reversal of removal, but adjust the cables as described in Chapter 1, and check for correct operation. Check that the rubber boots on the ends of the outer cable are correctly located, otherwise it is possible for water to cause corrosion and seizing. If the boots have become dislodged, attach them to the outer cable using cable-ties.

Secondary cable
Removal

8 Chock the front wheels, then jack up the rear of the vehicle and support on axle stands (see *"Jacking, towing and wheel changing"*). Fully release the handbrake lever.

9 Working under the vehicle, unhook the return spring from the pin on the secondary cable. Remove the pin, and disconnect the rear end of the primary cable.

10 Remove the rear brake shoes from both sides, with reference to Section 5.

11 Prise out the spring clips securing the rear ends of the secondary cable to the rear brake backplates, then pull the cables from the backplates (see illustrations). If they are tight, use a small drift to drive them out from the outside of the backplates.

12 Loosen the locknuts, release the cable from the supports, and withdraw it from under the vehicle. As the cable is being removed, note that it is located through guide straps attached to each rear leaf spring (see illustration).

15.11a Removing the handbrake secondary cable from the backplate

15.11b Entry point of the handbrake secondary inner cable in brake backplate

15.12 Handbrake cable guide straps attached to each rear leaf spring

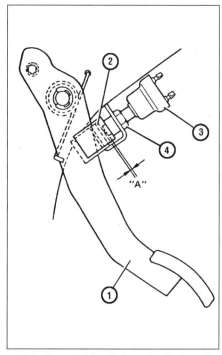

16.3a Stop light switch and adjustment dimension (A)

1 *Brake pedal*   3 *Stop-light switch*
2 *Contact plate*   4 *Locknut*

Refitting

13 Refitting is a reversal of removal, but before locating the rear ends of the secondary cable in the rear backplates, apply a little sealant to the end fittings, to prevent entry of water. Make sure that the clips are engaged correctly. Check that the rubber boots on the ends of the outer cables are correctly located, and if necessary, attach them using cable-ties as described in paragraph 7. Finally, adjust the cables as described in Chapter 1, and check for correct operation.

16.7 Disconnecting the wiring from the stop-light switch

16.3b Checking the clearance between the threaded end of the stop-light switch and the pedal contact plate

16 Stop-light switch - adjustment, removal and refitting

Adjustment

1 The stop-light switch is attached to the footbrake pedal bracket.
2 To check the adjustment of the switch, pull the brake pedal fully upwards, to ensure that it is fully released.
3 Using a feeler blade, check that the clearance between the threaded end of the switch and the pedal contact plate is between 0.5 mm and 1.0 mm (see illustrations). Note that the end of the switch is not parallel with the contact plate, and that the adjustment must be measured between the nearest part of the threaded end and the plate.
4 If adjustment is necessary, loosen the locknut, and turn the switch as required until the dimension is correct (see illustration). Tighten the locknut on completion.
5 With the ignition switched on, check that the brake lights operate when the pedal is depressed.

Removal

6 Disconnect the battery negative lead.

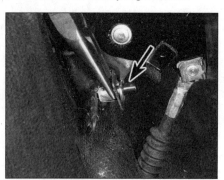

17.2 Using a pair of pliers to push the warning light switch (arrowed) out of the bracket

16.4 Adjusting the stop-light switch position

7 Reach up and disconnect the wiring from the switch (see illustration).
8 Loosen the locknut, then unscrew the switch from the pedal bracket.

Refitting

9 Refitting is a reversal of removal, but on completion, check the adjustment of the switch as described previously in this Section.

17 Handbrake lever warning light switch - removal and refitting

Removal

1 Remove the centre console as described in Chapter 11.
2 Using a pair of pliers, push the warning light switch out of the bracket located on the right-hand side of the handbrake lever (see illustration).
3 Withdraw the switch, and disconnect the wiring from it (see illustration).

Refitting

4 Refitting is a reversal of removal. Check the switch operation on completion.

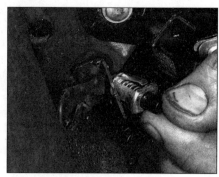

17.3 Withdraw the switch, and disconnect the wiring

Notes

Chapter 10 Suspension and steering

Contents

Degrees of difficulty

| Easy, suitable for novice with little experience | | Fairly easy, suitable for beginner with some experience | | Fairly difficult, suitable for competent DIY mechanic | | Difficult, suitable for experienced DIY mechanic | | Very difficult, suitable for expert DIY or professional | |

Specifications

Front suspension
Type .... Independent by MacPherson struts, with inclined coil springs and integral shock absorbers. Struts linked to crossmember by lower arms, and supported at the front by radius arms. Anti-roll bar on Van models, linked to lower arms, and supported by rubber bushes on the crossmember

Rear suspension
Type .... Rigid rear axle, with leaf springs and independent telescopic shock absorbers

Steering
Type .... Rack-and-pinion steering gear mounted at an angle, with centre lever located on top of the crossmember

Wheel alignment and steering angles
Front wheel camber angle .... 1° ± 45'
Front wheel castor angle .... 5° ± 1°
Kingpin inclination .... 11° 25' ± 2°
Front wheel toe setting .... 2.0 mm to 5.0 mm toe-in

Roadwheels
Type .... Pressed-steel
Size .... 4B x 12

Tyres
Tyre size .... 155R x 12
Pressures - refer to Chapter 1 Specifications.

Torque wrench settings

	Nm	lbf ft
Front suspension		
Steering knuckle clamp bolt to suspension strut	60	44
Front suspension strut location bolt	30	22
Front suspension strut piston upper nut	80	59
Front suspension strut upper mounting nut	25	18
Anti-roll bar to lower arm	23	17
Anti-roll bar clamp bolt	23	17
Radius arm front nut	80	59
Radius arm-to-lower arm nut	50	37
Front suspension lower arm to crossmember	50	37
Lower arm balljoint to steering knuckle	40 to 70	29 to 51
Front hub nut	150 to 270	109 to 195
Front brake caliper	85	63
Front brake disc to hub	50	37
Front suspension crossmember to underbody	50	37
Steering knuckle side locating bolt	29	21
Front brake backplate	23	17
Rear suspension		
Shock absorber upper mounting nut:		
Van models	29	21
Pickup models	13	10
Shock absorber lower mounting nut	13	10
Leaf spring-to-rear axle U-bolt nut	38	28
Leaf spring rear shackle nut	43	32
Leaf spring front mounting	60	44
Brake backplate to rear axle	23	17
Brake pipe union nut	16	12
Rear axle oil drain plug	6	4
Rear axle oil filler/level plug	4	3
Steering		
Track rod end balljoint locknut	60	44
Track rod end balljoint to steering knuckle	43	32
Steering wheel nut	33	24
Intermediate shaft universal joint clamp bolts	25	18
Intermediate shaft-to-pinion clamp bolt	25	18
Intermediate shaft flexible coupling bolts	20	15
Steering gear mounting bolts	50	37
Steering rack yoke:		
Right-hand drive models	80	59
Left-hand drive models	60	44
Centre lever retaining nut	80 to 150	59 to 111
Steering column mounting bolts	16	12
Drag link to steering rack yoke	50 to 80	37 to 59
Drag link to centre lever	30 to 55	22 to 41
Roadwheels		
Roadwheel nuts	65	48

1 General information

The independent front suspension is of MacPherson strut type, incorporating coil springs and integral telescopic shock absorbers **(see illustration)**. The MacPherson struts are located by transverse lower suspension arms with rubber inner mounting bushes and a balljoint at their outer ends, and also by front radius arms incorporating rubber bushes at their front ends. The front steering knuckles which carry the wheel bearings, brake components and hub assemblies, are attached to the bottom of the struts by clamp bolts - they are connected to the lower arms via balljoints. A front anti-roll bar is fitted to Van models. The anti-roll bar is rubber-mounted onto the front suspension crossmember and lower suspension arm.

The rear suspension incorporates a rigid axle with leaf springs **(see illustration)**.

The steering column has an intermediate shaft and universal joints fitted at its lower end, which is clamped to the steering gear pinion.

The steering gear is mounted at an angle on the front underbody, and unlike conventional systems, one end of the rack operates a centre lever mounted on the top of the front suspension crossmember **(see illustration)**. The rear end of the centre lever is connected to the two track rods, which in turn are connected to the front steering knuckles. The track rod ends and inner ends are threaded, to facilitate adjustment.

2 Front hub bearings - renewal

Note: *Ideally, a press will be required to dismantle and rebuild the assembly; if such a tool is not available, a large bench vice and spacers (such as large sockets) will serve as an adequate substitute.*

1 Apply the handbrake, then jack up the front of the vehicle and support on axle stands (see

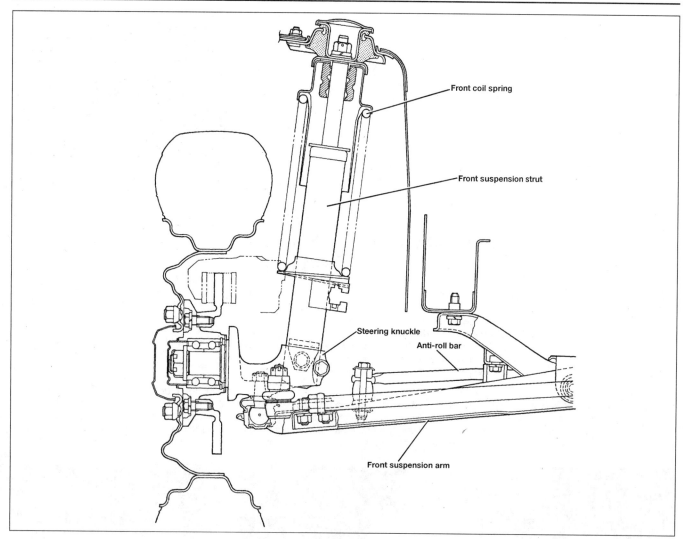

1.1 Cross-section of the front suspension

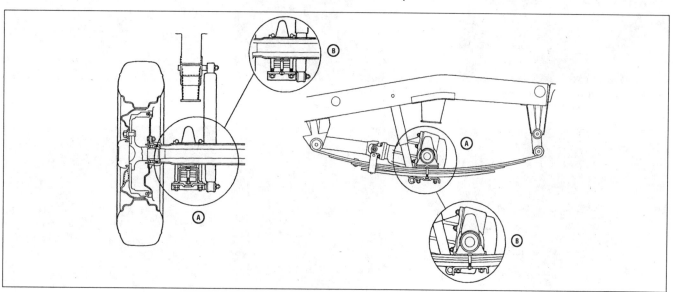

1.2 Cross-section of the rear suspension

A Van models   *B Pickup models*

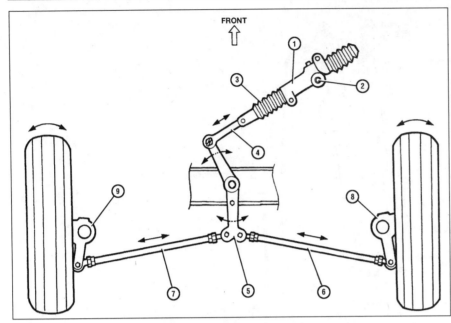

1.4 Diagram of the steering system

1 Steering gear	5 Centre lever	8 Steering knuckle (right-hand)
2 Pinion	6 Track rod (right-hand)	
3 Rubber gaiter	7 Track rod (left-hand)	9 Steering knuckle (left-hand)
4 Drag rod		

2.3 Suspend the brake caliper from the front suspension coil spring using a piece of wire

"Jacking, towing and wheel changing"). Remove the relevant front roadwheel.

2 If it is intended to separate the brake disc from the hub, have an assistant depress the brake pedal, then loosen (but do not remove) the bolts securing the brake disc to the hub.

3 Unscrew the brake caliper mounting bolts (see Chapter 9), move the caliper away from

the disc, then suspend it from the front suspension coil spring using a piece of wire **(see illustration)**.

⚠️ *Warning: Do not depress the brake pedal with the caliper removed from the disc.*

4 Unscrew the caliper bracket mounting bolts, and remove the bracket from the backplate **(see illustrations)**.

5 Carefully tap the dust cap from the centre of the hub using a screwdriver **(see illustrations)**. Turn the hub between each tap so that the cap is gradually released, and take care not to damage the cap or its seating.

6 Straighten the split pin, then extract it from the hole in the stub axle **(see illustration)**.

7 Unscrew and remove the hub nut, and recover the thrustwasher **(see illustrations)**.

2.4a Unscrew the caliper bracket mounting bolts . . .

2.4b . . . and remove the bracket from the backplate

2.5a Tap the dust cap with a screwdriver . . .

2.5b . . . and remove it from the hub

2.6 Extract the split pin . . .

2.7a . . . then use a socket to loosen the hub nut . . .

2.7b ... and remove the nut ...

2.7c ... and thrustwasher

2.8 Withdrawing the hub and disc from the stub axle

8 Withdraw the hub and disc from the stub axle **(see illustration)**. If the bearing inner races are tight on the stub axle, use a puller to remove it.

> **HAYNES HiNT** *If a puller is not available, temporarily refit the roadwheel to the hub to give extra leverage, but make sure that the vehicle is safely located on axle stands.*

9 If required, fully unscrew the bolts and separate the brake disc from the hub.
10 With the inside of the hub facing upwards on the bench, extract the bearing retaining circlip using circlip pliers **(see illustration)**.
11 The bearing must now be pressed out of the hub, using a suitable adapter located on the outer facing side of the bearing inner races. Refer to the note at the beginning of this Section. If the necessary tools are not available for pressing out the bearing, support the hub, and use a soft-metal drift to drive it out - work around the bearing, to ensure it is removed squarely from the hub. **Note:** *Since the bearing is removed by pressure on the inner races, it is not permitted to re-use the bearing again once removed.*
12 Wipe clean the inner surfaces of the hub, and coat them with a light film of oil. Support the hub on the bench with its inner side facing upwards, then locate the bearing in position.

13 Press the bearing fully into the hub using the same method as for removal, however **press only on the outer race,** to prevent damage to the ball bearings.
14 Insert the bearing retaining circlip in its groove in the hub. Make sure it is engaged with the groove, and not resting on the outer edge of the hub.
15 If the brake disc was removed, wipe clean the contact surfaces, then assemble the brake disc to the hub. Insert the retaining bolts loosely at this stage.
16 Locate the hub on the stub axle, and push it on fully. If the bearing inner races are tight, use a metal tube to drive on the hub while turning the hub frequently. The tube must only locate on the inner races.
17 Refit the thrustwasher, and screw on the hub nut.
18 Using a torque wrench, tighten the hub nut to within the specified torque tolerance, until the split pin holes are correctly aligned **(see illustration)**.
19 Insert a new split pin, and bend it over the nut to retain.
20 Locate the brake caliper and pads over the disc, then refit the caliper mounting bolts and tighten to the specified torque.
21 Tap the dust cap into the centre of the hub.
22 Depress the brake pedal several times to set the front disc pads in their normal position.
23 Have an assistant depress the brake

pedal, then tighten the bolts securing the brake disc to the hub to the specified torque.
24 Refit the front roadwheel, and lower the vehicle to the ground. Tighten the roadwheel nuts to the specified torque.

3 Front suspension strut - removal, overhaul and refitting

Removal

1 Chock the rear wheels, apply the handbrake, then jack up the front of the vehicle and support on axle stands (see *"Jacking, towing and wheel changing"*). Remove the appropriate roadwheel.
2 Remove the brake caliper with reference to Chapter 9, then pull out the special clip and detach the front brake hydraulic hose from the bracket on the front suspension strut **(see illustration)**. Support the caliper on an axle stand.
3 Lift and support the relevant front seat on Van models, or remove the seat on Pickup models, for access to the engine compartment.
4 Remove the plastic cap, then loosen but do not remove the strut piston rod nut located on the top of the strut. If the strut is not to be dismantled, then it is not necessary to loosen the nut.
5 Unscrew and remove the clamp bolt

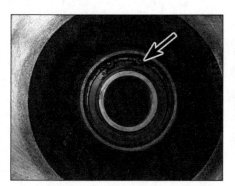

2.10 Bearing retaining circlip (arrowed)

2.18 Tightening the hub nut

3.2 Removing the special clip (arrowed) securing the front brake hydraulic hose to the strut

3.5 Removing the clamp bolt securing the steering knuckle to the bottom of the strut

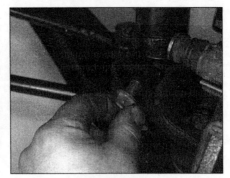

3.6 Removing the location bolt

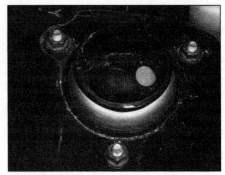

3.8 Front suspension strut upper mounting nuts

securing the steering knuckle to the bottom of the strut. Note which way round the bolt is fitted **(see illustration)**.

6 Unscrew and remove the location bolt which secures the bracket on the strut to the steering knuckle **(see illustration)**.

7 Support the weight of the front suspension lower arm on a trolley jack.

8 Working in the engine compartment, unscrew and remove the strut upper mounting nuts **(see illustration)**.

9 Support the strut, then lower the trolley jack a little, but make sure that the hydraulic brake hose is not stretched.

10 Pull the top of the strut down from the body, and withdraw it outwards, making sure that it clears the wing. Lift the strut from the steering knuckle **(see illustrations)**. If it is

tight in the knuckle, open up the knuckle clamp by inserting a suitable lever in the slot.

Overhaul

⚠️ *Warning: Before attempting to dismantle the front suspension strut, a suitable tool to hold the coil spring in compression must be obtained. Adjustable coil spring compressors are readily available, and are recommended for this operation. Any attempt to dismantle the strut without such a tool is likely to result in damage or personal injury.*

11 Fit the spring compressor(s), and compress the coil spring until all tension is relieved from the upper spring seat **(see illustration)**.

12 Unscrew and remove the strut top nut, using a pair of grips to hold the rebound stopper **(see illustration)**.

13 Noting the order of removal, remove the top mounting components, coil spring and rubber bumper **(see illustration)**.

14 With the strut assembly now dismantled, examine all the components for wear, damage or deformation. Renew any of the components as necessary. The manufacturers recommend that the upper bearing be washed, and lubricated with new grease.

3.10a Pull the front suspension strut downwards . . .

3.10b . . . and pull it up from the steering knuckle

3.11 Spring compressors fitted to the coil spring

3.12 Hold the rebound stopper while loosening the piston rod nut

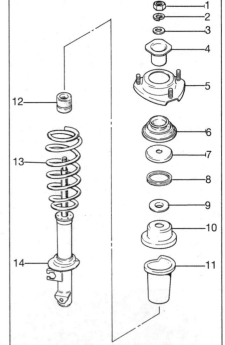

3.13 Front suspension strut components

1 Nut
2 Spring washer
3 Washer
4 Rebound stopper
5 Upper mounting bracket
6 Support rubber
7 Strut bearing upper seat
8 Dust seal
9 Bearing
10 Coil spring upper seat
11 Coil spring guide
12 Rubber bumper
13 Coil spring
14 Strut/shock absorber assembly

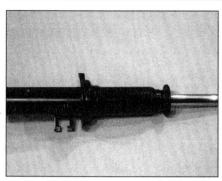

3.18a Make sure the strut is thoroughly cleaned before starting assembly

3.18b Locate the coil spring (compressed) on the strut, making sure that the lower end is engaged with the stepped part of the spring seat (arrowed)

3.18c Fit the rubber bumper onto the piston rod

15 Examine the strut for signs of fluid leakage. Check the strut piston for signs of pitting along its entire length, and check the strut body for signs of damage. While holding it in an upright position, test the operation of the strut by moving the piston through a full stroke, and then through short strokes of 50 to 100 mm. In both cases, the resistance felt should be smooth and continuous. If the resistance is jerky, or uneven, or if there is any visible sign of wear or damage to the strut, renewal is necessary. It is not possible to renew the shock absorber separately, and if faulty, the strut must be renewed complete.

16 If any doubt exists about the condition of the coil spring, carefully remove the spring compressor, and check the spring for distortion and signs of cracking. Renew the spring if it is damaged or distorted, or if there is any doubt as to its condition.

17 Inspect all other components for signs of damage or deterioration, and renew any that are suspect.

18 To reassemble the strut, follow the accompanying photo sequence, beginning with illustration 3.18a. Be sure to follow each step in sequence, and carefully read the caption beneath each photo **(see illustrations)**. Note the following points:

a) *Make sure that the rubber bumper is positioned with its groove towards the bottom of the strut.*

b) *Apply grease to all the surfaces of the bearing dust seal.*

3.18d Fit the coil spring guide, again making sure that the step (arrowed) engages the top end of the spring

3.18e Locate the coil spring upper seat on the guide

3.18f Grease the bearing . . .

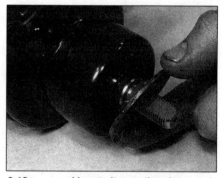

3.18g . . . and locate it over the piston rod, shouldered end first

3.18h Locate the dust seal over the bearing

3.18i Place the bearing upper seat over the bearing and seal

3.18j Locate the support rubber in the upper mounting bracket . . .

3.18k . . . then locate the mounting bracket over the piston rod

3.18l Fit the rebound stopper . . .

3.18m . . . followed by the plain washer . . .

3.18n . . . spring washer . . .

3.18o . . . and nut, tightened moderately at this stage

3.18p Remove the spring compressors, then tighten the nut to the specified torque while holding the rebound stopper with a pair of grips

c) *Compress the spring sufficiently to allow the top mounting components to be refitted - in practice, the coil spring must be compressed until its total length is 240 mm.*

d) *Make sure that the spring ends locate correctly in the stepped part of the spring seats.*

e) *The strut rod should be fully extended so that it protrudes through the upper mounting components. After tightening the strut rod nut to the specified torque, coat the nut and the end of the rod with paint or lacquer.*

Refitting

19 Manoeuvre the strut assembly into position under the vehicle, passing the mounting studs through the holes in the body turret, then refit the upper mounting nuts loosely.
20 Hold the front suspension lower arm down, then locate the bottom of the strut in the steering knuckle so that the location bolt holes are correctly aligned. Check also that the cut-out in the strut is correctly aligned with the clamp bolt hole. Insert and tighten the location bolt to the specified torque **(see illustration)**.
21 Insert and tighten the clamp bolt to the specified torque **(see illustration)**.
22 Tighten the strut upper mounting bolts to the specified torque.
23 Refit and secure the front seat.
24 Secure the front brake hydraulic hose to the bracket on the front suspension strut with the special clip. Do not twist the hose.

25 Refit the roadwheel, and lower the vehicle to the ground. Tighten the roadwheel nuts to the specified torque.

4 Front suspension steering knuckle - removal and refitting

Removal

1 If necessary, remove the front hub with reference to Section 2, but do not separate the brake disc from the hub. Leave the hub in position on the steering knuckle if there is no requirement to separate the two components.

3.18q Press the plastic cap into the mounting bracket

3.20 Tightening the strut location bolt

3.21 Tightening the strut clamp bolt

4.7 Extracting the split pin from the castellated nut

4.8 Using a balljoint separator tool to release the lower arm from the steering knuckle

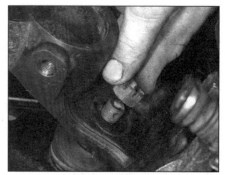

4.9a Remove the nut . . .

2 Straighten the split pin, and extract it from the track rod end castellated nut.

3 Unscrew and remove the castellated nut. Using a balljoint separator tool, separate the track rod end from the arm on the steering knuckle.

4 Unscrew and remove the location bolt which secures the bracket on the strut to the steering knuckle.

5 Unscrew and remove the clamp bolt securing the steering knuckle to the bottom of the strut. Note which way round the bolt is fitted.

6 Separate the steering knuckle from the bottom of the strut, and remove it from the vehicle. If it is tight in the strut, open up the knuckle clamp by inserting a suitable lever in the slot.

7 Straighten the split pin, and extract it from the castellated nut securing the front suspension lower arm to the steering knuckle **(see illustration)**. Unscrew the castellated nut until it is near the end of the balljoint stud.

8 Using a balljoint separator tool, release the lower arm from the steering knuckle **(see illustration)**. As access is limited, take care not to damage the threads of the balljoint stud.

9 Fully unscrew the nut, then separate the steering knuckle from the lower arm **(see illustrations)**.

10 Unscrew the four bolts, and remove the backplate from the steering knuckle **(see illustration)**.

Refitting

11 Refit the backplate, and tighten the bolts.

12 Locate the steering knuckle on the bottom of the strut, making sure that the location bolt holes are correctly aligned. Check also that the cut-out in the strut is correctly aligned with the clamp bolt hole. Insert and tighten the location bolt to the specified torque.

13 Insert and tighten the clamp bolt to the specified torque.

14 Hold the lower arm down with a suitable lever, then locate the balljoint stud in the steering knuckle. Apply pressure beneath the lower arm with a trolley jack, then refit and tighten the castellated nut within the specified torque tolerance until the split pin holes are aligned. Insert a new split pin, and bend it over the nut to retain.

15 Locate the track rod end in the arm on the steering knuckle, then refit and tighten the castellated nut within the specified torque tolerance until the split pin holes are aligned. Insert a new split pin, and bend it over the nut to retain.

16 Refit the front hub with reference to Section 2.

5 Front suspension lower arm - removal, overhaul and refitting

Removal

1 Chock the rear wheels, firmly apply the handbrake, then jack up the front of the vehicle and support on axle stands (see *"Jacking, towing and wheel changing"*). Remove the appropriate front roadwheel.

2 On models with a front anti-roll bar, unscrew the lower nut securing the anti-roll bar to the front suspension lower arm, and remove the washer and lower rubber bush. Remove the bolt from the top of the anti-roll bar, and recover the upper rubber bush and washer.

3 Unscrew the two bolts, and detach the radius arm from the top of the lower arm.

4 Straighten the split pin, and extract it from the castellated nut securing the front suspension lower arm to the steering knuckle. Unscrew and remove the castellated nut.

5 Using a balljoint separator tool, separate the lower arm from the steering knuckle. As access is limited, take care not to damage the threads of the balljoint stud.

6 Unscrew and remove the bolt securing the inner end of the lower arm to the crossmember **(see illustration)** and withdraw

4.9b . . . and remove the steering knuckle from the lower arm

4.10 Backplate mounting bolts

5.6 Bolt securing the inner end of the lower arm to the crossmember

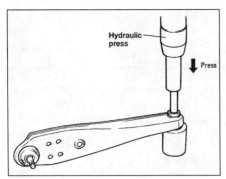

5.8 Using a hydraulic press to remove the rubber bush from the front suspension lower arm

6.2 Front mounting of the radius arm

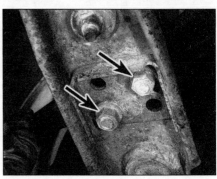

6.3 Radius arm mounting bolts (arrowed) on the front suspension lower arm

the arm from under the vehicle. Note that the head of the bolt is at the rear of the crossmember.

Overhaul

7 Check the lower arm for damage, particularly if the vehicle has been involved in an accident.

8 Check the condition of the lower arm inner rubber bush - if it is perished or has signs of excessive wear, it must be renewed. Ideally, a hydraulic press should be used to remove the bush **(see illustration)**. However, it can be removed using metal tubing and a long bolt, together with suitable washers. Alternatively, the bush can be pressed out using a vice.

9 Before fitting the new bush, clean the location bore. Dip the new bush in soapy water (washing-up liquid is ideal) before pressing it into position. Make sure that the bush is located centrally in the arm.

10 Check the balljoint for wear and/or seizure by articulating the stud, and attempting to press it in and out of its socket. Also check the dust cover for condition. It is not possible to renew the balljoint separately, but the dust cover is easily renewed by prising off the retaining clip and removing the cover from the top of the stud. If necessary, add grease to the balljoint before fitting the new dust cover and retaining with the clip.

Refitting

11 Locate the lower arm in the crossmember, and insert the bolt from the rear. Fit the washer and front nut, then position the arm so that it is pointing downwards from the horizontal at an angle of 11°, and fully tighten the nut to the specified torque. Make up a cardboard template with the required angle on it before setting the arm.

12 Locate the balljoint stud in the steering knuckle. Apply pressure beneath the lower arm with a trolley jack, then refit and tighten the castellated nut within the specified torque tolerance until the split pin holes are aligned. Insert a new split pin and bend it over the nut to retain.

13 Refit the radius arm to the top of the lower arm and tighten the bolts to the specified torque.

14 On models with a front anti-roll bar, refit the anti-roll bar to the lower arm, making sure that the short rubber bush is fitted on top of the bar. The long bush is located under the bar and on top of the lower arm, and the remaining short bush is located under the arm. Tighten the nut to the specified torque.

15 Refit the roadwheel, and lower the vehicle to the ground. Tighten the roadwheel nuts to the specified torque.

16 Check and if necessary adjust the front wheel toe setting.

---

6 Front suspension radius arm - removal and refitting

Removal

1 Chock the rear wheels, firmly apply the handbrake, then jack up the front of the vehicle and support on axle stands (see *"Jacking, towing and wheel changing"*). Remove the appropriate front roadwheel.

2 Unscrew and remove the nut from the front of the radius arm, and recover the washer and front rubber bush **(see illustration)**.

3 Unscrew the two bolts, and detach the radius arm from the top of the front suspension lower arm **(see illustration)**.

4 Withdraw the radius arm to the rear, and remove from under the vehicle.

5 Remove the rear rubber bush and spacer from the front of the radius arm.

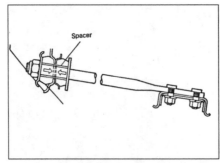

6.8 Showing the correct fitted position of the rubber bushes on the front suspension radius arm

6 Check the radius arm for damage, particularly if the vehicle has been involved in an accident.

7 Check the condition of the rubber bushes, and renew them if they are perished or excessively worn.

Refitting

8 Refitting is a reversal of removal, but note that the rubber bushes are not symmetrical, and must be fitted so that the arrows face each other (ie the arrows point towards the mounting bracket) **(see illustration)**.

---

7 Front suspension anti-roll bar - removal and refitting

Removal

1 Chock the rear wheels, firmly apply the handbrake, then jack up the front of the vehicle and support on axle stands (see *"Jacking, towing and wheel changing"*). Remove both front roadwheels.

2 Unscrew the nuts securing the anti-roll bar to the front suspension lower arms, and remove the washers and lower rubber bushes **(see illustration)**.

3 Remove the bolts from each end of the anti-roll bar, and recover the upper rubber bushes and washers.

4 Unscrew and remove the bolts from the

7.2 Anti-roll bar mounting on the front suspension lower arm

7.4 Anti-roll bar mounting clamp (located on the front crossmember)

8.7a Unscrew the bolts (one arrowed) securing the brake backplate to the rear axle . . .

8.7b . . . and remove the bolts

mounting clamps, and remove the clamps **(see illustration)**. The anti-roll bar is located inside the front suspension crossmember, and may be lowered onto this before removal.
5 Turn the anti-roll bar so that the ends point downwards, then feed it through the crossmember and withdraw it from under the vehicle.
6 Prise the split rubber bushes from the anti-roll bar, after noting their position for correct replacement.

Refitting

7 Examine the condition of all of the rubber bushes, and renew if necessary. Check the condition of the anti-roll bar itself - if it is bent or damaged, it must be renewed.
8 Locate the rubber bushes on the anti-roll bar, with their flat faces pointing upwards.
9 Feed the anti-roll bar through the crossmember, then locate it in position and refit the clamps and bolts. Note that the white painted area must face rearwards on the left-hand side of the bar, when viewed from the rear.
10 Tighten the clamp bolts to the specified torque.
11 Refit the anti-roll bar to the lower arms, making sure that the short rubber bushes are fitted on top of the bar. The long bushes are located under the bar and on top of the lower arms, and the remaining short bushes are located under the arms. Make sure that the special washers are fitted under the bolt heads and next to the nuts. Tighten the nuts to the specified torque.

12 Refit the roadwheels, and lower the vehicle to the ground. Tighten the roadwheel nuts to the specified torque.

8 Rear axle shaft and bearing - removal, bearing renewal, and refitting

Removal

Note: *A suitable slide hammer withdrawal tool will be required to remove the rear axle shaft and bearing assembly from the rear axle.*
1 Chock the front wheels, release the handbrake, then jack up the rear of the vehicle and support on axle stands (see *"Jacking, towing and wheel changing"*). Remove the relevant rear roadwheel.
2 Position a suitable clean container beneath the rear axle, then unscrew the oil drain plug, and drain the oil. To aid draining, also remove the filler plug. Refit and tighten the drain plug.
3 Remove the brake drum and rear brake shoes with reference to Chapter 9.
4 Extract the spring clip securing the handbrake cable to the rear brake backplate, then pull out the cable from the backplate.
5 Fit a brake hose clamp to the rear brake hose in front of the rear axle on the right-hand side.
6 Unscrew the union nut(s) securing the rear brake pipe(s) to the wheel cylinder. On the right-hand wheel there are two pipes, but on

the left-hand wheel there is only one pipe. Plug the end of the pipe with a suitable plastic or rubber cap, to prevent the escape of brake fluid or the ingress of dirt.
7 Unscrew and remove the nuts/bolts securing the brake backplate to the rear axle **(see illustrations)**.
8 The rear axle shaft must now be pulled from the rear axle. Attach a slide hammer removal tool to the studs on the rear axle shaft, using the wheel nuts to secure it. Pull the axle shaft from the rear axle and withdraw it, taking care not to damage the oil seal located near the outer end of the casing. The protector located on the inner side of the oil seal will prevent the axle shaft touching the oil seal, if the axle shaft is taken out carefully.
9 If there has been evidence of oil leakage from the rear axle casing, it will be necessary to renew the oil seal. Hook out the oil seal, followed by the protector, using a screwdriver or suitable lever **(see illustrations)**.

Bearing renewal

Note: *A suitable puller will be required to remove the bearing from the shaft.*
10 The bearing is retained with a metal ring which is pressed into position on the shaft. This ring must be removed by filing or grinding away before the bearing can be removed. Ideally, an angle grinder should be used at two opposite points on the ring, until the ring is thin enough to be broken with a cold chisel and removed from the shaft **(see illustration)**.

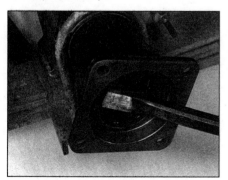

8.9a Hook out the old oil seal . . .

8.9b . . . and remove the protector

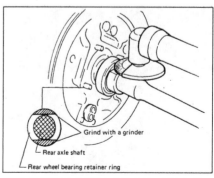

Grind with a grinder
Rear axle shaft
Rear wheel bearing retainer ring

8.10 Using an angle grinder to remove the bearing retaining metal ring

8.11a Locate the puller clamp under the bearing . . .

8.11b . . . and pull off the bearing

8.19 Locating the new oil seal in the rear axle casing

Alternatively, the ring can be filed or drilled, but make sure that the axle shaft itself it not damaged. Whichever method is used, take the necessary safety precautions (see "Safety first!").

11 Using a suitable puller, draw the bearing off the inner end of the shaft (see illustrations). The brake backplate and spacer can then be removed from the shaft.

12 Clean all of the components thoroughly, and check them for wear and damage. Renew as necessary.

13 Locate the spacer (tapered side first) onto the axle shaft, followed by the brake backplate.

14 Press the bearing onto the shaft, so that its sealed side faces the outer end of the shaft. To do this, support the bearing inner race on a suitable piece of metal tube located over the jaws of a vice, and press on the outer

8.20 Apply suitable sealant to the rear axle flange

end of the shaft until the inner race contacts the spacer.

15 Using the same method, press the metal retaining ring onto the shaft until it contacts the bearing inner race.

16 Check the outer surface of the retaining ring for nicks and damage, since the oil seal bears on this. If necessary, use emery tape to restore the surface to its original condition. Apply a little grease to the surface.

Refitting

17 Wipe clean the bearing and oil seal location inside the rear axle casing.

18 Locate the oil seal protector into the rear axle casing, convex side first.

19 Smear a little rear axle oil on the outer periphery and inner lip of the new oil seal, then press it into the casing with its sealed side facing outwards (ie its lip facing inwards) (see illustration).

20 Clean the outer flange of the axle casing, and apply a coating of suitable sealant to it (see illustration).

21 Insert the axle shaft in the axle casing, taking care not to damage the oil seal (see illustration). When the inner end of the shaft is near the differential, it will be necessary to turn the shaft so that its splines enter the side gear. At the same time, the bearing outer race must be located in the casing.

22 Using a soft-faced mallet, drive the shaft fully into position, then turn the brake backplate until the mounting holes are aligned

with the holes in the casing (see illustration). Insert the bolts from outside, screw on the nuts, and tighten to the specified torque.

23 Refit the brake pipe(s) to the wheel cylinder, then screw on the union nut(s) and tighten to the specified torque.

24 Apply sealant to the area of the outer handbrake cable which contacts the brake backplate, then insert the cable and secure with the clip.

25 Refit the rear brake shoes and drum with reference to Chapter 9.

26 Fill the rear axle with the correct quantity and grade of oil, with reference to Chapter 1. Tighten the filler/level plug.

27 Remove the brake hose clamp, then fill the master cylinder reservoir with fresh brake fluid, and bleed the system with reference to Chapter 9.

28 Refit the roadwheel, and lower the vehicle to the ground. Tighten the roadwheel nuts to the specified torque.

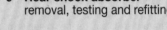

9 Rear shock absorber - removal, testing and refitting

Removal

1 Chock the front wheels, then jack up the rear of the vehicle and support it on axle stands (see "Jacking, towing and wheel changing"). Remove the relevant rear roadwheel.

2 Working under the vehicle, unscrew and

8.21 Inserting the axle shaft in the rear axle casing

8.22 Using a mallet to drive the shaft and bearing fully into the rear axle casing

9.2a Rear shock absorber upper mounting . . .

9.2b . . . and lower mounting

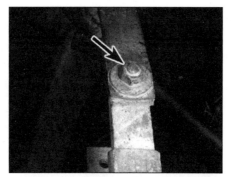

10.3 Handbrake secondary cable guide strap mounting bolt (arrowed) on the leaf spring

10.4 Rear suspension leaf spring U-bolt nuts and lower plate - note left-hand "L" and right-hand "R" orientation marks

remove the top and bottom mounting nuts, and recover the locking washers and outer plain washers **(see illustrations)**.

3 Withdraw the shock absorber from the mounting studs, and recover the inner plain washers. Where applicable, the tapered rubber bushes may come out as the shock absorber is being removed. On Pickup models, both the upper and lower rubber bushes may be removed, but on Van models, only the bottom bushes may be removed.

Testing

4 Examine the shock absorber for signs of fluid leakage or damage. Test the operation of the shock absorber while holding it in an upright position in a vice, by moving the piston through a full stroke, and then through short strokes of 50 to 100 mm. In both cases, the resistance felt should be smooth and continuous. If the resistance is jerky, or uneven, or if there is any visible sign of wear or damage, renewal is necessary. Also check the rubber mounting bushes for damage and deterioration. Renew the complete unit if any damage or excessive wear is evident; the mounting bushes are available separately, except for the upper mounting on Van models.

Refitting

5 Prior to refitting the shock absorber, mount it upright in the vice, and operate it fully through several strokes in order to prime it.
6 Locate the inner plain washers on the

mounting studs, then refit the shock absorber.
7 Locate the outer plain and locking washers on the studs, followed by the mounting nuts. Tighten the nuts to the specified torque.
8 Refit the roadwheel, then lower the vehicle to the ground. Tighten the roadwheel nuts to the specified torque.

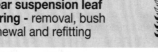

10 Rear suspension leaf spring - removal, bush renewal and refitting

Removal

1 Chock the front wheels, then jack up the rear of the vehicle and support it on axle stands (see *"Jacking, towing and wheel changing"*). **Do not** support the vehicle under the rear axle, but locate the axle stands under the rear chassis members. Remove the relevant rear roadwheel.
2 Support the weight of the rear axle on the relevant side with a further axle stand. **Do not** allow the rear axle to hang on the flexible rear brake hose.
3 Unbolt the handbrake secondary cable guide strap from the leaf spring bracket **(see illustration)**.
4 Unscrew and remove the nuts from the bottom of the U-bolts, and remove the U-bolts from the top of the rear axle **(see illustration)**. Recover the upper saddle/bump stop.

5 Move the lower plate to one side, leaving the shock absorber still attached to it. Recover the lower pad.
6 Unscrew the nuts from the leaf spring front mounting bolt and rear shackle **(see illustrations)**.
7 Support the leaf spring, then remove the front mounting bolt, and lower the front of the spring. Recover the saddle plate and upper pad from the top of the spring.
8 Remove the rear shackle outer plate, shackle pins and inner plate, then lower the leaf spring to the ground. Note which way round the shackle pins are fitted.

Bush renewal

9 Remove the bushes from the spring rear eye and body bracket, by prising out one bush, then driving out the remaining bush with a drift. Removal of the front bush will require a press. Alternatively, a home-made puller consisting of metal tubes, washers, and a nut and long bolt may be used.
10 Before pressing the new bushes into position, dip them in soapy water (washing-up liquid). Note that the front bush must be fitted with the narrow slit facing the front of the spring **(see illustration)** - make sure also that the bush is fitted centrally in the spring eye.
11 **Do not** apply mineral oil or grease to the bushes, as this will affect the rubber in the bushes. The manufacturers only recommend the use of silicone grease, and only then when the bushes are noisy during driving.

10.6a Rear leaf spring front mounting bolt

10.6b Rear leaf spring rear shackle

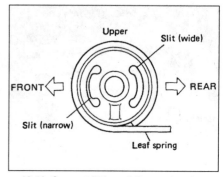

10.10 Correct fitting of the rear spring front bush

11.2a Remove the steering wheel centre pad . . .

11.2b . . . then unscrew the retaining nut . . .

11.2c . . . and remove the washer

Refitting

12 Before refitting the leaf spring, check that all of its leaves are undamaged and correctly aligned with each other. If any are displaced sideways, the spring is probably well worn and unserviceable. Note that exchange reconditioned springs may be obtained from specialist repairers. Check also that the centre bolt is tightened.

13 Insert the rear lower shackle pin through the inner plate, then assemble it to the rear spring eye from the inside of the spring. Loosely fit the outer plate and nut, complete with lockwasher.

14 Offer the rear of the spring to the body bracket, then insert the upper shackle pin through the inner plate, body bracket bushes, and outer plate. Fit the nut, complete with lockwasher. Note that both rear shackle pins **must** be fitted from the inside.

15 Locate the upper pad and saddle plate on the top of the leaf spring, making sure that the holes are over the top of the centre bolt.

16 Apply the handbrake, then raise the front of the spring, and locate it in the body bracket. Insert the front mounting bolt from the outside, and fit the nut complete with lockwasher.

17 Locate the lower pad on the bottom of the spring, then move the lower plate into position under the spring.

18 Locate the upper saddle/bump stop on the top of the rear axle, and refit the U-bolts through the lower plate. Fit the nuts to the U-

bolts, and progressively tighten them to the specified torque. With all the nuts tightened, check that the number of threads visible on the bottom of the U-bolts is the same on all of them.

19 Refit the handbrake secondary cable guide strap to the leaf spring, and tighten the retaining bolt.

20 Remove the support from the rear axle so that the spring is in its unladen position. Tighten all of the shackle pin nuts and the front mounting nut to the specified torque.

21 Refit the roadwheel, and lower the vehicle to the ground. Tighten the roadwheel nuts to the specified torque.

11 Steering wheel - removal and refitting

Removal

1 Set the front wheels in the straight-ahead position, and release the steering lock by inserting the ignition key.

2 Carefully ease off the steering wheel centre pad, then slacken and remove the steering wheel retaining nut. Recover the washer **(see illustrations)**.

3 Mark the steering wheel and steering column shaft in relation to each other **(see illustration)**, then lift the steering wheel off the column splines. If it is tight, twist it from side to side whilst pulling upwards to release it

from the shaft splines. If the steering wheel is very tight, it may be necessary to use a puller - note that if the special Vauxhall/Suzuki tool is used, it will be necessary to remove both the upper and lower steering column shrouds first.

Refitting

4 Refitting is a reversal of removal, but align the marks made on removal, and tighten the retaining nut to the specified torque. Note that if necessary, the position of the steering wheel on the column shaft can be altered in order to centralise the wheel (ensure that the front roadwheels are pointing in the straight-ahead position), by moving the wheel the required number of splines on the shaft.

12 Steering column - removal, inspection and refitting

Removal

1 Disconnect the battery negative lead.

2 Remove the steering wheel as described in Section 11, and remove the ignition key.

3 Unscrew the retaining screws, and remove the upper and lower steering column shrouds **(see illustrations)**.

4 Remove the steering column combination switch assembly, with reference to Chapter 12.

5 Unscrew the screw and remove the column

11.3 Mark the steering wheel and steering column shaft in relation to each other

12.3a Unscrew the retaining screws . . .

12.3b . . . and remove the upper and lower steering column shrouds

12.5 Removing the plastic column cover

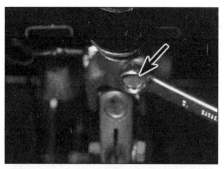

12.6 Unscrewing the intermediate shaft upper universal joint clamp bolt (arrowed)

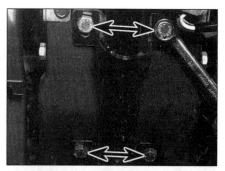

12.7a Unscrew the steering column mounting bolts (arrowed) . . .

cover **(see illustration)**, then disconnect the ignition switch wiring at the connector.

6 Unscrew the clamp bolt securing the intermediate shaft upper universal joint to the bottom of the inner steering column **(see illustration)**.

7 Unscrew and remove the steering column mounting bolts, and withdraw the steering column upwards from the intermediate shaft splines **(see illustrations)**. Remove the steering column from inside the vehicle.

Inspection

8 Check the steering shaft for signs of free play in the column bushes. If necessary, the bushes may be renewed by dismantling the steering column **(see illustration)**. The shaft and bushes are retained by circlips at the top and bottom of the inner column. Clean all components thoroughly, and apply a little grease to the inside and end faces of the new bushes before fitting them. Make sure that the circlips are located correctly in their grooves in the inner column.

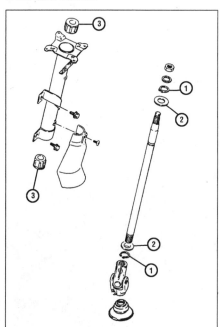

12.8 Exploded view of the steering column

1 Circlips   *3 Upper and lower bushes*
2 Washers

12.7b . . . and withdraw the steering column upwards

Refitting

9 Engage the splines on the bottom of the inner column with the splines in the intermediate shaft universal joint - the flat on the inner column must be aligned with the clamp bolt hole **(see illustration)**. Insert the clamp bolt loosely at this stage.

10 Locate the steering column on the mounting brackets, then insert the mounting bolts and tighten to the specified torque. The lower bolts should be fully tightened first, followed by the upper bolts.

11 Tighten the intermediate shaft universal joint clamp bolt to the specified torque.

12 Reconnect the ignition switch wiring, and refit the column cover.

13 Refit the steering column combination switch assembly, with reference to Chapter 12.

14 Refit the upper and lower steering column shrouds, and tighten the screws.

13.2a Depress the retaining pin . . .

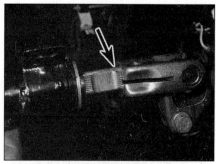

12.9 Engage the splines on the bottom of the inner column with the splines in the intermediate shaft universal joint (arrowed)

15 Refit the steering wheel with reference to Section 11.

16 Reconnect the battery negative lead.

13 Ignition switch/steering column lock -
removal and refitting

1 Remove the steering column as described in Section 12.

Ignition switch and barrel
Removal

2 The ignition switch key barrel may be removed from the casing by inserting the ignition key and turning it clockwise, then depressing the spring-tensioned retaining pin using a drill or suitable instrument through the hole in the casing **(see illustrations)**.

13.2b . . . and remove the ignition switch key barrel from the casing

13.3a Unscrew the single screw . . .

13.3b . . . and withdraw the switch from the casing

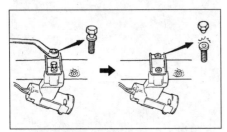

13.12 The shear-head bolts are tightened until their heads break off

3 The ignition switch may be removed by unscrewing the single retaining screw and withdrawing the switch from the casing **(see illustrations)**.

Refitting

4 Locate the ignition switch in the casing, then insert and tighten the retaining screw.
5 Insert the key barrel in the casing, making sure that it engages with the switch. Press it fully into the casing until the retaining pin locates in the casing hole.
6 Refit the steering column with reference to Section 12.

Steering column lock

Removal

7 The steering column lock housing is secured to the steering column with shear-head bolts. To remove them, use a centre-punch to turn them anti-clockwise. Alternatively, the bolts can be drilled out.

Refitting

8 Position the inner column shaft so that the cut-out for the steering lock is positioned centrally in the outer column hole.
9 With the ignition key inserted in the lock, turn it to the "locked" position and remove it.
10 Locate the steering column lock on the outer column, making sure that it is the correct way up. As the lock is being located, turn the inner shaft to ensure that the lock tab enters the cut-out in the inner column shaft. Insert the new shear-head bolts finger-tight.
11 Check that the inner column is held firmly in its locked position. Insert the ignition key, and turn it to release the lock, to check that the inner column is free to rotate.

12 Tighten each shear-head bolt until the head breaks off **(see illustration)**, then check the operation of the lock again.
13 Refit the steering column as described in Section 12.

---

14 Steering column intermediate shaft and universal joints - removal, checking and refitting

Upper universal joint

Removal

1 Remove the steering column as described in Section 12.
2 Unscrew the clamp bolt, and pull the universal joint from the splines on top of the intermediate shaft.

Checking

3 Check the universal joint for excessive wear and damage, and if necessary renew it.

Refitting

4 Fit the universal joint to the intermediate shaft splines, so that the flat is aligned with the clamp bolt hole. Insert and tighten the clamp bolt to the specified torque.
5 Refit the steering column with reference to Section 12.

Intermediate shaft and lower flexible coupling

Removal

6 Remove the steering gear as described in Section 15.
7 Working inside the vehicle, remove the column cover, then unscrew and remove the clamp bolt securing the upper universal joint to the top of the intermediate shaft.
8 Separate the intermediate shaft from the upper joint, and withdraw it from under the vehicle, complete with the lower flexible coupling.
9 Note how the flexible coupling is assembled, and if necessary mark the components to ensure that the steering wheel position is maintained on reassembly.

10 Unscrew the bolts, and separate the intermediate shaft from the flanged joint. Recover the flexible coupling, plates and spring.

Checking

11 Check the condition of the flexible coupling for perishing, deterioration and damage. Renew it if necessary.
12 Check the condition of the rubber grommet in the vehicle floor, and renew it if necessary. Apply a little silicone grease to the inner surface of the rubber grommet before refitting the intermediate shaft.

Refitting

13 Assemble the flexible coupling and flanged joint to the intermediate shaft in the previously-noted positions, and tighten the four bolts to the specified torque.
14 Insert the intermediate shaft upwards through the rubber grommet into the upper joint, making sure that the flat is aligned with the clamp bolt hole. Insert the clamp bolt loosely at this stage.
15 Refit the steering gear with reference to Section 15.
16 Tighten the upper clamp bolt to the specified torque.

---

15 Steering gear assembly - removal, overhaul and refitting

Removal

1 Set the front wheels in the straight-ahead position, and ensure that the steering lock is engaged by removing the ignition key.
2 Chock the rear wheels, firmly apply the handbrake, then jack up the front of the vehicle and support on axle stands (see *"Jacking, towing and wheel changing"*). Remove both front roadwheels.
3 Extract the split pin from the bolt securing the drag link to the steering rack **(see illustration)**. Unscrew the nut and remove the bolt.
4 Unscrew and remove the clamp bolt securing the intermediate shaft lower flanged joint to the

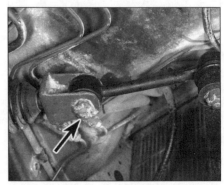

15.3 Bolt (arrowed) securing the drag link to the steering rack

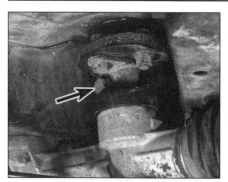

15.4 Clamp bolt (arrowed) securing the intermediate shaft lower flanged joint to the pinion on the steering gear

15.5 Steering gear mounting bolts (arrowed)

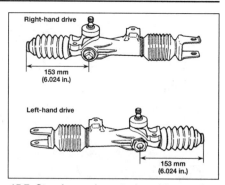

15.7 Steering rack central position setting dimension

pinion on the steering gear (see illustration). Mark the pinion and joint in relation to each other, to ensure correct refitting.

5 Unscrew and remove the mounting bolts, and lower the steering gear from the underbody (see illustration), at the same time releasing the pinion from the lower flanged joint. Withdraw the steering gear from under the vehicle.

Overhaul

6 Examine the steering gear assembly for signs of wear or damage, and check that the rack moves freely throughout the full length of its travel, with no signs of roughness or excessive free play between the steering gear pinion and rack. It is possible to overhaul the steering gear assembly housing components, but this task should be entrusted to a Vauxhall or Suzuki dealer. The only components which can be renewed easily by the home mechanic are the steering gear rubber gaiters, the track rod balljoints, the track rods, and the steering linkage centre lever. These procedures are covered in Sections 16, 17, 18 and 19 respectively.

Refitting

7 Check that the steering rack is placed in the central, straight-ahead position (see illustration).

8 Check that the front wheels are still in the straight-ahead position, then offer the steering gear into position, and engage the pinion with the intermediate shaft lower flanged joint. If the original steering gear is being refitted, make sure that the previously-made marks are aligned. Insert the clamp bolt loosely at this stage.

9 Insert the steering gear mounting bolts, and tighten to the specified torque.

10 Connect the drag link to the end of the steering gear rack. Insert the bolt, and tighten the nut to within the torque wrench tolerance until the split pin holes are aligned with each other. Insert a new split pin, and bend it over the nut and end of the bolt.

11 Tighten the intermediate shaft-to-pinion clamp bolt to the specified torque.

12 Refit both front roadwheels, and lower the vehicle to the ground. Tighten the roadwheel nuts to the specified torque.

16 Steering gear rubber gaiters - renewal

Drag link end gaiter

1 Set the front wheels in the straight-ahead position, and ensure that the steering lock is engaged by removing the ignition key.

2 Chock the rear wheels, firmly apply the handbrake, then jack up the front of the vehicle and support on axle stands (see "Jacking, towing and wheel changing"). For improved access, remove both front roadwheels.

3 Extract the split pin from the bolt securing the drag link to the steering rack. Unscrew the nut and remove the bolt. Move the drag link to one side.

4 Unscrew the nut from the end of the steering gear rack, and remove the yoke.

5 Release the small outer spring clip, then release the large inner spring clip using a pair of grips; at the same time, remove the gaiter from the end of the rack and housing.

6 Wipe clean the end of the rack, and the end of the steering gear housing.

7 Locate the large inner spring clip on the new gaiter, then hold the clip opened-up with a pair of grips. Fit the inner end of the gaiter on the end of the housing, and release the clip to retain it. Make sure that gaiter is fully located on the housing.

8 Locate the outer small end of the gaiter in the groove in the end of the rack, and retain with the spring clip.

9 Refit the yoke, and tighten the retaining nut to the specified torque. Note that the upper face of the yoke must be parallel with the steering gear mounting face.

10 Connect the drag link to the end of the steering gear rack, insert the bolt, then tighten the nut to within the torque wrench tolerance until the split pin holes are aligned with each other. Insert a new split pin, and bend it over the nut and end of the bolt.

11 Refit both front roadwheels, and lower the vehicle to the ground. Tighten the roadwheel nuts to the specified torque.

Closed end gaiter

12 Set the front wheels in the straight-ahead position.

13 Chock the rear wheels, firmly apply the handbrake, then jack up the front of the vehicle and support on axle stands (see "Jacking, towing and wheel changing"). For improved access, remove both front roadwheels.

14 Using a pair of grips, release the small outer spring clip. Similarly release the large inner spring clip, and at the same time remove the gaiter from the end of the rack and housing.

15 Wipe clean the end of the rack, and the end of the steering gear housing.

16 Locate the large inner spring clip on the new gaiter, then hold the clip opened-up with a pair of grips. Fit the inner end of the gaiter on the end of the housing, and release the clip to retain it. Make sure that the gaiter is fully located on the housing.

17 Locate the outer small end of the gaiter in the groove in the end of the rack, and retain with the spring clip.

18 Refit both front roadwheels, and lower the vehicle to the ground. Tighten the roadwheel nuts to the specified torque.

17 Track rod end balljoint - removal and refitting

Note: A balljoint separator tool will be required to disconnect the track rod end from the steering knuckle or steering centre lever.

Removal

1 Chock the rear wheels, firmly apply the handbrake, then jack up the front of the vehicle and support on axle stands (see "Jacking, towing and wheel changing"). Remove the relevant front roadwheel.

2 Using a straight-edge and a scriber, or similar, mark the relationship of the track rod end balljoint to the track rod. This is not strictly necessary if the track rod end is being

17.3 Track rod end and locknut (arrowed)

17.4 Track rod end, showing castellated nut and split pin

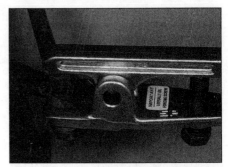

17.5 Using the balljoint separator tool to separate the track rod end from the steering arm

renewed, but the mark can be transferred to the new unit, to ensure that the new one is fitted in the correct position.

3 Hold the track rod with a spanner on the flats, and loosen the track rod end locknut by a quarter of a turn **(see illustration)**. Do not move the locknut from this position, as it will serve as a handy reference mark on refitting.

4 Extract the split pin, and unscrew the nut securing the track rod end to the steering arm on the steering knuckle, or on the centre lever, as applicable **(see illustration)**.

5 Use the balljoint separator tool to separate the track rod end from the steering arm **(see illustration)** or centre lever. To prevent any possible damage to the threaded shank of the balljoint, leave the nut in position until the shank is released.

6 Counting the **exact** number of turns necessary to do so, unscrew the track rod end balljoint from the track rod.

Refitting

7 If a new track rod end is being fitted, locate the locknut in the same position as noted on the old track rod end (ie with the same number of threads from the locknut to the end of the track rod end).

8 Screw the track rod end into the track rod the same number of turns as noted during removal.

9 Clean the taper surfaces, then fit the track rod end to the steering arm or centre lever. Tighten the nut to within the specified torque tolerance, until the split pin holes are aligned

with each other. Insert a new split pin, and bend it over the nut and end of the bolt.

10 Hold the track rod with a spanner on the flats, then tighten the locknut. Make sure that the previously-made alignment marks are lined up.

11 Refit the roadwheel, and lower the car to the ground. Tighten the roadwheel nuts to the specified torque.

12 Have the front wheel alignment checked at the earliest opportunity (see Section 20).

18 Track rod - removal and refitting

Removal

1 Chock the rear wheels, firmly apply the handbrake, then jack up the front of the vehicle and support on axle stands (see *"Jacking, towing and wheel changing"*). Remove the relevant front roadwheel.

2 Extract the split pin, and unscrew the nut securing the track rod end to the steering arm on the steering knuckle. Using a balljoint separator tool, separate the track rod end from the steering arm. To prevent any possible damage to the threaded shank of the balljoint, leave the nut in position until the shank is released.

3 Using the same method described in paragraph 2, separate the other end of the track rod from the centre lever, and remove the track rod.

4 Remove the track rod ends from the track rod with reference to Section 17; however, before doing so, measure the length of the track rod between the balljoint stud centres. This will help when fitting the track rod ends to the new track rod.

Refitting

5 Fit the track rod ends to the new track rod, so that the length of the track rod between the balljoint centres is the same as noted during removal. Make sure that the track rod ends are located the same distance in each end of the track rods.

6 Locate the inner track rod end ballstud in the centre lever, and tighten the nut to within the specified torque tolerance until the split pin holes are aligned. Fit a new split pin, and bend it over the nut and end of the ballstud to lock.

7 Using the same method described in paragraph 6, refit the outer track rod end ballstud to the steering knuckle.

8 Refit the roadwheel, and lower the vehicle to the ground. Tighten the roadwheel nuts to the specified torque.

9 Have the front wheel alignment checked at the earliest opportunity (see Section 20).

19 Steering linkage centre lever - removal, bush renewal and refitting

Removal

1 Chock the rear wheels, firmly apply the handbrake, then jack up the front of the vehicle and support on axle stands (see *"Jacking, towing and wheel changing"*). For improved access, remove both front roadwheels.

2 Extract the split pins, and unscrew the nuts securing the inner ends of the track rod ends to the rear of the centre lever **(see illustration)**. Use a balljoint separator tool to separate the track rod ends from the centre lever. To prevent any possible damage to the threaded shank of the balljoints, leave the nuts in position until the shank is released.

3 Extract the split pin, and unscrew the nut securing the steering drag link to the front of the centre lever **(see illustration)**. Use the

19.2 Inner ends of the track rods connected to the steering linkage centre lever - nuts arrowed

19.3 Nut securing the steering drag link to the front of the centre lever

19.5 Steering centre lever retaining nut (arrowed)

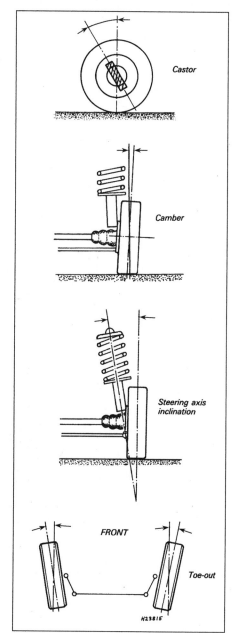

20.1 Wheel alignment and steering angle measurements

balljoint separator tool to separate the link from the lever.

4 Before removing the centre lever and bush from the stud, check the bush for wear by attempting to rock the lever. If there is appreciable free play, the bush and/or the centre lever is worn, and must be renewed.

5 Unscrew and remove the centre lever retaining nut from the stud on top of the front suspension crossmember **(see illustration)**. Recover the lockwasher and the dust cover.

6 Remove the centre lever from the stud, and recover the bush and lower thrustwasher.

7 Clean the stud, bush and the bore of the centre lever, and examine all components for wear and damage. Renew as necessary.

Refitting

8 Lubricate the new bush and the inner bore of the centre lever with suitable grease.

9 Locate the lower thrustwasher on the stud, followed by the bush and the centre lever. Make sure that the lever is located with the extended side facing upwards.

10 Refit the lockwasher and dust cover, then refit the centre lever retaining nut and tighten to the specified torque.

11 Refit the steering drag link to the front of the centre lever. Tighten the nut to within the torque wrench tolerance until the split pin holes are aligned. Fit a new split pin, and bend it over the nut and end of the ballstud.

12 Using the same procedure described in paragraph 11, refit the inner ends of the track rods to the centre lever.

13 Refit the front roadwheels, and lower the vehicle to the ground. Tighten the roadwheel nuts to the specified torque.

20 Wheel alignment and steering angles - general information

Definitions

1 A vehicle's steering and suspension geometry is defined in four basic settings - all angles are expressed in degrees (toe settings are expressed in degrees, or as a measurement); the steering axis is defined as an imaginary line drawn through the axis of the suspension strut, extended where necessary to contact the ground **(see illustration)**.

2 **Camber** is the angle between each roadwheel and a vertical line drawn through its centre and tyre contact patch, when viewed from the front or rear of the car. "Positive" camber is when the roadwheels are tilted outwards from the vertical at the top; "negative" camber is when they are tilted inwards.

3 Camber is not adjustable, and is given for reference only; while it can be checked using a camber checking gauge, if the figure obtained is significantly different from that specified, the vehicle must be taken for

careful checking by a professional, as the fault can only be caused by wear or damage to the body or suspension components.

4 **Castor** is the angle between the steering axis and a vertical line drawn through each roadwheel centre and tyre contact patch, when viewed from the side of the car. "Positive" castor is when the steering axis is tilted so that it contacts the ground ahead of the vertical; "negative" castor is when it contacts the ground behind the vertical.

5 Castor is not adjustable, and is given for reference only; while it can be checked using a castor checking gauge, if the figure obtained is significantly different from that specified, the vehicle must be taken for careful checking by a professional, as the fault can only be caused by wear or damage to the body or suspension components.

6 **Steering axis inclination/SAI** - also known as **kingpin inclination/KPI** - is the angle between the steering axis and a vertical line drawn through each roadwheel centre and tyre contact patch, when viewed from the front of the car.

7 SAI/KPI is not adjustable, and is given for reference only.

8 **Toe** is the difference between lines drawn through the roadwheel centres and the car's centre-line. "Toe-in" is when the roadwheels point inwards, towards each other at the front, while "toe-out" is when they splay outwards from each other at the front.

9 The front wheel toe setting is adjusted by screwing the track rods onto or away from the track rod ends, to alter the effective length of the track rod assemblies.

10 Rear wheel toe setting is not applicable to models in this manual, as a rigid rear axle is fitted.

Checking - general

11 Due to the special measuring equipment necessary to check the wheel alignment, and the skill required to use it properly, the checking and adjustment of these settings is best left to a Vauxhall or Suzuki dealer, or similar expert. Note that most tyre-fitting centres now possess sophisticated checking equipment.

12 For **accurate** checking, the vehicle **must** be at the kerb weight, ie unladen and with a full tank of fuel.

13 Before starting work, check first that the tyre sizes and types are as specified, then check the tyre pressures and tread wear, the roadwheel run-out, the condition of the hub bearings, and the condition of the front suspension components (Chapter 1). Correct any faults found.

14 Park the vehicle on level ground, check that the front roadwheels are in the straight-ahead position, then rock the vehicle front end to settle the suspension. Release the handbrake, and roll the vehicle backwards approximately 1 metre, then forwards again the same distance, to relieve any stresses in the steering and suspension components.

Toe setting - checking and adjusting

15 The front wheel toe setting is checked by measuring the distance between the front and rear inside edges of the roadwheel rims. Proprietary toe measurement gauges are available from motor accessory shops.

16 Prepare the vehicle as described in paragraphs 12 to 14 above.

17 Measure the distance between the front edges of the wheel rims and the rear edges of the rims. Subtract the front measurement from the rear measurement, and check that the toe-in result is within the specified range.

18 If adjustment is necessary, it is preferable to position the vehicle on a ramp; alternatively, raise the front of the vehicle and support on axle stands, since the locknuts on both the inner and outer ends of the track rods must be loosened. First check that the number of exposed threads visible on all four track rod ends is the same. If not, it will be necessary to disconnect the track rod(s) from the steering knuckle and/or the steering centre lever, and re-position the incorrect track rod end accordingly. **Note:** *It is most important that after adjustment, the length of each track rod (including the ends) is the same on each side.*

19 Loosen the track rod end locknuts (ie the two locknuts on each track rod) while holding the track rods with a spanner on the flats, and turn the track rods equally. Only turn them a quarter of a turn at a time before rechecking the alignment. Shortening the track rods will reduce toe-in/increase toe-out, and vice versa.

20 When the setting is correct, hold the track rods using a spanner on the flats, and securely tighten the locknuts. Where applicable, lower the vehicle to the ground.

Chapter 11 Bodywork and fittings

Contents

Degrees of difficulty

 Easy, suitable for novice with little experience | **Fairly easy,** suitable for beginner with some experience | 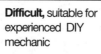 **Fairly difficult,** suitable for competent DIY mechanic | **Difficult,** suitable for experienced DIY mechanic | **Very difficult,** suitable for expert DIY or professional

1 General information

The bodyshell is made of pressed-steel sections, which are welded together to form an integral unit. A chassis section forms the base for the floor and body sections, and the main body sections are welded to it.

Plastic bumpers are fitted, constructed to provide maximum absorbing of minor accident damage.

The Van version is available with two sliding side doors and a wide opening, top mounted rear tailgate. Pickup models have a flat cargo bed, with fold-down sides and tailboard.

2 Maintenance - bodywork and underframe
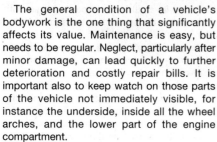

The general condition of a vehicle's bodywork is the one thing that significantly affects its value. Maintenance is easy, but needs to be regular. Neglect, particularly after minor damage, can lead quickly to further deterioration and costly repair bills. It is important also to keep watch on those parts of the vehicle not immediately visible, for instance the underside, inside all the wheel arches, and the lower part of the engine compartment.

The basic maintenance routine for the bodywork is washing - preferably with a lot of water, from a hose. This will remove all the loose solids which may have stuck to the vehicle. It is important to flush these off in such a way as to prevent grit from scratching the finish. The wheel arches and underframe need washing in the same way, to remove any accumulated mud, which will retain moisture and tend to encourage rust. Paradoxically enough, the best time to clean the underframe and wheel arches is in wet weather, when the mud is thoroughly wet and soft. In very wet weather, the underframe is usually cleaned of large accumulations automatically, and this is a good time for inspection.

Periodically, except on vehicles with a wax-based underbody protective coating, it is a good idea to have the whole of the underframe of the vehicle steam-cleaned, engine compartment included, so that a thorough inspection can be carried out to see what minor repairs and renovations are necessary. Steam-cleaning is available at many garages, and is necessary for the removal of the accumulation of oily grime, which sometimes is allowed to become thick in certain areas. If steam-cleaning facilities are not available, there are some excellent grease solvents available which can be brush-applied; the dirt can then be simply hosed off. Note that these methods should not be used on vehicles with wax-based underbody protective coating, or the coating will be removed. Such vehicles should be inspected annually, preferably just prior to Winter, when the underbody should be washed down, and any damage to the wax coating repaired. Ideally, a completely fresh coat should be applied. It would also be worth considering the use of such wax-based protection for injection into door panels, sills, box sections, etc, as an additional safeguard against rust damage, where such protection is not provided by the vehicle manufacturer.

After washing paintwork, wipe off with a chamois leather to give an unspotted clear finish. A coat of clear protective wax polish will give added protection against chemical pollutants in the air. If the paintwork sheen has dulled or oxidised, use a cleaner/polisher combination to restore the brilliance of the shine. This requires a little effort, but such dulling is usually caused because regular washing has been neglected. Care needs to be taken with metallic paintwork, as special non-abrasive cleaner/polisher is required to avoid damage to the finish. Always check that the door and ventilator opening drain holes and pipes are completely clear, so that water can be drained out. Brightwork should be treated in the same way as paintwork. Windscreens and windows can be kept clear of the smeary film which often appears, by the use of proprietary glass cleaner. Never use any form of wax or other body or chromium polish on glass.

3 Maintenance - upholstery and carpets

Mats and carpets should be brushed or vacuum-cleaned regularly, to keep them free of grit. If they are badly stained, remove them from the vehicle for scrubbing or sponging, and make quite sure they are dry before refitting. Seats and interior trim panels can be kept clean by wiping with a damp cloth. If they do become stained (which can be more apparent on light-coloured upholstery), use a little liquid detergent and a soft nail brush to scour the grime out of the grain of the material. Do not forget to keep the headlining clean in the same way as the upholstery. When using liquid cleaners inside the vehicle, do not over-wet the surfaces being cleaned. Excessive damp could get into the seams and padded interior, causing stains, offensive odours or even rot.

> **HAYNES HiNT** *If the inside of the vehicle gets wet accidentally, it is worthwhile taking some trouble to dry it out properly, particularly where carpets are involved. Do not leave oil or electric heaters inside the vehicle for this purpose.*

4 Minor body damage - repair

Note: *For more detailed information about bodywork repair, Haynes Publishing produce a book by Lindsay Porter called "The Car Bodywork Repair Manual". This incorporates information on such aspects as rust treatment, painting and glass-fibre repairs, as well as details on more ambitious repairs involving welding and panel beating.*

Repairs of minor scratches in bodywork

If the scratch is very superficial, and does not penetrate to the metal of the bodywork, repair is very simple. Lightly rub the area of the scratch with a paintwork renovator, or a very fine cutting paste, to remove loose paint from the scratch, and to clear the surrounding bodywork of wax polish. Rinse the area with clean water.

Apply touch-up paint to the scratch using a fine paint brush; continue to apply fine layers of paint until the surface of the paint in the scratch is level with the surrounding paintwork. Allow the new paint at least two weeks to harden, then blend it into the surrounding paintwork by rubbing the scratch area with a paintwork renovator or a very fine cutting paste. Finally, apply wax polish.

Where the scratch has penetrated right through to the metal of the bodywork, causing the metal to rust, a different repair technique is required. Remove any loose rust from the bottom of the scratch with a penknife, then apply rust-inhibiting paint to prevent the formation of rust in the future. Using a rubber or nylon applicator, fill the scratch with bodystopper paste. If required, this paste can be mixed with cellulose thinners to provide a very thin paste which is ideal for filling narrow scratches. Before the stopper-paste in the scratch hardens, wrap a piece of smooth cotton rag around the top of a finger. Dip the finger in cellulose thinners, and quickly sweep it across the surface of the stopper-paste in the scratch; this will ensure that the surface of the stopper-paste is slightly hollowed. The scratch can now be painted over as described earlier in this Section.

Repairs of dents in bodywork

When deep denting of the vehicle's bodywork has taken place, the first task is to pull the dent out, until the affected bodywork almost attains its original shape. There is little point in trying to restore the original shape completely, as the metal in the damaged area will have stretched on impact, and cannot be reshaped fully to its original contour. It is better to bring the level of the dent up to a point which is about 3 mm below the level of the surrounding bodywork. In cases where the dent is very shallow anyway, it is not worth trying to pull it out at all. If the underside of the dent is accessible, it can be hammered out gently from behind, using a mallet with a wooden or plastic head. Whilst doing this, hold a suitable block of wood firmly against the outside of the panel, to absorb the impact from the hammer blows and thus prevent a large area of the bodywork from being "belled-out".

Should the dent be in a section of the bodywork which has a double skin, or some other factor making it inaccessible from behind, a different technique is called for. Drill several small holes through the metal inside the area - particularly in the deeper section. Then screw long self-tapping screws into the holes, just sufficiently for them to gain a good purchase in the metal. Now the dent can be pulled out by pulling on the protruding heads of the screws with a pair of pliers.

The next stage of the repair is the removal of the paint from the damaged area, and from an inch or so of the surrounding "sound" bodywork. This is accomplished most easily by using a wire brush or abrasive pad on a power drill, although it can be done just as effectively by hand, using sheets of abrasive paper. To complete the preparation for filling, score the surface of the bare metal with a screwdriver or the tang of a file, or alternatively, drill small holes in the affected area. This will provide a really good "key" for the filler paste.

To complete the repair, see the Section on filling and respraying.

Repairs of rust holes or gashes in bodywork

Remove all paint from the affected area, and from an inch or so of the surrounding "sound" bodywork, using an abrasive pad or a wire brush on a power drill. If these are not available, a few sheets of abrasive paper will do the job most effectively. With the paint removed, you will be able to judge the severity of the corrosion, and therefore decide whether to renew the whole panel (if this is possible) or to repair the affected area. New body panels are not as expensive as most people think, and it is often quicker and more satisfactory to fit a new panel than to attempt to repair large areas of corrosion.

Remove all fittings from the affected area, except those which will act as a guide to the original shape of the damaged bodywork (eg headlight shells etc). Then, using tin snips or a hacksaw blade, remove all loose metal and any other metal badly affected by corrosion. Hammer the edges of the hole inwards, in order to create a slight depression for the filler paste.

Wire-brush the affected area to remove the powdery rust from the surface of the remaining metal. Paint the affected area with rust-inhibiting paint, if the back of the rusted area is accessible, treat this also.

Before filling can take place, it will be necessary to block the hole in some way. This can be achieved by the use of aluminium or plastic mesh, or aluminium tape.

Aluminium or plastic mesh, or glass-fibre matting, is probably the best material to use for a large hole. Cut a piece to the approximate size and shape of the hole to be filled, then position it in the hole so that its edges are below the level of the surrounding bodywork. It can be retained in position by several blobs of filler paste around its periphery.

Aluminium tape should be used for small or very narrow holes. Pull a piece off the roll, trim it to the approximate size and shape required, then pull off the backing paper (if used) and stick the tape over the hole; it can be overlapped if the thickness of one piece is insufficient. Burnish down the edges of the tape with the handle of a screwdriver or similar, to ensure that the tape is securely attached to the metal underneath.

Bodywork repairs - filling and respraying

Before using this Section, see the Sections on dent, deep scratch, rust holes and gash repairs.

Many types of bodyfiller are available, but generally speaking, those proprietary kits which contain a tin of filler paste and a tube of resin hardener are best for this type of repair. A wide, flexible plastic or nylon applicator will be found invaluable for imparting a smooth and well-contoured finish to the surface of the filler.

Mix up a little filler on a clean piece of card or board - measure the hardener carefully (follow the maker's instructions on the pack), otherwise the filler will set too rapidly or too slowly. Using the applicator, apply the filler paste to the prepared area; draw the applicator across the surface of the filler to achieve the correct contour and to level the surface. As soon as a contour that approximates to the correct one is achieved, stop working the paste - if you carry on too long, the paste will become sticky and begin to "pick-up" on the applicator. Continue to add thin layers of filler paste at 20-minute intervals, until the level of the filler is just proud of the surrounding bodywork.

Once the filler has hardened, the excess can be removed using a metal plane or file. From then on, progressively-finer grades of abrasive paper should be used, starting with a 40-grade production paper, and finishing with a 400-grade wet-and-dry paper. Always wrap the abrasive paper around a flat rubber, cork, or wooden block - otherwise the surface of the filler will not be completely flat. During the smoothing of the filler surface, the wet-and-dry paper should be periodically rinsed in water. This will ensure that a very smooth finish is imparted to the filler at the final stage.

At this stage, the "dent" should be surrounded by a ring of bare metal, which in turn should be encircled by the finely "feathered" edge of the good paintwork. Rinse the repair area with clean water, until all of the dust produced by the rubbing-down operation has gone.

Spray the whole area with a light coat of primer - this will show up any imperfections in the surface of the filler. Repair these imperfections with fresh filler paste or bodystopper, and once more smooth the surface with abrasive paper. Repeat this spray-and-repair procedure until you are satisfied that the surface of the filler, and the feathered edge of the paintwork, are perfect. Clean the repair area with clean water, and allow to dry fully.

 If bodystopper is used, it can be mixed with cellulose thinners to form a really thin paste which is ideal for filling small holes

The repair area is now ready for final spraying. Paint spraying must be carried out in a warm, dry, windless and dust-free atmosphere. This condition can be created artificially if you have access to a large indoor working area, but if you are forced to work in the open, you will have to pick your day very carefully. If you are working indoors, dousing the floor in the work area with water will help to settle the dust which would otherwise be in the atmosphere. If the repair area is confined to one body panel, mask off the surrounding panels; this will help to minimise the effects of a slight mis-match in paint colours. Bodywork fittings (eg chrome strips, door handles etc) will also need to be masked off. Use genuine masking tape, and several thicknesses of newspaper, for the masking operations.

Before commencing to spray, agitate the aerosol can thoroughly, then spray a test area (an old tin, or similar) until the technique is mastered. Cover the repair area with a thick coat of primer; the thickness should be built up using several thin layers of paint, rather than one thick one. Using 400-grade wet-and-dry paper, rub down the surface of the primer until it is really smooth. While doing this, the work area should be thoroughly doused with water, and the wet-and-dry paper periodically rinsed in water. Allow to dry before spraying on more paint.

Spray on the top coat, again building up the thickness by using several thin layers of paint. Start spraying at one edge of the repair area, and then, using a side-to-side motion, work until the whole repair area and about 2 inches of the surrounding original paintwork is covered. Remove all masking material 10 to 15 minutes after spraying on the final coat of paint.

Allow the new paint at least two weeks to harden, then, using a paintwork renovator, or a very fine cutting paste, blend the edges of the paint into the existing paintwork. Finally, apply wax polish.

Plastic components

With the use of more and more plastic body components by the vehicle manufacturers (eg bumpers. spoilers, and in some cases major body panels), rectification of more serious damage to such items has become a matter of either entrusting repair work to a specialist in this field, or renewing complete components. Repair of such damage by the DIY owner is not really feasible, owing to the cost of the equipment and materials required for effecting such repairs. The basic technique involves making a groove along the line of the crack in the plastic, using a rotary burr in a power drill. The damaged part is then welded back together, using a hot-air gun to heat up and fuse a plastic filler rod into the groove. Any excess plastic is then removed, and the area rubbed down to a smooth finish. It is important that a filler rod of the correct plastic is used, as body components can be made of a variety of different types (eg polycarbonate, ABS, polypropylene).

Damage of a less serious nature (abrasions, minor cracks etc) can be repaired by the DIY owner using a two-part epoxy filler repair material. Once mixed in equal proportions, this is used in similar fashion to the bodywork filler used on metal panels. The filler is usually cured in twenty to thirty minutes, ready for sanding and painting.

If the owner is renewing a complete component himself, or if he has repaired it with epoxy filler, he will be left with the problem of finding a suitable paint for finishing which is compatible with the type of plastic used. At one time, the use of a universal paint was not possible, owing to the complex range of plastics encountered in body component applications. Standard paints, generally speaking, will not bond to plastic or rubber satisfactorily. However, it is now possible to obtain a plastic body parts finishing kit which consists of a pre-primer treatment, a primer and coloured top coat. Full instructions are normally supplied with a kit, but basically, the method of use is to first apply the pre-primer to the component concerned, and allow it to dry for up to 30 minutes. Then the primer is applied, and left to dry for about an hour before finally applying the special-coloured top coat. The result is a correctly-coloured component, where the paint will flex with the plastic or rubber, a property that standard paint does not normally possess.

5 Major body damage - repair

Where serious damage has occurred, or large areas need renewal due to neglect, it means that complete new panels will need welding-in, and this is best left to professionals. If the damage is due to impact, it will also be necessary to check completely the alignment of the bodyshell, and this can only be carried out accurately by a Vauxhall/Suzuki dealer, using special jigs. If the body is left misaligned, it is primarily dangerous, as the vehicle will not handle properly; secondly, uneven stresses will be imposed on the steering, suspension and possibly transmission, causing abnormal wear, or complete failure, particularly to such items as the tyres.

6 Front bumper - removal and refitting

Removal

1 Remove the front indicator/sidelight units, with reference to Chapter 12. Alternatively, leave the light units in the front bumper, and disconnect the wiring under the front of the vehicle. If this option is taken, unscrew the bolt securing the earth wires to the underbody.
2 Where necessary, release the clutch and/or choke cable from the support bracket on the front bumper.
3 Where necessary, unscrew and remove the bolts securing the lower edge of the front bumper to the underbody.
4 Inside the vehicle, unscrew the bumper side mounting nuts **(see illustration)**.

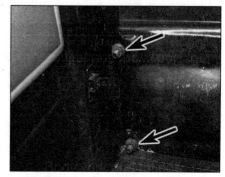
6.4 Front bumper side mounting nuts (arrowed)

6.6 Removing the front bumper centre mounting bolt

7.2 Rear bumper upper mounting screw

7.4a Rear bumper side mounting screw . . .

5 Have an assistant support the front bumper.
6 At the front of the bumper, remove the number plate, then prise out the plastic cover and unscrew the centre front bumper mounting bolt **(see illustration)**.
7 Withdraw the front bumper from the vehicle.

Refitting

8 Refitting is a reversal of removal. Check that the front indicator/sidelight units operate correctly on completion.

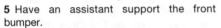

7   Rear bumper - removal and refitting

Removal

1 For improved access, chock the front wheels, then jack up the rear of the vehicle and support on axle stands (see *"Jacking, towing and wheel changing"*).

Van models

2 Open the tailgate, then unscrew and remove the screws securing the top of the bumper to the body rear panel **(see illustration)**.
3 Have an assistant support the rear bumper.
4 Unscrew and remove the two lower side mounting screws and the central nuts, then withdraw the bumper from the rear of the vehicle **(see illustrations)**.

7.4b . . . and central mounting nut

Pickup models

5 From under the rear bumper, unscrew the lower mounting bolts securing the rear bumper to the rear brackets.
6 Have an assistant support the rear bumper.
7 Unscrew and remove the upper mounting bolts, and withdraw the rear bumper from the rear of the vehicle.

Refitting

All models

8 Refitting is a reversal of removal.

8   Door (front and side loading) - removal, refitting and adjustment

Front door

Removal

1 The door hinges are bolted to the front doors and to the A-pillars **(see illustration)**. The door may be removed either together with the hinges, or leaving the hinges on the A-pillars. If it is required to remove the door with the hinges, refer to paragraph 9.

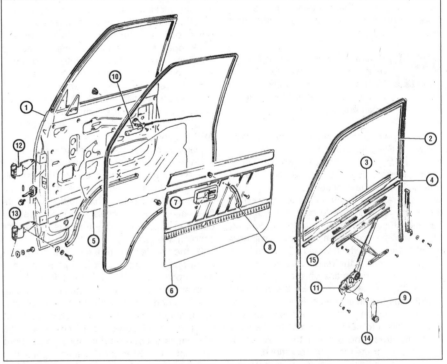

8.1 Front door components

1 *Door panel*	7 *Inner door handle*	12 *Door upper hinge*
2 *Window glass*	*surround*	13 *Door lower hinge*
3 *Outer weatherstrip*	8 *Door pull*	14 *Window regulator handle*
4 *Inner weatherstrip*	9 *Window regulator handle*	*retaining spring*
5 *Plastic insulation membrane*	10 *Inner door handle*	15 *Window glass bottom*
6 *Inner trim panel*	11 *Window regulator*	*channel*

8.5 Door check strap and roll pin

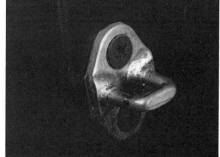

8.12a Door striker

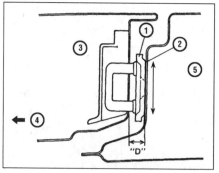

8.12b Front door striker adjustment (D)

1 Striker
2 Spacer
3 Front door
4 Front of vehicle
5 B-pillar/body side
   panel
D See text

2 Remove the door inner trim panel as described in Section 9.

3 Carefully peel away the front of the plastic insulation membrane, to give access to the door hinge bolts through the special holes.

4 Prise the plugs from the door hinge bolt access holes.

5 Using a suitable punch, drive out the door check strap roll pin upwards through the bracket on the A-pillar **(see illustration)**.

6 With the help of an assistant, support the weight of the door, using blocks of wood and axle stands or a trolley jack. Take care not to damage the door paintwork.

7 Using a socket through the access holes, unscrew and remove the door mounting bolts.

8 Withdraw the door rearwards from the hinges, and lift it away from the vehicle.

9 If it is required to remove the hinges, it will be necessary to remove the front bumper as described in Section 6, and the headlight surround with reference to Chapter 12, Section 7, for access to the hinge mounting bolts. The bolt heads are concealed in holes in the body, which are covered with adhesive tape.

10 With the door removed from the vehicle, check the weatherseal for condition; if it is at all damaged or deteriorated, renew it.

Refitting and adjustment

11 Refit the door using a reversal of the removal procedure. Make sure that the mounting bolts are tightened securely.

12 Close the door slowly, and check that the lock engages centrally with the striker on the B-pillar **(see illustration)**. With the door fully closed, the door outer skin should be level with the outer surface of the B-pillar. If adjustment is necessary, loosen the striker mounting screws a little, so that it is held in position, but may be moved by light tapping with a small hammer. Reposition the striker as necessary, and check the adjustment by closing the door slowly. On completion, fully tighten the striker screws. If necessary, the door striker should be adjusted in the fore-and-aft position by adding or removing spacers - the dimension "D" **(see illustration)** should be between 12.7 and 14.7 mm.

Side loading door

Removal

13 Unscrew the screw, and remove the plastic cover from the rear end of the lower guide rail **(see illustrations)**.

14 Open the sliding door, and support its weight.

15 Mark the position of the lower guide arm, then unscrew the bolt fixing the door to the arm **(see illustration)**.

16 Release the lower guide bracket from the body channel, then lower the door guide arm from the upper rail, and slide the hinge from the rear guide. Remove the side loading door from the vehicle **(see illustrations)**.

17 With the door removed from the vehicle, check the weatherseal for condition; if it is at all damaged or deteriorated, renew it.

8.13a Remove the screw . . .

8.13b . . . and remove the guide rail plastic cover

8.15 Unscrew the bolt fixing the door to the arm

8.16a Release the lower guide bracket from the body channel . . .

8.16b . . . then lower the door guide arm from the upper rail . . .

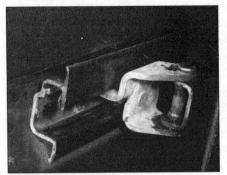

8.16c . . . and slide the hinge from the rear guide

8.23a Front stopper on the side loading door (door on bench)

8.23b Contact plate on the B-pillar

Refitting and adjustment

18 Before refitting the door, apply a little grease to the sliding surfaces on the rear guide rail, and to the spring surfaces on the lower entry valance.

19 Refit the side loading door using a reversal of the removal procedure, then check and adjust its position as follows.

20 With the door shut, check that the door front edge outer skin is level with the door pillar outer skin. If not, open the door and slightly loosen the bolt fixing the door to the lower guide arm. Move the door in or out as necessary, then tighten the bolt.

21 With the door shut, check that the door rear edge outer skin is level with the rear body side panel. If not, remove the door inner trim panel as described in Section 9, then peel away the plastic membrane for access to the slide hinge mounting bolts. Loosen the mounting bolts, and adjust the rear edge of the sliding door until it is aligned with the body panel, then tighten the bolts.

22 With the door shut, check that it is positioned centrally in the body aperture (ie the clearance at the front and rear of the door is equal). Adjustment is also made on the slide hinge mounting bolts.

23 Close the door slowly, and check that the front stoppers engage the contact plates centrally **(see illustrations)**. If necessary, adjust the stoppers by loosening the mounting bolts, re-positioning the stoppers, then re-tightening the bolts. Also check the rear upper and lower rubber buffers for condition, and renew them if necessary.

24 Close the door slowly, and check that the lock on the rear edge of the door engages centrally with the striker on the B-pillar. If adjustment is necessary, loosen the striker mounting screws a little, so that it is held in position, but may be moved by light tapping with a small hammer. Reposition the striker as necessary, and check the adjustment by closing the door slowly. On completion, fully tighten the screws. If necessary, the door striker should be adjusted in the fore-and-aft position by adding or removing spacers - dimension "D" (see illustration 8.12b) should be between 14.6 and 16.6 mm.

25 Refit the door inner trim panel with reference to Section 9.

9 Door inner trim panels - removal and refitting

Front door trim panel

Removal

1 Remove the retaining screws, and withdraw the door pull from the panel **(see illustration)**.

2 Remove the screw retaining the inner door handle surround. Withdraw the surround over the inner door handle **(see illustrations)**.

3 With the window fully closed, note the position of the regulator handle - it should be pointing upwards and facing forwards by approximately 45°. The handle is retained on

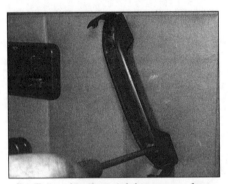

9.1 Removing the retaining screws from the door pull

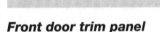

9.2a Remove the screw . . .

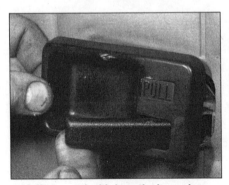

9.2b . . . and withdraw the inner door handle surround

9.3a Draw a piece of cloth sideways along the window regulator handle . . .

9.3b . . . pull the handle off the splines . . .

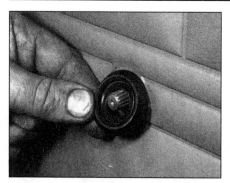

9.3c . . . and recover the embellisher

9.5 Unclipping the trim panel from the front door

9.6 Removing the plastic insulation membrane

the spindle with a spring clip - to release the clip, draw a piece of cloth sideways along the handle, and pull the handle off the splines at the same time. Recover the embellisher **(see illustrations)**.

4 Where fitted, unscrew the retaining screws and remove the armrest.

5 The trim panel can now be carefully prised free and removed using a wide-bladed screwdriver **(see illustration)**. Prise it free near the clips, to prevent damage to the panel.

6 Access to the inner door components can be made by carefully peeling free the plastic insulation membrane from the door **(see illustration)**.

Refitting

7 Refit in the reverse order of removal.

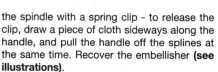

9.8a Unscrew the mounting screws . . .

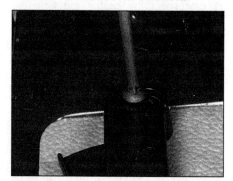

9.8b . . . and remove the interior door handle

Side loading door inner trim panel
Removal

8 Note the fitted position of the interior door handle, then unscrew the mounting screws and remove it **(see illustrations)**.

9 Where fitted, remove the ashtray.

10 The trim panel can now be carefully prised free and removed using a wide-bladed screwdriver. Prise it free near the clips, to prevent damage to the panel.

Refitting

11 Refit in the reverse order of removal, but adjust the interior door handle as described in Section 10.

---

10 Door handle and lock components - removal and refitting

Front door interior handle
Removal

1 Remove the door inner trim panel and plastic insulation membrane, as described in Section 9.

2 Remove the retaining screws, then release the control rod from the clip, and withdraw the interior door handle assembly a little way from the door **(see illustrations)**.

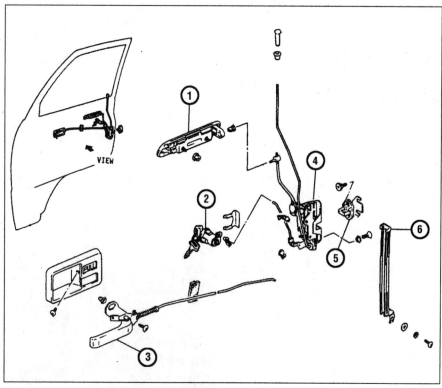

10.2a Front door handles and lock components

1 *Exterior door handle*
2 *Lock cylinder*
3 *Interior door handle*
4 *Lock assembly*
5 *Striker*
6 *Plastic cover strip*

10.2b Unscrewing the interior door handle
assembly retaining screws

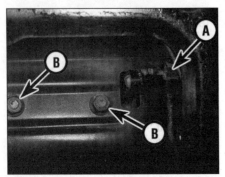

10.6 Removing the control rod from the
exterior door handle

A Control rod
B Exterior door handle mounting nuts

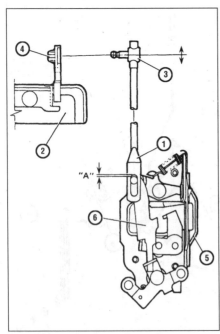

10.8 Front door exterior handle
adjustment

1 Control rod   5 Lock assembly
2 Exterior door handle 6 Link
3 Adjustment joint   A 0 to 2 mm
4 Adjustment joint retainer

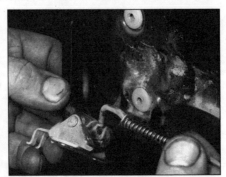

10.3 Disconnecting the control rod from
the interior door handle

3 Disconnect the control rod from the interior
door handle (see illustration).

Refitting and adjustment

4 Refitting is a reversal of removal, but before
fully tightening the retaining screws, adjust
the handle as follows. Move the handle
forward or rearward as required until the
clearance "B" between the lever on the lock is
as shown (see illustration). Make sure that
the plastic clip securing the control rod to the
lock is firmly pressed together.

Front door exterior handle

Removal

5 Remove the door inner trim panel and
plastic insulation membrane, as described in
Section 9.
6 Prise the control rod from the exterior door
handle (see illustration). Note that the joint
on the control rod is adjustable, so do not
move it up or down the rod.
7 Unscrew the mounting nuts, and withdraw
the exterior door handle from the outside of
the door.

Refitting

8 Refitting is a reversal of removal, but check
that the joint on the control rod is correctly
positioned, as follows. Check that the
clearance "A" between the link on the lock
and the top of the slot on the control rod is as
shown (see illustration). If adjustment is
necessary, prise off the joint, re-position it on
the control rod, and press it on again. While
making the adjustment, make sure that the
lock link is not pressed downwards.

10.11 Removing the locking knob

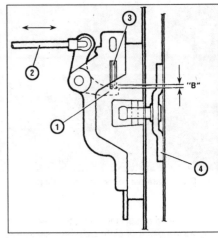

10.4 Interior door handle adjustment
dimension (B)

1 Lever (for control rod)   4 Striker
2 Control rod   B 0 to 2 mm
3 Lever (for exterior handle)

Front door lock

Removal

9 Remove the door inner trim panel and
plastic insulation membrane, as described in
Section 9.
10 Where necessary, remove the single
screw, and withdraw the plastic cover strip
from the rear edge of the front door.
11 Unscrew the locking knob from the top of
the locking rod (see illustration).
12 Disconnect the control rod from the
exterior door handle.
13 Disconnect the interior door handle
control rod from the lock.
14 Release the control rods from their clips
as necessary, then unscrew the mounting
screws and remove the front door lock from
inside the door (see illustrations).

Refitting

15 Refitting is a reversal of the removal
procedure, but adjust the position of the
control rod joint on the exterior door handle as
described previously. Also check the
adjustment of the interior door handle as
previously described. Ensure that the plastic
clip securing the interior door handle control
rod is pressed firmly together.

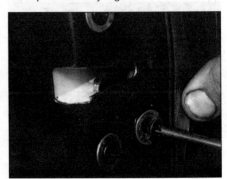

10.14a Unscrew the mounting screws . . .

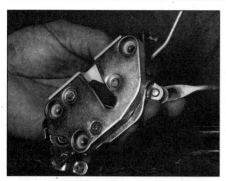

10.14b . . . and remove the front door lock

10.18 Disconnecting the control rod (arrowed) from the lock cylinder

10.19a Extract the retaining spring . . .

10.19b . . . then withdraw the lock cylinder

16 Check and if necessary adjust the position of the lock striker as previously described.

Front door lock cylinder

Removal

17 Remove the door inner trim panel and plastic insulation membrane, as described in Section 9.

18 Disconnect the control rod from the lock cylinder by prising it from the plastic clip **(see illustration)**.

19 Using a pair of pliers, extract the lock cylinder retaining spring, then withdraw the cylinder from the outside of the door **(see illustrations)**.

Refitting

20 Refitting is a reversal of the removal procedure. Make sure that the control rod plastic clip is firmly pressed together.

Side loading door interior door handle

Removal

21 Open the side loading door, then remove the two mounting screws and withdraw the handle.

Refitting and adjustment

22 Refit the door handle, and lightly tighten the two mounting screws. Adjust the position of the handle in its fully-open position so that it is just touching the remote control lever, then tighten the mounting screws.

Side loading door exterior door handle

Removal

23 Remove the door inner trim panel and plastic insulation membrane, as described in Section 9.

24 Prise the control rod from the exterior door handle, using a wide-bladed screwdriver **(see illustrations)**.

25 Remove the retaining screws, and withdraw the handle from the outside of the door **(see illustrations)**.

Refitting

26 Refitting is a reversal of removal, but check that the joint on the control rod is

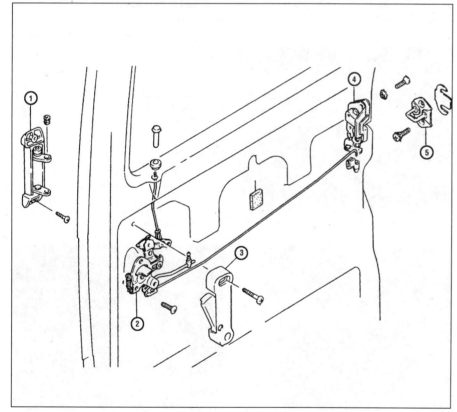

10.24a Side loading door handle and lock components

1 Exterior handle   2 Remote control assembly   3 Interior handle   4 Lock assembly   5 Striker

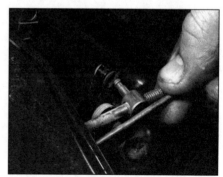

10.24b Removing the control rod from the exterior door handle

10.25a Remove the retaining screws . . .

10.25b . . . and withdraw the handle from the outside of the door

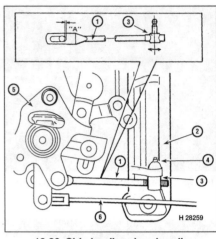

10.26 Side loading door handle adjustment

1 Exterior handle control rod
2 Exterior handle
3 Adjustment joint
4 Adjustment joint retainer
5 Remote control assembly
6 Lock control rod
A 0 to 2 mm

correctly positioned, as follows. Check that the clearance "A" between the horizontal link on the lock and the slot on the control rod is as shown (see illustration). The clearance is hidden from view, but the amount of play can be felt by moving the handle. If adjustment is necessary, prise off the joint, re-position it on the control rod, and press it on again. While making the adjustment, make sure that the lock link is not pressed sideways.

Side loading door remote control assembly

Removal

27 Remove the door inner trim panel and plastic insulation membrane, as described in Section 9.
28 Unscrew the locking knob from the top of the locking rod (see illustration).

29 Prise the control rod from the exterior door handle.
30 Disconnect the control rod from the rear lock by prising apart the plastic clip.
31 Unscrew the mounting screws, and remove the remote control assembly from inside the door (see illustrations).

Refitting

32 Refitting is a reversal of the removal procedure, but adjust the position of the control rod joint on the exterior door handle as described previously. Also check the adjustment of the interior door handle as previously described.

Side loading door lock assembly

Removal

33 Remove the door inner trim panel and plastic insulation membrane, as described in Section 9.

34 Disconnect the control rod from the lock by prising apart the plastic clip.
35 Unscrew the mounting screws, and remove the lock assembly from inside the door (see illustrations).

Refitting

36 Refitting is a reversal of the removal procedure.

11 Front door window glass and regulator - removal and refitting

Removal

1 Remove the door inner trim panel and plastic insulation membrane, as described in Section 9.
2 Fully open the window, then prise the inner and outer weatherstrips off the top of the door

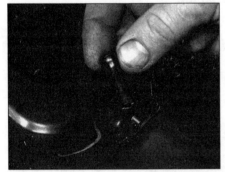

10.28 Removing the locking knob

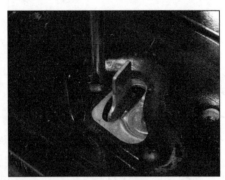

10.31a Unscrew the mounting screws . . .

10.35b . . . and remove the lock assembly

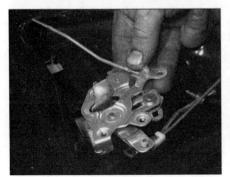

10.31b . . . and remove the remote control assembly

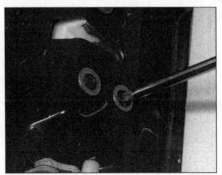

10.35a Unscrew the mounting screws . . .

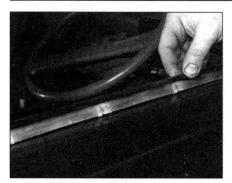

11.2 Removing the weatherstrips from the top of the door

11.3a Removing the screws securing the glass support channel to the window regulator

11.3b Glass support channel separated from the regulator

(see illustration). Use a wide-bladed screwdriver if necessary. Take care not to damage the door paintwork.
3 Working through the holes in the inner door, unscrew the two screws securing the glass support channel to the window regulator (see illustrations).
4 Carefully tilt the window glass forwards, then lift it upwards from the outside of the door (see illustration).
5 If necessary, the support channel may be removed from the bottom of the glass.
6 Unscrew the mounting screws, and manoeuvre window regulator unit from the door (see illustrations).

Refitting

7 Refitting is a reversal of removal, but first apply a little grease to the gear teeth, the centre pivot and the sliding surfaces. If the support channel is being refitted, make sure that it is located on the glass as shown (see illustration), with the rear mounting hole centre the specified distance from the rear edge of the glass. Apply soapy water (washing-up liquid) to the channel before tapping it carefully onto the glass with a plastic hammer. Check that the window moves easily in the side channels - if not, adjust the position of the lower equaliser bar, as this determines the glass position, and the relation of the top edge of the glass to the upper sealing channel. The equaliser bar is retained with two bolts.

<h2>12 Tailgate and support struts - removal and refitting</h2>

Tailgate
Removal

1 Open the tailgate, then carefully prise off the inner trim panel using a wide-bladed screwdriver. Only prise the panel near the clips, otherwise there is a risk of damaging the panel. Recover the clips, then pull back the plastic membrane (see illustration).
2 Have an assistant support the tailgate, then disconnect the struts by prising out the spring clips and pulling the struts off the ball pivot. Lower the struts onto the rear panel.

11.6a Unscrew the mounting screws . . .

11.4 Removing the window glass

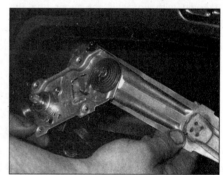

11.6b . . . and manoeuvre the window regulator unit from the door

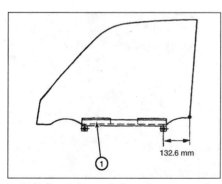

11.7 Front door window glass support channel (1) location dimension

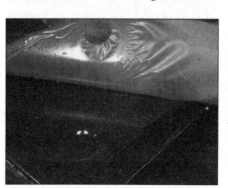

12.1 Removing the plastic membrane from the inside of the tailgate

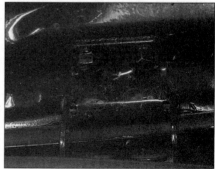

12.4 Tailgate hinge

132.6 mm

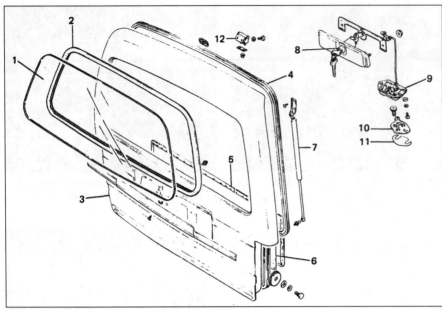

12.6 Tailgate components

1 Glass	5 Inner trim panel	9 Lock
2 Glass weatherstrip	6 Cover	10 Striker
3 Tailgate	7 Strut	11 Adjustment shims
4 Tailgate weatherstrip	8 Lock cylinder assembly	12 Hinge

3 As applicable, disconnect the wiring for the heated rear window and tailgate wiper motor. Also detach the washer tube.

4 Mark the position of the hinges on the tailgate using a marker pen **(see illustration)**.

5 Again with an assistant supporting the tailgate, unscrew the mounting bolts and remove the tailgate from the rear of the vehicle.

6 With the tailgate removed from the vehicle, check the weatherseal for condition; if it is at all damaged or deteriorated, renew it **(see**

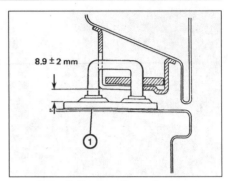

12.7a Tailgate striker adjustment dimension

1 Shim

illustration). Also check the condition of the stoppers on each side, and renew them if necessary.

Refitting

7 Refit in the reverse order of removal, but check that the jaw of the lock passes centrally over the striker. If not, loosen the striker bolts, re-position the striker as necessary, then tighten the bolts. Check that the tailgate is held firmly shut by the striker, so that it is pressed against the weatherstrip. Adjustment for this is made by adding or removing shims from under the striker. With the tailgate shut, the clearance between the lock mounting panel and the flat face of the striker should be as shown. Make sure that the wiring connector is fully engaged, and check the number plate lights, tailgate wiper and heated rear window for correct operation as applicable. Check that the circular guides on the sides of the tailgate are secure and in good condition **(see illustrations)**.

Support struts

Removal

8 Support the tailgate in the open position with the help of an assistant, or using a stout piece of wood.

9 Prise out the spring clip, and pull the strut from the ball pivot **(see illustrations)**.

10 To remove the ball pivot, prise off the inner trim panel using a wide-bladed screwdriver, and recover the clips. Pull back

12.7b Tailgate striker

12.7c Circular guides on the tailgate

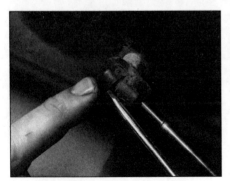

12.9a Prise out the spring clip . . .

12.9b . . . and pull the strut from the ball pivot

12.11 Strut mounting on the rear body panel

13.2 Disconnecting the control rod from the lock cylinder

13.3 Removing the tailgate lock

13.6a Tailgate lock cylinder assembly mounting nuts (arrowed) inside the tailgate

the plastic membrane. Unscrew the mounting nut, and disconnect the strut from the tailgate.
11 Unbolt the strut from the rear body panel **(see illustration)**.

> ⚠ *Warning: The strut is filled with gas under high pressure, and no attempt must be made to dismantle it. Do not rotate the piston rod within the cylinder, or expose the strut to excessive heat.*

Refitting

12 Refitting is a reversal of removal.

---

13 Tailgate lock components - removal and refitting

Tailgate lock

Removal

1 Open the tailgate, then prise off the inner trim panel using a wide-bladed screwdriver. Only prise the panel near the clips, otherwise there is a risk of damaging the panel. Recover the clips.
2 Inside the tailgate, disconnect the control rod from the lock cylinder **(see illustration)**.
3 Unscrew the mounting bolts, and withdraw the lock from the tailgate **(see illustration)**.

Refitting

4 Refitting is a reversal of removal. If necessary, adjust the position of the striker as described in Section 12.

Tailgate lock cylinder

Removal

5 Carry out the procedure given in paragraphs 1 and 2.
6 Unscrew the mounting nuts/screws, and withdraw the lock cylinder assembly from the tailgate. Recover the gasket **(see illustrations)**.
7 Check the condition of the gasket, and renew it if necessary.
8 If necessary, the lock cylinder barrel may be removed by extracting the circlip and lifting out the components **(see illustrations)**.

Refitting

9 Refitting is a reversal of removal.

13.6b Unscrewing the lock cylinder assembly mounting screws

13.6c Removing the lock cylinder assembly

13.8a Extract the circlip . . .

13.8b . . . and remove the linkage . . .

13.8c . . . spring . . .

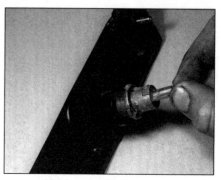

13.8d . . . and lock cylinder

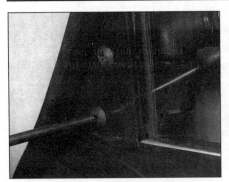

14.2a Removing the exterior mirror mounting screws

14.2b Removing the exterior mirror and plastic plate

14 Exterior mirror -
removal and refitting

Removal

1 Open the front door. The exterior mirror mounting screws are located in the small triangular area just forward of the window.
2 Support the mirror on the outside, then unscrew the mounting screws and withdraw the mirror. Recover the plastic plate. **(see illustrations)**.

Refitting

3 Refitting is a reversal of removal.

15 Windscreen, tailgate and rear cab windows -
general information

These areas of glass are secured by the tight fit of the weatherstrip in the body aperture. Renewal of such fixed glass is a difficult, messy and time-consuming task, which is considered beyond the scope of the home mechanic. It is difficult, unless one has plenty of practice, to obtain a secure, waterproof fit. Furthermore, the task carries a high risk of breakage; this applies especially to the laminated glass windscreen. In view of this, owners are strongly advised to have this sort of work carried out by one of the many specialist windscreen fitters.

16 Body exterior fittings -
removal and refitting

Front panel cover

1 Remove both headlight surrounds, with reference to Chapter 12, Section 7.
2 Unscrew the two screws, and remove the front panel cover from the front body panel.
3 Refitting is a reversal of removal.

Mudflaps

4 Unscrew the bolts securing the clamp bar and mudflap to the body bracket, and lift away the bar and mudflap. If necessary, the bracket may be unbolted from the body.
5 Refitting is a reversal of removal.

17 Seats -
removal and refitting

Van models

Removal

1 The seat retaining catches are located on the fronts of the seats. Pull the top of each catch to release the front of the seat.
2 Unscrew the mounting bolts located at the rear of the seat, then lift the seat out of the vehicle.
3 If necessary, the insulation plate (engine

cover) may be removed from the bottom of the seat by unscrewing the nuts.

Refitting

4 Refitting is a reversal of the removal procedure.

Pickup models

Removal

5 The seat retaining catches are located on the fronts of the seats. Pull the top of each catch to release the front of the seat.
6 Pull the seat forwards, then lift it so that the rear retaining pegs are released from the slots in the crosspanel.
7 If necessary, the insulation plate (engine cover) may be removed from the bottom of the seat by unscrewing the nuts.

Refitting

8 Refitting is a reversal of the removal procedure, but make sure that the rear pegs are correctly engaged with the slots before securing the front catches.

18 Seat belt components -
general

1 The seat belts do not normally require any attention, apart from periodically checking their condition and security. However, if the vehicle is ever involved in an accident, note that the seat belts should be checked particularly carefully. In the event of a frontal impact, they should be renewed as a matter of course, as they will have been subjected to severe loading.
2 The seat belt stalks are mounted in the centre of the vehicle, to the rear of the centre console **(see illustration)**.
3 The shoulder and lap seat belt is mounted at its bottom end on the outer body valance. On the static type belt, the upper mounting is at the top of the body B-pillar. On the inertia reel type belt, the upper buckle is mounted at the top of the B-pillar, and the lower inertia reel at the bottom of the B-pillar, beneath a plastic cover **(see illustrations)**.
4 Access to the mounting bolts is straight-forward; it will be necessary to prise off the

18.2 Seat belt stalk mounting bolts (shown with the centre console removed)

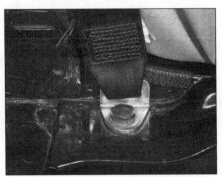

18.3a Seat belt lower mounting on the outer body valance

18.3b Seat belt upper mounting on the B-pillar (cover being removed)

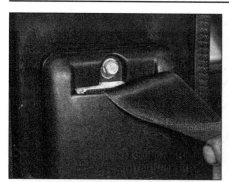

18.3c Unscrew the bolt . . .

18.3d . . . to remove the cover from the lower inertia reel assembly

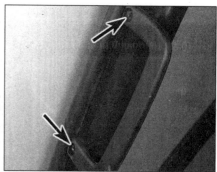

19.6 Cab hand grip and mounting screws (arrowed)

upper mounting cover, and to remove the cover screw, for access to the lower reel cover. Access to the seat belt stalks is gained by removing the centre console filler panel (see illustration 20.4).

5 Whenever the belt is removed and refitted, tighten all mounting bolts securely, and check it for satisfactory operation. Check the operation of the inertia reel type by gripping the webbing and pulling it sharply - the inertia reel must lock.

19 Interior trim panels and components - removal and refitting

Door inner trim panels

1 Refer to Section 9.

Rear load area inner trim panel (Van models)

2 The trim panel can be carefully prised free and removed using a wide-bladed screwdriver. Prise it free near the clips, to prevent damage to the panel. Where fitted, remove the plastic membrane.

3 Renew any clips which are damaged, then refit the panel using a reversal of the removal

procedure. Make sure that the clips are pressed fully in.

Sunvisors

4 Unscrew the mounting screws, and remove the sunvisor from the front roof panel.
5 Refitting is a reversal of removal.

Cab hand grips

6 Unscrew the mounting screws, and remove the hand grip from the A-pillar **(see illustration)**.
7 Refitting is a reversal of removal.

Front floor mat

8 The passenger compartment floor mat is in one piece, and is secured at its edges by screws. To remove it, first remove both front seats and the centre console (Sections 17 and 20 respectively).
9 Unscrew the retaining screws, and remove the mat from the passenger compartment.
10 Refitting is a reversal of removal.

Headlining

11 It is recommended that this work be carried out by a Vauxhall or Suzuki dealer. The headlining is attached to the roof with adhesive; before removing the old headlining, it is necessary to remove the roof strengthening bars by unbolting them from the side panels.

20 Centre console - removal and refitting

Removal

1 Remove one of the front seats, as described in Section 17.
2 Unscrew the knob from the top of the gear lever **(see illustration)**.
3 Prise the rubber boot from the centre console, and withdraw it over the gear lever **(see illustration)**.
4 Prise the plastic filler panel from the centre console **(see illustration)**.
5 Unscrew the centre console mounting screws, and lift the assembly over the gear lever and seat belt stalks **(see illustrations)**.

Refitting

6 Refitting is a reversal of removal.

21 Facia panel assembly - removal and refitting

Removal

1 Disconnect the battery negative lead.
2 Referring to Chapter 10, remove the steering column.

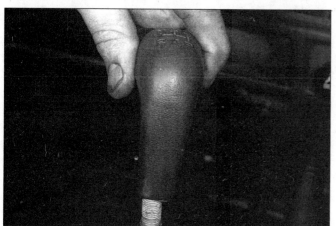

20.2 Removing the gear lever knob

20.3 Removing the rubber boot from the centre console

20.4 Removing the filler panel from the centre console

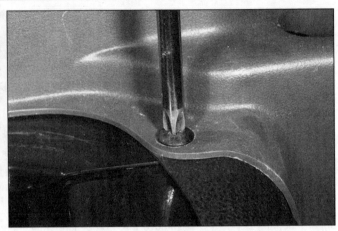

20.5a Centre console front top mounting screw . . .

20.5b . . . rear mounting screw . . .

20.5c . . . and front lower mounting screw

20.5d Lifting the centre console over the gear lever and seat belt stalks

3 Remove the small bracket fitted above the pedal mounting bracket from the facia as follows. Unscrew and remove the two lower bolts, then loosen (but do not remove) the upper bolts. Slide the bracket downwards, then out from the facia panel **(see illustrations)**.
4 Remove the instrument panel with reference to Chapter 12.
5 Remove the radio with reference to Chapter 12.
6 Pull the knobs from the heater control

levers (and fan motor switch, if applicable), then carefully press out the panel from behind **(see illustrations)**.
7 Unscrew the screws securing the heater control bracket to the facia panel **(see illustration)**.
8 Remove the choke cable with reference to Chapter 4.
9 Pull out the air vent tubes from the sides of the heater unit **(see illustrations)**. The tubes can remain attached to the facia until it is removed.

10 Prise out the plastic covers along the front of the facia near the windscreen, then unscrew and remove the front mounting screws **(see illustrations)**.
11 Open both front doors, then unscrew and remove the facia side mounting screws **(see illustration)**.
12 Withdraw the facia from the bulkhead **(see illustration)**, until it is possible to disconnect the wiring connectors. On right-hand-drive models, there are three connectors at the right-hand end of the facia.

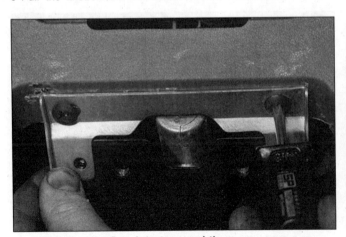

21.3a Loosen (but do not remove) the upper screws . . .

21.3b . . . and slide the bracket downwards from the facia

21.6a Removing the fan motor control knob from the switch

21.6b Removing the knobs from the heater control levers

21.6c Removing the heater control panel - press it out from behind, to release the securing clips

21.7 Removing the screws securing the heater control bracket to the facia panel

21.9a Pulling out the left-hand air vent tube from the heater

21.9b Pulling out the right-hand air vent tube from the heater

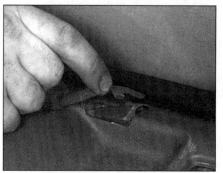

21.10a Remove the covers . . .

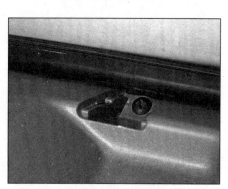

21.10b . . . for access to the facia front mounting screws

21.11 Removing the facia side mounting screws

Refitting

13 Refitting is a reversal of the removal procedure, but note the following additional points:

a) *Ensure that all wiring connections are correctly and securely made.*

b) *Refit the choke cable with reference to Chapter 4.*

c) *Refit the radio and instrument panel with reference to Chapter 12.*

d) *Refit the steering column with reference to Chapter 10.*

e) *On completion, check for satisfactory operation of all components.*

21.12 Withdrawing the facia from the bulkhead

Notes

Chapter 12 Body electrical systems

Contents

Degrees of difficulty

Easy, suitable for novice with little experience		Fairly easy, suitable for beginner with some experience		Fairly difficult, suitable for competent DIY mechanic	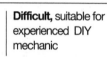	Difficult, suitable for experienced DIY mechanic		Very difficult, suitable for expert DIY or professional	

Specifications

Bulbs

	Wattage
Headlight	40/45, 50/60 or 55/65
Front sidelight	5
Stop-light/tail light	21/5
Front/rear direction indicator light	21
Direction indicator side repeater light	5
Rear number plate light	5
Rear foglight	21
Reversing light	21
Interior light	5
Instrument illumination	3.4
Instrument panel warning light	1.4

Fuses (Van models)

Left-hand row (from top)

Rating (amps)	Circuit(s) protected
15	Engine electrics, fuel pump, instruments and warning lights
15	Interior heater motor
15	Heated tailgate window (where applicable)
15	Windscreen wiper and washers, tailgate wiper and washers (where applicable)
10	Direction indicators and reversing lights
10	Hazard warning lights and horn
15	Cigarette lighter and radio

Right-hand row (from top)

Rating (amps)	Circuit(s) protected
10	Right-hand headlight
10	Left-hand headlight
10	Stop-lights
10	Interior light(s), rear foglight
5	Rear number plate light, instruments and clock illumination light
5	Right-hand side and tail lights
5	Left-hand side and tail lights

Fuses (Pickup models)

Left-hand row (from top)

Rating (amps)		Circuit(s) protected
15	. . . .	Engine electrics, fuel pump, instruments and warning lights
15	. . . .	Interior heater motor
15	. . . .	Not used
10	. . . .	Windscreen wiper and washers
10	. . . .	Direction indicators and reverse lights

Right-hand row (from top)

Rating (amps)		Circuit(s) protected
10	. . . .	Right-hand headlight
10	. . . .	Left-hand headlight
10	. . . .	Stop/tail lights, side lights, rear number plate light, rear foglight, interior lights
15	. . . .	Hazard warning lights and horn
15	. . . .	Cigarette lighter and radio

1 General information and precautions

General information

The body electrical system consists of all lights, wash/wipe equipment, interior electrical equipment, and associated switches and wiring.

The electrical system is of the 12-volt negative earth type. Power to the system is provided by a 12-volt battery, which is charged by the alternator (see Chapter 5A).

The engine electrical system (battery, alternator, starter motor, ignition system, etc) is covered separately in Chapter 5, Parts A and B.

Precautions

⚠️ **Warning: Before carrying out any work on the electrical system, read through the precautions given in "Safety first!" at the beginning of this manual, and in Chapter 5.**

⚠️ **Caution: If the radio/cassette player fitted to the vehicle has an anti-theft security code, refer to the information given in the preliminary Sections of this manual before disconnecting the battery.**

Prior to working on any component in the electrical system, the battery negative lead should first be disconnected, to prevent the possibility of electrical short-circuits and/or fires.

2 Electrical fault-finding - general information

Note: *Refer to the precautions given in "Safety first!" and in Section 1 of this Chapter before starting work. The following tests relate to testing of the main electrical circuits, and should not be used to test delicate electronic circuits (such as anti-lock braking systems), especially not those where an electronic control unit is used.*

General

1 A typical electrical circuit consists of an electrical component, any switches, relays, motors, fuses, fusible links or circuit breakers related to that component, and the wiring and connectors which link the component to both the battery and the chassis. To help to pinpoint a problem in an electrical circuit, wiring diagrams are included at the end of this manual.

2 Before attempting to diagnose an electrical fault, first study the appropriate wiring diagram, to obtain a more complete understanding of the components included in the particular circuit. The possible sources of a fault can be narrowed down by noting whether other components related to the circuit are operating properly. If several components or circuits fail at one time, the problem is likely to be related to a shared fuse or earth connection.

3 Electrical problems usually stem from simple causes, such as loose or corroded connections, a faulty earth connection, a blown fuse, a melted fusible link, or a faulty relay (refer to Section 3 for details of testing relays). Visually inspect the condition of all fuses, wires and connections in a problem circuit before testing the components. Use the wiring diagrams at the end of this Chapter to determine which terminal connections will need to be checked, in order to pinpoint the trouble-spot.

4 The basic tools required for electrical fault-finding include a circuit tester or voltmeter (a 12-volt bulb with a set of test leads can also be used for certain tests); a self-powered test light (or continuity tester); an ohmmeter (to measure resistance); a battery and set of test leads; and a jumper wire, preferably with a circuit breaker or fuse incorporated, which can be used to bypass suspect wires or electrical components. Before attempting to locate a problem with test instruments, use the wiring diagram to determine where to make the connections.

5 To find the source of an intermittent wiring fault (usually due to a poor or dirty connection, or damaged wiring insulation), a "wiggle" test can be performed on the wiring. This involves wiggling the wiring by hand, to see if the fault occurs as the wiring is moved. It should be possible to narrow down the source of the fault to a particular section of wiring. This method of testing can be used in conjunction with any of the tests described in the following sub-Sections.

6 Apart from problems due to poor connections, two basic types of fault can occur in an electrical circuit - open-circuit, or short-circuit.

7 Open-circuit faults are caused by a break somewhere in the circuit, which prevents current from flowing. An open-circuit fault will prevent a component from working, but will not cause the relevant circuit fuse to blow.

8 Short-circuit faults are caused by a "short" somewhere in the circuit, which allows the current flowing in the circuit to "escape" along an alternative route, usually to earth. Short-circuit faults are normally caused by a breakdown in wiring insulation, which allows a feed wire to touch either another wire, or an earthed component such as the bodyshell. A short-circuit fault will normally cause the relevant circuit fuse to blow.

Finding an open-circuit

9 To check for an open-circuit, connect one lead of a circuit tester or voltmeter to either the negative battery terminal or a known good earth.

10 Connect the other lead to a connector in the circuit being tested, preferably nearest to the battery or fuse.

11 Switch on the circuit, bearing in mind that some circuits are live only when the ignition switch is moved to a particular position.

12 If voltage is present (indicated either by the tester bulb lighting or a voltmeter reading, as applicable), this means that the section of the circuit between the relevant connector and the battery is problem-free.

13 Continue to check the remainder of the circuit in the same fashion.

14 When a point is reached at which no voltage is present, the problem must lie between that point and the previous test point

with voltage. Most problems can be traced to a broken, corroded or loose connection.

Finding a short-circuit

15 To check for a short-circuit, first disconnect the load(s) from the circuit (loads are the components which draw current from a circuit, such as bulbs, motors, heating elements, etc).

16 Remove the relevant fuse from the circuit, and connect a circuit tester or voltmeter to the fuse connections.

17 Switch on the circuit, bearing in mind that some circuits are live only when the ignition switch is moved to a particular position.

18 If voltage is present (indicated either by the tester bulb lighting or a voltmeter reading, as applicable), this means that there is a short-circuit. If voltage is present with the switch in its off position, then there is a short-circuit between the fuse and the switch.

19 If no voltage is present, but the fuse still blows with the load(s) connected, this indicates an internal fault in the load(s).

Finding an earth fault

20 The battery negative terminal is connected to "earth" - the metal of the engine/transmission and the vehicle body - and most systems are wired so that they only receive a positive feed, the current returning via the metal of the vehicle body. This means that the component mounting and the body form part of that circuit. Loose or corroded mountings can therefore cause a range of electrical faults, ranging from total failure of a circuit, to a puzzling partial fault. In particular, lights may shine dimly (especially when another circuit sharing the same earth point is in operation), motors (eg wiper motors or the radiator cooling fan motor) may run slowly, and the operation of one circuit may have an apparently-unrelated effect on another. Note that on many vehicles, earth straps are used between certain components, such as the engine/transmission and the body, usually where there is no metal-to-metal contact between components, due to flexible rubber mountings, etc.

21 To check whether a component is properly earthed, disconnect the battery, and connect one lead of an ohmmeter to a known good earth point. Connect the other lead to the wire or earth connection being tested. The resistance reading should be zero; if not, check the connection as follows.

22 If an earth connection is thought to be faulty, dismantle the connection, and clean back to bare metal both the bodyshell and the wire terminal, or the component earth connection mating surface. Be careful to remove all traces of dirt and corrosion, then use a knife to trim away any paint, so that a clean metal-to-metal joint is made. On reassembly, tighten the joint fasteners securely; if a wire terminal is being refitted, use serrated washers between the terminal and the bodyshell, to ensure a clean and

secure connection. When the connection is remade, prevent the onset of corrosion in the future by applying a coat of petroleum jelly or silicone-based grease, or by spraying on (at regular intervals) a proprietary ignition sealer or a water-dispersant lubricant.

3 Fuses and relays - general information

Fuses

1 Fuses are designed to break a circuit when a predetermined current is reached, in order to protect the components and wiring which could be damaged by excessive current flow. Any excessive current flow will be due to a fault in the circuit, usually a short-circuit (see Section 2).

2 The fusebox is located beneath the facia panel, to the left-hand side of the steering column.

3 Access to the fuses inside the fusebox is gained by carefully pulling off the plastic cover **(see illustration)**.

4 In addition to the fuses in the fusebox, a fusible link wire is located in the main wiring harness negative lead near the battery. The link is designed as an overall protection, and in the event of an electrical overload, it will melt and break the circuit to the main wiring harness.

5 A blown fuse can be recognised from its melted or broken wire.

6 To remove a fuse, first ensure that the relevant circuit is switched off.

7 Carefully pull the fuse from its location. The circuits are marked on the outside of the cover.

8 Spare fuses are provided in the plastic cover.

9 Before renewing a blown fuse, trace and rectify the cause, and always use a fuse of the correct rating. Never substitute a fuse of a higher rating, or make temporary repairs using wire or metal foil; more serious damage, or even fire, could result.

10 Note that the fuses are colour-coded as follows. Refer to the Specifications at the

beginning of this Chapter for details of the fuse ratings and the circuits protected:

Colour	Rating
Brown or orange	5A
Red	10A
Blue	15A

Relays

11 A relay is an electrically-operated switch, which is used for the following reasons:
a) *A relay can switch a heavy current remotely from the circuit in which the current is flowing, allowing the use of lighter-gauge wiring and switch contacts.*
b) *A relay can receive more than one control input, unlike a mechanical switch.*
c) *A relay can have a timer function - for example, the intermittent wiper relay.*

13 The direction indicator/hazard warning relay is located beneath the facia next to the steering column.

14 The dim-dip controlling relay (where applicable) is located on the front panel beneath the facia **(see illustration)**.

15 Where fitted, the carburettor controlling relay is located in a special container beneath the front of the vehicle.

16 The fuel solenoid controlling relay is located beneath the left-hand side of the facia.

15 If a circuit or system controlled by a relay develops a fault, and the relay is suspect, operate the system. If the relay is functioning, it should be possible to hear it "click" as it is energised. If this is the case, the fault lies with the components or wiring of the system. If the relay is not being energised, then either the relay is not receiving a main supply or a switching voltage, or the relay itself is faulty. Testing is by the substitution of a known good unit.

16 To remove a relay, first ensure that the relevant circuit is switched off, then disconnect the wiring and unscrew the retaining screw(s).

17 On UK models, a dim-dip headlight system may be fitted. With this system, if the sidelights are switched on with the engine running, the headlights will be illuminated with reduced voltage. The controller for this system is located on a bracket beneath the centre of the facia.

3.3 Removing the cover from the fusebox

3.14 Dim-dip controlling relay (arrowed) on the front panel

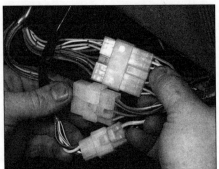

4.4 Disconnecting the combination switch wiring plugs

4.5a Unscrew the combination switch mounting screws (arrowed) . . .

4.5b . . . and withdraw the combination switch

4 Switches - removal and refitting

Note: *Disconnect the battery negative lead before removing any switch, and reconnect the lead after refitting the switch.*

Ignition switch/steering column lock

1 Refer to Chapter 10.

Steering column combination switches

2 Remove the steering wheel as described in Chapter 10.
3 Remove the steering column shroud securing screws, using a screwdriver from under the steering column, and lift off the upper and lower shrouds.

4.7 Prising a switch from the facia

4 Disconnect the combination switch wiring plugs **(see illustration)**, and where necessary, release the wire from the clamp/tie.
5 Unscrew the mounting screws, and withdraw the combination switch upwards over the top of the steering column **(see illustrations)**.
6 Refitting is a reversal of the removal procedure, but make sure that the wiring is not trapped between the upper shroud and bracket. Refit the steering wheel with reference to Chapter 10.

Facia-mounted pushbutton switches

7 Using a screwdriver, carefully prise the switch from the facia (or instrument panel surround) **(see illustration)**. Where necessary, protect the surrounding trim using card or a pad of cloth.
8 Disconnect the wiring from the rear of the switch **(see illustration)**.
9 Refitting is a reversal of removal, but press the switch into position until the plastic clips engage.

Heater blower motor switch

10 Remove the heating/ventilation control panel, as described in Chapter 3.
11 Remove the switch from the panel.
12 Refitting is a reversal of removal.

Courtesy light switches

13 Open the door/tailgate, then where necessary prise the switch from the side panel

or rear panel (as applicable), and withdraw it. Disconnect the wiring connector as it becomes accessible **(see illustration)**.

HAYNES HiNT *Tape the wiring to the door pillar, to prevent it falling into the door pillar. Alternatively, tie a piece of string to the wiring, to retrieve it.*

14 Refitting is a reversal of removal, but where necessary ensure that the rubber gaiter is correctly seated on the switch.

5 Bulbs (exterior lights) - renewal

General

1 Whenever a bulb is renewed, note the following points:
a) Remember that, if the light has just been in use, the bulb (and its holder) may be extremely hot.
b) Always check the bulb contacts and holder, ensuring that there is clean metal-to-metal contact between the bulb and its live contact(s) and earth. Clean off any corrosion or dirt before fitting a new bulb.
c) Wherever bayonet-type bulbs are fitted, ensure that the live contact(s) bear firmly against the bulb contact.
d) Always ensure that the new bulb is of the

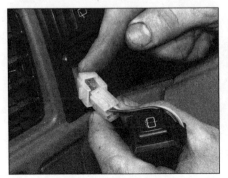

4.8 Disconnecting the wiring from a facia-mounted switch

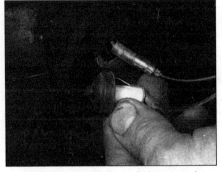

4.13 Courtesy light switch removal

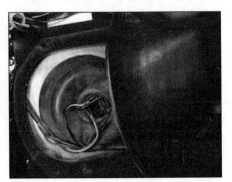

5.2 Removing the plastic cover for access to the rear of the headlight

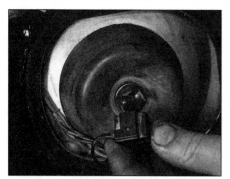

5.3 Disconnecting the wiring plug from the headlight bulb

5.4 Removing the rubber cover from the rear of the headlight

5.5 Pull back the spring clips . . .

correct rating, and that it is completely clean before fitting it; this applies particularly to headlight/foglight bulbs (see following paragraphs).

Headlight

2 Working inside the vehicle beneath the facia, remove the four screws and withdraw the plastic cover from beneath the relevant side of the facia panel for access to the rear of the headlight **(see illustration)**.

3 Pull the wiring plug from the terminals on the rear of the bulb **(see illustration)**.

4 Pull the rubber cover from the rear of the headlight **(see illustration)**.

5 Two types of bulb retainer are fitted. Either depress and twist the bulb retainer from the rear of the headlight, or pull back the spring clips with a screwdriver **(see illustration)**.

6 Withdraw the bulb from the aperture in the headlight **(see illustration)**.

7 When handling the new bulb, use a tissue or clean cloth, to avoid touching the glass with the fingers; moisture and grease from the skin can cause premature failure of the bulb.

> **HAYNES HiNT** *If the headlight bulb glass is accidentally touched, wipe it clean using methylated spirit.*

8 Install the new bulb, ensuring that the projection on the bulb flange locates in the cut-out in the headlight aperture. Refit the

retainer, then refit the rubber cover, wiring plug, and trim panel.

Front sidelight (located in the rear of the headlight unit)

9 Working at the front of the vehicle, unscrew the four retaining screws and remove the surround from the headlight.

10 Carefully press the headlight unit inwards, and turn it anti-clockwise in order to release it from the beam adjustment screws. **Do not** unscrew the beam adjustment screws, otherwise the beam setting will be altered.

11 Withdraw the headlight unit until it is possible to pull out the sidelight bulbholder **(see illustration)**.

12 Pull the wedge-type bulb from the bulbholder.

13 Install the new bulb using a reversal of the removal procedure. Make sure that the headlight is fully seated on the beam adjustment screws.

Front sidelight (located in the headlight surround)

14 Working at the front of the vehicle, unscrew the four retaining screws and remove the surround from the headlight.

15 Press and twist the bulbholder, and separate it from the surround.

16 Pull the wedge-type bulb from the bulbholder.

17 Install the new bulb using a reversal of the removal procedure.

Front sidelight (located in the direction indicator/sidelight unit)

18 Unscrew the two screws, and remove the lens from the front of the light unit.

19 Depress and twist the bulb to remove it.

20 Install the new bulb using a reversal of the removal procedure. Do not over-tighten the lens retaining screws, as there is a risk of cracking the lens.

Front direction indicator

21 Unscrew the two screws, and remove the lens from the front of the light unit **(see illustrations)**.

22 Depress and twist the bulb to remove it **(see illustration)**.

5.6 . . . and withdraw the bulb from the headlight

5.11 Removing a sidelight bulbholder from the headlight

5.21a Remove the screws . . .

5.21b . . . and remove the lens from the front direction indicator light unit

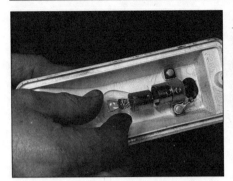

5.22 Removing a front indicator bulb

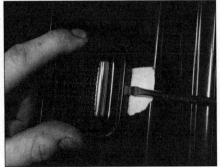

5.24 Prise the side repeater light from the B-pillar, using a screwdriver and piece of card

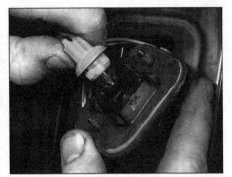

5.25 Removing the side repeater light bulbholder

23 Install the new bulb using a reversal of the removal procedure. Do not over-tighten the lens retaining screws, as there is a risk of cracking the lens.

Front direction indicator side repeater

24 Prise the side repeater light from the B-pillar, using a screwdriver and piece of card to prevent damage to the paintwork **(see illustration)**.
25 Pull out the bulbholder, then pull out the wedge-type bulb from the body **(see illustration)**.
26 Press in the new bulb, then press on the lens until it clicks into position.

Rear light cluster (Van models)

27 Open the tailgate, then remove the retaining screw from the top of the relevant cluster. Lift the unit to release it from the bottom of the body aperture, and withdraw it for access to the rear. If necessary, disconnect the wiring for the light unit **(see illustrations)**.
28 Twist the relevant bulbholder anti-clockwise, and remove it from the light unit **(see illustration)**.
29 Depress and twist the bulb to remove it from the bulbholder **(see illustration)**.
30 Check the condition of the sealing gasket. If necessary, the gasket may be renewed separately.

31 Install the new bulb using a reversal of the removal procedure. Note that the double-filament stop/tail light bulb has offset pins, to ensure that it locates in one position only. The other single-filament bulbs have parallel pins, and may be located either way round.

Rear light cluster (Pickup models)

32 Unscrew the two screws, and remove the lens from the light unit **(see illustrations)**.
33 Depress and twist the relevant bulb to remove it **(see illustration)**.
34 Install the new bulb using a reversal of the removal procedure. Note that the double-filament stop/tail light bulb has offset pins, to

5.27a On Van models, unscrew the top retaining screw . . .

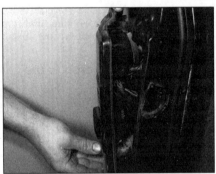

5.27b . . . and withdraw the rear light cluster

5.27c Disconnecting the wiring from the rear light cluster (Van models)

5.28 On Van models, remove the bulbholder . . .

5.29 . . . and remove the bulb

5.32a On Pickup models, unscrew the retaining screws . . .

5.32b . . . and remove the lens from the rear light cluster

5.33 Removing a rear light cluster bulb (Pickup models)

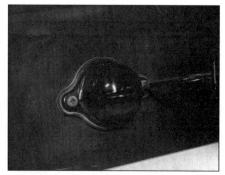

5.36a Unscrew the two screws . . .

ensure that it locates in one position only. The other single-filament bulbs have parallel pins, and may be located either way round.

Rear number plate light

35 On Van models, it will be necessary to remove the tailgate lock cylinder and plastic cover assembly first, with reference to Chapter 11, Section 13.

36 Unscrew the two screws, and remove the lens/cover **(see illustrations)**.

37 Pull the wedge-type bulb from the bulbholder **(see illustration)**.

38 Press the new bulb into the bulbholder, then refit the lens/cover and tighten the screws. **Do not** over-tighten the screws, otherwise the lens/cover may crack.

Rear foglight

39 Unscrew the two screws, and remove the lens **(see illustrations)**.

40 Depress and twist the bulb anti-clockwise to remove it.

41 Check the condition of the sealing gasket. If necessary, the gasket may be renewed separately.

42 Install the new bulb using a reversal of the removal procedure. **Do not** over-tighten the lens retaining screws, otherwise the lens may crack.

Reversing light (Pickup models)

Note: *On Van models, the reversing light is integral with the rear light cluster.*

43 Unscrew the two screws, and remove the lens. Note that the screws also secure the light body to the rear panel **(see illustration)**.

44 Hold the rear of the reversing light body, then depress and twist the bulb to remove it **(see illustration)**.

45 Install the new bulb using a reversal of the removal procedure. Before tightening the lens securing screws, make sure that the light body is correctly aligned with the aperture in the bumper.

5.36b . . . and remove the lens/cover

5.37 Pull the wedge-type bulb from the bulbholder

5.39a Rear foglight (Pickup model shown)

5.39b Removing the rear foglight lens (Pickup model shown)

5.43 Removing the reversing light lens/unit (Pickup models)

5.44 Reversing light bulb removal (Pickup models)

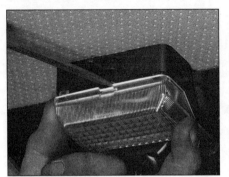

6.2a Use a screwdriver . . .

6.2b . . . to prise off the interior light lens

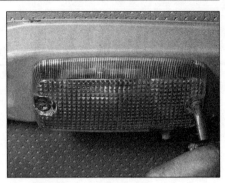

6.5a Unscrew the two screws . . .

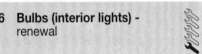

6 Bulbs (interior lights) - renewal

General

1 Refer to Section 5, paragraph 1.

Driving compartment interior light

2 Carefully prise the lens from the interior light body, using a screwdriver (see illustrations).
3 Remove the festoon-type bulb from the terminals in the light unit.
4 Install the new bulb using a reversal of the removal procedure. Make sure that the

terminals hold the bulb securely, and bend them if necessary.

Load compartment interior light

5 Where the lens is secured by screws, unscrew the two screws and lift off the lens (see illustrations). Where the lens is clipped into position, carefully pull it from the light body. If it is tight, use a wide-bladed screwdriver to prise it off.
6 Remove the festoon-type bulb from the terminals in the light unit. If necessary, the light may be completely removed by disconnecting the wiring (see illustration).
7 Install the new bulb using a reversal of the removal procedure. Make sure that the terminals hold the bulb securely, and bend them if necessary. Where the lens is secured by screws, do not over-tighten the screws, otherwise the lens may crack.

Instrument panel lights

8 Remove the instrument panel as described in Section 9.
9 Twist the relevant bulbholder anti-clockwise, and withdraw it from the rear of the panel (see illustrations).
10 Pull the wedge-type bulb from the bulbholder.
11 Press the new bulb into the bulbholder, then tighten the bulbholder into the instrument panel.
12 Refit the instrument panel with reference to Section 9.

Switch illumination bulbs

13 Some of the switches are fitted with illuminating bulbs. Access to the bulbs is gained by first removing the switch as described earlier.
14 Pull the bulb from the rear of the switch.
15 Install the bulb using a reversal of the removal procedure.

7 Exterior light units - removal and refitting

Headlight

Removal

1 To remove a headlight unit, first unscrew the screws and remove the headlight surround panel (see illustration).
2 Depress the headlight unit (using both

6.5b . . . and lift the lens from the load compartment interior light

6.6 Load compartment interior light and wiring

7.1 Removing a headlight surround panel

6.9a Removal of an instrument panel warning light bulb . . .

6.9b . . . and illumination bulb

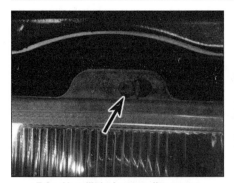

7.2a Headlight beam adjustment screw/headlight unit mounting (arrowed)

7.2b Releasing the headlight unit from the beam adjustment screws

7.3a Disconnecting the wiring from the headlight

hands, to ensure that it is pressed uniformly onto the beam adjustment screw springs), then rotate it anti-clockwise so that it is released from the beam adjustment screws **(see illustrations)**. On models with a facia-mounted headlight beam level adjustment system, it will be necessary to remove the screw from the control unit located next to the headlight.

3 Disconnect the headlight wiring (and, where necessary, the sidelight wiring), and withdraw the unit. Remove the headlight and sidelight bulbs (as applicable) as described in Section 5. The headlight mounting plate may be removed from the headlight, by unscrewing the four screws and removing the clamps **(see illustrations)**.

Refitting

4 Refitting is a reversal of removal. Provided the beam adjustment screws have not been turned, it should not be necessary to re-adjust the beam alignment.

Front direction indicator light

Removal

5 Remove the front direction indicator light bulb as described in Section 5.
6 Working behind the front bumper, release the retaining clamp, then withdraw the light.
7 Disconnect the wiring at the connector, and unscrew the earth wire bolt from the body **(see illustrations)**. Note that on the left-hand

side, the earth wire is attached to the horn mounting bolt.
8 Refitting is a reversal of removal.

Front direction indicator side repeater light

Removal

9 Remove the direction indicator side repeater bulb as described in Section 5.
10 Unscrew the mounting screws, and withdraw the light.
11 Disconnect the wiring at the connector. Tape the wiring harness to the body, to prevent it dropping back into the body.

Refitting

12 Refitting is a reversal of removal.

7.3b Release the spring clips . . .

7.3c . . . and remove the headlight bulb

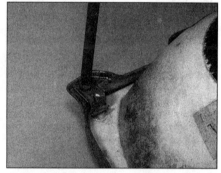

7.3d Remove the screws and clamps . . .

7.3e . . . and remove the headlight from the mounting plate

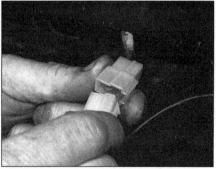

7.7a Disconnect the front indicator wiring at the connector . . .

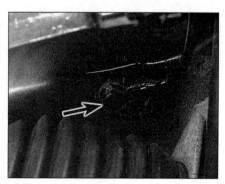

7.7b . . . and unscrew the earth wire bolt from the body

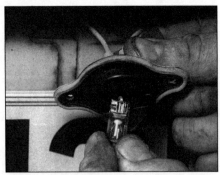

7.25 Number plate light unit removed (and new bulb being fitted) - Pickup models

Rear light cluster (Van models)

Removal

13 Remove all of the rear light cluster bulbs, as described in Section 5.
14 If necessary, disconnect the wiring from the main harness.

Refitting

15 Refitting is a reversal of removal.

Rear light cluster (Pickup models)

Removal

16 Remove all of the rear light cluster bulbs, as described in Section 5.
17 Remove the screws, and withdraw the light unit from the rear panel.
18 Disconnect the wiring at the connector.

Refitting

19 Refitting is a reversal of the removal procedure.

Rear number plate light (Van models)

Removal

20 Remove the rear number plate light bulb as described in Section 5.
21 Open the rear tailgate and remove the inner trim panel.
22 Disconnect the rear number plate wiring inside the tailgate and withdraw the bulbholder from the rear of the vehicle.

Refitting

23 Refitting is a reversal of the removal procedure.

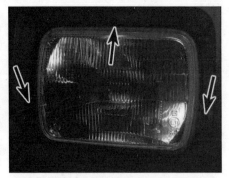

8.2 The headlight beam adjustment screws are located as shown by the arrows

Rear number plate light (Pickup models)

Removal

24 Remove the rear number plate light bulb as described in Section 5.
25 Reach up above the number plate, and pull down the light unit **(see illustration)**.
26 Disconnect the number plate wiring as it becomes accessible, and withdraw the bulbholder from the rear of the vehicle.

Refitting

27 Refitting is a reversal of the removal procedure.

Rear foglight

Removal

28 Remove the rear foglight bulb as described in Section 5.
29 Working beneath the rear of the vehicle, disconnect the wiring to the foglight at the connector.
30 Unscrew the mounting nut, and remove the foglight from the mounting bracket.

Refitting

31 Refitting is a reversal of the removal procedure.

Reversing light (Pickup models)

Removal

32 Remove the reversing light bulb as described in Section 5. Note that removal of the lens releases the light unit from the rear panel.

33 Working beneath the rear of the vehicle, disconnect the wiring at the connector, and withdraw the light unit.

Refitting

34 Refitting is a reversal of the removal procedure.

8 Headlight beam alignment - general information

1 Accurate adjustment of the headlight beams is only possible using optical beam-setting equipment, and this work should therefore be carried out by a Vauxhall/Suzuki dealer or suitably-equipped workshop.
2 Adjustment of the headlight beams is made by turning the headlight mounting screws as necessary **(see illustration)**. The headlight is held in contact with the screw heads by tension springs.
3 Certain models may be fitted with a headlight beam adjustment system operated by the driver, which allows the aim of the headlights to be adjusted to compensate for the varying loads carried in the vehicle. A switch is provided on the facia, which enables beam adjustment via electric adjuster motors attached to the rear of the headlight assemblies.

9 Instrument panel - removal and refitting

Removal

1 Disconnect the battery negative lead.
2 If required for improved access, remove the steering wheel as described in Chapter 10.
3 Unscrew the screws, and remove the upper steering column shroud. This is necessary for access to the lower instrument panel surround screws.
4 Unscrew the retaining screws, and withdraw the instrument panel surround sufficiently to disconnect the switch wiring **(see illustrations)**.
5 Unscrew the instrument panel mounting screws, and withdraw the panel sufficiently to

9.4a Unscrew the screws . . .

9.4b . . . and withdraw the instrument panel surround

9.4c Disconnecting the switch wiring

9.5a Unscrewing the instrument panel mounting screws

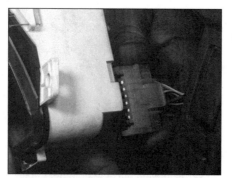

9.5b Disconnecting the wiring from the right-hand side of the instrument panel

9.5c Disconnecting the wiring from the left-hand side of the instrument panel

disconnect the wiring from the terminals on the rear face **(see illustrations)**.

6 Disconnect the speedometer cable **(see illustration)**, and withdraw the instrument panel from the facia. If it is not possible to withdraw the instrument panel sufficiently to disconnect the speedometer cable, it may be necessary to create some slack by pulling the cable through the floor, after releasing it from the clips in the engine compartment.

Refitting

7 Refitting is a reversal of removal, but make sure that the speedometer cable and wiring plugs are correctly connected. Check the operation of the various instruments on the panel on completion. If the speedometer

cable was released from any clips, make sure that it is correctly relocated in the clips.

10 Instrument panel components - general

1 Individual components (ie speedometer, fuel/temperature gauge, printed circuit etc) are available separately from Vauxhall/Suzuki dealers, and their removal is straightforward. A small and medium-size screwdriver, and a pair of pliers, are the only tools required to remove the instruments **(see illustrations)**. Instrument panel bulb renewal is covered in Section 6.

11 Cigarette lighter - removal and refitting

Removal

1 Remove the ashtray. For improved access, also remove the radio as described in Section 18.
2 Disconnect the wiring from the rear of the cigarette lighter.
3 Release the retainer from the rear of the cigarette lighter, then withdraw the unit from the facia.

Refitting

4 Refitting is a reversal of removal.

9.6 Disconnecting the speedometer cable from the instrument panel

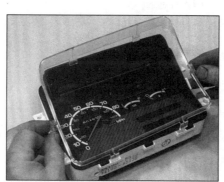

10.1a Removing the instrument panel outer cover . . .

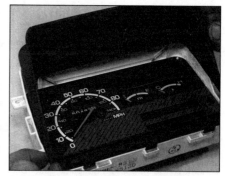

10.1b . . . and inner surround

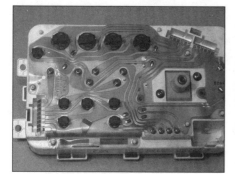

10.1c Rear of the instrument panel, showing component retaining screws

10.1d Removing the speedometer and facia panel

10.1e Removing the fuel and temperature gauge units

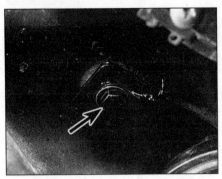

12.3 Horn mounting bolt (arrowed)

13.2 Removing the speedometer cable end fitting from the left-hand side of the transmission

14.3 Unscrewing the windscreen wiper spindle nut

12 Horn - removal and refitting

Removal

1 The horn is located behind the front left-hand side of the lower body valance. If necessary, apply the handbrake, then raise the front of the vehicle and support on axle stands.
2 Disconnect the wiring from the rear of the horn.
3 Unscrew the mounting bolt **(see illustration)**, and withdraw the horn from under the vehicle. Note that a front indicator light earth wire is attached to the mounting bolt.

Refitting

4 Refitting is a reversal of the removal procedure.

13 Speedometer drive cable - removal and refitting

Removal

1 Remove the instrument panel, as described in Section 9.
2 Working beneath the vehicle, unscrew the retaining bolt and withdraw the speedometer cable end fitting from the left-hand side of the transmission **(see illustration)**. For improved access to the transmission, apply the handbrake, then raise the front of the vehicle and support on axle stands (see *"Jacking, towing and wheel changing"*).
3 Release the cable from the clips on the underbody.
4 Prise out the cable grommet located inside the vehicle in the centre front of the floor, then withdraw the cable from inside the vehicle.

Refitting

5 Refitting is a reversal of the removal procedure, but check the condition of the rubber O-ring on the cable end fitting, and renew it if necessary.

14 Wiper arm - removal and refitting

Removal

1 Operate the wiper motor, then switch it off so that the wiper arm returns to the at-rest ("parked") position.
2 Stick a piece of tape along the edge of the wiper blade, to use as an alignment aid when refitting.
3 To remove the windscreen wiper arm, lift up the spindle nut cover, then unscrew and remove the spindle nut **(see illustration)**. Lift the blade off the glass, and pull the wiper arm off its spindle. If necessary, the arm can be levered off the spindle using a suitable flat-bladed screwdriver.
4 To remove the tailgate wiper arm, lift the blade off the glass, then unscrew the clamp bolt and pull the wiper arm off its spindle **(see illustration)**.

Refitting

5 Refitting is a reversal of removal, but align the wiper blade with the tape before tightening the spindle nut/bolt.

15 Windscreen wiper motor and linkage - removal and refitting

Removal

1 Remove the facia panel with reference to Chapter 11.

Wiper motor

2 Disconnect the motor wiring plug **(see illustration)**.
3 Unscrew the mounting bolts, and remove the wiper motor and bracket from the front body panel **(see illustration)**.

14.4 Removing the tailgate wiper arm from the spindle

15.2 Disconnecting the wiper motor wiring plug

15.3 Unscrewing the wiper motor and bracket mounting bolts (arrowed)

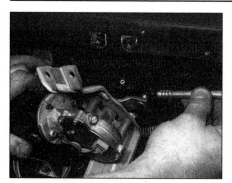

15.4 Releasing the linkage arm from the wiper motor crank

15.5 Wiper motor crank and bracket mounting bolts

15.7a Remove the rubber caps . . .

4 Release the linkage arm from the motor crank **(see illustration)**.
5 The motor can be removed from the bracket by removing the crank and unscrewing the three mounting bolts **(see illustration)**.

Wiper linkage

6 Remove the wiper blades and arms, as described in Section 14.
7 Remove the rubber caps from the spindles, then unscrew the retaining nuts and recover the washers **(see illustrations)**.
8 Withdraw the linkage from the inner side of the front panel, then disconnect the linkage from the cranks **(see illustrations)**.

Refitting

9 Refitting is a reversal of removal, but note the following additional points:
a) *Check the condition of the bushes, and renew them if necessary.*
b) *Before refitting the linkage, apply a little grease to the bushes and motor pivot ball.*
c) *When locating the linkage on the front panel, make sure that the spindle boxes are located in the special square sections.*
d) *Before refitting the nuts to the spindles, apply a little locking fluid to the threads of the spindles.*
e) *On completion, check the operation of the wipers.*

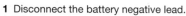

16 Tailgate wiper motor and linkage - removal and refitting

Removal

1 Disconnect the battery negative lead.
2 With the tailgate open, carefully prise free the trim panel using a wide-bladed screwdriver (or suitable forked tool) inserted next to each clip **(see illustration)**. Recover the clips.
3 Release the linkage arm from the motor by pressing it firmly off **(see illustration)**.

15.7b . . . unscrew the retaining nuts . . .

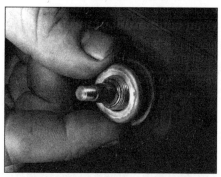

15.7c . . . then recover the metal washers . . .

15.7d . . . and rubber washers

15.8a Withdraw the linkage from the inner side of the front panel . . .

15.8b . . . then disconnect the linkage from the cranks

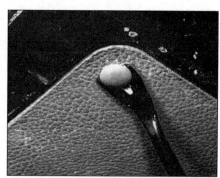

16.2 Prise free the trim panel using a wide-bladed screwdriver or (preferably) a suitable forked tool

16.3 Disconnecting the tailgate wiper motor linkage

16.4a Unscrew the bracket mounting screws (arrowed) . . .

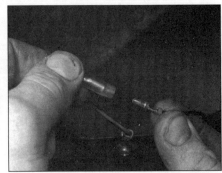

16.4b . . . and disconnect the motor earth lead

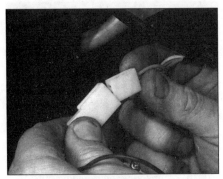

16.5 Disconnecting the tailgate wiper motor wiring plug

Wiper motor

4 Unscrew the bracket mounting screws and disconnect the motor earth lead, then remove the wiper motor together with the bracket **(see illustrations)**.
5 Disconnect the motor wiring plug **(see illustration)**.
6 Unbolt the wiper motor from the bracket **(see illustration)**.

Wiper linkage

7 Remove the tailgate wiper arm, as described in Section 14.
8 Inside the tailgate, pull the linkage arm from the spindle crank **(see illustration)**.

9 Prise off the spindle dust cover, then unscrew the nut, and remove the washer and packing **(see illustrations)**.
10 Withdraw the spindle assembly from inside the tailgate **(see illustrations)**.

Refitting

11 Refitting is a reversal of removal, but note the following additional points:
a) *Make sure that the spindle assembly is correctly located in the metal guides inside the tailgate before refitting the nut **(see illustration)**.*
b) *Before refitting the linkage, apply a little grease to the motor pivot ball.*
c) *Before refitting the nut to the spindle,*

16.6 Tailgate wiper motor and bracket

16.8 Removing the linkage arm (arrowed) from the spindle crank

16.9a Prise off the spindle dust cover . . .

16.9b . . . then unscrew the nut . . .

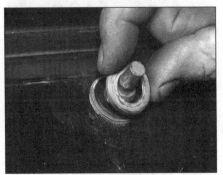

16.9c . . . and remove the washer and packing

16.10a Removing the spindle assembly from inside the tailgate

16.10b Tailgate wiper spindle assembly

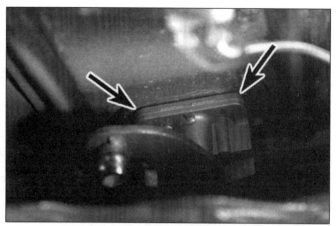

16.11 Metal guides (arrowed) inside the tailgate

apply a little locking fluid to the threads of the spindle.
d) On completion, check the operation of the wiper.

17 Windscreen/tailgate washer system components - removal and refitting

Washer fluid reservoir

Removal

1 Make sure that the ignition is switched off.
2 Raise or remove the left-hand seat (according to model) for access to the engine compartment.
3 Pull the reservoir firmly upwards to detach it from the bracket on the bodywork.
4 Remove the filler cap, then invert the reservoir and pour the contents into a suitable container.
5 Disconnect the wiring from the pumps on the reservoir, noting the location of each wire.

Refitting

6 Refitting is a reversal of removal. Refill the reservoir with washer fluid.

Washer pumps

Removal

7 Remove the fluid reservoir as described previously in this Section.
8 The washer pumps are a push fit in the reservoir.

Refitting

9 Refitting is a reversal of removal, but check the condition of the mounting grommet in the reservoir, and renew if necessary.

Windscreen washer jet

Removal

10 Remove the facia panel as described in Chapter 11.
11 Disconnect the washer tube from the rear of the jet (or at the connector). Unscrew the mounting nut, and remove the jet and gasket from the front panel **(see illustrations)**.

Refitting

12 Refitting is a reversal of removal. Adjust the aim of the jets as follows. Insert a pin into the jet nozzle, and turn the jet end as necessary, so that the spray hits the middle of the wiper blades' swept area.

Tailgate washer jet

Removal

13 Open the tailgate, and prise off the inner trim panel using a wide-bladed screwdriver (or suitable forked tool) located near the retaining clips.
14 Disconnect the washer tube from the jet assembly (or at the connector), working through the aperture in the tailgate.
15 Unscrew the nut, and remove the jet from the outside of the tailgate.

Refitting

16 Refitting is a reversal of removal, but adjust the jet as necessary, as described in paragraph 12.

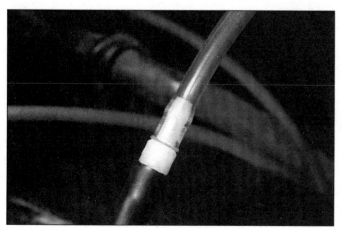

17.11a Windscreen washer tube connector

17.11b Removing the windscreen washer jet and gasket from the front panel

18 Radio/cassette player - removal and refitting

Removal

1 Where fitted, the radio (or radio/cassette) is located in the centre of the facia.

2 The aerial is located on the right-hand A-pillar, and the speaker is located in the facia.

3 Early radios may be secured by a surround; this can be removed by pulling off the control knobs and unscrewing the mounting nuts. With the surround removed, pull the radio out, and disconnect the wiring and aerial lead.

4 The later type radio may be fixed by means of concealed side clips, and access is gained by inserting special release keys through the slotted holes in the front face of the unit. These keys are obtainable from car radio specialists. Insert the keys into the release access holes each side, release the clips and withdraw the radio unit. With the radio removed, disconnect the wiring and aerial lead.

Refitting

5 Refit in the reverse order of removal, making sure (where applicable) that the radio is fully engaged with its retaining clips. Check that the wiring is positioned correctly behind the radio, to allow space for the unit to be pushed into position.

19 Speakers - removal and refitting

Removal

1 The speakers are located inside the facia panel **(see illustration)**. Remove the facia panel as described in Chapter 11.

2 Unscrew the mounting screws, release the clips, disconnect the wiring (noting the location of each wire, for refitting), and remove the speakers.

Refitting

3 Refitting is a reversal of removal.

20 Radio aerial - removal and refitting

Removal

1 Remove the radio and disconnect the aerial as described in Section 18.

2 Remove the facia panel as described in Chapter 11.

19.1 The speakers are located inside the facia panel

3 Unscrew the cross-head screws securing the aerial to the front A-pillar. There are two screws - one at the base of the aerial, and the other at the upper support block.

4 Attach a suitable length of string to the radio end of the aerial, then feed the aerial cable through the A-pillar from the inside, and withdraw it from outside the vehicle. Disconnect the string, leaving it in place in the A-pillar. The string can then be used on refitting, to guide the aerial lead into place.

Refitting

5 Refitting is a reversal of the removal procedure, using the string to pull the aerial through the A-pillar.

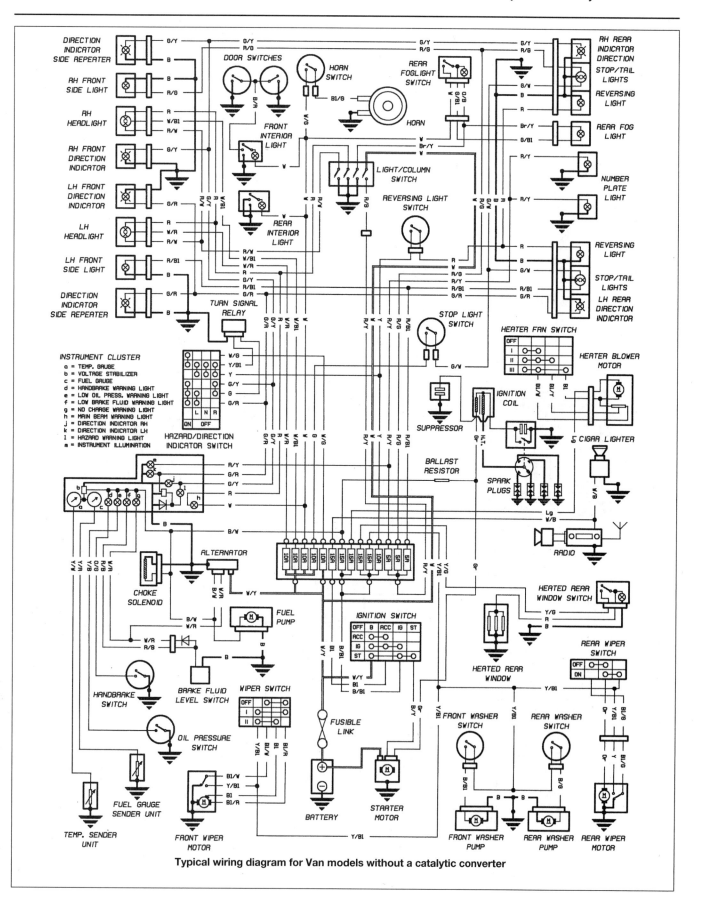

Typical wiring diagram for Van models without a catalytic converter

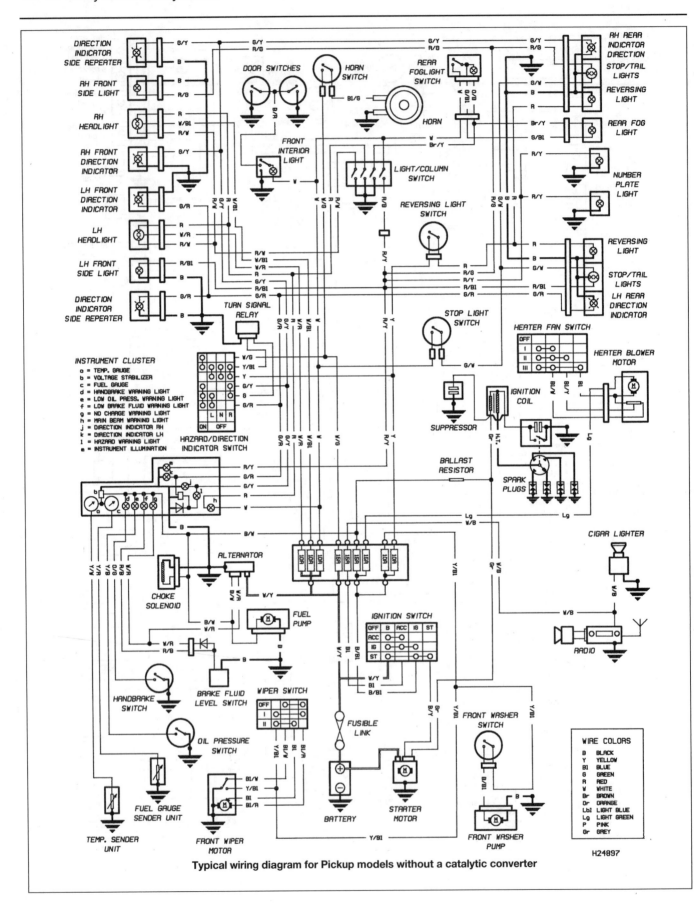

Typical wiring diagram for Pickup models without a catalytic converter

H24897

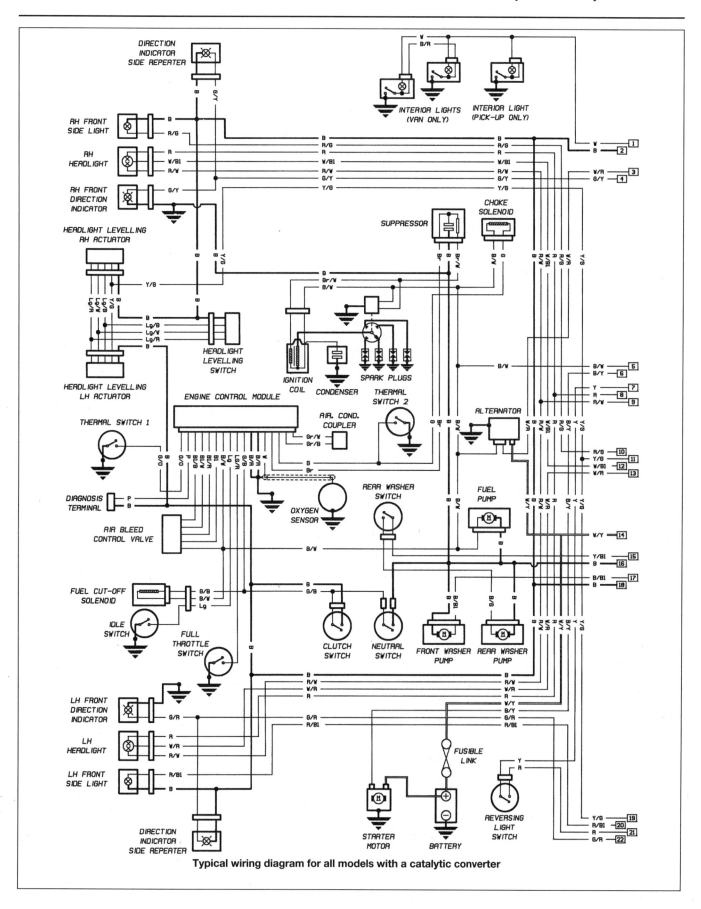

Typical wiring diagram for all models with a catalytic converter

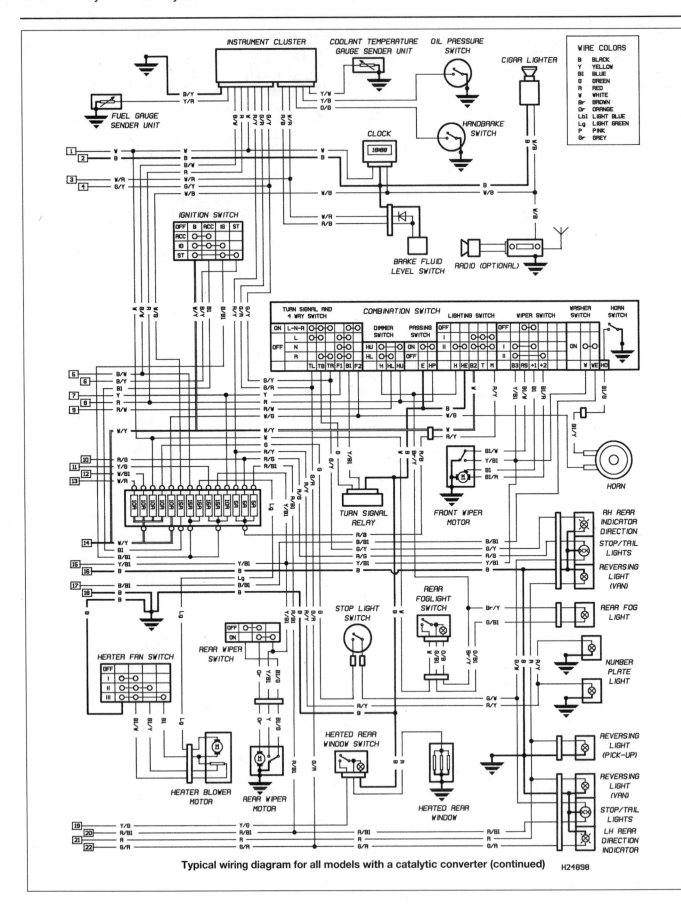

Typical wiring diagram for all models with a catalytic converter (continued)   H24898

This is a guide to getting your vehicle through the MOT test. Obviously it will not be possible to examine the vehicle to the same standard as the professional MOT tester. However, working through the following checks will enable you to identify any problem areas before submitting the vehicle for the test.

Where a testable component is in borderline condition, the tester has discretion in deciding whether to pass or fail it. The basis of such discretion is whether the tester would be happy for a close relative or friend to use the vehicle with the component in that condition. If the vehicle presented is clean and evidently well cared for, the tester may be more inclined to pass a borderline component than if the vehicle is scruffy and apparently neglected.

It has only been possible to summarise the test requirements here, based on the regulations in force at the time of printing. Test standards are becoming increasingly stringent, although there are some exemptions for older vehicles.

An assistant will be needed to help carry out some of these checks.

The checks have been sub-divided into four categories, as follows:

1 Checks carried out **FROM THE DRIVER'S SEAT**

2 Checks carried out **WITH THE VEHICLE ON THE GROUND**

3 Checks carried out **WITH THE VEHICLE RAISED AND THE WHEELS FREE TO TURN**

4 Checks carried out on **YOUR VEHICLE'S EXHAUST EMISSION SYSTEM**

---

1 Checks carried out **FROM THE DRIVER'S SEAT**

Handbrake

☐ Test the operation of the handbrake. Excessive travel (too many clicks) indicates incorrect brake or cable adjustment.

☐ Check that the handbrake cannot be released by tapping the lever sideways. Check the security of the lever mountings.

Footbrake

☐ Depress the brake pedal and check that it does not creep down to the floor, indicating a master cylinder fault. Release the pedal, wait a few seconds, then depress it again. If the pedal travels nearly to the floor before firm resistance is felt, brake adjustment or repair is necessary. If the pedal feels spongy, there is air in the hydraulic system which must be removed by bleeding.

☐ Check that the brake pedal is secure and in good condition. Check also for signs of fluid leaks on the pedal, floor or carpets, which would indicate failed seals in the brake master cylinder.

☐ Check the servo unit (when applicable) by operating the brake pedal several times, then keeping the pedal depressed and starting the engine. As the engine starts, the pedal will move down slightly. If not, the vacuum hose or the servo itself may be faulty.

Steering wheel and column

☐ Examine the steering wheel for fractures or looseness of the hub, spokes or rim.

☐ Move the steering wheel from side to side and then up and down. Check that the steering wheel is not loose on the column, indicating wear or a loose retaining nut. Continue moving the steering wheel as before, but also turn it slightly from left to right.

☐ Check that the steering wheel is not loose on the column, and that there is no abnormal

movement of the steering wheel, indicating wear in the column support bearings or couplings.

Windscreen, mirrors and sunvisor

☐ The windscreen must be free of cracks or other significant damage within the driver's field of view. (Small stone chips are acceptable.) Rear view mirrors must be secure, intact, and capable of being adjusted.

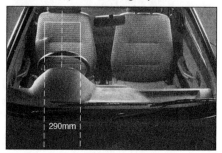

290mm

☐ The driver's sunvisor must be capable of being stored in the "up" position.

Seat belts and seats

Note: *The following checks are applicable to all seat belts, front and rear.*

☐ Examine the webbing of all the belts (including rear belts if fitted) for cuts, serious fraying or deterioration. Fasten and unfasten each belt to check the buckles. If applicable, check the retracting mechanism. Check the security of all seat belt mountings accessible from inside the vehicle.

☐ Seat belts with pre-tensioners, once activated, have a "flag" or similar showing on the seat belt stalk. This, in itself, is not a reason for test failure.

☐ The front seats themselves must be securely attached and the backrests must lock in the upright position.

Doors

☐ Both front doors must be able to be opened and closed from outside and inside, and must latch securely when closed.

2 Checks carried out WITH THE VEHICLE ON THE GROUND

Vehicle identification

☐ Number plates must be in good condition, secure and legible, with letters and numbers correctly spaced – spacing at (A) should be at least twice that at (B).

☐ The VIN plate and/or homologation plate must be legible.

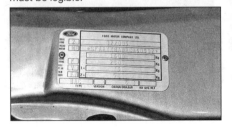

Electrical equipment

☐ Switch on the ignition and check the operation of the horn.

☐ Check the windscreen washers and wipers, examining the wiper blades; renew damaged or perished blades. Also check the operation of the stop-lights.

☐ Check the operation of the sidelights and number plate lights. The lenses and reflectors must be secure, clean and undamaged.

☐ Check the operation and alignment of the headlights. The headlight reflectors must not be tarnished and the lenses must be undamaged.

☐ Switch on the ignition and check the operation of the direction indicators (including the instrument panel tell-tale) and the hazard warning lights. Operation of the sidelights and stop-lights must not affect the indicators - if it does, the cause is usually a bad earth at the rear light cluster.

☐ Check the operation of the rear foglight(s), including the warning light on the instrument panel or in the switch.

☐ The ABS warning light must illuminate in accordance with the manufacturers' design. For most vehicles, the ABS warning light should illuminate when the ignition is switched on, and (if the system is operating properly) extinguish after a few seconds. Refer to the owner's handbook.

Footbrake

☐ Examine the master cylinder, brake pipes and servo unit for leaks, loose mountings, corrosion or other damage.

☐ The fluid reservoir must be secure and the fluid level must be between the upper (**A**) and lower (**B**) markings.

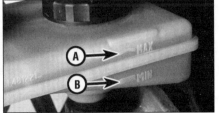

☐ Inspect both front brake flexible hoses for cracks or deterioration of the rubber. Turn the steering from lock to lock, and ensure that the hoses do not contact the wheel, tyre, or any part of the steering or suspension mechanism. With the brake pedal firmly depressed, check the hoses for bulges or leaks under pressure.

Steering and suspension

☐ Have your assistant turn the steering wheel from side to side slightly, up to the point where the steering gear just begins to transmit this movement to the roadwheels. Check for excessive free play between the steering wheel and the steering gear, indicating wear or insecurity of the steering column joints, the column-to-steering gear coupling, or the steering gear itself.

☐ Have your assistant turn the steering wheel more vigorously in each direction, so that the roadwheels just begin to turn. As this is done, examine all the steering joints, linkages, fittings and attachments. Renew any component that shows signs of wear or damage. On vehicles with power steering, check the security and condition of the steering pump, drivebelt and hoses.

☐ Check that the vehicle is standing level, and at approximately the correct ride height.

Shock absorbers

☐ Depress each corner of the vehicle in turn, then release it. The vehicle should rise and then settle in its normal position. If the vehicle continues to rise and fall, the shock absorber is defective. A shock absorber which has seized will also cause the vehicle to fail.

Exhaust system

☐ Start the engine. With your assistant holding a rag over the tailpipe, check the entire system for leaks. Repair or renew leaking sections.

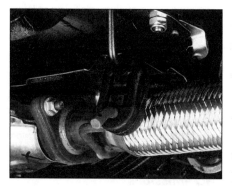

3 Checks carried out **WITH THE VEHICLE RAISED AND THE WHEELS FREE TO TURN**

Jack up the front and rear of the vehicle, and securely support it on axle stands. Position the stands clear of the suspension assemblies. Ensure that the wheels are clear of the ground and that the steering can be turned from lock to lock.

Steering mechanism

☐ Have your assistant turn the steering from lock to lock. Check that the steering turns smoothly, and that no part of the steering mechanism, including a wheel or tyre, fouls any brake hose or pipe or any part of the body structure.

☐ Examine the steering rack rubber gaiters for damage or insecurity of the retaining clips. If power steering is fitted, check for signs of damage or leakage of the fluid hoses, pipes or connections. Also check for excessive stiffness or binding of the steering, a missing split pin or locking device, or severe corrosion of the body structure within 30 cm of any steering component attachment point.

Front and rear suspension and wheel bearings

☐ Starting at the front right-hand side, grasp the roadwheel at the 3 o'clock and 9 o'clock positions and rock gently but firmly. Check for free play or insecurity at the wheel bearings, suspension balljoints, or suspension mountings, pivots and attachments.

☐ Now grasp the wheel at the 12 o'clock and 6 o'clock positions and repeat the previous inspection. Spin the wheel, and check for roughness or tightness of the front wheel bearing.

☐ If excess free play is suspected at a component pivot point, this can be confirmed by using a large screwdriver or similar tool and levering between the mounting and the component attachment. This will confirm whether the wear is in the pivot bush, its retaining bolt, or in the mounting itself (the bolt holes can often become elongated).

☐ Carry out all the above checks at the other front wheel, and then at both rear wheels.

Springs and shock absorbers

☐ Examine the suspension struts (when applicable) for serious fluid leakage, corrosion, or damage to the casing. Also check the security of the mounting points.

☐ If coil springs are fitted, check that the spring ends locate in their seats, and that the spring is not corroded, cracked or broken.

☐ If leaf springs are fitted, check that all leaves are intact, that the axle is securely attached to each spring, and that there is no deterioration of the spring eye mountings, bushes, and shackles.

☐ The same general checks apply to vehicles fitted with other suspension types, such as torsion bars, hydraulic displacer units, etc. Ensure that all mountings and attachments are secure, that there are no signs of excessive wear, corrosion or damage, and (on hydraulic types) that there are no fluid leaks or damaged pipes.

☐ Inspect the shock absorbers for signs of serious fluid leakage. Check for wear of the mounting bushes or attachments, or damage to the body of the unit.

Driveshafts (fwd vehicles only)

☐ Rotate each front wheel in turn and inspect the constant velocity joint gaiters for splits or damage. Also check that each driveshaft is straight and undamaged.

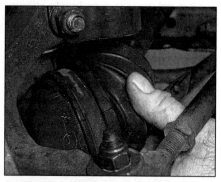

Braking system

☐ If possible without dismantling, check brake pad wear and disc condition. Ensure that the friction lining material has not worn excessively, (A) and that the discs are not fractured, pitted, scored or badly worn (B).

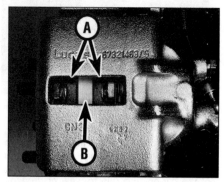

☐ Examine all the rigid brake pipes underneath the vehicle, and the flexible hose(s) at the rear. Look for corrosion, chafing or insecurity of the pipes, and for signs of bulging under pressure, chafing, splits or deterioration of the flexible hoses.

☐ Look for signs of fluid leaks at the brake calipers or on the brake backplates. Repair or renew leaking components.

☐ Slowly spin each wheel, while your assistant depresses and releases the footbrake. Ensure that each brake is operating and does not bind when the pedal is released.

☐ Examine the handbrake mechanism, checking for frayed or broken cables, excessive corrosion, or wear or insecurity of the linkage. Check that the mechanism works on each relevant wheel, and releases fully, without binding.

☐ It is not possible to test brake efficiency without special equipment, but a road test can be carried out later to check that the vehicle pulls up in a straight line.

Fuel and exhaust systems

☐ Inspect the fuel tank (including the filler cap), fuel pipes, hoses and unions. All components must be secure and free from leaks.

☐ Examine the exhaust system over its entire length, checking for any damaged, broken or missing mountings, security of the retaining clamps and rust or corrosion.

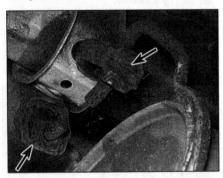

Wheels and tyres

☐ Examine the sidewalls and tread area of each tyre in turn. Check for cuts, tears, lumps, bulges, separation of the tread, and exposure of the ply or cord due to wear or damage. Check that the tyre bead is correctly seated on the wheel rim, that the valve is sound and properly seated, and that the wheel is not distorted or damaged.

☐ Check that the tyres are of the correct size for the vehicle, that they are of the same size and type on each axle, and that the pressures are correct.

☐ Check the tyre tread depth. The legal minimum at the time of writing is 1.6 mm over at least three-quarters of the tread width. Abnormal tread wear may indicate incorrect front wheel alignment.

Body corrosion

☐ Check the condition of the entire vehicle structure for signs of corrosion in load-bearing areas. (These include chassis box sections, side sills, cross-members, pillars, and all suspension, steering, braking system and seat belt mountings and anchorages.) Any corrosion which has seriously reduced the thickness of a load-bearing area is likely to cause the vehicle to fail. In this case professional repairs are likely to be needed.

☐ Damage or corrosion which causes sharp or otherwise dangerous edges to be exposed will also cause the vehicle to fail.

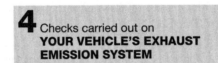

4 Checks carried out on **YOUR VEHICLE'S EXHAUST EMISSION SYSTEM**

Petrol models

☐ Have the engine at normal operating temperature, and make sure that it is in good tune (ignition system in good order, air filter element clean, etc).

☐ Before any measurements are carried out, raise the engine speed to around 2500 rpm, and hold it at this speed for 20 seconds. Allow the engine speed to return to idle, and watch for smoke emissions from the exhaust tailpipe. If the idle speed is obviously much too high, or if dense blue or clearly-visible black smoke comes from the tailpipe for more than 5 seconds, the vehicle will fail. As a rule of thumb, blue smoke signifies oil being burnt (engine wear) while black smoke signifies unburnt fuel (dirty air cleaner element, or other carburettor or fuel system fault).

☐ An exhaust gas analyser capable of measuring carbon monoxide (CO) and hydrocarbons (HC) is now needed. If such an instrument cannot be hired or borrowed, a local garage may agree to perform the check for a small fee.

CO emissions (mixture)

☐ At the time of writing, for vehicles first used between 1st August 1975 and 31st July 1986 (P to C registration), the CO level must not exceed 4.5% by volume. For vehicles first used between 1st August 1986 and 31st July 1992 (D to J registration), the CO level must not exceed 3.5% by volume. Vehicles first

used after 1st August 1992 (K registration) must conform to the manufacturer's specification. The MOT tester has access to a DOT database or emissions handbook, which lists the CO and HC limits for each make and model of vehicle. The CO level is measured with the engine at idle speed, and at "fast idle". The following limits are given as a general guide:
> *At idle speed -*
>> CO level no more than 0.5%
> *At "fast idle" (2500 to 3000 rpm) -*
>> CO level no more than 0.3%
>> (Minimum oil temperature 60ºC)

☐ If the CO level cannot be reduced far enough to pass the test (and the fuel and ignition systems are otherwise in good condition) then the carburettor is badly worn, or there is some problem in the fuel injection system or catalytic converter (as applicable).

HC emissions

☐ With the CO within limits, HC emissions for vehicles first used between 1st August 1975 and 31st July 1992 (P to J registration) must not exceed 1200 ppm. Vehicles first used after 1st August 1992 (K registration) must conform to the manufacturer's specification. The MOT tester has access to a DOT database or emissions handbook, which lists the CO and HC limits for each make and model of vehicle. The HC level is measured with the engine at "fast idle". The following is given as a general guide:
> *At "fast idle" (2500 to 3000 rpm) -*
>> HC level no more than 200 ppm
>> (Minimum oil temperature 60ºC)

☐ Excessive HC emissions are caused by incomplete combustion, the causes of which can include oil being burnt, mechanical wear and ignition/fuel system malfunction.

Diesel models

☐ The only emission test applicable to Diesel engines is the measuring of exhaust smoke density. The test involves accelerating the engine several times to its maximum unloaded speed.

Note: *It is of the utmost importance that the engine timing belt is in good condition before the test is carried out.*

☐ The limits for Diesel engine exhaust smoke, introduced in September 1995 are:
Vehicles first used before 1st August 1979:
> Exempt from metered smoke testing, but must not emit "dense blue or clearly visible black smoke for a period of more than 5 seconds at idle" or "dense blue or clearly visible black smoke during acceleration which would obscure the view of other road users".
Non-turbocharged vehicles first used after
> *1st August 1979:* 2.5m-1
Turbocharged vehicles first used after
> *1st August 1979:* 3.0m-1

☐ Excessive smoke can be caused by a dirty air cleaner element. Otherwise, professional advice may be needed to find the cause.

Introduction

A selection of good tools is a fundamental requirement for anyone contemplating the maintenance and repair of a motor vehicle. For the owner who does not possess any, their purchase will prove a considerable expense, offsetting some of the savings made by doing-it-yourself. However, provided that the tools purchased meet the relevant national safety standards and are of good quality, they will last for many years and prove an extremely worthwhile investment.

To help the average owner to decide which tools are needed to carry out the various tasks detailed in this manual, we have compiled three lists of tools under the following headings: *Maintenance and minor repair, Repair and overhaul,* and *Special.* Newcomers to practical mechanics should start off with the *Maintenance and minor repair* tool kit, and confine themselves to the simpler jobs around the vehicle. Then, as confidence and experience grow, more difficult tasks can be undertaken, with extra tools being purchased as, and when, they are needed. In this way, a *Maintenance and minor repair* tool kit can be built up into a *Repair and overhaul* tool kit over a considerable period of time, without any major cash outlays. The experienced do-it-yourselfer will have a tool kit good enough for most repair and overhaul procedures, and will add tools from the *Special* category when it is felt that the expense is justified by the amount of use to which these tools will be put.

Maintenance and minor repair tool kit

The tools given in this list should be considered as a minimum requirement if routine maintenance, servicing and minor repair operations are to be undertaken. We recommend the purchase of combination spanners (ring one end, open-ended the other); although more expensive than open-ended ones, they do give the advantages of both types of spanner.

☐ *Combination spanners:*
Metric - 8 to 19 mm inclusive
☐ *Adjustable spanner - 35 mm jaw (approx.)*
☐ *Spark plug spanner (with rubber insert) - petrol models*
☐ *Spark plug gap adjustment tool - petrol models*
☐ *Set of feeler gauges*
☐ *Brake bleed nipple spanner*
☐ *Screwdrivers:*
Flat blade - 100 mm long x 6 mm dia
Cross blade - 100 mm long x 6 mm dia
Torx - various sizes (not all vehicles)
☐ *Combination pliers*
☐ *Hacksaw (junior)*
☐ *Tyre pump*
☐ *Tyre pressure gauge*
☐ *Oil can*
☐ *Oil filter removal tool*
☐ *Fine emery cloth*
☐ *Wire brush (small)*
☐ *Funnel (medium size)*
☐ *Sump drain plug key (not all vehicles)*

Repair and overhaul tool kit

These tools are virtually essential for anyone undertaking any major repairs to a motor vehicle, and are additional to those given in the *Maintenance and minor repair* list. Included in this list is a comprehensive set of sockets. Although these are expensive, they will be found invaluable as they are so versatile - particularly if various drives are included in the set. We recommend the half-inch square-drive type, as this can be used with most proprietary torque wrenches.

The tools in this list will sometimes need to be supplemented by tools from the *Special* list:

☐ *Sockets (or box spanners) to cover range in previous list (including Torx sockets)*
☐ *Reversible ratchet drive (for use with sockets)*
☐ *Extension piece, 250 mm (for use with sockets)*
☐ *Universal joint (for use with sockets)*
☐ *Flexible handle or sliding T "breaker bar" (for use with sockets)*
☐ *Torque wrench (for use with sockets)*
☐ *Self-locking grips*
☐ *Ball pein hammer*
☐ *Soft-faced mallet (plastic or rubber)*
☐ *Screwdrivers:*
Flat blade - long & sturdy, short (chubby), and narrow (electrician's) types
Cross blade – long & sturdy, and short (chubby) types
☐ *Pliers:*
Long-nosed
Side cutters (electrician's)
Circlip (internal and external)
☐ *Cold chisel - 25 mm*
☐ *Scriber*
☐ *Scraper*
☐ *Centre-punch*
☐ *Pin punch*
☐ *Hacksaw*
☐ *Brake hose clamp*
☐ *Brake/clutch bleeding kit*
☐ *Selection of twist drills*
☐ *Steel rule/straight-edge*
☐ *Allen keys (inc. splined/Torx type)*
☐ *Selection of files*
☐ *Wire brush*
☐ *Axle stands*
☐ *Jack (strong trolley or hydraulic type)*
☐ *Light with extension lead*
☐ *Universal electrical multi-meter*

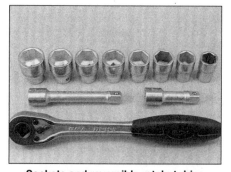

Sockets and reversible ratchet drive

Brake bleeding kit

Torx key, socket and bit

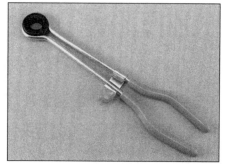

Hose clamp

Angular-tightening gauge

Tools and Working Facilities

Special tools

The tools in this list are those which are not used regularly, are expensive to buy, or which need to be used in accordance with their manufacturers' instructions. Unless relatively difficult mechanical jobs are undertaken frequently, it will not be economic to buy many of these tools. Where this is the case, you could consider clubbing together with friends (or joining a motorists' club) to make a joint purchase, or borrowing the tools against a deposit from a local garage or tool hire specialist. It is worth noting that many of the larger DIY superstores now carry a large range of special tools for hire at modest rates.

The following list contains only those tools and instruments freely available to the public, and not those special tools produced by the vehicle manufacturer specifically for its dealer network. You will find occasional references to these manufacturers' special tools in the text of this manual. Generally, an alternative method of doing the job without the vehicle manufacturers' special tool is given. However, sometimes there is no alternative to using them. Where this is the case and the relevant tool cannot be bought or borrowed, you will have to entrust the work to a dealer.

- [ ] Angular-tightening gauge
- [ ] Valve spring compressor
- [ ] Valve grinding tool
- [ ] Piston ring compressor
- [ ] Piston ring removal/installation tool
- [ ] Cylinder bore hone
- [ ] Balljoint separator
- [ ] Coil spring compressors (where applicable)
- [ ] Two/three-legged hub and bearing puller
- [ ] Impact screwdriver
- [ ] Micrometer and/or vernier calipers
- [ ] Dial gauge
- [ ] Stroboscopic timing light
- [ ] Dwell angle meter/tachometer
- [ ] Fault code reader
- [ ] Cylinder compression gauge
- [ ] Hand-operated vacuum pump and gauge
- [ ] Clutch plate alignment set
- [ ] Brake shoe steady spring cup removal tool
- [ ] Bush and bearing removal/installation set
- [ ] Stud extractors
- [ ] Tap and die set
- [ ] Lifting tackle
- [ ] Trolley jack

Buying tools

Reputable motor accessory shops and superstores often offer excellent quality tools at discount prices, so it pays to shop around.

Remember, you don't have to buy the most expensive items on the shelf, but it is always advisable to steer clear of the very cheap tools. Beware of 'bargains' offered on market stalls or at car boot sales. There are plenty of good tools around at reasonable prices, but always aim to purchase items which meet the relevant national safety standards. If in doubt, ask the proprietor or manager of the shop for advice before making a purchase.

Care and maintenance of tools

Having purchased a reasonable tool kit, it is necessary to keep the tools in a clean and serviceable condition. After use, always wipe off any dirt, grease and metal particles using a clean, dry cloth, before putting the tools away. Never leave them lying around after they have been used. A simple tool rack on the garage or workshop wall for items such as screwdrivers and pliers is a good idea. Store all normal spanners and sockets in a metal box. Any measuring instruments, gauges, meters, etc, must be carefully stored where they cannot be damaged or become rusty.

Take a little care when tools are used. Hammer heads inevitably become marked, and screwdrivers lose the keen edge on their blades from time to time. A little timely attention with emery cloth or a file will soon restore items like this to a good finish.

Working facilities

Not to be forgotten when discussing tools is the workshop itself. If anything more than routine maintenance is to be carried out, a suitable working area becomes essential.

It is appreciated that many an owner-mechanic is forced by circumstances to remove an engine or similar item without the benefit of a garage or workshop. Having done this, any repairs should always be done under the cover of a roof.

Wherever possible, any dismantling should be done on a clean, flat workbench or table at a suitable working height.

Any workbench needs a vice; one with a jaw opening of 100 mm is suitable for most jobs. As mentioned previously, some clean dry storage space is also required for tools, as well as for any lubricants, cleaning fluids, touch-up paints etc, which become necessary.

Another item which may be required, and which has a much more general usage, is an electric drill with a chuck capacity of at least 8 mm. This, together with a good range of twist drills, is virtually essential for fitting accessories.

Last, but not least, always keep a supply of old newspapers and clean, lint-free rags available, and try to keep any working area as clean as possible.

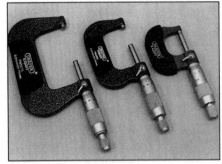

Micrometers

Dial test indicator ("dial gauge")

Strap wrench

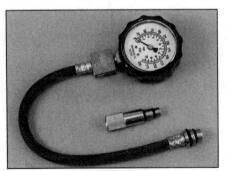

Compression tester

Fault code reader

Whenever servicing, repair or overhaul work is carried out on the car or its components, observe the following procedures and instructions. This will assist in carrying out the operation efficiently and to a professional standard of workmanship.

Joint mating faces and gaskets

When separating components at their mating faces, never insert screwdrivers or similar implements into the joint between the faces in order to prise them apart. This can cause severe damage which results in oil leaks, coolant leaks, etc upon reassembly. Separation is usually achieved by tapping along the joint with a soft-faced hammer in order to break the seal. However, note that this method may not be suitable where dowels are used for component location.

Where a gasket is used between the mating faces of two components, a new one must be fitted on reassembly; fit it dry unless otherwise stated in the repair procedure. Make sure that the mating faces are clean and dry, with all traces of old gasket removed. When cleaning a joint face, use a tool which is unlikely to score or damage the face, and remove any burrs or nicks with an oilstone or fine file.

Make sure that tapped holes are cleaned with a pipe cleaner, and keep them free of jointing compound, if this is being used, unless specifically instructed otherwise.

Ensure that all orifices, channels or pipes are clear, and blow through them, preferably using compressed air.

Oil seals

Oil seals can be removed by levering them out with a wide flat-bladed screwdriver or similar implement. Alternatively, a number of self-tapping screws may be screwed into the seal, and these used as a purchase for pliers or some similar device in order to pull the seal free.

Whenever an oil seal is removed from its working location, either individually or as part of an assembly, it should be renewed.

The very fine sealing lip of the seal is easily damaged, and will not seal if the surface it contacts is not completely clean and free from scratches, nicks or grooves. If the original sealing surface of the component cannot be restored, and the manufacturer has not made provision for slight relocation of the seal relative to the sealing surface, the component should be renewed.

Protect the lips of the seal from any surface which may damage them in the course of fitting. Use tape or a conical sleeve where possible. Lubricate the seal lips with oil before fitting and, on dual-lipped seals, fill the space between the lips with grease.

Unless otherwise stated, oil seals must be fitted with their sealing lips toward the lubricant to be sealed.

Use a tubular drift or block of wood of the appropriate size to install the seal and, if the seal housing is shouldered, drive the seal down to the shoulder. If the seal housing is unshouldered, the seal should be fitted with its face flush with the housing top face (unless otherwise instructed).

Screw threads and fastenings

Seized nuts, bolts and screws are quite a common occurrence where corrosion has set in, and the use of penetrating oil or releasing fluid will often overcome this problem if the offending item is soaked for a while before attempting to release it. The use of an impact driver may also provide a means of releasing such stubborn fastening devices, when used in conjunction with the appropriate screwdriver bit or socket. If none of these methods works, it may be necessary to resort to the careful application of heat, or the use of a hacksaw or nut splitter device.

Studs are usually removed by locking two nuts together on the threaded part, and then using a spanner on the lower nut to unscrew the stud. Studs or bolts which have broken off below the surface of the component in which they are mounted can sometimes be removed using a stud extractor. Always ensure that a blind tapped hole is completely free from oil, grease, water or other fluid before installing the bolt or stud. Failure to do this could cause the housing to crack due to the hydraulic action of the bolt or stud as it is screwed in.

When tightening a castellated nut to accept a split pin, tighten the nut to the specified torque, where applicable, and then tighten further to the next split pin hole. Never slacken the nut to align the split pin hole, unless stated in the repair procedure.

When checking or retightening a nut or bolt to a specified torque setting, slacken the nut or bolt by a quarter of a turn, and then retighten to the specified setting. However, this should not be attempted where angular tightening has been used.

For some screw fastenings, notably cylinder head bolts or nuts, torque wrench settings are no longer specified for the latter stages of tightening, "angle-tightening" being called up instead. Typically, a fairly low torque wrench setting will be applied to the bolts/nuts in the correct sequence, followed by one or more stages of tightening through specified angles.

Locknuts, locktabs and washers

Any fastening which will rotate against a component or housing during tightening should always have a washer between it and the relevant component or housing.

Spring or split washers should always be renewed when they are used to lock a critical component such as a big-end bearing retaining bolt or nut. Locktabs which are folded over to retain a nut or bolt should always be renewed.

Self-locking nuts can be re-used in non-critical areas, providing resistance can be felt when the locking portion passes over the bolt or stud thread. However, it should be noted that self-locking stiffnuts tend to lose their effectiveness after long periods of use, and should then be renewed as a matter of course.

Split pins must always be replaced with new ones of the correct size for the hole.

When thread-locking compound is found on the threads of a fastener which is to be re-used, it should be cleaned off with a wire brush and solvent, and fresh compound applied on reassembly.

Special tools

Some repair procedures in this manual entail the use of special tools such as a press, two or three-legged pullers, spring compressors, etc. Wherever possible, suitable readily-available alternatives to the manufacturer's special tools are described, and are shown in use. In some instances, where no alternative is possible, it has been necessary to resort to the use of a manufacturer's tool, and this has been done for reasons of safety as well as the efficient completion of the repair operation. Unless you are highly-skilled and have a thorough understanding of the procedures described, never attempt to bypass the use of any special tool when the procedure described specifies its use. Not only is there a very great risk of personal injury, but expensive damage could be caused to the components involved.

Environmental considerations

When disposing of used engine oil, brake fluid, antifreeze, etc, give due consideration to any detrimental environmental effects. Do not, for instance, pour any of the above liquids down drains into the general sewage system, or onto the ground to soak away. Many local council refuse tips provide a facility for waste oil disposal, as do some garages. If none of these facilities are available, consult your local Environmental Health Department, or the National Rivers Authority, for further advice.

With the universal tightening-up of legislation regarding the emission of environmentally-harmful substances from motor vehicles, most vehicles have tamperproof devices fitted to the main adjustment points of the fuel system. These devices are primarily designed to prevent unqualified persons from adjusting the fuel/air mixture, with the chance of a consequent increase in toxic emissions. If such devices are found during servicing or overhaul, they should, wherever possible, be renewed or refitted in accordance with the manufacturer's requirements or current legislation.

OIL CARE

OIL BANK LINE
0800 66 33 66
www.oilbankline.org.uk

Note: It is antisocial and illegal to dump oil down the drain. To find the location of your local oil recycling bank, call this number free.

Engine

- ☐ Engine fails to rotate when attempting to start
- ☐ Engine rotates, but will not start
- ☐ Engine difficult to start when cold
- ☐ Engine difficult to start when hot
- ☐ Starter motor noisy or excessively-rough in engagement
- ☐ Engine starts, but stops immediately
- ☐ Engine idles erratically
- ☐ Engine misfires at idle speed
- ☐ Engine misfires throughout the driving speed range
- ☐ Engine hesitates on acceleration
- ☐ Engine stalls
- ☐ Engine lacks power
- ☐ Engine backfires
- ☐ Oil pressure warning light illuminated with engine running
- ☐ Engine runs-on after switching off
- ☐ Engine noises

Cooling system

- ☐ Overheating
- ☐ Overcooling
- ☐ External coolant leakage
- ☐ Internal coolant leakage
- ☐ Corrosion

Fuel and exhaust systems

- ☐ Excessive fuel consumption
- ☐ Fuel leakage and/or fuel odour
- ☐ Excessive noise or fumes from exhaust system

Clutch

- ☐ Pedal travels to floor - no pressure or very little resistance
- ☐ Clutch fails to disengage (unable to select gears)
- ☐ Clutch slips (engine speed increases, with no increase in vehicle speed)
- ☐ Judder as clutch is engaged
- ☐ Noise when depressing or releasing clutch pedal

Manual transmission

- ☐ Noisy in neutral with engine running
- ☐ Noisy in one particular gear
- ☐ Difficulty engaging gears
- ☐ Jumps out of gear
- ☐ Vibration
- ☐ Lubricant leaks

Driveshafts

- ☐ Clicking or knocking noise on turns (at slow speed on full-lock)
- ☐ Vibration when accelerating or decelerating

Braking system

- ☐ Vehicle pulls to one side under braking
- ☐ Noise (grinding or high-pitched squeal) when brakes applied
- ☐ Excessive brake pedal travel
- ☐ Brake pedal feels spongy when depressed
- ☐ Excessive brake pedal effort required to stop vehicle
- ☐ Judder felt through brake pedal or steering wheel when braking
- ☐ Brakes binding
- ☐ Rear wheels locking under normal braking

Suspension and steering systems

- ☐ Vehicle pulls to one side
- ☐ Wheel wobble and vibration
- ☐ Excessive pitching and/or rolling around corners, or during braking
- ☐ Wandering or general instability
- ☐ Excessively-stiff steering
- ☐ Excessive play in steering
- ☐ Lack of power assistance
- ☐ Tyre wear excessive

Electrical system

- ☐ Battery will not hold a charge for more than a few days
- ☐ Ignition/no-charge warning light remains illuminated with engine running
- ☐ Ignition/no-charge warning light fails to come on
- ☐ Lights inoperative
- ☐ Instrument readings inaccurate or erratic
- ☐ Horn inoperative, or unsatisfactory in operation
- ☐ Windscreen/tailgate wipers inoperative, or unsatisfactory in operation
- ☐ Windscreen/tailgate washers inoperative, or unsatisfactory in operation

The vehicle owner who does his or her own maintenance according to the recommended service schedules should not have to use this section of the manual very often. Modern component reliability is such that, provided those items subject to wear or deterioration are inspected or renewed at the specified intervals, sudden failure is comparatively rare. Faults do not usually just happen as a result of sudden failure, but develop over a period of time. Major mechanical failures in particular are usually preceded by characteristic symptoms over hundreds or even thousands of miles. Those components which do occasionally fail without warning are often small and easily carried in the vehicle.

With any fault-finding, the first step is to decide where to begin investigations. Sometimes this is obvious, but on other occasions, a little detective work will be necessary. The owner who makes half-a-dozen haphazard adjustments or replacements may be successful in curing a fault (or its symptoms), but will be none the wiser if the fault recurs, and ultimately may have spent more time and money than was necessary. A calm and logical approach will be found to be more satisfactory in the long run. Always take into account any warning signs or abnormalities that may have been noticed in the period preceding the fault - power loss, high or low gauge readings, unusual smells, etc - and remember that failure of components such as fuses or spark plugs may only be pointers to some underlying fault.

The pages which follow provide an easy-reference guide to the more common problems which may occur during the operation of the vehicle. These problems and their possible causes are grouped under headings denoting various components or systems, such as Engine, Cooling system, etc. The Chapter and/or Section which deals with the problem is also shown in brackets. Whatever the fault, certain basic principles apply. These are as follows:

Verify the fault. This is simply a matter of being sure that you know what the symptoms are before starting work. This is particularly important if you are investigating a fault for someone else, who may not have described it very accurately.

Don't overlook the obvious. For example, if the vehicle won't start, is there petrol in the tank? (Don't take anyone else's word on this particular point, and don't trust the fuel gauge either!) If an electrical fault is indicated, look for loose or broken wires before digging out the test gear.

Cure the disease, not the symptom. Substituting a flat battery with a fully-charged one will get you off the hard shoulder, but if the underlying cause is not attended to, the new battery will go the same way. Similarly, changing oil-fouled spark plugs (petrol models) for a new set will get you moving again, but remember that the reason for the fouling (if it wasn't simply an incorrect grade of plug) will have to be established and corrected.

Don't take anything for granted. Particularly, don't forget that a "new" component may itself be defective (especially if it's been rattling around in the boot for months), and don't leave components out of a fault diagnosis sequence just because they are new or recently-fitted. When you do finally diagnose a difficult fault, you'll probably realise that all the evidence was there from the start.

Engine

Engine fails to rotate when attempting to start

☐ Battery terminal connections loose or corroded (Chapter 1).
☐ Battery discharged or faulty (Chapter 5A).
☐ Broken, loose or disconnected wiring in the starting circuit (Chapter 5A).
☐ Defective starter solenoid or switch (Chapter 5A).
☐ Defective starter motor (Chapter 5A).
☐ Starter pinion or flywheel ring gear teeth loose or broken (Chapter 5A or 2A).
☐ Engine earth strap broken or disconnected (Chapter 5A).

Engine rotates, but will not start

☐ Fuel tank empty.
☐ Battery discharged (engine rotates slowly) (Chapter 5A).
☐ Battery terminal connections loose or corroded (Chapter 1).
☐ Ignition components damp or damaged (Chapters 1 and 5B).
☐ Broken, loose or disconnected wiring in the ignition circuit (Chapters 1 and 5B).
☐ Worn, faulty or incorrectly-gapped spark plugs (Chapter 1).
☐ Choke mechanism incorrectly adjusted, worn or sticking (Chapter 4).
☐ Faulty fuel cut-off solenoid (Chapter 4).
☐ Major mechanical failure (eg camshaft drive) (Chapter 2A or 2B).

Engine difficult to start when cold

☐ Battery discharged (Chapter 5A).
☐ Battery terminal connections loose or corroded (Chapter 1).
☐ Worn, faulty or incorrectly-gapped spark plugs (Chapter 1).
☐ Choke mechanism incorrectly adjusted, worn or sticking (Chapter 4).
☐ Other ignition system fault (Chapters 1 and 5B).
☐ Low cylinder compressions (Chapter 2A).

Engine difficult to start when hot

☐ Air filter element dirty or clogged (Chapter 1).
☐ Choke mechanism incorrectly adjusted, worn or sticking (Chapter 4).
☐ Low cylinder compressions (Chapter 2A).

Starter motor noisy or excessively-rough in engagement

☐ Starter pinion or flywheel ring gear teeth loose or broken (Chapter 5A or 2A).
☐ Starter motor mounting bolts loose or missing (Chapter 5A).
☐ Starter motor internal components worn or damaged (Chapter 5A).

Engine starts, but stops immediately

☐ Loose or faulty electrical connections in the ignition circuit (Chapters 1 and 5B).
☐ Vacuum leak at the carburettor or inlet manifold (Chapter 4).
☐ Blocked carburettor jet(s) or internal passages (Chapter 4).

Engine idles erratically

☐ Air filter element clogged (Chapter 1).
☐ Vacuum leak at the carburettor, inlet manifold or associated hoses (Chapter 4).
☐ Worn, faulty or incorrectly-gapped spark plugs (Chapter 1).
☐ Uneven or low cylinder compressions (Chapter 2A).
☐ Camshaft lobes worn (Chapter 2B).
☐ Timing belt incorrectly tensioned (Chapter 2A).
☐ Blocked carburettor jet(s) or internal passages (Chapter 4).
☐ Blocked injector/fuel injection system fault (Chapter 4).

Engine misfires at idle speed

☐ Worn, faulty or incorrectly-gapped spark plugs (Chapter 1).
☐ Faulty spark plug HT leads (Chapter 1).
☐ Vacuum leak at the carburettor, inlet manifold or associated hoses (Chapter 4).
☐ Blocked carburettor jet(s) or internal passages (Chapter 4).
☐ Distributor cap cracked or tracking internally (Chapter 1).
☐ Uneven or low cylinder compressions (Chapter 2A).
☐ Disconnected, leaking, or perished crankcase ventilation hoses (Chapter 6).

Engine misfires throughout the driving speed range

☐ Fuel filter choked (Chapter 1).
☐ Fuel pump faulty, or delivery pressure low (Chapter 4).
☐ Fuel tank vent blocked, or fuel pipes restricted (Chapter 4).
☐ Vacuum leak at the carburettor, inlet manifold or associated hoses (Chapter 4).
☐ Worn, faulty or incorrectly-gapped spark plugs (Chapter 1).
☐ Faulty spark plug HT leads (Chapter 1).
☐ Distributor cap cracked or tracking internally (Chapter 1).
☐ Faulty ignition coil (Chapter 5B).
☐ Uneven or low cylinder compressions (Chapter 2A).
☐ Blocked carburettor jet(s) or internal passages (Chapter 4).

Engine hesitates on acceleration

☐ Worn, faulty or incorrectly-gapped spark plugs (Chapter 1).
☐ Vacuum leak at the carburettor, inlet manifold or associated hoses (Chapter 4).
☐ Blocked carburettor jet(s) or internal passages (Chapter 4).

Engine stalls

☐ Vacuum leak at the carburettor, inlet manifold or associated hoses (Chapter 4).
☐ Fuel filter choked (Chapter 1).
☐ Fuel pump faulty, or delivery pressure low (Chapter 4).
☐ Fuel tank vent blocked, or fuel pipes restricted (Chapter 4).
☐ Blocked carburettor jet(s) or internal passages (Chapter 4).

Engine lacks power

☐ Timing belt incorrectly fitted or tensioned (Chapter 2A).
☐ Fuel filter choked (Chapter 1).
☐ Fuel pump faulty, or delivery pressure low (Chapter 4).
☐ Uneven or low cylinder compressions (Chapter 2A).
☐ Worn, faulty or incorrectly-gapped spark plugs (Chapter 1).
☐ Vacuum leak at the carburettor, inlet manifold or associated hoses (Chapter 4).
☐ Blocked carburettor jet(s) or internal passages (Chapter 4).
☐ Brakes binding (Chapters 1 and 9).
☐ Clutch slipping (Chapter 7).

Engine backfires

☐ Timing belt incorrectly fitted or tensioned (Chapter 2A).
☐ Vacuum leak at the carburettor, inlet manifold or associated hoses (Chapter 4).
☐ Blocked carburettor jet(s) or internal passages (Chapter 4).

Oil pressure warning light illuminated with engine running

☐ Low oil level, or incorrect oil grade (Chapter 1).
☐ Faulty oil pressure sensor (Chapter 5A).
☐ Worn engine bearings and/or oil pump (Chapter 2B).
☐ High engine operating temperature (Chapter 3).
☐ Oil pickup strainer clogged (Chapter 2A).

Engine runs-on after switching off

☐ Excessive carbon build-up in engine (Chapter 2A or 2B).
☐ High engine operating temperature (Chapter 3).
☐ Faulty fuel cut-off solenoid (Chapter 4).

Engine noises

Pre-ignition (pinking) or knocking during acceleration or under load

☐ Ignition timing incorrect/ignition system fault (Chapter 1 and 5B).
☐ Incorrect grade of spark plug (Chapter 1).
☐ Incorrect grade of fuel (Chapter 1 and 4).
☐ Vacuum leak at the carburettor, inlet manifold or associated hoses (Chapter 4).
☐ Excessive carbon build-up in engine (Chapter 2A or 2B).
☐ Blocked carburettor jet(s) or internal passages (Chapter 4).

Whistling or wheezing noises

☐ Leaking inlet manifold or carburettor gasket (Chapter 4).
☐ Leaking exhaust manifold gasket or pipe-to-manifold joint (Chapter 4).
☐ Leaking vacuum hose (Chapters 4, 5B and 9).
☐ Blowing cylinder head gasket (Chapter 2A).

Tapping or rattling noises

☐ Worn valve gear or camshaft (Chapter 2A or 2B).
☐ Ancillary component fault (water pump, alternator, etc) (Chapters 3, 5A, etc).

Knocking or thumping noises

☐ Worn big-end bearings (regular heavy knocking, perhaps less under load) (Chapter 2B).
☐ Worn main bearings (rumbling and knocking, perhaps worsening under load) (Chapter 2B).
☐ Piston slap (most noticeable when cold) (Chapter 2B).
☐ Ancillary component fault (water pump, alternator, etc) (Chapters 3, 5A, etc).

Cooling system

Overheating

☐ Insufficient coolant in system (Chapter 1).
☐ Thermostat faulty (Chapter 3).
☐ Radiator core blocked, or grille restricted (Chapter 3).
☐ Pressure cap faulty (Chapter 3).
☐ Ignition timing incorrect/ignition system fault (Chapters 1 and 5B).
☐ Inaccurate temperature gauge sender unit (Chapter 3).
☐ Airlock in cooling system (Chapter 1).

Overcooling

☐ Thermostat faulty (Chapter 3).
☐ Inaccurate temperature gauge sender unit (Chapter 3).

Internal coolant leakage

☐ Leaking cylinder head gasket (Chapter 2A).
☐ Cracked cylinder head or cylinder bore (Chapter 2A or 2B).

External coolant leakage

☐ Deteriorated or damaged hoses or hose clips (Chapter 1).
☐ Radiator core or heater matrix leaking (Chapter 3).
☐ Pressure cap faulty (Chapter 3).
☐ Water pump seal leaking (Chapter 3).
☐ Boiling due to overheating (Chapter 3).
☐ Core plug leaking (Chapter 2B).

Corrosion

☐ Infrequent draining and flushing (Chapter 1).
☐ Incorrect coolant mixture or inappropriate coolant type (Chapter 1).

Fuel and exhaust systems

Excessive fuel consumption
- [ ] Air filter element dirty or clogged (Chapter 1).
- [ ] Choke cable incorrectly adjusted, or choke sticking (Chapter 4).
- [ ] Ignition timing incorrect/ignition system fault (Chapters 1 and 5B).
- [ ] Tyres under-inflated (Chapter 1).

Fuel leakage and/or fuel odour
- [ ] Damaged or corroded fuel tank, pipes or connections (Chapter 4).
- [ ] Carburettor float chamber flooding (float height incorrect) (Chapter 4).

Excessive noise or fumes from exhaust system
- [ ] Leaking exhaust system or manifold joints (Chapters 1 and 4).
- [ ] Leaking, corroded or damaged silencers or pipe (Chapters 1 and 4).
- [ ] Broken mountings causing body or suspension contact (Chapter 1).

Clutch

Pedal travels to floor - no pressure or very little resistance
- [ ] Broken clutch cable (Chapter 7).
- [ ] Incorrect clutch cable adjustment (Chapter 7).
- [ ] Broken clutch release bearing or fork (Chapter 7).
- [ ] Broken diaphragm spring in clutch pressure plate (Chapter 7).

Clutch fails to disengage (unable to select gears)
- [ ] Incorrect clutch cable adjustment (Chapter 7).
- [ ] Clutch disc sticking on gearbox input shaft splines (Chapter 7).
- [ ] Clutch disc sticking to flywheel or pressure plate (Chapter 7).
- [ ] Faulty pressure plate assembly (Chapter 7).
- [ ] Clutch release mechanism worn or incorrectly assembled (Chapter 7).

Clutch slips (engine speed increases, with no increase in vehicle speed)
- [ ] Incorrect clutch cable adjustment (Chapter 7).
- [ ] Clutch disc linings excessively worn (Chapter 7).
- [ ] Clutch disc linings contaminated with oil or grease (Chapter 7).
- [ ] Faulty pressure plate or weak diaphragm spring (Chapter 7).

Judder as clutch is engaged
- [ ] Clutch disc linings contaminated with oil or grease (Chapter 7).
- [ ] Clutch disc linings excessively worn (Chapter 7).
- [ ] Clutch cable sticking or frayed (Chapter 7).
- [ ] Faulty or distorted pressure plate or diaphragm spring (Chapter 7).
- [ ] Worn or loose engine or gearbox mountings (Chapter 2A).
- [ ] Clutch disc hub or gearbox input shaft splines worn (Chapter 7 or 8).

Noise when depressing or releasing clutch pedal
- [ ] Worn clutch release bearing (Chapter 7).
- [ ] Worn or dry clutch pedal bushes (Chapter 7).
- [ ] Faulty pressure plate assembly (Chapter 7).
- [ ] Pressure plate diaphragm spring broken (Chapter 7).
- [ ] Broken clutch disc cushioning springs (Chapter 7).

Manual transmission

Noisy in neutral with engine running
- [ ] Input shaft bearings worn (noise apparent with clutch pedal released, but not when depressed) (Chapter 8).*
- [ ] Clutch release bearing worn (noise apparent with clutch pedal depressed, possibly less when released) (Chapter 7).

Noisy in one particular gear
- [ ] Worn, damaged or chipped gear teeth (Chapter 8).*

Difficulty engaging gears
- [ ] Clutch fault (Chapter 7).
- [ ] Worn or damaged gear linkage (Chapter 8).
- [ ] Incorrectly-adjusted gear linkage (Chapter 8).
- [ ] Worn synchroniser units (Chapter 8).*

Vibration
- [ ] Lack of oil (Chapter 1).
- [ ] Worn bearings (Chapter 8).*

Jumps out of gear
- [ ] Worn or damaged gear linkage (Chapter 8).
- [ ] Incorrectly-adjusted gear linkage (Chapter 8).
- [ ] Worn synchroniser units (Chapter 8).*
- [ ] Worn selector forks (Chapter 8).*

Lubricant leaks
- [ ] Leaking differential output oil seal (Chapter 8).
- [ ] Leaking housing joint (Chapter 8).*
- [ ] Leaking input shaft oil seal (Chapter 8).*

*Although the corrective action necessary to remedy the symptoms described is beyond the scope of the home mechanic, the above information should be helpful in isolating the cause of the condition, so that the owner can communicate clearly with a professional mechanic.

Propeller shaft/differential

Vibration when accelerating or decelerating
- [ ] Worn universal joint (Chapter 7).
- [ ] Bent or distorted propeller shaft (Chapter 7).

Low-pitched whining, increasing with road speed
- [ ] Worn differential (Chapter 7)

Braking system

Note: *Before assuming that a brake problem exists, make sure that the tyres are in good condition and correctly inflated, that the front wheel alignment is correct, and that the vehicle is not loaded with weight in an unequal manner.*

Vehicle pulls to one side under braking

- ☐ Worn, defective, damaged or contaminated front brake pads or rear brake shoes on one side (Chapters 1 and 9).
- ☐ Seized or partially-seized front brake caliper or rear wheel cylinder piston (Chapters 1 and 9).
- ☐ A mixture of brake pad/shoe lining materials fitted between sides (Chapters 1 and 9).
- ☐ Front brake caliper mounting bolts loose (Chapter 9).
- ☐ Rear brake backplate mounting bolts loose (Chapter 9).
- ☐ Worn or damaged steering or suspension components (Chapters 1 and 10).

Noise (grinding or high-pitched squeal) when brakes applied

- ☐ Brake pad or shoe friction lining material worn down to metal backing (Chapters 1 and 9).
- ☐ Excessive corrosion of brake disc or drum. May be apparent after the vehicle has been standing for some time (Chapters 1 and 9).
- ☐ Foreign object (stone chipping, etc) trapped between brake disc and shield (Chapters 1 and 9).

Brakes binding

- ☐ Seized brake caliper or wheel cylinder piston(s) (Chapter 9).
- ☐ Incorrectly-adjusted handbrake mechanism (Chapter 1).
- ☐ Faulty master cylinder (Chapter 9).

Rear wheels locking under normal braking

- ☐ Rear brake shoe linings contaminated (Chapters 1 and 9).
- ☐ Faulty brake pressure regulator (Chapter 9).

Excessive brake pedal travel

- ☐ Inoperative rear brake self-adjust mechanism (Chapters 1 and 9).
- ☐ Faulty master cylinder (Chapter 9).
- ☐ Air in hydraulic system (Chapters 1 and 9).
- ☐ Faulty vacuum servo unit (Chapter 9).

Brake pedal feels spongy when depressed

- ☐ Air in hydraulic system (Chapters 1 and 9).
- ☐ Deteriorated flexible rubber brake hoses (Chapters 1 and 9).
- ☐ Faulty master cylinder (Chapter 9).

Excessive brake pedal effort required to stop vehicle

- ☐ Faulty vacuum servo unit (Chapter 9).
- ☐ Disconnected, damaged or insecure brake servo vacuum hose (Chapter 9).
- ☐ Primary or secondary hydraulic circuit failure (Chapter 9).
- ☐ Seized brake caliper or wheel cylinder piston(s) (Chapter 9).
- ☐ Brake pads or brake shoes incorrectly fitted (Chapters 1 and 9).
- ☐ Incorrect grade of brake pads or brake shoes fitted (Chapters 1 and 9).
- ☐ Brake pads or brake shoe linings contaminated (Chapters 1 and 9).

Judder felt through brake pedal or steering wheel when braking

- ☐ Excessive run-out or distortion of front discs or rear drums (Chapters 1 and 9).
- ☐ Brake pad or brake shoe linings worn (Chapters 1 and 9).
- ☐ Brake caliper or rear brake backplate mounting bolts loose (Chapter 9).
- ☐ Wear in suspension or steering components or mountings (Chapters 1 and 10).

Suspension and steering

Note: *Before diagnosing suspension or steering faults, be sure that the trouble is not due to incorrect tyre pressures, mixtures of tyre types, or binding brakes.*

Vehicle pulls to one side

- ☐ Defective tyre (Chapter 1).
- ☐ Excessive wear in suspension or steering components (Chapters 1 and 10).
- ☐ Incorrect front wheel alignment (Chapter 10).
- ☐ Accident damage to steering or suspension components (Chapter 1).

Wheel wobble and vibration

- ☐ Front roadwheels out of balance (vibration felt mainly through the steering wheel) (Chapters 1 and 10).
- ☐ Rear roadwheels out of balance (vibration felt throughout the vehicle) (Chapters 1 and 10).
- ☐ Roadwheels damaged or distorted (Chapters 1 and 10).
- ☐ Faulty or damaged tyre (Chapter 1).
- ☐ Worn steering or suspension joints, bushes or components (Chapters 1 and 10).
- ☐ Wheel bolts loose (Chapters 1 and 10).

Excessive pitching and/or rolling around corners, or during braking

- ☐ Defective shock absorbers (Chapters 1 and 10).
- ☐ Broken or weak spring and/or suspension component (Chapters 1 and 10).
- ☐ Worn or damaged anti-roll bar or mountings, where applicable (Chapter 10).

Wandering or general instability

- ☐ Incorrect front wheel alignment (Chapter 10).
- ☐ Worn steering or suspension joints, bushes or components (Chapters 1 and 10).
- ☐ Roadwheels out of balance (Chapters 1 and 10).
- ☐ Faulty or damaged tyre (Chapter 1).
- ☐ Wheel bolts loose (Chapters 1 and 10).
- ☐ Defective shock absorbers (Chapters 1 and 10).

Excessively-stiff steering

- ☐ Lack of steering gear lubricant (Chapter 10).
- ☐ Seized track rod end balljoint or suspension balljoint (Chapters 1 and 10).
- ☐ Incorrect front wheel alignment (Chapter 10).
- ☐ Steering rack or column bent or damaged (Chapter 10).

Excessive play in steering

☐ Worn steering column intermediate shaft universal joint (Chapter 10).
☐ Worn steering track rod end balljoints (Chapters 1 and 10).
☐ Worn rack-and-pinion steering gear (Chapter 10).
☐ Worn steering or suspension joints, bushes or components (Chapters 1 and 10).

Tyre wear excessive

Tyres worn on inside or outside edges

☐ Tyres under-inflated (wear on both edges) (Chapter 1).
☐ Incorrect camber or castor angles (wear on one edge only) (Chapter 10).
☐ Worn steering or suspension joints, bushes or components (Chapters 1 and 10).
☐ Excessively-hard cornering.
☐ Accident damage.

Tyre treads exhibit feathered edges

☐ Incorrect toe setting (Chapter 10).

Tyres worn in centre of tread

☐ Tyres over-inflated (Chapter 1).

Tyres worn on inside and outside edges

☐ Tyres under-inflated (Chapter 1).

Tyres worn unevenly

☐ Tyres/wheels out of balance (Chapter 1).
☐ Excessive wheel or tyre run-out (Chapter 1).
☐ Worn shock absorbers (Chapters 1 and 10).
☐ Faulty tyre (Chapter 1).

Electrical system

Note: *For problems associated with the starting system, refer to the faults listed under "Engine".*

Battery will not hold a charge for more than a few days

☐ Battery defective internally (Chapter 5A).
☐ Battery terminal connections loose or corroded (Chapter 1).
☐ Auxiliary drivebelt worn or incorrectly adjusted (Chapter 1).
☐ Alternator not charging at correct output (Chapter 5A).
☐ Alternator or voltage regulator faulty (Chapter 5A).
☐ Short-circuit causing continual battery drain (Chapters 5A and 12).

Ignition/no-charge warning light remains illuminated with engine running

☐ Auxiliary drivebelt broken, worn, or incorrectly adjusted (Chapter 1).
☐ Alternator brushes worn, sticking, or dirty (Chapter 5A).
☐ Alternator brush springs weak or broken (Chapter 5A).
☐ Internal fault in alternator or voltage regulator (Chapter 5A).
☐ Broken, disconnected, or loose wiring in charging circuit (Chapter 5A).

Ignition/no-charge warning light fails to come on

☐ Warning light bulb blown (Chapter 12).
☐ Broken, disconnected, or loose wiring in warning light circuit (Chapter 12).
☐ Alternator faulty (Chapter 5A).

Lights inoperative

☐ Bulb blown (Chapter 12).
☐ Corrosion of bulb or bulbholder contacts (Chapter 12).
☐ Blown fuse (Chapter 12).
☐ Faulty relay (Chapter 12).
☐ Broken, loose, or disconnected wiring (Chapter 12).
☐ Faulty switch (Chapter 12).

Instrument readings inaccurate or erratic

Instrument readings increase with engine speed

☐ Faulty voltage regulator (Chapter 12).

Fuel or temperature gauges give no reading

☐ Faulty gauge sender unit (Chapter 3 or 4).
☐ Wiring open-circuit (Chapter 12).
☐ Faulty gauge (Chapter 12).

Fuel or temperature gauges give continuous maximum reading

☐ Faulty gauge sender unit (Chapter 3 or 4).
☐ Wiring short-circuit (Chapter 12).
☐ Faulty gauge (Chapter 12).

Horn inoperative, or unsatisfactory in operation

Horn operates all the time

☐ Horn push either earthed or stuck down (Chapter 12).
☐ Horn cable-to-horn push earthed (Chapter 12).

Horn fails to operate

☐ Blown fuse (Chapter 12).
☐ Cable or cable connections loose, broken or disconnected (Chapter 12).
☐ Faulty horn (Chapter 12).

Horn emits intermittent or unsatisfactory sound

☐ Cable connections loose (Chapter 12).
☐ Horn mountings loose (Chapter 12).
☐ Faulty horn (Chapter 12).

Windscreen/tailgate wipers inoperative, or unsatisfactory in operation

Wipers fail to operate, or operate very slowly

☐ Wiper blades stuck to screen, or linkage seized or binding (Chapters 1 and 12).
☐ Blown fuse (Chapter 12).
☐ Cable or cable connections loose, broken or disconnected (Chapter 12).
☐ Faulty relay (Chapter 12).
☐ Faulty wiper motor (Chapter 12).

Wiper blades sweep over too large or too small an area of the glass

☐ Wiper arms incorrectly positioned on spindles (Chapter 1).
☐ Excessive wear of wiper linkage (Chapter 12).
☐ Wiper motor or linkage mountings loose or insecure (Chapter 12).

Wiper blades fail to clean the glass effectively

☐ Wiper blade rubbers worn or perished (Chapter 1).
☐ Wiper arm tension springs broken, or arm pivots seized (Chapter 12).
☐ Insufficient windscreen washer additive to adequately remove road film (Chapter 1).

Windscreen/tailgate washers inoperative, or unsatisfactory in operation

One or more washer jets inoperative

☐ Blocked washer jet (Chapter 1).
☐ Disconnected, kinked or restricted fluid hose (Chapter 12).
☐ Insufficient fluid in washer reservoir (Chapter 1).

Washer pump fails to operate

☐ Broken or disconnected wiring or connections (Chapter 12).
☐ Blown fuse (Chapter 12).
☐ Faulty washer switch (Chapter 12).
☐ Faulty washer pump (Chapter 12).

Washer pump runs for some time before fluid is emitted from jets

☐ Faulty one-way valve in fluid supply hose (Chapter 12).

Conversion Factors

Length (distance)

Inches (in)	25.4	=	Millimetres (mm)	x 0.0394	=	Inches (in)
Feet (ft)	0.305	=	Metres (m)	x 3.281	=	Feet (ft)
Miles	1.609	=	Kilometres (km)	x 0.621	=	Miles

Volume (capacity)

Cubic inches (cu in; in^3)	x 16.387	=	Cubic centimetres (cc; cm^3)	x 0.061	=	Cubic inches (cu in; in^3)
Imperial pints (Imp pt)	x 0.568	=	Litres (l)	x 1.76	=	Imperial pints (Imp pt)
Imperial quarts (Imp qt)	x 1.137	=	Litres (l)	x 0.88	=	Imperial quarts (Imp qt)
Imperial quarts (Imp qt)	x 1.201	=	US quarts (US qt)	x 0.833	=	Imperial quarts (Imp qt)
US quarts (US qt)	x 0.946	=	Litres (l)	x 1.057	=	US quarts (US qt)
Imperial gallons (Imp gal)	x 4.546	=	Litres (l)	x 0.22	=	Imperial gallons (Imp gal)
Imperial gallons (Imp gal)	x 1.201	=	US gallons (US gal)	x 0.833	=	Imperial gallons (Imp gal)
US gallons (US gal)	x 3.785	=	Litres (l)	x 0.264	=	US gallons (US gal)

Mass (weight)

Ounces (oz)	x 28.35	=	Grams (g)	x 0.035	=	Ounces (oz)
Pounds (lb)	x 0.454	=	Kilograms (kg)	x 2.205	=	Pounds (lb)

Force

Ounces-force (ozf; oz)	x 0.278	=	Newtons (N)	x 3.6	=	Ounces-force (ozf; oz)
Pounds-force (lbf; lb)	x 4.448	=	Newtons (N)	x 0.225	=	Pounds-force (lbf; lb)
Newtons (N)	x 0.1	=	Kilograms-force (kgf; kg)	x 9.81	=	Newtons (N)

Pressure

Pounds-force per square inch (psi; lbf/in^2; lb/in^2)	x 0.070	=	Kilograms-force per square centimetre (kgf/cm^2; kg/cm^2)	x 14.223	=	Pounds-force per square inch (psi; lbf/in^2; lb/in^2)
Pounds-force per square inch (psi; lbf/in^2; lb/in^2)	x 0.068	=	Atmospheres (atm)	x 14.696	=	Pounds-force per square inch (psi; lbf/in^2; lb/in^2)
Pounds-force per square inch (psi; lbf/in^2; lb/in^2)	x 0.069	=	Bars	x 14.5	=	Pounds-force per square inch (psi; lbf/in^2; lb/in^2)
Pounds-force per square inch (psi; lbf/in^2; lb/in^2)	x 6.895	=	Kilopascals (kPa)	x 0.145	=	Pounds-force per square inch (psi; lbf/in^2; lb/in^2)
Kilopascals (kPa)	x 0.01	=	Kilograms-force per square centimetre (kgf/cm^2; kg/cm^2)	x 98.1	=	Kilopascals (kPa)
Millibar (mbar)	x 100	=	Pascals (Pa)	x 0.01	=	Millibar (mbar)
Millibar (mbar)	x 0.0145	=	Pounds-force per square inch (psi; lbf/in^2; lb/in^2)	x 68.947	=	Millibar (mbar)
Millibar (mbar)	x 0.75	=	Millimetres of mercury (mmHg)	x 1.333	=	Millibar (mbar)
Millibar (mbar)	x 0.401	=	Inches of water (inH$_2$O)	x 2.491	=	Millibar (mbar)
Millimetres of mercury (mmHg)	x 0.535	=	Inches of water (inH$_2$O)	x 1.868	=	Millimetres of mercury (mmHg)
Inches of water (inH$_2$O)	x 0.036	=	Pounds-force per square inch (psi; lbf/in^2; lb/in^2)	x 27.68	=	Inches of water (inH$_2$O)

Torque (moment of force)

Pounds-force inches (lbf in; lb in)	x 1.152	=	Kilograms-force centimetre (kgf cm; kg cm)	x 0.868	=	Pounds-force inches (lbf in; lb in)
Pounds-force inches (lbf in; lb in)	x 0.113	=	Newton metres (Nm)	x 8.85	=	Pounds-force inches (lbf in; lb in)
Pounds-force inches (lbf in; lb in)	x 0.083	=	Pounds-force feet (lbf ft; lb ft)	x 12	=	Pounds-force inches (lbf in; lb in)
Pounds-force feet (lbf ft; lb ft)	x 0.138	=	Kilograms-force metres (kgf m; kg m)	x 7.233	=	Pounds-force feet (lbf ft; lb ft)
Pounds-force feet (lbf ft; lb ft)	x 1.356	=	Newton metres (Nm)	x 0.738	=	Pounds-force feet (lbf ft; lb ft)
Newton metres (Nm)	x 0.102	=	Kilograms-force metres (kgf m; kg m)	x 9.804	=	Newton metres (Nm)

Power

Horsepower (hp)	x 745.7	=	Watts (W)	x 0.0013	=	Horsepower (hp)

Velocity (speed)

Miles per hour (miles/hr; mph)	x 1.609	=	Kilometres per hour (km/hr; kph)	x 0.621	=	Miles per hour (miles/hr; mph)

Fuel consumption*

Miles per gallon (mpg)	x 0.354	=	Kilometres per litre (km/l)	x 2.825	=	Miles per gallon (mpg)

* It is common practice to convert from miles per gallon (mpg) to litres/100 kilometres (l/100km), where mpg x l/100 km = 282

Temperature

Degrees Fahrenheit = (°C x 1.8) + 32   Degrees Celsius (Degrees Centigrade; °C) = (°F - 32) x 0.56

A

ABS (Anti-lock brake system) A system, usually electronically controlled, that senses incipient wheel lockup during braking and relieves hydraulic pressure at wheels that are about to skid.

Air bag An inflatable bag hidden in the steering wheel (driver's side) or the dash or glovebox (passenger side). In a head-on collision, the bags inflate, preventing the driver and front passenger from being thrown forward into the steering wheel or windscreen.

Air cleaner A metal or plastic housing, containing a filter element, which removes dust and dirt from the air being drawn into the engine.

Air filter element The actual filter in an air cleaner system, usually manufactured from pleated paper and requiring renewal at regular intervals.

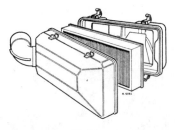

Air filter

Allen key A hexagonal wrench which fits into a recessed hexagonal hole.

Alligator clip A long-nosed spring-loaded metal clip with meshing teeth. Used to make temporary electrical connections.

Alternator A component in the electrical system which converts mechanical energy from a drivebelt into electrical energy to charge the battery and to operate the starting system, ignition system and electrical accessories.

Ampere (amp) A unit of measurement for the flow of electric current. One amp is the amount of current produced by one volt acting through a resistance of one ohm.

Anaerobic sealer A substance used to prevent bolts and screws from loosening. Anaerobic means that it does not require oxygen for activation. The Loctite brand is widely used.

Antifreeze A substance (usually ethylene glycol) mixed with water, and added to a vehicle's cooling system, to prevent freezing of the coolant in winter. Antifreeze also contains chemicals to inhibit corrosion and the formation of rust and other deposits that would tend to clog the radiator and coolant passages and reduce cooling efficiency.

Anti-seize compound A coating that reduces the risk of seizing on fasteners that are subjected to high temperatures, such as exhaust manifold bolts and nuts.

Asbestos A natural fibrous mineral with great heat resistance, commonly used in the composition of brake friction materials.

Asbestos is a health hazard and the dust created by brake systems should never be inhaled or ingested.

Axle A shaft on which a wheel revolves, or which revolves with a wheel. Also, a solid beam that connects the two wheels at one end of the vehicle. An axle which also transmits power to the wheels is known as a live axle.

Axleshaft A single rotating shaft, on either side of the differential, which delivers power from the final drive assembly to the drive wheels. Also called a driveshaft or a halfshaft.

B

Ball bearing An anti-friction bearing consisting of a hardened inner and outer race with hardened steel balls between two races.

Bearing The curved surface on a shaft or in a bore, or the part assembled into either, that permits relative motion between them with minimum wear and friction.

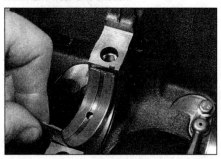

Bearing

Big-end bearing The bearing in the end of the connecting rod that's attached to the crankshaft.

Bleed nipple A valve on a brake wheel cylinder, caliper or other hydraulic component that is opened to purge the hydraulic system of air. Also called a bleed screw.

Brake bleeding Procedure for removing air from lines of a hydraulic brake system.

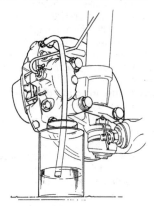

Brake bleeding

Brake disc The component of a disc brake that rotates with the wheels.

Brake drum The component of a drum brake that rotates with the wheels.

Brake linings The friction material which contacts the brake disc or drum to retard the vehicle's speed. The linings are bonded or riveted to the brake pads or shoes.

Brake pads The replaceable friction pads that pinch the brake disc when the brakes are applied. Brake pads consist of a friction material bonded or riveted to a rigid backing plate.

Brake shoe The crescent-shaped carrier to which the brake linings are mounted and which forces the lining against the rotating drum during braking.

Braking systems For more information on braking systems, consult the *Haynes Automotive Brake Manual*.

Breaker bar A long socket wrench handle providing greater leverage.

Bulkhead The insulated partition between the engine and the passenger compartment.

C

Caliper The non-rotating part of a disc-brake assembly that straddles the disc and carries the brake pads. The caliper also contains the hydraulic components that cause the pads to pinch the disc when the brakes are applied. A caliper is also a measuring tool that can be set to measure inside or outside dimensions of an object.

Camshaft A rotating shaft on which a series of cam lobes operate the valve mechanisms. The camshaft may be driven by gears, by sprockets and chain or by sprockets and a belt.

Canister A container in an evaporative emission control system; contains activated charcoal granules to trap vapours from the fuel system.

Canister

Carburettor A device which mixes fuel with air in the proper proportions to provide a desired power output from a spark ignition internal combustion engine.

Castellated Resembling the parapets along the top of a castle wall. For example, a castellated balljoint stud nut.

Castor In wheel alignment, the backward or forward tilt of the steering axis. Castor is positive when the steering axis is inclined rearward at the top.

Catalytic converter A silencer-like device in the exhaust system which converts certain pollutants in the exhaust gases into less harmful substances.

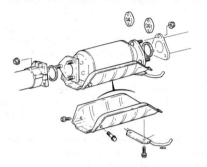

Catalytic converter

Circlip A ring-shaped clip used to prevent endwise movement of cylindrical parts and shafts. An internal circlip is installed in a groove in a housing; an external circlip fits into a groove on the outside of a cylindrical piece such as a shaft.

Clearance The amount of space between two parts. For example, between a piston and a cylinder, between a bearing and a journal, etc.

Coil spring A spiral of elastic steel found in various sizes throughout a vehicle, for example as a springing medium in the suspension and in the valve train.

Compression Reduction in volume, and increase in pressure and temperature, of a gas, caused by squeezing it into a smaller space.

Compression ratio The relationship between cylinder volume when the piston is at top dead centre and cylinder volume when the piston is at bottom dead centre.

Constant velocity (CV) joint A type of universal joint that cancels out vibrations caused by driving power being transmitted through an angle.

Core plug A disc or cup-shaped metal device inserted in a hole in a casting through which core was removed when the casting was formed. Also known as a freeze plug or expansion plug.

Crankcase The lower part of the engine block in which the crankshaft rotates.

Crankshaft The main rotating member, or shaft, running the length of the crankcase, with offset "throws" to which the connecting rods are attached.

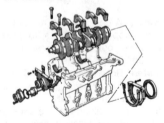

Crankshaft assembly

Crocodile clip See Alligator clip

D

Diagnostic code Code numbers obtained by accessing the diagnostic mode of an engine management computer. This code can be used to determine the area in the system where a malfunction may be located.

Disc brake A brake design incorporating a rotating disc onto which brake pads are squeezed. The resulting friction converts the energy of a moving vehicle into heat.

Double-overhead cam (DOHC) An engine that uses two overhead camshafts, usually one for the intake valves and one for the exhaust valves.

Drivebelt(s) The belt(s) used to drive accessories such as the alternator, water pump, power steering pump, air conditioning compressor, etc. off the crankshaft pulley.

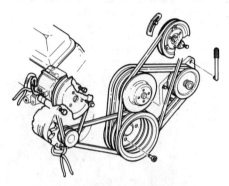

Accessory drivebelts

Driveshaft Any shaft used to transmit motion. Commonly used when referring to the axleshafts on a front wheel drive vehicle.

Drum brake A type of brake using a drum-shaped metal cylinder attached to the inner surface of the wheel. When the brake pedal is pressed, curved brake shoes with friction linings press against the inside of the drum to slow or stop the vehicle.

E

EGR valve A valve used to introduce exhaust gases into the intake air stream.

Electronic control unit (ECU) A computer which controls (for instance) ignition and fuel injection systems, or an anti-lock braking system. For more information refer to the *Haynes Automotive Electrical and Electronic Systems Manual.*

Electronic Fuel Injection (EFI) A computer controlled fuel system that distributes fuel through an injector located in each intake port of the engine.

Emergency brake A braking system, independent of the main hydraulic system, that can be used to slow or stop the vehicle if the primary brakes fail, or to hold the vehicle stationary even though the brake pedal isn't depressed. It usually consists of a hand lever that actuates either front or rear brakes mechanically through a series of cables and linkages. Also known as a handbrake or parking brake.

Endfloat The amount of lengthwise movement between two parts. As applied to a crankshaft, the distance that the crankshaft can move forward and back in the cylinder block.

Engine management system (EMS) A computer controlled system which manages the fuel injection and the ignition systems in an integrated fashion.

Exhaust manifold A part with several passages through which exhaust gases leave the engine combustion chambers and enter the exhaust pipe.

F

Fan clutch A viscous (fluid) drive coupling device which permits variable engine fan speeds in relation to engine speeds.

Feeler blade A thin strip or blade of hardened steel, ground to an exact thickness, used to check or measure clearances between parts.

Feeler blade

Firing order The order in which the engine cylinders fire, or deliver their power strokes, beginning with the number one cylinder.

Flywheel A heavy spinning wheel in which energy is absorbed and stored by means of momentum. On cars, the flywheel is attached to the crankshaft to smooth out firing impulses.

Free play The amount of travel before any action takes place. The "looseness" in a linkage, or an assembly of parts, between the initial application of force and actual movement. For example, the distance the brake pedal moves before the pistons in the master cylinder are actuated.

Fuse An electrical device which protects a circuit against accidental overload. The typical fuse contains a soft piece of metal which is calibrated to melt at a predetermined current flow (expressed as amps) and break the circuit.

Fusible link A circuit protection device consisting of a conductor surrounded by heat-resistant insulation. The conductor is smaller than the wire it protects, so it acts as the weakest link in the circuit. Unlike a blown fuse, a failed fusible link must frequently be cut from the wire for replacement.

G

Gap The distance the spark must travel in jumping from the centre electrode to the side electrode in a spark plug. Also refers to the spacing between the points in a contact breaker assembly in a conventional points-type ignition, or to the distance between the reluctor or rotor and the pickup coil in an electronic ignition.

Adjusting spark plug gap

Gasket Any thin, soft material - usually cork, cardboard, asbestos or soft metal - installed between two metal surfaces to ensure a good seal. For instance, the cylinder head gasket seals the joint between the block and the cylinder head.

Gasket

Gauge An instrument panel display used to monitor engine conditions. A gauge with a movable pointer on a dial or a fixed scale is an analogue gauge. A gauge with a numerical readout is called a digital gauge.

H

Halfshaft A rotating shaft that transmits power from the final drive unit to a drive wheel, usually when referring to a live rear axle.

Harmonic balancer A device designed to reduce torsion or twisting vibration in the crankshaft. May be incorporated in the crankshaft pulley. Also known as a vibration damper.

Hone An abrasive tool for correcting small irregularities or differences in diameter in an engine cylinder, brake cylinder, etc.

Hydraulic tappet A tappet that utilises hydraulic pressure from the engine's lubrication system to maintain zero clearance (constant contact with both camshaft and valve stem). Automatically adjusts to variation in valve stem length. Hydraulic tappets also reduce valve noise.

I

Ignition timing The moment at which the spark plug fires, usually expressed in the number of crankshaft degrees before the piston reaches the top of its stroke.

Inlet manifold A tube or housing with passages through which flows the air-fuel mixture (carburettor vehicles and vehicles with throttle body injection) or air only (port fuel-injected vehicles) to the port openings in the cylinder head.

J

Jump start Starting the engine of a vehicle with a discharged or weak battery by attaching jump leads from the weak battery to a charged or helper battery.

L

Load Sensing Proportioning Valve (LSPV) A brake hydraulic system control valve that works like a proportioning valve, but also takes into consideration the amount of weight carried by the rear axle.

Locknut A nut used to lock an adjustment nut, or other threaded component, in place. For example, a locknut is employed to keep the adjusting nut on the rocker arm in position.

Lockwasher A form of washer designed to prevent an attaching nut from working loose.

M

MacPherson strut A type of front suspension system devised by Earle MacPherson at Ford of England. In its original form, a simple lateral link with the anti-roll bar creates the lower control arm. A long strut - an integral coil spring and shock absorber - is mounted between the body and the steering knuckle. Many modern so-called MacPherson strut systems use a conventional lower A-arm and don't rely on the anti-roll bar for location.

Multimeter An electrical test instrument with the capability to measure voltage, current and resistance.

N

NOx Oxides of Nitrogen. A common toxic pollutant emitted by petrol and diesel engines at higher temperatures.

O

Ohm The unit of electrical resistance. One volt applied to a resistance of one ohm will produce a current of one amp.

Ohmmeter An instrument for measuring electrical resistance.

O-ring A type of sealing ring made of a special rubber-like material; in use, the O-ring is compressed into a groove to provide the sealing action.

Overhead cam (ohc) engine An engine with the camshaft(s) located on top of the cylinder head(s).

Overhead valve (ohv) engine An engine with the valves located in the cylinder head, but with the camshaft located in the engine block.

Oxygen sensor A device installed in the engine exhaust manifold, which senses the oxygen content in the exhaust and converts this information into an electric current. Also called a Lambda sensor.

P

Phillips screw A type of screw head having a cross instead of a slot for a corresponding type of screwdriver.

Plastigage A thin strip of plastic thread, available in different sizes, used for measuring clearances. For example, a strip of Plastigage is laid across a bearing journal. The parts are assembled and dismantled; the width of the crushed strip indicates the clearance between journal and bearing.

Plastigage

Propeller shaft The long hollow tube with universal joints at both ends that carries power from the transmission to the differential on front-engined rear wheel drive vehicles.

Proportioning valve A hydraulic control valve which limits the amount of pressure to the rear brakes during panic stops to prevent wheel lock-up.

R

Rack-and-pinion steering A steering system with a pinion gear on the end of the steering shaft that mates with a rack (think of a geared wheel opened up and laid flat). When the steering wheel is turned, the pinion turns, moving the rack to the left or right. This movement is transmitted through the track rods to the steering arms at the wheels.

Radiator A liquid-to-air heat transfer device designed to reduce the temperature of the coolant in an internal combustion engine cooling system.

Refrigerant Any substance used as a heat transfer agent in an air-conditioning system. R-12 has been the principle refrigerant for many years; recently, however, manufacturers have begun using R-134a, a non-CFC substance that is considered less harmful to the ozone in the upper atmosphere.

Rocker arm A lever arm that rocks on a shaft or pivots on a stud. In an overhead valve engine, the rocker arm converts the upward movement of the pushrod into a downward movement to open a valve.

Rotor In a distributor, the rotating device inside the cap that connects the centre electrode and the outer terminals as it turns, distributing the high voltage from the coil secondary winding to the proper spark plug. Also, that part of an alternator which rotates inside the stator. Also, the rotating assembly of a turbocharger, including the compressor wheel, shaft and turbine wheel.

Runout The amount of wobble (in-and-out movement) of a gear or wheel as it's rotated. The amount a shaft rotates "out-of-true." The out-of-round condition of a rotating part.

S

Sealant A liquid or paste used to prevent leakage at a joint. Sometimes used in conjunction with a gasket.

Sealed beam lamp An older headlight design which integrates the reflector, lens and filaments into a hermetically-sealed one-piece unit. When a filament burns out or the lens cracks, the entire unit is simply replaced.

Serpentine drivebelt A single, long, wide accessory drivebelt that's used on some newer vehicles to drive all the accessories, instead of a series of smaller, shorter belts. Serpentine drivebelts are usually tensioned by an automatic tensioner.

Serpentine drivebelt

Shim Thin spacer, commonly used to adjust the clearance or relative positions between two parts. For example, shims inserted into or under bucket tappets control valve clearances. Clearance is adjusted by changing the thickness of the shim.

Slide hammer A special puller that screws into or hooks onto a component such as a shaft or bearing; a heavy sliding handle on the shaft bottoms against the end of the shaft to knock the component free.

Sprocket A tooth or projection on the periphery of a wheel, shaped to engage with a chain or drivebelt. Commonly used to refer to the sprocket wheel itself.

Starter inhibitor switch On vehicles with an automatic transmission, a switch that prevents starting if the vehicle is not in Neutral or Park.

Strut See MacPherson strut.

T

Tappet A cylindrical component which transmits motion from the cam to the valve stem, either directly or via a pushrod and rocker arm. Also called a cam follower.

Thermostat A heat-controlled valve that regulates the flow of coolant between the cylinder block and the radiator, so maintaining optimum engine operating temperature. A thermostat is also used in some air cleaners in which the temperature is regulated.

Thrust bearing The bearing in the clutch assembly that is moved in to the release levers by clutch pedal action to disengage the clutch. Also referred to as a release bearing.

Timing belt A toothed belt which drives the camshaft. Serious engine damage may result if it breaks in service.

Timing chain A chain which drives the camshaft.

Toe-in The amount the front wheels are closer together at the front than at the rear. On rear wheel drive vehicles, a slight amount of toe-in is usually specified to keep the front wheels running parallel on the road by offsetting other forces that tend to spread the wheels apart.

Toe-out The amount the front wheels are closer together at the rear than at the front. On front wheel drive vehicles, a slight amount of toe-out is usually specified.

Tools For full information on choosing and using tools, refer to the *Haynes Automotive Tools Manual*.

Tracer A stripe of a second colour applied to a wire insulator to distinguish that wire from another one with the same colour insulator.

Tune-up A process of accurate and careful adjustments and parts replacement to obtain the best possible engine performance.

Turbocharger A centrifugal device, driven by exhaust gases, that pressurises the intake air. Normally used to increase the power output from a given engine displacement, but can also be used primarily to reduce exhaust emissions (as on VW's "Umwelt" Diesel engine).

U

Universal joint or U-joint A double-pivoted connection for transmitting power from a driving to a driven shaft through an angle. A U-joint consists of two Y-shaped yokes and a cross-shaped member called the spider.

V

Valve A device through which the flow of liquid, gas, vacuum, or loose material in bulk may be started, stopped, or regulated by a movable part that opens, shuts, or partially obstructs one or more ports or passageways. A valve is also the movable part of such a device.

Valve clearance The clearance between the valve tip (the end of the valve stem) and the rocker arm or tappet. The valve clearance is measured when the valve is closed.

Vernier caliper A precision measuring instrument that measures inside and outside dimensions. Not quite as accurate as a micrometer, but more convenient.

Viscosity The thickness of a liquid or its resistance to flow.

Volt A unit for expressing electrical "pressure" in a circuit. One volt that will produce a current of one ampere through a resistance of one ohm.

W

Welding Various processes used to join metal items by heating the areas to be joined to a molten state and fusing them together. For more information refer to the *Haynes Automotive Welding Manual*.

Wiring diagram A drawing portraying the components and wires in a vehicle's electrical system, using standardised symbols. For more information refer to the *Haynes Automotive Electrical and Electronic Systems Manual*.

Note: *References throughout this index relate to Chapter•page number*

Preserving Our Motoring Heritage

<
The Model J Duesenberg Derham Tourster. Only eight of these magnificent cars were ever built – this is the only example to be found outside the United States of America

Almost every car you've ever loved, loathed or desired is gathered under one roof at the Haynes Motor Museum. Over 300 immaculately presented cars and motorbikes represent every aspect of our motoring heritage, from elegant reminders of bygone days, such as the superb Model J Duesenberg to curiosities like the bug-eyed BMW Isetta. There are also many old friends and flames. Perhaps you remember the 1959 Ford Popular that you did your courting in? The magnificent 'Red Collection' is a spectacle of classic sports cars including AC, Alfa Romeo, Austin Healey, Ferrari, Lamborghini, Maserati, MG, Riley, Porsche and Triumph.

A Perfect Day Out

Each and every vehicle at the Haynes Motor Museum has played its part in the history and culture of Motoring. Today, they make a wonderful spectacle and a great day out for all the family. Bring the kids, bring Mum and Dad, but above all bring your camera to capture those golden memories for ever. You will also find an impressive array of motoring memorabilia, a comfortable 70 seat video cinema and one of the most extensive transport book shops in Britain. The Pit Stop Cafe serves everything from a cup of tea to wholesome, home-made meals or, if you prefer, you can enjoy the large picnic area nestled in the beautiful rural surroundings of Somerset.

>
John Haynes O.B.E., Founder and Chairman of the museum at the wheel of a Haynes Light 12.

<
Graham Hill's Lola Cosworth Formula 1 car next to a 1934 Riley Sports.

The Museum is situated on the A359 Yeovil to Frome road at Sparkford, just off the A303 in Somerset. It is about 40 miles south of Bristol, and 25 minutes drive from the M5 intersection at Taunton.
Open 9.30am - 5.30pm (10.00am - 4.00pm Winter) 7 days a week, *except Christmas Day, Boxing Day and New Years Day*
Special rates available for schools, coach parties and outings Charitable Trust No. 292048